SENSE AND STYLE
The Craft of the Essay

SENSE
AND STYLE

The Craft of the Essay

SUZANNE SILBERSTEIN
HOFSTRA COLLEGE

MARIAN SELDIN
QUEENSBOROUGH COMMUNITY COLLEGE

RANDOM HOUSE · NEW YORK

FIRST PRINTING

© Copyright, 1962, by Random House, Inc.

All rights reserved under International and Pan-American Copyright
Conventions. Published in New York by Random House, Inc., and
simultaneously in Toronto, Canada, by Random House of Canada, Limited.
Library of Congress Catalog Card Number: 62-10670
Manufactured in the United States of America by The Colonial Press, Clinton,
Massachusetts

Design by Joan Wall

Foreword

THIS BOOK is an anthology of essays for courses in learning to read with sophistication and to write with effectiveness. The essential requirement for such material is that it be itself excellent, that it introduce the student to English beautifully written and ideas cogently developed to give him models from which he can learn. But in addition to excellence of form and presentation, these essays offer a sufficiently wide range of topic, style, and opinion to attract students with varied interests and to extend their horizons to fields they have never considered.

The essays have been arranged according to subject matter, in an order which, we believe, provides a valid teaching plan. However, since most of the essays are related not only to others in their category but also to material in other sections, they can be used in a number of ways, according to the needs and interests of teachers and classes. Some instructors, for example, may wish to try other arrangements based on subject matter, and to study, for instance, C. P. Snow's essay in the section on "Knowledge and Learning" with the pieces by Bertrand Russell and Julian Huxley in the "Perspectives" section: all three are concerned with the impact of science upon modern man. Or some of the essays may be studied primarily from the point of view of rhetoric and style.

Because we are convinced that most instructors—and students —would prefer a compact, inexpensive book to one elaborately equipped with "study aids" and other impedimenta, we have included a minimum of editorial apparatus. An introduction to each essay gives pertinent information about the author and the essay itself. The brief "Notes and Comments" after each selection discuss matters of interpretation and style, including questions on the essay, suggestions for the student's own writing or, in a few cases, for his research.

A final note: the nature of the text suggests the use of very few translations. We have included only four, all of them worthy of originals too good to omit.

Acknowledgments

EVERY ANTHOLOGY, if the truth were told, has an anthology of collectors. Those to whom we are particularly indebted are our colleagues at Hofstra College, especially Dr. Edward Chalfant, Dr. Wiebur Scott, and Stanley Brodwin. Gilbert Hoover gave us invaluable assistance and encouragement, and in its early stages Professor A. Kent Hieatt of Columbia University read the plan for the book and offered judicious praise and useful criticism. The members of Columbia's 1960-61 seminar in eighteenth-century literature were kind enough to devote a large part of one session to several of our problems, and their assistance—particularly that of Thomas Steiner, Kenneth Craven, and Professor James L. Clifford, the director of the seminar—has done much to enrich the volume. Charles Lieber and Anne Murphy, together with other members of the editorial staff of Random House, have devoted to us more than our fair share of their patience, time, and skill. Richard Cohn of Welco Associates arranged for the typing of the manuscript. And for encouragement and the sort of help one can't ask even of one's friends—although only friends will provide it—we are indeed in debt to Leonard Koppett and Charles Burkhart.

Contents

Contents

OF ESSAYS

"Essay"—from the French *essai*—means "trial," "attempt," "experiment," and when Montaigne originally used the word in 1580 to describe his adventures in soul-searching, he stressed its tentativeness. He was a man who probed, suggested, sent up trial balloons to feel out the stresses in his relationship to the world he knew. His focus of interest was himself. He made no pronouncements of general truth; his civilized airing of ideas, his playing with fancy seek not to persuade but rather to set the reader meditating. He is, in short, a conversationalist on paper. His very rambling is, to use Aldous Huxley's phrase, "Free association artistically controlled. . . . One damned thing after another—but in a sequence that in some almost miraculous way develops a central theme and relates it to the rest of human experience."

Montaigne's *genre*, or the name he gave it, appeared in England a few years later with the publication of the essays of Francis Bacon (1561-1626), whose short, pithy pieces entitled "Of Study" or "Of Revenge" or "Of Truth" share some of the qualities of their French counterparts. For instance, though Bacon's essays cannot be said to "reach not their end, but their suspension in full career," as Virginia Woolf said of Montaigne, they do suggest more than they say. They are tightly reasoned, yet this very condensation has some of the same effect as Montaigne's wandering, for the reader is stimulated to reply, to develop the ideas he encounters. But Bacon does not have the quality of tentativeness: "Revenge is a kind of wild justice; which the more man's nature runs to, the more ought law to weed it out." "Studies serve for delight, for ornament, and for ability." "It is generally better to deal by speech than by letter; and by the mediation of a third than by man's self." These are the pronouncements of a man who *knows*, not the doubts of one who probes. If Montaigne charms, Bacon compels.

Bacon was, nonetheless, experimenting. English prose was in its infancy when he wrote, and his "attempts" helped to form it into an instrument to express and develop abstract ideas with brevity, balance, and clarity. His immediate successors in the early seventeenth century tended less to this kind of prose than to a prose like John Donne's, rich in images and allusions, more Latinate in structure, more nearly allied to poetry (see page 346). But later in the century essayists mined a vein of English closer to Bacon's. John Dryden (1631-1700), who was also a poet, ushered in the Age of Prose in an idiom today's reader recognizes as his own. In syntax, in vocabulary, in rhythm, Dryden's style is "modern." And in helping English prose come of age, he also helped develop the essay.

One of Dryden's most famous prose works is "An Essay of Dramatic Poesy," rightly named, for in it he was *trying* to set forth a critical view of the drama which would be relevant to the English stage. Critical principles of his day were drawn from the theories of the "Ancients"—Aristotle, Horace, Longinus—or from the French. Reputable sources all, but Dryden was aware that critics who relied upon them used them more often to denigrate than to appreciate English dramatists. His essay in defense of English drama has affinity with both Bacon and Montaigne. He is discussing not himself, but an object of intellectual interest, as Bacon does, yet his tone has some of the tentativeness, some of the air of suggesting rather than declaring, that one finds in Montaigne.

But in spite of his roots in what was becoming a tradition, Dryden's "Essay of Dramatic Poesy" is in many ways the fruit of a very different plant. It is much longer than the essays of Bacon and Montaigne and far more elaborately organized; the subject is much more completely developed. Dryden, as a matter of fact, was cultivating a hybrid, borrowing his technique from an older tradition. His essay is a sort of Platonic dialogue among four critics who debate their differing positions as they float on a barge down the Thames. The form is appropriate, for Dryden, like Plato, was didactic: he sought to teach and to convince. The conversation in the essay is no longer between author and reader; it is *within* the piece. The reader listens, assents or disagrees, but his response is not really part of the essay. Whereas Montaigne and Bacon could be called masters of ceremonies for an audience-participation program, Dryden produced a play.

His production was unquestionably a success. His innovations in the essay were all adopted and developed in one way or another by writers in the eighteenth century. Didacticism appears in the work of Alexander Pope, in long poems like "An Essay on Criticism" and "An Essay on Man" (Pope's "essays in verse"). Didacticism was also the *raison d'être* of the century's most fruitful contribution to the *genre*, the periodical essay.

Sir Richard Steele (1672-1729), in deciding to publish periodical essays to amuse and inform members of the rising middle class on matters of taste, of morals, and especially of manners, embarked upon a notable experiment in adult education. He was the idea man, but it was his partner in the venture, Joseph Addison, whose steadier working habits and engaging style gave Steele's papers, *The Tatler* and *The Spectator*, their distinction.

Addison and Steele were far more frankly didactic than Dryden had been, for he had addressed an audience whose members were his equals, whereas theirs acknowledged its inferiority. It was, however, by no means a captive audience, and Addison and Steele had to develop techniques to hold their readers. Perhaps their most important asset was Addison's graceful style, which succeeded in discussing entertainingly the poetry of Milton and other topics not necessarily immediately attractive to an eighteenth-century burgher. Their most interesting invention, however, was the Sir Roger de Coverley Club, whose members suggested in their actions both the ideal of social conduct and the sort of behavior of which the authors disapproved. The device has some affinity with Dryden's dialogue, but the cast was larger, and each member of Sir Roger's set was well enough developed to be interesting in himself as well as for what he said. The doings of the club provided a remarkably flexible framework for indirect instruction, amusement, and the sort of gentle satire Addison practices in "The Cries of London" (see page 419). Ultimately the club's activities formed what might be called a proto-novel, since the same characters appeared in essay after essay in situations which continued from issue to issue. (Dickens exploited the narrative possibilities of the device in *The Pickwick Papers*.) Its usefulness to the essay itself appealed to such authors as Oliver Goldsmith (1730-1774), who introduced similar characters in his *Citizen of the World* essays, in which a Chinese writing letters home served as a detached observer and critic of English social customs.

Later in the century Samuel Johnson undertook *The Rambler* and *The Idler* with the same purpose as Addison and Steele: to enlighten the middle class. His essays in the two periodicals are weightier than Addison's or Steele's and contain some of the criticism on which his fame rests. In them he developed the style and dialectic method he uses with such superb effect in his "Preface to Shakespeare" (see page 246).

Dryden's use of the essay to persuade was adopted in the eighteenth century particularly in the field of politics, where a widening franchise led political parties to appeal systematically for support. The greatest of the political journalists was Jonathan Swift, whose brilliance and intensity lifted what can be the most ephemeral of rhetoric to the level of high art. He used his gifts not only to edit *The Examiner* for the Tories from 1710 to 1714, but also in tracts, such as "The Abolishing of Christianity in England" (page 350), in which dramatic irony gives depth and power to his convictions about religion and the state. The most famous of his essays are those he wrote in later years on the Irish question. "A Modest Proposal," which suggests that poverty in Ireland could be mitigated if Irish "yearling" children were sold as delicacies to the English gentry, is unequalled in its searing indictment of the callousness and brutality of men who hold power without acknowledging responsibility.

Swift's irony brought into play again one of the early elements of the essay: the participation of the reader, whom Swift addresses through a spokesman or *persona*, and whose reaction is part of the artistry of the piece. But the reader is asked not to converse, as he was with Montaigne, or to think, as Bacon requested. In Swift's hands he is to be shocked into speechlessness when he sees the premises he acts upon without question carried out not just to their absurd but to their monstrous conclusions.

A survey of the essay in the first century and a half of its development reveals, then, works written in such a variety of forms and with such diverse techniques that one is justified in asking, what *is* an essay? But the *genre* seems to be too true to its name to be subject to specific definition. Something which is called a trial, an experiment, an attempt, *ought* to grow in diverse directions. It *ought* to grow experimentally. And some of its shoots may even be failures, at least in the sense of being dead ends, of providing no avenues for future experiment.

The early essayists we have been discussing were, however, on the right track. A survey of the present collection reveals the extent to which their ideas could bear fruit. Charles Lamb, G. K. Chesterton, E. B. White, and, in his way, Dylan Thomas go back to Montaigne's revelation of personality through written conversation. The essays by H. L. Mencken and Dwight Macdonald recall not only Swift's irony but his subjects. Clement Greenberg, Aldous Huxley, and John Ciardi are following Addison and Steele in directing and informing taste. Henry James, like Dryden, analyzes a literary form in an attempt to give it critical principles which can extend, not limit, its range. Belloc's

"The Apprentice," narrative in form, recalls the narrative elements Addison and Steele introduced. And the indirect comment on human foibles which gave the Sir Roger de Coverley Club its greatest fame appears again in James Thurber, in William E. Wilson's "Madeline Among the Midshipmen," and in Frank Sullivan's "A Garland of Ibids."

Granted that these experiments did succeed, what do the originators and their followers have in common? In the first place, they all know, as Virginia Woolf would have it, "The first essential—how to write." That would seem to be necessary for anyone who works in words, but to echo Mrs. Woolf again, an essayist has *only* words. He has no plot, no rhyme. Though he often gives information in his essays, he gives it to an audience that doesn't have to take it. He needs to hold his reader, and his best trap will always be the well-turned phrase, the well-woven paragraph.

The matter of writing well, of style, is a matter also of personality. Swift's laconic definition, "Proper words in proper places," is an admirable general description of good style, but what is proper and where is its proper place are as subject to variation as the essay itself. Shaw is witty and persuasive through extended metaphors. C. S. Lewis and Rebecca West move their readers with rhythmic prose that embodies their own intensity. Newman builds architectonically, in balanced sentences and paragraphs which even in their formality are the proper vehicle for his equally intense involvement in the subject he discusses. Virginia Woolf's style asks the reader for empathy, almost begs him to enter into Mary Wollstonecraft's heart, as she has done, and feel both with her subject and herself.

In other words, an essayist needs to write himself into his essay. The thread of the personal goes back to Montaigne, and though only a few writers represented here, like Lamb, Mark Twain or E. B. White, make themselves their subject as he did, any really good essayist is in his work in that he is personally committed. He has to care about what he discusses. His personality will determine his manner of caring, just as it determines his style. C. P. Snow, scientist and novelist, expresses his concern about the cultural dichotomy of the twentieth century as a scientist, through reasoned argument, without the overt, almost plainly stated emotion of Mrs. Woolf, but his essay would be a committee report were it not for the conviction that informs it and gives it power. In this connection it is pertinent to return briefly to the eighteenth century. It used to be said that Pope's "Essays" were not really poetry, that their rationality, their intellectual subjects—criticism, the nature of man, the right use of riches—made them prose in rhyme, fitly called "essays," for that was a prose form. Critics understand Pope well enough now to recognize that he was without doubt a poet. Maybe, then, the reverse of the original judgment is true. Pope's long poems were essays not because they were nearly prose, but because the essay, in its demand for personal involvement, is closely allied to poetry.

In all its successful experiments the essay has sustained one other element: it has always been written not to a coterie but to the general reader, or as Samuel Johnson and later Virginia Woolf called him, the Common Reader—the educated man who is not a specialist, but who wants to understand the specialist's knowledge, asking only that it be offered to him in his own language, not in a particularized technical jargon. The relationship between the essayist and his reader ought to be a relationship of equals. Addison and Steele skirted the edge of failure in their experiment, for they were educating an audience which joined them in considering itself their inferiors. If they succeeded, it was because they nonetheless treated their readers with respect. At their best they wrote well—in the full meaning of the term—in polished, exact prose, without condescension.

The essay, then, makes demands upon both writer and reader. It can exist, to quote David Daiches, only when there are "people who know enough about enough matters to afford an audience for the attractive discussion that is expert without being specialized." The "general" reader turns out to be a limited audience, since he needs, at least, really to *be* a reader. On the other hand, the essay form requires an author who is "at ease in the world of human thought . . . prepared to see the infinite relevance of any particular argument he might present." In this volume this aspect of the essay is perhaps best exemplified in Martin D'Arcy's experiment in relating scientific discovery to theological doctrine for the layman in either field, and Bertrand Russell's discussion of what relativity means to those of us who aren't Einstein.

All of which adds up to a form that bridges categories. Though it imposes some limits, the essay is eclectic. It tries almost anything, using, if a particular purpose seems to warrant it, tools to which another *genre* lays primary claim. It borrows narration and character development from fiction. It uses rhythm, metaphor, the connotative, emotion-charged words that seem to belong to poetry. It appropriates, on occasion, Platonic dialogue. And it establishes its right to these properties simply by using them well, by building with them wholes whose right to exist cannot be challenged. They exist too effectively to be denied.

To use De Quincey's terms (see page 127), the essay bridges two quite fundamental categories. It is both Literature of Knowledge and Literature of Power. It informs and it moves. Sometimes it is what has been rather foolishly called "pure" literature: Lamb, Twain, Chesterton, Thurber would appear to have no ulterior motives. They write simply to delight an audience, to move it to laughter, to sympathy, or to wonder. Hence, De Quincey would say theirs is a Literature of

Power. But those essays which have primarily an intellectual end, those which teach or analyze or persuade, like Macdonald's "The Responsibility of Peoples," Bergson's "Laughter," or Freud's "Why War?" are not just Literature of Knowledge. Their style, the extent to which they are profoundly personal, their serious relationship to the reader, make them Literature of Power, too. If they were not, they would have to be written off as more of the essay's unsuccessful experiments.

POLITICS AND
PEOPLE

◄§ The essays in this section treat, with a variety of styles and approaches, the theme of man as a social animal—in other terms, politics in the widest sense. Writers of the most disparate interests and temperament have always been attracted to this broad subject that touches on so many aspects of human life: of the authors represented here only Edmund Burke, the eighteenth-century British statesman, was concerned with politics as a profession.

The other writers bring to the subject diverse backgrounds and points of view. Freud, the psychoanalyst, discusses war in the light of his own discoveries about human instincts and motivation. Shaw, the dramatist, writes a witty critique of democracy. José Ortega y Gasset examines the role of the masses in modern society with a philosopher's insight. Dwight Macdonald and Rebecca West, both of them journalists and critics, write with differing styles but equal intensity about two of the great issues of our time: Macdonald about the concept of collective responsibility, Miss West about the value of loyalty. The three final essays present the reflections of three very dissimilar writers on the interaction of individuals and events: George Orwell writes on Gandhi, Hilaire Belloc on Charles I and one of his humbler subjects, Virginia Woolf on Mary Wollstonecraft, who faced in the eighteenth century problems we tend to think are peculiar to the modern woman.

DWIGHT MACDONALD

1906-

Dwight Macdonald is probably America's most independent-minded political thinker. He began his career on *Fortune,* but resigned in protest in 1936 when the magazine's editors deleted too much of his sharply critical analysis of the United States Steel Corporation. Because only the Communists seemed to be doing anything about the Depression, he became, as he says, "a mild fellow traveller," but grew disenchanted almost immediately over Stalin's purge of the Trotskyites. Subsequently, he helped revive *Partisan Review,* a defunct Communist literary magazine, as a politically independent journal which sought to defend, as its staff phrased it, the "Autonomy of Culture." In 1943, however, he parted company with his fellow editors. They supported World War II; Macdonald did not, partly because he was at that time a pacifist and partly because in his view alliance with Russia compromised too seriously the justice of the Allied position.

From 1944 to 1949 Macdonald was, in his words, "editor, publisher, owner, proofreader, layout man and chief contributor" to *Politics,* a magazine noted for its vigorous, highly personal, and unashamedly partisan commentary on the current scene. He gave it up after five years, not only because it lost money steadily but also because he needed time to investigate and reflect upon his "growing sense of ignorance . . . before sounding off in print." He has since written about social, cultural, and political topics, primarily for *The New Yorker.*

"The Responsibility of Peoples" appeared in *Politics* in 1945. It was reprinted in 1957 in *Memoirs of a Revolutionist,* a collection of Macdonald's essays. In the meantime Macdonald had reread the piece and added in footnotes some criticisms and amplifications. Thus the essay in its present form has something to say about the development of Macdonald's personal political philosophy as well as about one of the most serious problems of the twentieth century.

The Responsibility of Peoples

We talk of the Turks and abhor the cannibals; but may not some of them go to heaven before some of us? We may have civilized bodies and yet barbarous souls. We are blind to the real sights of this world; deaf to its voice; and dead to its death.

HERMAN MELVILLE

Germans have thought in politics what other peoples have done. . . .

Although Germany has only accompanied the development of nations with the abstract activity of thought, without taking an active part in the real struggles incident to this development, she has, on the other hand, shared in the suffering caused by national development without sharing in its enjoyments, or their partial satisfaction. Abstract activity on the one side corresponds to abstract suffering on the other side.

Consequently, one fine day Germany will find herself at the level of European decay before she has ever stood at the level of European emancipation. The phenomenon might be likened to a fetish-worshiper who succumbs to the diseases of Christianity. . . .

The only liberation of Germany that is practical or possible is a liberation motivated by the theory that declares man to be the Supreme Being of mankind. . . . In Germany, no brand of serfdom can be extirpated without extirpating every kind of serfdom. . . . The emancipation of Germans is the emancipation of mankind.

KARL MARX (1844)

Now I must say goodbye. Tomorrow mother goes into the gas chamber, and I will be thrown into the well.

FROM A LETTER WRITTEN BY A CHILD
IN A POLISH "DEATH CAMP"

"WE WERE a little nervous when she was taken," the girl's mother said afterwards. "You never know what will happen when they start to use the electric needle. But we should not have worried. She never gave the Germans a single name or address and no one was arrested."

The girl was a member of the French underground; she was caught by the Gestapo; she was tortured, while her mother was held in a nearby cell so she could hear her daughter's screams; and she died. This was Europe under the Nazis: the matter-of-fact reference to torture; the technological modernity of the instrument; the mother's politicalized attitude—"we should not have worried," since "she never gave a single name." Something has happened to the Germans—to some of them, at least; something has happened to Europe—to some of it, at least. What is it? Who or what is responsible? What does it mean about our civilization, our whole system of values? This is the great moral question of our times, and on what our hearts as well as our heads answer to it depends largely our answer to the great practical questions.

In this article, I want to consider this question as an aspect of the general problem of what my friend, Nicola Chiaromonte, calls "the responsibility of peoples."

In the last war, we believed many "atrocity stories" which later turned out to have been propaganda. Compared to the German atrocities which are reported by the press in this war, those of 1917, however revolting in detail, were (1) quantitatively negligible (rarely involving more than a score or so of alleged victims), and (2) deeds done in hot blood by individual soldiers using bayonets or guns rather than the systematic tortures and massacres with specially designed instruments that are now reported. So tender was the civilian mood of those days that the British were able to arouse great indignation over the execution of Edith Cavell, who, as a spy, by all the rules of warfare "deserved" her fate. Today we are more tough-minded—we have to be, or go crazy, so severe are the shocks administered to our moral sensibilities, indeed to our very nervous systems, by each morning's newspaper. Yet even so, one's heart fails at some of the reports.

The French War Crimes Commission recently estimated that between 200,000 and 250,000 French civilians had been killed by the Germans during their occupation of France. The Commission has also assembled a museum of torture devices: branding irons, pincers for pulling out fingernails, an "electrical shoe," a steel helmet studded with screws that can slowly be tightened. . . . Not

since the Spanish Inquisition has such an array been seen. Who
would have dared predict, in the 19th century, that one of the
most advanced nations in Europe would employ such instruments?
Marx himself might well have shrunk from the supposition. His
epigram of 1844 must now be reversed: the Germans have *done* in
politics what other peoples have up to now dared only to *think*.

In the last war, all this could have been dismissed as propaganda. But the great difference between the "atrocity stories" of
World War I and those of World War II is that the latter are as
convincingly authenticated as the former were not. To disbelieve
the accounts of today, one would have to assume that almost every
war correspondent is a liar on a Munchausen scale, that various
neutral observers are liars, that certain internationally known
religious and charitable institutions have fabricated detailed
reports. We know, also, from the Nazis' own theories and from
what they did in Germany itself that such horrors are not improbable.

Let us not only accept these horrors; let us insist on them.
Let us not turn aside even from the greatest of all: the execution
of half the Jewish population of Europe, some four million men,
women, and children, in Silesian and Polish "death factories." [1]
In the last war, the farthest our propagandists ventured was to
fabricate the tale of the German "corpse factories," in which the
bodies of dead soldiers were alleged to have been boiled down
for their fat and chemicals. Not only was this untrue, but it would
never have occurred to any one in 1917 even to *invent* a story
about abattoirs in which human beings took the place of cattle.
And yet we know, from irrefutable evidence, that *these things have
been done.* They are part of our world and we must try to come
to some kind of terms with them.

Detailed reports about the "death camps" have only come out

---

[1] *This essay appears here as published in* Politics, March 1945. *The following footnote was added in 1953:* Later estimates put it at six million. By an
ironical twist of history, the victims have now become oppressors in their turn.
Since 1948, some 800,000 Arab refugees, who fled from Palestine during the
fighting, have been living wretchedly in camps around the country's borders
maintained by UN charity. The Israeli government—opposed by no important
Jewish group that I know of—refuses to let them back and has given their
homes, farms, and villages to new Jewish settlers. This is rationalized by the
usual "collective responsibility" nonsense. This expropriation cannot, of course,
be put on the same plane as the infinitely greater crime of the Nazis. But
neither should it be passed over in silence.

within the past year. The chief ones I have seen are the descriptions of the camps at Auschwitz and Birkenau in Upper Silesia which appeared in the N. Y. *Times* of July 2 and 5, 1944, sent in from Switzerland; the stories in the *Times* (Aug. 27) and *Time* (Sept. 11) based on a Russian-conducted tour of the former death camp at Maidanek; and the report, based on stories by three eyewitnesses who were able to escape, of the Auschwitz and Birkenau camps that was released by the War Refugees Board, a Government agency, on Nov. 26, 1944. The first report is the most impressive, because it was put out by the well-known Swiss relief organization, the Fluchtlingshilfe of Zurich, whose head is the Rev. Paul Voght. It is also sponsored by the Ecumenical Refugee Committee of the World Council of Churches. But in all the reports, the atmosphere is the same: rationality and system gone mad; the discoveries of science, the refinements of modern mass organization applied to the murder of noncombatants on a scale unknown since Genghis Khan.

These camps, which the Nazis called "model extermination camps" and which were operated by specially trained *Judenvernichtung* (Jew-killing) experts, were literally "death factories," often with railroad sidings running into them for the transport of their raw materials. These "materials" were processed in an orderly fashion: shaved, bathed, deloused, each given a slip of paper with his or her number typed on it, then routed into another room where this number was tattooed on the body—on the breasts of the women. (So in Kafka's "The Penal Colony," the mechanism executes the criminal by tattooing the record of his crime on his body—one of too many modern instances in which reality has now caught up with Kafka's imagination.) The cooperation of the victims was necessary to save time (and make production records possible). By experiment, it was found that death came quicker when the body was warm, washed and wet. The execution buildings were therefore sometimes given the appearance of bathing establishments, the illusion being methodically carried out by having two attendants in white jackets give each victim a towel and a piece of soap. There were even simulated shower-entries in the death chamber itself: a concrete room into which as many naked persons were packed as possible. "When everybody is inside, the heavy doors are closed. Then there is a short pause, presumably to allow the room temperature to rise to a certain level,

after which SS men with gas masks climb the roof, open the traps
in the ceiling, and shake down a preparation in powder form
labeled 'Cyklon,' for use against vermin, which is manufactured
by a Hamburg concern. It is presumed that this is a cyanide
mixture of some sort which turns into a gas at a certain temperature. After three minutes, every one in the chamber is dead." The
bodies were then taken into the crematorium (which at Maidanek
looked like "a big bake shop or a very small blast furnace") where
they were cut up by butchers, loaded onto iron stretchers and
slid on rollers into the coke-fed ovens. With such methods, death
was produced on a mass scale: at Birkenau alone, over a million
and a half persons are estimated to have perished from April,
1942, to April, 1944.

As in the Chicago stockyards, no by-products were wasted.
The clothes and shoes were shipped into Germany to relieve the
shortage of consumption goods: "We came to a large warehouse.
It was full of shoes. A sea of shoes. . . . They were piled like
coal in a bin halfway up the walls. Boots. Rubbers. Leggings.
Slippers. Children's shoes, soldiers' shoes, old shoes, new shoes.
. . . In one corner, there was a stock of artificial limbs." Also:
"Near the ovens were the remains of a room with a big stone
table. Here gold fillings were extracted from the teeth. No corpse
could be burned without a stamp on the chest: 'INSPECTED FOR
GOLD FILLINGS.' " The ashes and bones of the burned bodies were
used to fertilize cabbage fields around the camps. Nor did the
Germans, devotees of science, lose the chance to advance human
knowledge. All identical twins that passed through Birkenau were
removed for "biological examination" at a German scientific
institute. In the Vosges section of France, a "laboratory camp"
was recently discovered, where thousands of persons were experi-
mented on, always with fatal results. Some were vivisected, some
were given leprosy and plague, some were blinded (to see if their
sight could be restored), many were put to death by gas while
observers watched their reactions through a window. Perhaps the
most humanly appalling details of all were certain juxtapositions
which one would be tempted to say showed a typical Germanic
tastelessness, were it not for our own "war-theme" advertisements.
Thus at a Dutch camp, there were found certain cells so con-
structed as to cause death by slow suffocation—and a nursery for
prisoners' children whose walls were decorated with scenes from

fairy tales. And at Maidanek, the camp loudspeaker blared out all day over the countryside . . . Viennese waltzes.

But enough! We may say that those who planned and carried out such things were insane. This may have often been true, in a medical sense. But once granted the ends, the means were rational enough—all too rational. The Nazis learned much from mass production, from modern business organization. It all reads like a sinister parody of Victorian illusions about scientific method and the desirability *in itself* of man's learning to control his environment. The environment was controlled at Maidanek. It was the human beings who ran amok.

1. THE GERMAN WAR CRIMES ARE UNIQUE. A considerable portion of the atrocious acts of the Germans in this war are chargeable rather to war in general than to any special inhumanity of the Germans.

There was much moral indignation, for example, about the robot bombs. But the effects of "saturation bombing," which the British and American air forces have brought to a high degree of perfection, are just as indiscriminate and much more murderous. "The Allied air chiefs," states this morning's paper, "have made the long-awaited decision to adopt deliberate terror bombing of German population centers. . . . The Allied view is that bombardment of large German cities creates immediate need for relief. This is moved into the bombed areas both by rail and road, and not only creates a traffic problem but draws transport away from the battle front. Evacuation of the homeless has the same result." The only mistake in the above is to say the decision has just been adopted; actually, the Allies have used "terror bombing" for several years. We might also recall the indignation we felt, in 1940, at the strafing of refugees by the Luftwaffe. "How typically Nazi!" we exclaimed—but we were more tender-minded in those days. The first contracts have already been let for the manufacture of our own robot bombs, and no one at all conversant with modern warfare doubts that the robot bomb will be a key weapon in World War III.[1]

---

[1] Six months after this was written, "we" humane and democratic Americans dropped atomic bombs on Hiroshima and Nagasaki, destroying in the twinkling of an eye some 90,000 civilians—men, women and children. This was the climax of the Anglo-American policy of massacring civilian populations from the air, a policy which later evidence shows to have been morally

The ruthless economic exploitation, accompanied by mass starvation, to which the Nazis subjected Europe when they held it was deplorable. But our own press for many months now has carried articles about the failure of the Allies to provide any more food to the "liberated" (and hungry) Europeans than the Germans did (and often, as in Italy and Belgium, not as much). "Military necessity" apparently rules "us" as absolutely as it ruled "them," and with the same terrible results for the peoples of Europe.

Some of the most horrible brutalities chargeable to the Nazis have been committed in their attempts to deal with the maquis. Throughout military history, franc-tireurs have always been dealt with severely; the Hague rules of warfare even authorize the shooting of civilian hostages in reprisal for franc-tireur attacks on the invading soldiery. One should not forget that the Germans occupied almost all of Europe for four years, and that our own armies are only just beginning to occupy enemy territory. If a German resistance movement materializes that is anything like as determined as the one the Nazis had to deal with, we shall probably see our own armies climbing down a bit from their present pinnacle of moral superiority.[1]

Even the extermination of large numbers of helpless people is not so unknown in modern times as our own propagandists would have us think. Great numbers of the colored races have been wiped out since 1800 by the whites: the "rubber atrocities" of the Amazon and the Belgian Congo (cf. Conrad's *Heart of Darkness*); the large scale executions that followed the Boxer Rebellion in China; the slaughter of the bulk of the Australian Black-fellows and the American Indians; not to mention dozens of lesser "episodes" throughout Asia and Africa. In England itself, furthermore, in the first half of the last century, millions of men, women and children of the working class were starved and worked

---

indefensible, politically disastrous, and militarily of dubious value. (*Footnote added in 1953*)

[1] The resistance did not materialize, and, on the whole, the conduct of the American and British armies in Germany was no worse than that of most conquerors—a modest enough standard. The Red Army, however, sunk far below even this standard. The first few weeks of the Russian occupation of Eastern Germany, Austria, and Hungary were an orgy of unrestrained and wholesale raping and killing on a scale unknown in the West for many centuries. See the four terrible first-hand reports by survivors I printed in *Politics* (January 1946, pp. 4-8; October 1946, pp. 315-319). (1953)

to death in conditions which were often almost as brutal and de-grading as those of Maidanek and which had the disadvantage of prolonging the victims' suffering much longer (cf. the Parlia-mentary "Blue Books" of the period, Engels' *Condition of the English Working Class* in 1844, or J. L. and Barbara Hammond's *Lord Shaftesbury*). And in Soviet Russia in the last fifteen years, millions of peasants and political prisoners have been starved to death in State-created famines or worked to death on forced-labor projects.

After the acids of sophisticated inquiry have done their worst, however, a considerable residue remains. It is this residue which makes the German atrocities in this war a phenomenon unique at least in modern history.

It is partly a question of the intimate individual cruelty shown in much of the Germans' behavior. That the Allied forces will execute hostages and burn down towns if "necessary" I have no doubt; but I should be surprised if they do it on the scale the Germans did (50 lives for one was the lowest "rate of exchange") or with the brutality and sadism shown in the extermination of whole villages and the common use of the most revolting tortures.

But it is mostly what might be called the "gratuitous" charac-ter of the worst atrocities. What has been done by other peoples as an unpleasant by-product of the attainment of certain ends has been done by the Germans at Maidanek and Auschwitz as an end in itself. What has been done elsewhere in violation of the doer's code of ethics, and hence in a shamefaced way draped over with hypocritical apologies, has been done here in conformance with the avowed Nazi moral code, and thus done as publicly and proclaimed as exultantly as the winning of a great battle.[1] The

---

[1] Untrue, indeed the reverse of the truth. "Why I wrote so false a state-ment, I don't know," I wrote later. "There was no evidence for it: the intoxi-cation of rhetoric must be my only feeble excuse." Another excuse was that I failed to make a crucial distinction (that others also often fail to make) between the *death* camps (as: Maidanek, Auschwitz, Oswiecim) and the *concentration camps* (as: Buchenwald, Dachau, Sachsenhausen). The latter existed through the Hitler regime; the death rate in them was very high, but their aim was to terrorize, torture, and demoralize the prisoners, and also, dur-ing the war, to exploit their labor, rather than just to kill them. Their existence was no secret—the Nazis indeed took care to let the Germans know about them—in general, not in revolting detail—as a means of intimidating opposi-tion. They could not have been kept secret anyway, since they were all in Germany itself and since, up to 1940, their prisoners were all Germans. But

Allied bombing of German cities killed many innocent civilians
(though not as many as a single one of the German death camps),
but there was at least this much humane rationality about it; that
it was thought necessary to the winning of the war, which in turn
was thought necessary to the self-preservation of the Allied nations. Furthermore, some kind of an argument could be made
that it *was* necessary. But the extermination of the Jews of Europe
was not a means to any end one can accept as even plausibly
rational. The Jews constituted no threat to their executioners; no
military purpose was served by their extermination; the "racial
theory" behind it is scientifically groundless and humanly abhorrent and can only be termed, in the strictest sense of the term,
neurotic. The Jews of Europe were murdered to gratify a paranoiac
hatred (as the robot bomb was christened "V" for "Vengeance")
but for no reason of policy or advantage that I can see.[1]

---

the death camps were mostly in Poland, and they "processed" only Jews, most
of them Polish, and other non-Germans. So they could be kept secret, and they
were. Only Germans with very good connections with the high army staff ever
learned of their existence. For their aim was simply to kill all the Jews, male
and female, adults and children, for no alleged political or criminal offenses,
but just because they were Jews. And this aim would have disgusted and
shocked everybody, in Germany or out of it, except fanatical Nazis.

The blueprints for "mobile gas chambers" (closed trucks specially
equipped to asphyxiate people) were approved by Hitler in the fall of 1941, and
the first units began operating in occupied Russian territory in the spring of
1942. The first death camps were opened in the fall of 1942 and operated to
the fall of 1944, when Himmler closed them down, without telling Hitler, as
part of his preparations to open negotiations with the Anglo-Americans, behind Hitler's back, for a truce. Rumors began circulating about the mobile
gas chambers and later the death camps in 1942, and the British Foreign
Office almost certainly was informed by Moscow about the camps early in
1943. *The Black Book of Polish Jewry* appeared that year, with sensational
reports of the camps. But precisely because the whole thing *was* so sensational,
so beyond all Western experience—indeed beyond good and evil, as the acts
of an insane person are juridically recognized to be—these reports for some
time were simply not believed. There are even many stories of Jews who were
warned but refused to believe it, and dutifully reported for shipment to
Maidanek. It was not till the summer of 1944 that the non-German world
began to believe it, and if some Germans then heard about the death camps
from Allied broadcasts, what wonder if they discounted it as enemy "atrocity
stuff"? But most were not even that much informed. (Best source on the
death camps is Leon Poliakov's *Bréviaire de la Haine*, Paris, 1951.) (1953)

[1] This statement provoked much dissent at the time, but I have become
more and more convinced of its truth, especially after reading Hannah Arendt's
brilliant and profound *The Origins of Totalitarianism* (Harcourt Brace, 1951).
(1953)

Or consider the Stalin regime's massacres, the only other ones of our day which have been on the Nazi scale. In Russia today there is much less respect for human life and less ideological resistance to acts of violence on a mass scale than there is in the bourgeois democracies. Yet even here, there is at least the justification for, say, the State-induced famine of 1932 that it represented the carrying out, by brutal and abhorrent means (which of course corrupted the ends—but that is another story) an agricultural policy whose aim was to increase productivity. This may not be a good end in itself, but it is certainly not a bad one. It is, in any case, rational. And the kulaks were starved incident to this aim, not because there was any desire to exterminate them in themselves. It may be said, justly, that it makes little difference to the dead kulak or to the dead Jew what the motives of his executioners were. But it makes a great deal of difference to the executioners, and to our evaluation of their act.[1]

To put it briefly: the English mill-owners in the last century and the Russian bureaucrats in this one showed a disregard for human life which was shocking enough. But the Nazis have not *disregarded* human life. They have, on the contrary, paid close attention to it. They have taken it for the pure, disinterested pleasure of taking it. There was no ulterior motive behind Maidanek, no possible advantage to its creators beyond the gratification of neurotic racial hatreds. What has previously been done only by individual psychopathic killers has now been done by the rulers and servants of a great modern State. This *is* something new.

We now come to the question: who is responsible for these horrors?

2. GERMAN ANTI-SEMITISM IS NOT A "PEOPLE'S ACTION." If we can conceive of a modern people as collectively responsible in a moral sense at all, then it must be held accountable only for actions which it takes spontaneously and as a whole, actions which are approved by the popular *mores*. It cannot be indicted for things done by sharply differentiated sub-groups.

How does this apply to the Germans and the Jews? It is true there was and is widespread anti-Semitism in Germany, as in this

---

[1] I now think I overestimated the rationality of Stalin's policy. At first it was more rational than Hitler's but the dynamic of totalitarianism seems to lead towards irrationality, and by 1945 there was less to choose between the two horrors, in this respect, than I then thought. (1953)

country. But anti-Semitism is one thing and violent persecution of
Jews is another. If the German people as a whole had approved of
the Nazis' Jewish policy, one would expect that between 1933 and
the present, a period in which the Nazis used the State power to
place the Jews outside the pale of legality and indeed of humanity
itself, there would have been many mob attacks on Jewish institutions and individuals. Actually, as far as I can recall, the American
press reported none. And I remember distinctly that in 1938
when the Nazis took advantage of the assassination, by a Jew, of
their Parisian diplomatic agent, Vom Rath, to intensify the anti-
Jewish terror in Germany, the press reports stressed that there was
very little hostility shown by the street crowds against the Jews.
The controlled German press was filled with incitements to anti-
Jewish violence. Storm troopers and SS men arrested thousands of
Jews with great publicity, wrecked Jewish stores, burned syna-
gogues; but the crowds that watched these organized atrocities
were silent and withdrawn when they did not venture to express
their disapproval. There were many more cases reported of Germans who dared to help Jews than of those who helped the Nazi
pogromists—and this, too, in papers like the N. Y. Times which
were not at all friendly to Nazi Germany.

In contrast, the constant and widespread acts of violence
against Negroes throughout the South, culminating in lynching,
may be considered real "people's actions," for which the Southern
whites bear collective responsibility. As Dollard showed in Caste
and Class in a Southern Town, the brutality with which Negroes are
treated is not the work of a differentiated minority or of individual
sadists but is participated in, actively or with passive sympathy, by
the entire white community. "White aggression against Negroes
and the social patterns which permit it are forms of social control.
They are instrumentalities for keeping the Negro in his place and
maintaining the supraordinate position of the white caste. . . . It
must not be supposed that the major or perhaps even the most
significant part of white aggression against Negroes consists of the
few dramatic acts of lynching featured in the newspapers. Massive
and continuous pressures of other types are far more important in
achieving social stability." (My italics.)

So too with the 1943 Detroit race riot, in which hundreds of
Negroes were killed or horribly beaten up by large mobs of whites,
in the very heart of the city. This kind of behavior has the general

support of the Southern white people, and has enough popular support even in a Northern city like Detroit to allow it to be carried out without interference from the police. This latter point suggests that whereas anti-Negro violence in America is a real "folk" activity, carried on *against* the State and its police (which, of course, wink at it), in Germany it is the reverse: pogroms are carried out by the State and the forces of "law and order" *against* the folkways.[1]

But *someone* killed the Jews of Europe? And those who did were Germans. True. But a particular kind of Germans, specialists in torture and murder, whom it would be as erroneous to confuse with the general run of Germans as it would be to confuse the brutality-specialists who form so conspicuous a part of our own local police forces (and who occasionally burst out in such sensational horrors as the Chicago Memorial Day massacre) with the average run of Americans. It is of capital significance that the death camps for Jews and the mass killings of Russian prisoners of war have apparently not been entrusted to regular German Army units but rather to specially selected and trained SS squads. The Swedish journalist, Avid Fredborg, for example, has this interesting description in his book, *Behind the Steel Wall*:

> SS soldiers forming the execution squads in the East are carefully chosen. They are recruited from the most brutal elements and are gradually trained to become harder and more ruthless. At first

---

[1] This is, I think, one of my shrewdest points. But I must add that the Negroes have made remarkable gains since 1945: Jim Crow segregation in the armed forces has been largely abolished; the Supreme Court for the first time has begun to enforce the 14th and 15th Amendments and even the Civil Rights Acts of 1866, 1870, and 1875, so that the whole structure of "white supremacy" in the South is cracking, and Negroes are *beginning to vote* in large numbers, to be admitted to hitherto all-white Southern universities, and to travel unsegregated on interstate trains. Lynchings have become very rare (sometimes a whole year goes by without one, as against the old days when several hundred Negroes died annually *"pour encourager les autres"*), and several cases have arisen in which white men have actually been punished for murdering Negroes. These post-1945 advances toward racial equality have come because a more determined assertion of their rights by Negroes has coincided with a less determined denial of those rights by the whites, who now show a (belated) bad conscience that may be somewhat connected with the necessity for a united nation to face the Nazi and now the Soviet threat. There is still plenty of "folk activity" against Negroes, as the recent episode in Cicero, Ill., showed, but on the governmental level there has been a notable improvement since 1945. (1953)

they may only have to take Jews out for street cleaning and snow shoveling. After a time they are assigned to perform single executions. Only after this training is completed are they ordered to do mass executions.
Many have refused to take part in these and have been shot. . . . Others have had nervous breakdowns and have been sent to asylums. Even the most hardened have at times caved in. Time and again, physicians have been called to attend soldiers on leave who have had severe attacks of hysteria or prolonged insomnia or delirium tremens (soldiers in the firing squads often get intoxicated before executions, and many stay so continually). . . .
The chief instrument for these ghastly practices is the SS. Sometimes it seems that the SS is driving the policy beyond the intention of the Party leaders. In any case, it is certain the German public has little real knowledge of what is going on.

Bruno Bettelheim's article on Nazi concentration camp life in the August 1944 issue [of *Politics—Ed.*] shows in detail how *given complete control over the individual,* it is possible to condition even anti-Nazis to accept Nazi values. Major Applegate's little treatise, *Kill—or Be Killed,*[1] indicates that it is not only the Nazis who are consciously trying to break down the civilized individual's inhibitions against taking life.

But if the Nazis can thus condition their SS men and their concentration camp prisoners, cannot they—and have they not in fact—so conditioned the German people as a whole? To some extent, of course they can and have, especially in the case of the youth. Hitler said in 1937:

"We still have among us old-fashioned people who are not fit for anything. They get in our way like cats and dogs. But this does not worry us. *We will take away their children.* We will not permit them to lapse into the old way of thinking. We will take them away when they are ten years old and bring them up in the spirit of nationalism until they are eighteen. They shall not escape us. They will join the Party, the SA, the SS and other formations. Later on they will do two years of military service. Who shall dare say that such a training will not produce a nation?"

But we must remember that the great majority of present-day

[1 *Kill—or Get Killed; a Manual of Hand-to-Hand Fighting,* by Major Rex Applegate, was a quasi-official manual for use in the training of troops. In September 1944 Macdonald had commented in *Politics* on the brutality and ruthlessness the book sought to inculcate.—*Ed.*]

Germans were adults when Hitler came to power, and that even what the Nazis called their "conquest of youth" (a revealing phrase, by the way) is not complete, judging from reports of executions of university students. More important, it would seem probable that the kind of extreme *behavior* required of mass-executioners and torturers can only be psychologically conditioned by extreme *situations*, as Bettelheim calls them, involving cither complete physical control of the individual in a prison camp or else his willing cooperation in a lengthy and rigorous training process. Neither of these conditions is possible in the case of the average German: eighty million people, or even ten or five million can neither be subjected to concentration-camp control nor can they be put through any elaborate training course (even if they consented to be). Propaganda and force are not adequate substitutes for the more intimate types of conditioning; their effect is weakened and even negated constantly by the family and working life of the individual, which goes on still along the traditional lines of Western civilization.[1]

Nazi Germany is often called "one big concentration camp," but one should not forget that this is a metaphor and not a literal description. Misled by the metaphor, some *Politics* readers have drawn—from Bettelheim's article, for instance—the unwarranted conclusion that the whole German population—and even that of the occupied Europe of 1940-1943, which journalists also have called "one big concentration camp"—was being conditioned by the Nazis as effectively as the prisoners Bettelheim writes about. The fallacy in the case of Europe is apparent at a glance: as "Gallicus" showed in the January, 1945 issue, the Nazis failed to make much impression even on the youth, and soon found themselves confronted by an overwhelmingly hostile population—and, worse, corrupted by it. In Germany itself, the Nazis obviously could make more progress, since the German people were offered superior material rewards and since national hatred of a foreign conqueror was not involved. But even there it seems unlikely that propaganda and terrorism applied to a population still working

[1] Stalin's regime has gone much further toward subjecting the whole population to "extreme situations" by "concentration-camp control" and "the more intimate types of conditioning" than Hitler's did. Morally, this makes the Russian people no more "responsible" than the German people were, but practically it does present a problem that, however painful, must be faced up to by pacifists and other men of good will. (1953)

and living in comparative (by concentration-camp standards)
freedom have been sufficient to effectively Nazify a people the
majority of whom were definitely anti-Nazi when Hitler assumed
power in 1933. The very fact that concentration camps have continued to exist on a large scale is one proof of a continued popular
opposition to Nazism, as are the scores of executions for "treason"
which are still announced daily.[1]

3. THINGS HAPPEN *to* PEOPLE. All this is not to deny that
Nazism has had a great effect on the German people. It is simply
to deny that this effect has as yet changed the average German's
attitudes enough to cause him to commit pogroms or to approve
of them when his Nazi rulers commit them; and to indicate the
limitations on Nazi indoctrination outside the concentration camp
and the special training schools. The Germans have been changed
by Nazism, but it has been a slower process and has gone less far
than concentration-camp analogies would suggest, and certainly
less far than our own Teutonophobes claim.[2]

---

[1] A wrong inference, I now believe. Perplexing though it is, the fact seems
to be that, as Hannah Arendt writes in *The Origins of Totalitarianism* (p.
379): "Terror increased both in Soviet Russia and Nazi Germany in inverse
ratio to the existence of internal political opposition, so that it looks as though
political opposition had not been the pretext of terror (as liberal accusers of the
regimes were wont to assert) but rather the last impediment to its full fury."
Viz.: the Nazis killed six million Jews not when they were fighting to con-
solidate their power in 1933-36 but in 1942-44, when they had long since
destroyed effective opposition, when the Jews offered no threat to them at all,
and when the German people were forced to back them in the war as a matter
of national survival. And viz.: Lenin's "Red Terror" of 1918-20, when internal
opposition was still strong and the Red Army was fighting defensively on
Russian soil against a half dozen invading armies, was minuscule compared to
the terror Stalin unleashed in 1937-39, years after forced-collectivization had
crushed the peasants into shape, the first Five Year Plan the workers, and
Stalin's intra-party tactics the Old Bolsheviks (the Moscow Trials were merely
the juridical ratification of a *fait* long ago *accompli*). In more normal or at
least familiar kinds of societies, even dictatorships like Peron's or Mussolini's,
repression is used to overcome resistance. In the irrational world of totalitarianism, it is sometimes so used (executions soared after the 1944 attempt on
Hitler's life), but in general it increases as the opposition weakens, since the
rulers are chiefly concerned not with just keeping their power but with a
laboratory experiment in changing men into bundles of conditioned reflexes.
(1953)
[2] The more virulent of them, like Vansittart and Rex Stout, have
concocted a theory of German "responsibility" which is just the reverse of the
one discussed here: that the German people, far from having been conditioned to Nazi attitudes by external pressure (which of course implies

It is a process, furthermore, which is also going on in our own society, in England, and in Russia—in the last-named perhaps[1] even faster and farther than in Germany itself. Modern society has become so tightly organized, so rationalized and routinized that it has the character of a mechanism which grinds on without human consciousness or control. The individual, be he "leader" or mass-man, is reduced to powerlessness vis-à-vis the mechanism. More and more, things happen TO people.

Some examples, mostly drawn from the "democratic" side in this war, may suggest what I mean:

A. The *New Yorker* of Aug. 12, 1944 ran a profile of a 22-year-old lieutenant in the Army Air Force who had just completed thirty bombing missions in the European theater. He seemed to be of superior intelligence, not politically radical; his main personal interest was in jazz music. "Whatever I tell you," he said to the interviewer, "boils down to this: I'm a cog in one hell of a big machine. The more I think about it, and I've thought about it a lot lately, the more it looks as if I'd been a cog in one thing after another since the day I was born. Whenever I get set to do what I want to do, something a whole lot bigger than me comes along and shoves me back into place. It's not especially pleasant, but there it is." The lieutenant's personal aspirations would seem modest and attainable enough: to live with his wife, to have a home, to play and hear good jazz. Our society has been unable to give him these satisfactions. Instead, it puts him in the plexiglass nose of a bomber and sends him out to kill his fellow men and destroy their homes, at the most terrible psychological cost to himself, as the profile makes clear. Society is not ungrateful, however: the lieutenant wears the Purple Heart, the Distinguished Flying Cross, and the Air Medal with three oak-leaf clusters.

B. At the Mare Island, California, naval base last summer two munitions ships blew up while they were being loaded. In a

---

they were decent people *before* Hitler) have been warlike barbarians throughout European history. This is such an obvious inversion of Nazi racial theory, and is so wide open to the same scientific refutations that it does not seem worth wasting any more space on here. Combating it is a task for the propagandist, not for the analyst: like the Nazis' ideas on the Jewish people, it is as easy to refute on the scientific plane as it is difficult to combat on the psychological level. It seems more fruitful here to discuss a more sophisticated and tenable theory of German collective responsibility.

[1] I would now delete this word. (1953)

twinkling, the blast leveled everything for miles around and killed some three hundred sailors. The next day, the admiral in charge issued an Order of the Day in which he paid tribute to the "heroism" and "self-sacrifice" of the dead.

Now obviously the men who were killed were killed because they happened to be around when the explosives went off, and not because of any decision or action of their own. (So, too, civilians die in air raids; and so, too, nine out of ten soldiers die in a modern battle because they happen to be around when a bomb or shell lands.) The dead had no choice but to be "heroic," in the admiral's concept of heroism: TNT offers no surrender terms. These particular sailors had not even a choice about being around so dangerous a neighborhood: they were mostly Negroes, and they were assigned to this dirty and dangerous work because of their race (about which they had had no choice either). Indeed, they most definitely did not want the job. The fifty Negro sailors who were recently convicted and sentenced to long prison terms for mutiny were all employed at Mare Island unloading munitions and most of them were survivors of last summer's blast. They felt so strong a disinclination, after the tragedy, towards sharing their dead comrades' "heroic" fate that they risked a possible death penalty for mutiny.

The admiral's Order of the Day was thus a fantastic distortion of reality. Yet the administrative reflex which prompted him to issue it was sound. Instinctively, he felt it necessary to give to something which was non-purposive and impersonal a *human* meaning, to maintain the fiction that men who die in modern war do so not as chance victims but as active "patriots," who heroically *choose* to sacrifice their lives for their countries. It was his misfortune that the Mare Island explosion did not even superficially lend itself to this purpose. It is the good fortune of our war correspondents that battle deaths can be given at least a superficial plausibility along these lines.

C. The people of London are constantly being applauded for their "heroism" by war propagandists, and doubtless many individual Londoners did show heroic qualities during the bombing raids. But others doubtless also showed mean and cowardly traits. Insofar as the concept of heroism can be applied, it must be used on an individual not a collective basis. But when journalists salute the "heroism" of the Londoners or of the Russian people

—they really mean a kind of collective heroism which can never exist actually, since as a collectivity the people of London had no alternative except to endure the bombings. As a Cockney retorted to a war correspondent: "Everyone's sticking it? And just what the bloody hell do you think anyone can do? You'd think we had some bloody choice in the matter!"

D. Perhaps the most heavily bombed community in this war is the strategic British-held island of Malta, which in a 28-month period had 2,315 air-raid alerts, or an average of three a day. One in 200 of the civilian population died during these raids. Some time ago the British Government awarded a collective Victoria Cross to the people of Malta for their "heroism"— which, once more, consisted in simply enduring what they had to endure, since their British masters would not have allowed them to leave the island anyway. And only the other day the same Government issued a booklet on the "siege of Malta" full of the usual nonsense, on which the N. Y. *Times* commented with the usual idiocy: "The island remained unconquered, a light and a symbol."

An incident reported in *Time* of Aug. 7, 1944 illuminates the myth of Malta. It seems that on July 14, 1943, a British army captain caught a Maltese citizen looting his parked car. He took him to the Maltese police, who promptly freed the thief and put the captain in jail—for false arrest. When it appeared that the Maltese authorities planned to keep the captain in jail indefinitely, his commanding officer appealed to the British Governor (without result) and finally direct to London. The British Government replied that "in view of the present tense relations with the Maltese population and urgent military necessities, it is impossible to intervene." The captain remained in solitary confinement for nine months, until April, 1944, when his case came up in a Maltese civil court. He was then sentenced to thirteen *additional* months imprisonment at hard labor. Lord Gort, the British Military Governor, ventured to reduce the sentence, on appeal, to three months.

"We walk on tiptoe in Malta," explained an English officer. "We dare not cross a Maltese citizen in any way. Military experience demands appeasement of the pro-Fascist population." Whether the Maltese are pro-Fascist or anti-British or both is not the present point. The thing is that the collectively decorated

people of "heroic Malta" detest their British "allies." We may be
sure that the British don't allow their army officers to be treated
this way by "natives" unless there are compelling reasons.
E. With their customary thoroughness, the Germans have
carried what might be called "collective irresponsibility" to its
logical extreme. To cope with the Anglo-American armies poured
into France after D-Day, they impressed great numbers of Poles,
Russians, Frenchmen, Italians, Czechs, Georgians, Mongolians—
most of them war prisoners given a choice between starvation and
service in the Reichswehr. In some German regiments, the colonel
needed an interpreter to make his commands understood. Even
crack SS divisions were filled out with these foreign conscripts, all
of whom, even the Mongolians, were officially listed as "Volksdeutsche." The Allies in France found themselves confronted by
a veritable International in Reichswehr uniforms. Many of these
"Volksdeutsche" shot their officers and came over to the Allied
side at the first chance, giving our High Command a typical modern problem. Were they allies? (But they wore the German
uniform.) Or were they prisoners? (But they hated the uniform
they wore.) All that could be said with certainty is that they were
fought on the German side. The passive verb is intentional: the
modern soldier does not "fight"; he "is fought," like a battleship
or other inanimate mechanism.[1]

The following story was related by George Orwell in his
column in the Oct. 13, 1944 London *Tribune*:

Among the German prisoners captured in France there are a
certain number of Russians. Some time back two were captured who

---

[1] The Communist soldier also "is fought." At this writing, the Korean
truce negotiations have been hung up for a year on the issue of whether
prisoners shall be forcibly repatriated. The Communists insist they shall be;
the UN that they be allowed to choose whether to go back or not. The
firmness of the UN position may be partly due to memories of the shameful
forced repatriation of Russian prisoners by the West in 1945-46. This was
one of the dirty deals at Yalta between Stalin and Roosevelt, and it was
dishonorably honored by the West until the political break with Russia in
the fall of 1946. British and American MP's (who "were fought" also by
their commanders) performed the noble work of herding and dragging Russian prisoners—some of whom cut their throats rather than return—into
trains to be shipped back to the land of socialism, where they were punished
because (a) they had been taken prisoner, and (b) they were assumed to be
"unreliable elements," since they had lived beyond the Iron Curtain and so
had a standard of comparison with conditions in Soviet Russia. (1953)

did not speak Russian or any other language that was known either to their captors or their fellow-prisoners. They could, in fact, only converse with one another. A professor of Slavonic languages, brought down from Oxford, could make nothing of what they were saying. Then it happened that a sergeant who had served on the frontiers of India overheard them talking and recognized their language, which he was able to speak a little. It was Tibetan! After some questioning he managed to get their story out of them.

Some years earlier they had strayed over the frontier into the Soviet Union and been conscripted into a labour battalion, afterwards being sent to western Russia when the war with Germany broke out. They were taken prisoner by the Germans and sent to North Africa; later they were sent to France, then exchanged into a fighting unit when the Second Front opened, and taken prisoner by the British. All this time they had been able to speak to nobody but one another, and had no notion of what was happening or who was fighting whom.

It would round the story off neatly if they were now conscripted into the British Army and sent to fight the Japanese, ending up somewhere in Central Asia, quite close to their native village, but still very much puzzled as to what it is all about.

4. POLITICAL ANIMISM—THE THEORY OF THE "ORGANIC STATE." The above instances suggest that the difference between "civilized" and "primitive" social organization is growing less. The great circle is slowly closing, and a contemporary Soviet or German citizen would feel more in common with an Australian bushman in many ways than with, let us say, a French *philosophe* of 1780 or a Jeffersonian democrat of 1810. In place of the rigid, unexamined customs which determine the individual's behavior in primitive communities, there is substituted today a complex politico-economic organization which is equally "given" and not-to-be-criticized in its ultimate aims and assumptions, and which overrides with equal finality the individual's power of choice.

The parallel goes farther. As primitive man endowed natural forces with human animus, so modern man attributes to a nation or a people qualities of will and choice that belong in reality only to individuals. The reasons are the same in both cases: to reduce mysterious and uncontrollable forces to a level where they may be dealt with. The cave dweller feels much more comfortable about a thunderstorm if he can explain it as the rage of someone like himself only bigger, and the urban cave dwellers of our time feel much better about war if they can think of the enemy nation as a

person like themselves only bigger, which can be collectively
punched in the nose for the evil actions it collectively chooses to
do. If the German people are not "responsible" for "their" nation's
war crimes, the world becomes a complicated and terrifying place,
in which un-understood social forces move men puppetlike to
perform terrible acts, and in which guilt is at once universal and
meaningless. Unhappily, the world is in fact such a place.

One of the reasons anthropology is so interesting to the politi-
cally-minded today is because its method of observation, already
used successfully on primitive societies, can be applied very use-
fully to contemporary society, and is already being so applied by
Dollard, Benedict, the Lynds and others. May we not, indeed,
expect some future historian to write of us as one scholar has
written of the ancient Hebrews:

"They explained nearly all phenomena by the direct action of
superhuman and invisible persons and powers, resembling the
human spirit. Like the 'primitives,' they recognized no essential
difference between the spiritual and the material. Like them, too,
they conceived of a solidarity, or more accurately, a practical
identity, between many beings, events and things which we regard
as absolutely distinct."

This animistic confusion marks the common man's thinking
(with plenty of help from his political rulers) not only on relations
between nations but also on the relation between the State and
the individual citizen. Precisely because in this sphere the individual is most powerless in reality, do his rulers make their greatest
efforts to present the State not only as an instrument for *his*
purposes but as an extension of *his* personality. They have to try
to do this because of the emphasis on the free individual which the
bourgeois revolution has made part of our political assumptions
(for how long?).

Hegel, who developed an anti-individualist theory of Statism
while the cannons of the Napoleonic wars were still echoing, saw
the problem clearly and tried to meet it in such terms as these:

In the State, everything depends upon the unity of the universal
and the particular. In the ancient States, the subjective purpose was
absolutely one with the will of the State. In modern times, on the
contrary, we demand an individual opinion, an individual will and
conscience. The ancients had none of these in the modern sense; the

final thing for them was the will of the State.[1] While in Asiatic despotisms, the individual had no inner self and no self-justification, in the modern world man demands to be honored for the sake of his subjective individuality.

The union of duty and right has the twofold aspect that what the State demands as duty should directly be the right of the individual, since the State is nothing but the organization of the concept of freedom. The determinations of the individual will are given by the State objectivity, and it is through the State alone that they attain truth and realization. . . .

To the complete State belongs, essentially, consciousness and thought. The State knows thus what it wills, and it knows it under the form of thought. . . . The State must be regarded as a great architectonic edifice, a hieroglyph of reason, manifesting itself in reality. . . . That the State is the self-determining and the completely sovereign will, the final decision being necessarily referred to it—that is easy to comprehend. (Hegel: *The Philosophy of Law*.)

We may be sure, at any rate, that Stalin—or Roosevelt—would find these animistic formulations of the great philosopher of modern reaction "easy to comprehend." Nor would they be at all fazed by another passage in the same essay:

The people without its monarch and without that whole organization necessarily and directly connected with him is a formless mass, which is no longer a State. In a people, not conceived in a lawless and unorganized condition, but as a self-developed and truly organic totality—in such a people, sovereignty is the personality of the whole, and this is represented in reality by the person of the monarch.

Will, consciousness, conscience, thought, personality—these are the attributes of the Hegelian State, the whole theory culminating in the "person of the monarch" as the symbol and expression of the "organic totality." The "responsibility of peoples" is direct and all-embracing, according to such a theory.

---

[1] Hegel fails to mention the great and shining exception: the Greeks, who, to Plato's disgust, were individualistic and democratic to what today would be considered an insane degree. They found the State sometimes boring, sometimes absurd, and sometimes hateful, but never worthy of a man's respect. For an informative, learned, witty, and fascinating account of these curious folk, to whom we are still indebted for most of the few decent and agreeable aspects our culture still retains, see H. D. F. Kitto's *The Greeks* (Penguin Books). There were only a few hundred thousand of them, and their society lasted only a century or so, but never in history have so many owed so much to so few. (1953)

"Lives of nations," said Roosevelt in his 1940 Inaugural Address, "are determined not by the count of years, but by the lifetime of the human spirit. The life of a man is three-score years and ten. . . . The life of a nation is the fulness of the measure of its will to live. . . . A nation, like a person, has a body. A nation, like a person, has a mind. . . . A nation, like a person, has something deeper, something more permanent. . . . It is that something which matters most to its future, which calls for the most sacred guarding of its present."

5. IF EVERYONE IS GUILTY, NO ONE IS GUILTY. From the "Organic State" conception, it follows that no individual citizen or group of citizens may think or act otherwise than in accordance with the policies laid down by those in control of the State apparatus. When cells in a biological organism cut loose from their organic function, the result is cancer. Similar behavior by the citizen-cells of the Organic State is political cancer. The old Roman fable of the belly and the members by which the patricians defended their position against the plebs, this is still the basic argument of the "organicists."

In an organism, obviously no line can be drawn between the whole (the nation, or the people) and the parts (the individual citizens, the specific classes and interest-groups). The hands that strangle are no more guilty than the belly which nourishes them; the specialized "Jew-killing experts" are no more guilty than the peasants who raise the food they eat or the metalworkers who forge their instruments.

Thus the theory is convenient for those in power on two scores: internally, it preserves the ladder of hierarchy, making rebellious behavior treason not only to those in authority but also to the alleged common interests of everybody, to what is reverently termed "national unity" these days; in time of war, it makes it possible to treat the enemy population as a homogeneous single block, all of them equally wicked and detestable. This second use is what concerns us here: it is the theoretical underpinning of the concept that the German people are responsible for the horrors of Nazism.

But if everyone is guilty, then no one is guilty. The dialectics of this are wonderfully illustrated in an anecdote quoted by Hannah Arendt ("Organized Guilt and Universal Responsibility," *Jewish Frontier*, January, 1945) from *PM* of Nov. 12, 1944. An

American correspondent interviews an official of a "death camp" who had fallen into the hands of the Russians:

Q. Did you kill people in the camp? A. Yes.
Q. Did you poison them with gas? A. Yes.
Q. Did you bury them alive? A. It sometimes happened.
Q. Did you personally help to kill people? A. Absolutely not.
I was only paymaster in the camp.
Q. What did you think of what was going on? A. It was bad at first, but we got used to it.
Q. Do you know the Russians will hang you? A. (bursting into tears) Why should they? What have I done?

What have I done? These words ring true. One feels that the worthy paymaster—imagine the civilization that has produced the job of paymaster in a death camp!—is sincerely outraged by the proposal to hang him for his part in killing several million human beings. What had he done indeed? Simply obeyed orders and kept his mouth shut. It was what he had *not* done that shocks our moral sensibilities. But from the standpoint of the Organic State he is no more and no less guilty than every other person in Germany and deserves hanging no more and no less. Soldiers must obey their officers, just as citizens must obey the law. Stalin and Roosevelt would certainly not permit their own soldiers to discriminate, on the frivolous grounds of personal conscience, between one military order and another. Harold Denny in the N. Y. *Times* of Feb. 17, 1945 tells about a captured noncom who had witnessed the execution of forty Jewish men, women and children in Brest-Litovsk. "The only thoughts I had about it," he said, "were that it was ordered from above and that those who ordered it must have had their important reasons. By now we have been educated in such a manner that we no longer discuss given orders but agree to them without question." Asked whether he himself would be capable of carrying out such an order, he replied, after reflection, that he thought he would be, adding: "I cannot say I would have had fun doing it—not the least little bit. It could only be under the compulsion of an order. To volunteer for it, that I could not do."

It is not the law-breaker we must fear today so much as he who obeys the law. The Germans have long been noted for their deep respect for law and order. This foible, which one could smile at as an amiable weakness in the past, has assumed a sinister aspect under the Nazis. One of the most hopeful auguries for the future of this country, with the Permanent War Economy taking shape, is that we Americans have a long and honorable tradition of lawlessness and disrespect for authority.

Only those who are willing to resist authority themselves when it conflicts too intolerably with their personal moral code, only they have the right to condemn the death-camp paymaster. Certainly those who preach, or practice, the Organic State have no such right. (For all that, the Russian authorities, untroubled by such nice points, have probably long since hung the fellow— while we agonize over the rights and wrongs of the case.) Yet can even *we* really condemn the paymaster? For the Organic State is by no means only an ideological slogan devised by those in authority; it also corresponds to the real arrangement of things in the modern world. The principles on which our mass-industry economy is built—centralization of authority, division of labor (or specialization of function), rigid organization from the top down into which each worker fits at his appointed hierarchical level —these have been carried over into the political sphere. The result is that, as we have seen above, the individual has little choice about his behavior, and can be made to function, by the pressure and terror wielded by the masters of the Organic State, in ways quite opposed to any he would voluntarily choose. I have been told that the Nazis created a Jewish section of the Gestapo and that these creatures were much more feared by their fellow Jews than were the regular Gestapo men, since they would never dare take a bribe or show the slightest good nature. There were also Jewish policemen in the Warsaw ghetto, working loyally with the Nazis. We may imagine the pressure against these individuals, and their families, which produced this behavior. And doubtless some Jews refused to play the role, and took the consequences. But probably not very many, for such Jews were heroes, and there are not many heroes among the Jews or among any other peoples today (except primitive folk like the Greeks and the Poles). Our paymaster was not a hero, and the Russians hung him for not being one—as they would have hung him for being one in *their* State.[1]

---

[1] Since the war ended, we have had much experience, most of it depressing, in trying to assess criminal responsibility for political crimes. The de-

With their usual unerring cynicism, the Nazis exploit this moral weakness in the German people—that they are not heroes. The official SS organ recently editorialized:

There are no innocents in Germany. We have not yet met a single German who for political reasons had refused marriage, children, family support, reductions of taxes or paid vacations only because National Socialism had made them possible. On the contrary, they grew fat and stout under the prosperity of National Socialism. They felt no pangs of conscience at the "Aryanization" of Jewish businesses. They had their full share in the prosperity. And they shouted "Hurrah" to our victories. . . . There were, it is true, lamblike innocents who did not want to declare war upon any country and who did for the German war effort only as much as they had to. But even these did not object to making money from the war or from National Socialism. They liked to ride in their new cars on our new highways and to travel on our "Strength through Joy" excursions. Nobody, after all, has preferred a democratic death to a National Socialist life.

(Editorial in *Das Schwarze Korps,* quoted in the *Neue Volkszeitung,* New York City, for Feb. 10, 1945.)

The *Schwarze Korps,* of course, exaggerates: as we shall presently see, scores of Germans every day "prefer" (at least get—which I admit is not necessarily quite the same thing) a "democratic death" to a "National Socialist life." But, from the Organic standpoint, it is quite true that "no one is innocent." With their customary political logic, the Nazis of late have deliberately tried to involve the whole German people in the moral responsibility for their crimes. In her brilliant article in the *Jewish Frontier,* Hannah Arendt describes this process and its political consequences.

The terror-organizations, which were at first strictly separated from the mass of the people, admitting only persons who could show a criminal past or prove their preparedness to become criminals, have since been continually expanded. . . . Whereas those crimes which have always been a part of the daily routine of concentration camps since the beginning of the Nazi regime were at first a jealously guarded monopoly of the SS and Gestapo, today members of the Wehrmacht are assigned at will to the duties of mass murder. These

Nazification program and the Nuremberg Trials got all snarled up in the Responsibility of Peoples. That bewildering concept also transmuted the whole population of Berlin in three years from Nazi beasts to democratic heroes. (1953)

crimes were at first kept secret by every possible means and any publication of such reports was made punishable as atrocity propaganda. Later, however, such reports were spread by Nazi-organized whispering campaigns and today these crimes are openly proclaimed under the title of "measures of liquidation" in order to force "Volksgenossen" [1] whom difficulties of organization made it impossible to induct into the "Volksgemeinschaft" [2] of crime at least to bear the onus of complicity and awareness of what was going on. These tactics resulted in a victory for the Nazis, and the Allies abandoned the distinction between Germans and Nazis. . . .

National Socialism's chances of organizing an underground movement in the future depends on there being no visible signs of distinction any longer, and above all on the victorious powers' being convinced that there really are no differences between Germans.

6. WE, TOO, ARE GUILTY. If "they," the German people, are responsible for the atrocious policies and actions of "their" (in the possessive and possessing sense, again) government, then "we," the peoples of Russia, England and America, must also take on a big load of responsibility.

We forced defeated Germany, after World War I, into a blind alley from which the only escape was another blind alley, Nazism; this we did by throwing our weight against socialist revolution. After Hitler took power, more or less with our blessing as a lesser evil to revolution, we allowed him to rearm Germany in the hopes we could turn him against Russia, and we used "nonintervention" to aid him and Mussolini to overthrow the Spanish Republic in the "dress rehearsal" for World War II.

In the present war, we have carried the saturation bombing of German cities to a point where "military objectives" are secondary to the incineration or suffocation of great numbers of civilians; we have betrayed the Polish underground fighters in Warsaw into the hands of the Nazis, have deported hundreds of thousands of Poles to slow-death camps in Siberia, and have taken by force a third of Poland's territory; we have conducted a civil war against another ally, Greece, in order to restore a reactionary and unpopular monarch; we have starved those parts of Europe our armies have "liberated" almost as badly as the Nazis did, and if we explain that the shipping was needed for our armies, they

---

[1 Comrades (Nazi terminology).—*Ed.*]
[2 National community (Nazi terminology).—*Ed.*]

can retort that the food was needed for *their* armies; we have followed Nazi racist theories in segregating Negro soldiers in our military forces and in deporting from their homes on the West Coast to concentration camps in the interior tens of thousands of citizens who happened to be of Japanese ancestry; we have made ourselves the accomplice of the Maidanek butchers by refusing to permit more than a tiny trickle of the Jews of Europe to take refuge inside our borders; we have ruled India brutally, imprisoning the people's leaders, denying the most elementary civil liberties, causing a famine last year in which hundreds of thousands perished; we have—

But this is monstrous, you say? We, the people, didn't do these things. They were done by a few political leaders, and the majority of Americans, Englishmen and (perhaps—who knows?) Russians deplore them and favor quite different policies. Or if they don't, then it is because they have not had a chance to become aware of the real issues and to act on them. In any case, *I* can accept no responsibility for such horrors. I and most of the people I know are vigorously opposed to such policies and have made our disapproval constantly felt in the pages of the *Nation* and on the speaker's platforms of the Union for Democratic Action.

Precisely. And the Germans could say the same thing. And if you say, but why didn't you get rid of Hitler if you didn't like his policies, they can say: But you people (in America and England, at least) merely had to vote against your Government to overthrow it, while we risked our necks if we even talked against ours. Yet you Britishers have tolerated Churchill for five years, and you Americans have thrice re-elected Roosevelt by huge majorities.

It is a terrible fact, but it is a fact, that few people have the imagination or the moral sensitivity to get very excited about actions which they don't participate in themselves (and hence about which they feel no personal responsibility). The scale and complexity of modern Governmental organization, and the concentration of political power at the top, are such that the vast majority of people are excluded from this participation. How many votes did Roosevelt's refugee policy cost him? What political damage was done the Churchill-Labor government by its treatment of India, or by last year's Bombay famine? What percentage of the American electorate is deeply concerned about the mass starva-

tion of the Italians under the Allied occupation? As the French
say, to ask such questions is to answer them.

7. THE POLITICAL MEANING OF COLLECTIVE WAR GUILT. The
theory of the German people's collective responsibility for Nazi
policies not only (1) ignores the deep cleavages between the
Nazis and the people, but also (2) cements these cracks up again.

(1) If the theory were correct, one would expect to find the
German people following the Nazis' war leadership with docility
if not with enthusiasm. Actually, according to official German
figures (N. Y. *Times*, Dec. 20, 1944), "People's Courts" executions (mostly involving treason and other offenses against the
State) rose 5,000% in the first four years of the war: from 99 in
1939 to 1,292 in 1941 to 5,336 in 1943. These figures don't include
the death sentences passed in the regular courts, nor the thousands
of Germans executed annually without trial by the Gestapo, the
Elite Guard, etc. The 1944 figures are unavailable but are probably
much higher than 1943: estimates of the executions after last
summer's attempt on Hitler's life run into the tens of thousands.
"After the proclamation of total mobilization as a link in 'the
holy war of the entire people,' " writes a neutral correspondent
just back from Germany (N. Y. *Times Magazine*, Sept. 24, 1944),
"Nazi leaders ordered all Nazis to report immediately to the
Gestapo any defeatist utterances. . . . Well above a hundred of
my worker friends and their acquaintances have recently disappeared, 'spurlos versenkt.' " [1] Facts like these, even if we grant
there is little organized opposition to the Nazis inside Germany,
suggests the fuel is ready from which might spring the flames of
an anti-Nazi revolution, if the right spark were provided. But it
would be difficult to say which dreads such a spark the most, the
Nazis or the Big Three.

(2) It is likely that not since 1934 have the Nazis commanded
the popular support they have today. Goebbels and Roosevelt are
agreed on one thing at least: that the German people's destiny is
identical with that of the Nazis. On the one hand, we have the
Nazis organizing a popular *maquis* to carry on the struggle against
the Allies for years after the war, pointing to the Morgenthau
Plan as conclusive evidence of the Jewish plot against Germany,
and telling the German people—with the novel advantage that

[1 *Spurlos versenkt*, sunk without a trace.—*Ed.*]

the propaganda is true—that there is no alternative except a fight to the bitter end under Hitler's leadership. On the other hand, we have the Big Three insisting on "unconditional surrender" (a formula, let us note, which was evolved not by the totalitarian Stalin nor the Tory Churchill but by the common man's friend, Roosevelt), proposing to enslave millions of German males, to reduce Germany to a semi-agricultural status, etc. Thus from both sides of the battle-lines, the German people are told that the Nazis' survival is their only hope of survival, that the Nazis *are Germany* (a claim the Nazis have long made but up to now have been unable to get generally accepted).

For one curious result of the "all-are-guilty" line, which is put forward by those who profess the utmost detestation of Nazism, is that it makes Nazism (or its equivalent called by some other name) the logical *postwar* form of regime for defeated Germany. This comes out nakedly if one considers the most fully developed "organic" theory on Germany—that, fittingly enough, propounded by the Nazis' fellow totalitarian regime in Russia. One finds Moscow promoting hatred of Germans as Germans (not only as Nazis) and proposing the most Draconic treatment of Germany after the war, and at the same time encouraging German military nationalism through the Von Seidlitz officers' committee. A contradiction? Only superficially. The "organic" theory leads precisely to the retention of the Nazis and *junkers* as the German people's rulers. The logic: all are guilty; therefore no one is more guilty than another, therefore, the Nazis and the *junkers* are no more guilty than their opponents; therefore, if it is convenient—and it *is* convenient —it is permissible to keep the Nazis and *junkers* (except a few that are hung for demonstration purposes) in power. Thus we have Stalin using the generals and Eisenhower using the SS and the Nazi police. "In Germany there will be no fraternization," proclaimed Eisenhower's Order of the Day of Oct. 12, 1944. "We go in as conquerors." [1] The logical result of this Order was reported in

---

[1] Eisenhower's Order of the Day resulted in such edifying scenes as the following, reported by a private in the occupation forces in the Sept. 1945 *Politics:* "We had finished eating and there was a large amount left over. Children of between six and ten were standing around hoping to catch a morsel. We then proceeded to dig a hole and bury the food." For, according to the purest form of the Responsibility of Peoples doctrine, no moral distinction is made between children and grown-ups. "Would not the punishment of all Germans inflict needless hardship on millions of German children who can

the London *Tribune* of Nov. 24, 1944: "Front-line correspondents report that posters have been put up everywhere in the British and American zones announcing that 52 different Nazi organizations are to be disbanded. This figure does not, however, include all Nazi organizations. Some of these have been ordered to their stations and barracks, to await further orders. Among them are the Hitler Youth, the Nazi Police, and the SS." Some all-are-guilty enthusiasts even insist that the German people are so despicable that they *deserve* to be ruled forever by the Nazis! Thus the most extreme anti-Nazism turns into its dialectical opposite.

So much for the effect on the German people of the collective responsibility theory. It is equally disastrous for the Allied peoples. Last summer everyone thought the war in Europe would be over by the fall. The Anglo-Americans had broken out of Normandy and were racing across France in pursuit of the disorganized German armies; the Russians were advancing on all their fronts; an attempt on Hitler's life was almost successful; the popular mood inside Germany was one of panic and loss of confidence in Hitler's leadership. At that moment, it would not have taken much political pressure to pry loose the people from the Nazis and to bring the whole structure down. Instead of applying this pressure, the Allies reiterated the "unconditional surrender" line, embellished with such grace notes as the Morgenthau Plan. They succeeded in con-

---

in no way be held responsible for the crimes of their elders?" a man in the audience asked Major Erwin Lessner during a 1945 Town-Meeting-of-the-Air debate between the major and Dorothy Thompson. "Of course it would," admitted, or rather insisted, the major. "These innocent German children are the potential soldiers of World War III, just as the innocent German children who had been fed after 1918 later served in Hitler's army and did remarkably well." Today, General Eisenhower (and doubtless the major too) thinks highly of the German people, since he needs them desperately in his NATO army, and it is a plus and not a minus for German kids that they are "potential soldiers of World War III." In seven years, the German people have risen from beasts to defenders of democracy, and the Russian people have changed as radically in the reverse direction.

Personally, I find the attitude of Louis XIV more congenial. France was at war with England when the second Eddystone Lighthouse was being built, early in the eighteenth century. A French privateer carried off the builders to France, where they were imprisoned. Louis XIV learned of this action when the French captain applied to him for a reward. *Le Roi Soleil* was indignant. "I am at war with England, not with mankind," he declared, in the grand manner. And he sent the Eddystone builders back to England with rich presents, thoughtfully filling their prison cells with the French captain and crew. (1953)

vincing the German people, as Hitler's most frenetic orations could not have convinced them, that their only hope was to stand firm behind the Nazis. To make sure the Germans didn't miss the point, the American High Command staged a special demonstration at Aachen, the first sizable German city our troops reached. Aachen was defended by a single second-rate division, reinforced by one SS unit and a few fortress troops. The defenders cooperated splendidly with the attackers: for one week, the city, ringed with American divisions and artillery units, was bombed and shelled. It was finally taken "the hard way," by an all-out infantry assault backed up by tanks and God knows what else. Militarily, not exactly brilliant. But politically sound enough, for the city was reduced to rubble, thousands of its inhabitants were killed (and a good many American soldiers, too), and notice was served on all Germany (and on the Americans) of what was in store for it (and them).

It is not worth wasting printer's ink to prove that, militarily, the "Aachen policy" is inferior to a policy which would split the German people from the Nazis, and that such a policy would save an enormous number of American, British and Russian lives. But when have military considerations been allowed to interfere with the more serious business of politics (except, of course, when bestarred generals urge strikers not to interfere with the "war effort")? The Big Three want things to be done in an orderly way, with the masses' properly constituted rulers remaining on top; they don't want any unauthorized popular movements behind their own lines and they don't want them behind the enemy lines either. Only a liberal editor would seriously point out to them that military victory could be had more rapidly by encouraging the internal break up of Germany. They are well aware of that fact, but, as responsible, ruling-class leaders, they are unwilling to abandon their principles for the sake of military expediency.[1]

---

[1] No! No! Marxistical baby-talk! Not a question of "the masses' properly constituted rulers remaining on top" at all; goes much deeper than these antiquated class-war concepts, profound a century ago but now superficial and misleading. The only serious threat to Nazi rule from within Germany during the war came not from the masses, but from the upper class: the conspiracy of generals and Junker aristocrats, plus a couple of liberal politicians, which culminated in the near-assassination of Hitler in August, 1944. The conspirators wanted to overthrow the Nazis and make peace simply because they were (correctly) convinced that Hitler was leading Germany to ruin. They en-

"Modern war," wrote Simone Weil, "appears as a struggle led by all the State apparatuses and their general staffs against all men old enough to bear arms. . . . The great error of nearly all studies of war . . . has been to consider war as an episode in foreign policies, when it is especially an act of interior politics, and the most atrocious act of all." (*Politics*, February, 1945.)

The common peoples of the world are coming to have less and less control over the policies of "their" governments, while at the same time they are being more and more closely identified with those governments. Or to state it in slightly different terms: as the common man's *moral* responsibility diminishes (assuming agreement that the degree of moral responsibility is in direct proportion to the degree of freedom of choice), his *practical* responsibility increases. Not for many centuries have individuals been at once so powerless to influence what is done by the national collectivities to which they belong, and at the same time so generally held responsible for what is done by those collectivities.

Where can the common peoples look for relief from this intolerable agonizing contradiction? Not to their traditional defender, the labor movement. This no longer exists in Russia, and in the two great bourgeois democracies, it has quite lost touch with the humane and democratic ideals it once believed in. Last fall, the British Trade Union Congress endorsed, 5 to 1, a statement that the German people are responsible for the crimes of Nazism; and a few weeks later the CIO convention over here resolved: "The German people must . . . atone for the crimes and horrors which they have visited on the earth." Such international working-class solidarity as once existed has vanished, and the workers of the world, including and especially those of the Soviet Union, are as brutally and rabidly nationalistic—*in their capacity as organized workers*—as their own ruling classes are.

We must look both more widely and more deeply for relief from the dilemma of increasing political impotence accompanied by increasing political responsibility. To our essential humanity

---

visaged a capitalist democracy not very different from our own (or from the present Bonn Government, for that matter), and certainly no revolutionary upheaval. Yet the concept of the Responsibility of Peoples, as expressed in Roosevelt's "unconditional surrender" line, was so strong that they got no encouragement or support from the Allies in their effort to destroy Hitler's rule from within. (1953)

and to a more sensitive and passionate respect for our own and other people's humanity.

Harold Denny in the N. Y. *Times* of Feb. 18, 1945, tells the story of a captured SS private. He was a young Ukrainian farmer who was impressed into the SS when the Germans retreated from Russia last summer. Fed up, apathetic, without interest even in tracing his family, he "appears to have no hatreds, no likes and little resentment. . . . To all questions he replies, 'I cannot know anything about that. Everything's so mixed up.' He looks and acts like a man in a profound state of shock." But the Ukrainian-farmer-SS-man had learned one thing, and he gave it as his only value-judgment:

"We are all human beings. If we had peace, if people would work together, they'd perhaps be comrades. But now—."

NOTES AND COMMENTS

Though Macdonald seeks to convince his readers, many of them probably not sympathetic to his view, that the German people ought not to bear collective responsibility for Nazi horrors, he devotes the first two sections of his essay to a demonstration that German war crimes were far worse than any others to which they might be compared. How does this strategy aid the development of his argument? Consider also the effect of the footnotes to see if his discussion with his earlier self strengthens or weakens the case the essay builds.

Macdonald's opposition to so many aspects of Allied strategy suggests research to discover what military or moral justification was offered at the time for the siege of Aachen, the bombing of Dresden, the withholding of assistance from the Polish underground, or the bombing of Nagasaki and Hiroshima. You may also wish to investigate the Morgenthau Plan and the policy of non-fraternization which required soldiers to destroy food rather than offer it to starving enemy civilians.

GEORGE BERNARD SHAW

1856-1950

George Bernard Shaw achieved unparalleled success as playwright, essayist, and critic while preaching ideas that were in themselves thoroughly unpalatable to a majority of his audience. In everything he wrote he advocated socialism, creative evolution, and unadulterated rationalism. The irony—often noted by Shaw himself—is that his witty aphorisms are quoted as often as his serious teaching is ignored. For though it was his success as a playwright that made him universally famous, he did not feel that he was primarily a "man of the theater." He considered himself a writer on political, economic, and sociological subjects who preferred to write plays rather than textbooks.

When Shaw first came to London from his native Dublin in 1876, he devoted himself to writing treatises and making public speeches for the socialist Fabian Society. In 1885 he turned to journalism as a music and drama critic, and his pieces were so perceptive and so brilliantly written that they are still widely read, although the performers and events they deal with are more than half a century behind us. When his first play, *Widowers' Houses*, was produced in 1892, he was already thirty-six and a noted critic, famous for championing the music of Wagner, the dramas of Ibsen, and the painting of Whistler. But he did not have a major theatrical triumph until 1904, when *John Bull's Other Island* started a long series of successes.

The Preface to *The Apple Cart*, written in 1929, is a typical Shavian preface. It states directly the views (in this case, on democracy) that the play illustrates obliquely.

FROM *Preface to The Apple Cart*

ON THE SUBJECT of Democracy generally I have nothing to say that can take the problem farther than I have already carried it in my Intelligent Woman's Guide to Socialism and Capitalism. We have to solve two inseparable main problems: the economic problem of how to produce and distribute our subsistence, and the political problem of how to select our rulers and prevent them from abusing their authority in their own interests or those of their class or religion. Our solution of the economic problem is the Capitalist system, which achieves miracles in production, but fails so ludicrously and disastrously to distribute its products rationally, or to produce in the order of social need, that it is always complaining of being paralysed by its 'overproduction' of things of which millions of us stand in desperate want. Our solution of the political problem is Votes for Everybody and Every Authority Elected by Vote, an expedient originally devised to prevent rulers from tyrannizing by the very effectual method of preventing them from doing anything, and thus leaving everything to irresponsible private enterprise. But as private enterprise will do nothing that is not profitable to its little self, and the very existence of civilization now depends on the swift and unhampered public execution of enterprises that supersede private enterprise and are not merely profitable but vitally necessary to the whole community, this purely inhibitive check on tyranny has become a stranglehold on genuine democracy. Its painfully evolved machinery of parliament and Party System and Cabinet is so effective in obstruction that we take thirty years by constitutional methods to do thirty minutes work, and shall presently be forced to clear up thirty years arrears in thirty minutes by unconstitutional ones unless we pass a Reform Bill that will make a complete revolution in our political machinery and procedure. When we see parliaments like ours kicked into the gutter by dictators, both in kingdoms and republics, it is foolish to wait until the dictator dies or collapses, and then do nothing but pick the poor old things up and try to scrape the mud off them: the only sane course is to take the step by which the dictatorship could have been anticipated and averted, and construct a political system for rapid positive work instead of slow nugatory work, made to fit into the twentieth century instead of into the sixteenth.

Until we face this task and accomplish it we shall not be able to produce electorates capable of doing anything by their votes except pave the way to their own destruction. An election at present, considered as a means of selecting the best qualified rulers, is so absurd that if the last dozen parliaments had consisted of the candidates who were at the foot of the poll instead of those who were at the head of it there is no reason to suppose that we should have been a step more or less advanced than we are today. In neither case would the electorate have had any real choice of representatives. If it had, we might have had to struggle with parliaments of Titus Oateses and Lord George Gordons dominating a few generals and artists, with Cabinets made up of the sort of orator who is said to carry away his hearers by his eloquence because, having first ascertained by a few cautious feelers what they are ready to applaud, he gives it to them a dozen times over in an overwhelming crescendo, and is in effect carried away by them. As it is, the voters have no real choice of candidates: they have to take what they can get and make the best of it according to their lights, which is often the worst of it by the light of heaven. By chance rather than by judgment they find themselves represented in parliament by a fortunate proportion of reasonably honest and public spirited persons who happen to be also successful public speakers. The rest are in parliament because they can afford it and have a fancy for it or an interest in it.

Last October (1929) I was asked to address the enormous audience created by the new invention of Wireless Broadcast on a range of political and cultural topics introduced by a previous speaker under the general heading of Points of View. Among the topics was Democracy, presented, as usual, in a completely abstract guise as an infinitely beneficent principle in which we must trust though it slay us. I was determined that this time Votes for Everybody and Every Authority Elected by Vote should not escape by wearing its imposing mask. I delivered myself as follows:

Your Majesties, your Royal Highnesses, your Excellencies,

your Graces and Reverences, my Lords, Ladies and Gentlemen, fellow-citizens of all degrees: I am going to talk to you about Democracy objectively: that is, as it exists and as we must all reckon with it equally, no matter what our points of view may be. Suppose I were to talk to you not about Democracy, but about the sea, which is in some respects rather like Democracy! We all have our own views of the sea. Some of us hate it and are never well when we are at it or on it. Others love it, and are never so happy as when they are in it or on it or looking at it. Some of us regard it as Britain's natural realm and surest bulwark: others want a Channel Tunnel. But certain facts about the sea are quite independent of our feelings towards it. If I take it for granted that the sea exists, none of you will contradict me. If I say that the sea is sometimes furiously violent and always uncertain, and that those who are most familiar with it trust it least, you will not immediately shriek out that I do not believe in the sea; that I am an enemy of the sea; that I want to abolish the sea; that I am going to make bathing illegal; that I am out to ruin our carrying trade and lay waste all our seaside resorts and scrap the British Navy. If I tell you that you cannot breathe in the sea, you will not take that as a personal insult and ask me indignantly if I consider you inferior to a fish. Well, you must please be equally sensible when I tell you some hard facts about Democracy. When I tell you that it is sometimes furiously violent and always dangerous and treacherous, and that those who are familiar with it as practical statesmen trust it least, you must not at once denounce me as a paid agent of Benito Mussolini, or declare that I have become a Tory Die-hard in my old age, and accuse me of wanting to take away your votes and make an end of parliament, and the franchise, and free speech, and public meeting, and trial by jury. Still less must you rise in your places and give me three rousing cheers as a champion of medieval monarchy and feudalism. I am quite innocent of any such extravagances. All I mean is that whether we are Democrats or Tories, Catholics or Protestants, Communists or Fascists, we are all face to face with a certain force in the world called Democracy; and we must understand the nature of that force whether we want to fight it or to forward it. Our business is not to deny the perils of Democracy, but to provide against them as far as we can, and then consider whether the risks we cannot provide against are worth taking.

Democracy, as you know it, is seldom more than a long word beginning with a capital letter, which we accept reverently or disparage contemptuously without asking any questions. Now we should never accept anything reverently until we have asked it a great many very searching questions, the first two being What are you? and Where do you live? When I put these questions to Democracy the answer I get is 'My name is Demos; and I live in the British Empire, the United States of America, and wherever the love of liberty burns in the heart of man. You, my friend Shaw, are a unit of Democracy: your name is also Demos: you are a citizen of a great democratic community: you are a potential constituent of the Parliament of Man, the Federation of the World.' At this I usually burst into loud cheers, which do credit to my enthusiastic nature. Tonight, however, I shall do nothing of the sort: I shall say 'Dont talk nonsense. My name is not Demos: it is Bernard Shaw. My address is not the British Empire, nor the United States of America, nor wherever the love of liberty burns in the heart of man: it is at such and such a number in such and such a street in London; and it will be time enough to discuss my seat in the Parliament of Man when that celebrated institution comes into existence. I don't believe your name is Demos: nobody's name is Demos; and all I can make of your address is that you have no address, and are just a tramp—if indeed you exist at all.'

You will notice that I am too polite to call Demos a windbag or a hot air merchant; but I am going to ask you to begin our study of Democracy by considering it first as a big balloon, filled with gas or hot air, and sent up so that you shall be kept looking up at the sky whilst other people are picking your pockets. When the balloon comes down to earth every five years or so you are invited to get into the basket if you can throw out one of the people who are sitting tightly in it; but as you can afford neither the time nor the money, and there are forty millions of you and hardly room for six hundred in the basket, the balloon goes up again with much the same lot in it and leaves you where you were before. I think you will admit that the balloon as an image of Democracy corresponds to the parliamentary facts.

Now let us examine a more poetic conception of Democracy. Abraham Lincoln is represented as standing amid the carnage of the battlefield of Gettysburg, and declaring that all that slaughter of Americans by Americans occurred in order that Democracy, defined as government *of* the people *for* the people *by* the people, should not perish from the earth. Let us pick this famous peroration to pieces and see what there really is inside it. (By the way, Lincoln did not really declaim it on the field of Gettysburg; and the American Civil War was not fought in defence of any such principle, but, on the contrary, to enable one half of the United States to force the other half to be governed as they did not wish to be governed. But never mind that. I mentioned it only to remind you that it seems impossible for statesmen to make speeches about Democracy, or journalists to report them, without obscuring it in a cloud or humbug.)

Now for the three articles of the definition. Number One: Government *of* the people: that, evidently, is necessary: a human community can no more exist without a government than a human being can exist without a co-ordinated control of its breathing and blood circulation. Number Two: Government *for* the people, is most important. Dean Inge put it perfectly for us when he called Democracy a form of society which means equal consideration for all. He added that it is a Christian principle, and that, as a Christian, he believes in it. So do I. That is why I insist on equality of income. Equal consideration for a person with a hundred a year and one with a hundred thousand is impossible. But Number Three: Government *by* the people, is quite a different matter. All the monarchs, all the tyrants, all the dictators, all the Die-hard Tories are agreed that we must be governed. Democrats like the Dean and myself are agreed that we must be governed with equal consideration for everybody. But we repudiate Number Three on the ground that the people cannot govern. The thing is a physical impossibility. Every citizen cannot be a ruler any more than every boy can be an engine driver or a pirate king. A nation of prime ministers or dictators is as absurd as an army of field marshals. Government by the people is not and never can be a reality: it is only a cry by which demagogues humbug us into voting for them. If you doubt this—if you ask me 'Why should not the people make their own laws?' I need only ask you 'Why should not the people write their own plays?' They cannot. It is much easier to write a good play than to make a good law. And there are not a hundred men in the world who can write a play good enough to stand daily wear and tear as long as a law must.

Now comes the question, If we cannot govern ourselves, what can we do to save ourselves from being at the mercy of those who *can* govern, and who may quite possibly be thoroughpaced grafters and scoundrels? The primitive answer is that as we are always in a huge majority we can, if rulers oppress us intolerably, burn their houses and tear them to pieces. This is not satisfactory. Decent people never do it until they have quite lost their heads; and when they have lost their heads they are as likely as not to burn the wrong house and tear the wrong man to pieces. When we have what is called a popular movement very few people who take part in it know what it is all about. I once saw a real popular movement in London. People were running excitedly through the streets. Everyone who saw them doing it immediately joined in the rush. They ran simply because everyone else was doing it. It was most impressive to see thousands of people sweeping along at full speed like that. There could be no doubt that it was literally a popular movement. I ascertained afterwards that it was started by a runaway cow. That cow had an important share in my education as a political philosopher; and I can assure you that if you will study crowds, and lost and terrified animals, and things like that, instead of reading books and newspaper articles, you will learn a great deal about politics from them. Most general elections, for instance, are nothing but stampedes. Our last but one was a conspicuous example of this. The cow was a Russian one.

I think we may take it that neither mob violence nor popular movements can be depended on as checks upon the abuse of power by governments. One might suppose that at least they would act as a last resort when an autocrat goes mad and commits outrageous excesses of tyranny and cruelty. But it is a curious fact that they never do. Take two famous cases: those of Nero and Tsar Paul the First of Russia. If Nero had been an ordinary professional fiddler he would probably have been no worse a man than any member of the wireless orchestra. If Paul had been a lieutenant in a line regiment we should never have heard of him. But when these two poor fellows were invested with absolute powers over their fellow-creatures they went mad, and did such appalling things that they had to be killed like mad dogs. Only, it was not the people that rose up and killed them. They were dispatched quite privately by a very select circle of their own bodyguards. For a genuinely democratic execution of unpopular statesmen we must turn to the brothers De Witt, who were torn to pieces by a Dutch mob in the seventeenth century. They were neither tyrants nor autocrats. On the contrary, one of them had been imprisoned and tortured for his resistance to the despotism of William of Orange; and the other had come to meet him as he came out of prison. The mob was on the side of the autocrat. We may take it that the shortest way for a tyrant to get rid of a troublesome champion of liberty is to raise a hue and cry against him as an unpatriotic person, and leave the mob to do the rest after supplying them with a well tipped ringleader. Nowadays this is called direct action by the revolutionary proletariat. Those who put their faith in it soon find that proletariats are never revolutionary, and that their direct action, when it is controlled at all, is usually controlled by police agents.

Democracy, then, cannot be government by the people: it can only be government by consent of the governed. Unfortunately, when democratic statesmen propose to govern us by our own consent, they find that we dont want to be governed at all, and that we regard rates and taxes and rents and death duties as intolerable burdens. What we want to know is how little government we can get along with without being murdered in our beds. That question cannot be answered until we have explained what we mean by getting along. Savages manage to get along. Unruly Arabs and Tartars get along. The only rule in the matter is that the civilized way of getting along is the way of corporate action, not individual action; and corporate action involves more government than individual action.

Thus government, which used to be a comparatively simple affair, today has to manage an enormous development of Socialism and Communism. Our industrial and social life is set in a huge communistic framework of public roadways, streets, bridges, water supplies, power supplies, lighting, tramways, schools, dockyards, and public aids and conveniences, employing a prodigious army of police, inspectors, teachers, and officials of all grades in hundreds of departments. We have found by bitter experience that it is impossible to trust factories, workshops, and mines to private management. Only by stern laws enforced by constant inspection have we stopped the monstrous waste of human life and welfare it cost when it was left uncontrolled by the Government. During the war our attempt to leave the munitioning of the army to pri-

vate enterprise led us to the verge of defeat and caused an appalling slaughter of our soldiers. When the Government took the
work out of private hands and had it done in national factories
it was at once successful. The private firms were still allowed to
do what little they could; but they had to be taught to do it economically, and to keep their accounts properly, by Government
officials. Our big capitalist enterprises now run to the Government
for help as a lamb runs to its mother. They cannot even make an
extension of the Tube railway in London without Government aid.
Unassisted private capitalism is breaking down or getting left behind in all directions. If all our Socialism and Communism and
the drastic taxation of unearned incomes which finances it were to
stop, our private enterprises would drop like shot stags, and we
should all be dead in a month. When Mr Baldwin tried to win
the last election by declaring that Socialism had been a failure
whenever and wherever it had been tried, Socialism went over him
like a steam roller and handed his office to a Socialist Prime Minister. Nothing could save us in the war but a great extension of
Socialism; and now it is clear enough that only still greater exten-
sions of it can repair the ravages of the war and keep pace with
the growing requirements of civilization.

What we have to ask ourselves, then, is not whether we will
have Socialism and Communism or not, but whether Democracy
can keep pace with the developments of both that are being forced
on us by the growth of national and international corporate action.

Now corporate action is impossible without a governing body.
It may be the central Government: it may be a municipal corporation, a county council, a district council, or a parish council. It
may be the board of directors of a joint stock company, or of a
trust made by combining several joint stock companies. Such
boards, elected by the votes of the shareholders, are little States
within the State, and very powerful ones, too, some of them. If
they have not laws and kings, they have by-laws and chairmen. And
you and I, the consumers of their services, are more at the mercy
of the boards that organize them than we are at the mercy of
parliament. Several active politicians who began as Liberals and
are now Socialists have said to me that they were converted by
seeing that the nation had to choose, not between governmental
control of industry and control by separate private individuals kept
in order by their competition for our custom, but between govern-

mental control and control by gigantic trusts wielding great power without responsibility, and having no object but to make as much money out of us as possible. Our Government is at this moment having much more trouble with the private corporations on whom we are dependent for our coals and cotton goods than with France or the United States of America. We are in the hands of our corporate bodies, public or private, for the satisfaction of our everyday needs. Their powers are life and death powers. I need not labor this point: we all know it.

But what we do not all realize is that we are equally dependent on corporate action for the satisfaction of our religious needs. Dean Inge tells us that our general elections have become public auctions at which the contending parties bid against one another for our votes by each promising us a larger share than the other of the plunder of the minority. Now that is perfectly true. The contending parties do not as yet venture to put it exactly in those words; but that is what it comes to. And the Dean's profession obliges him to urge his congregation, which is much wider than that of St Paul's (it extends across the Atlantic), always to vote for the party which pledges itself to go farthest in enabling those of us who have great possessions to sell them and give the price to the poor. But we cannot do this as private persons. It must be done by the Government or not at all. Take my own case. I am not a young man with great possessions; but I am an old man paying enough in income tax and surtax to provide doles for some hundreds of unemployed and old age pensioners. I have not the smallest objection to this: on the contrary, I advocated it strongly for years before I had any income worth taxing. But I could not do it if the Government did not arrange it for me. If the Government ceased taxing my superfluous money and redistributing it among people who have no incomes at all, I could do nothing by myself. What could I do? Can you suggest anything? I could send my war bonds to the Chancellor of the Exchequer and invite him to cancel the part of the National Debt that they represent; and he would undoubtedly thank me in the most courteous official terms for my patriotism. But the poor would not get any of it. The other payers of surtax and income tax and death duties would save the interest they now have to pay on it: that is all. I should only have made the rich richer and myself poorer. I could burn all my share certificates and inform the secretaries of the companies that they might write off that much of their capital indebtedness. The result would be a bigger dividend for the rest of the shareholders, with the poor out in the cold as before. I might sell my war bonds and share certificates for cash, and throw the money into the street to be scrambled for; but it would be snatched up, not by the poorest, but by the best fed and most able-bodied of the scramblers. Besides, if we all tried to sell our bonds and shares—and this is what you have to consider; for Christ's advice was not addressed to me alone but to all who have great possessions—the result would be that their value would fall to nothing, as the Stock Exchange would immediately become a market in which there were all sellers and no buyers. Accordingly, any spare money that the Government leaves me is invested where I can get the highest interest and the best security, as thereby I can make sure that it goes where it is most wanted and gives immediate employment. This is the best I can do without Government interference: indeed any other way of dealing with my spare money would be foolish and demoralizing; but the result is that I become richer and richer, and the poor become relatively poorer and poorer. So you see I cannot even be a Christian except through Government action; and neither can the Dean.

Now let us get down to our problem. We cannot govern ourselves; yet if we entrust the immense powers and revenues which are necessary in an effective modern Government to an absolute monarch or dictator, he goes more or less mad unless he is a quite extraordinary and therefore very seldom obtainable person. Besides, modern government is not a one-man job: it is too big for that. If we resort to a committee or parliament of superior persons, they will set up an oligarchy and abuse their power for their own benefit. Our dilemma is that men in the lump cannot govern themselves; and yet, as William Morris put it, no man is good enough to be another man's master. We need to be governed, and yet to control our governors. But the best governors will not accept any control except that of their own consciences; and, as we who are governed are also apt to abuse any power of control we have, our ignorance, our passions, our private and immediate interests are constantly in conflict with the knowledge, the wisdom, and the public spirit and regard for the future of our best qualified governors.

Still, if we cannot control our governors, can we not at least choose them and change them if they do not suit?

Let me invent a primitive example of democratic choice. It is always best to take imaginary examples: they offend nobody. Imagine then that we are the inhabitants of a village. We have to elect somebody for the office of postman. There are several candidates; but one stands out conspicuously, because he has frequently treated us at the public-house, has subscribed a shilling to our little flower show, has a kind word for the children when he passes, and is a victim of oppression by the squire because his late father was one of our most successful poachers. We elect him triumphantly; and he is duly installed, uniformed, provided with a red bicycle, and given a batch of letters to deliver. As his motive in seeking the post has been pure ambition, he has not thought much beforehand about his duties; and it now occurs to him for the first time that he cannot read. So he hires a boy to come round with him and read the addresses. The boy conceals himself in the lane whilst the postman delivers the letters at the house, takes the Christmas boxes, and gets the whole credit of the transaction. In course of time he dies with a high reputation for efficiency in the discharge of his duties; and we elect another equally illiterate successor on similar grounds. But by this time the boy has grown up and become an institution. He presents himself to the new postman as an established and indispensable feature of the postal system, and finally becomes recognized and paid by the village as such.

Here you have the perfect image of a popularly elected Cabinet Minister and the Civil Service department over which he presides. It may work very well; for our postman, though illiterate, may be a very capable fellow; and the boy who reads the addresses for him may be quite incapable of doing anything more. But this does not always happen. Whether it happens or not, the system is not a democratic reality: it is a democratic illusion. The boy, when he has ability enough to take advantage of the situation, is the master of the man. The person elected to do the work is not really doing it: he is a popular humbug who is merely doing what a permanent official tells him to do. That is how it comes about that we are now governed by a Civil Service which has such enormous power that its regulations are taking the place of the laws of

England, though some of them are made for the convenience of
the officials without the slightest regard to the convenience or
even the rights of the public. And how are our Civil Servants selected? Mostly by an educational test which nobody but an ex-
pensively schooled youth can pass, thus making the most powerful
and effective part of our government an irresponsible class government.

Now, what control have you or I over the Services? We have
votes. I have used mine a few times to see what it is like. Well,
it is like this. When the election approaches, two or three persons
of whom I know nothing write to me soliciting my vote and en-
closing a list of meetings, an election address, and a polling card.
One of the addresses reads like an article in *The Morning Post*,
and has a Union Jack on it. Another is like *The Daily News* or
Manchester Guardian. Both might have been compiled from the
editorial waste paper baskets of a hundred years ago. A third address, more up-to-date and much better phrased, convinces me that
the sender has had it written for him at the headquarters of the
Labor Party. A fourth, the most hopelessly out of date of them
all, contains scraps of the early English translations of the Communist Manifesto of 1848. I have no guarantee that any of these
documents were written by the candidates. They convey nothing
whatever to me as to their character or political capacity. The half-
tone photographic portraits which adorn the front pages do not
even tell me their ages, having been taken twenty years ago. If I
go to one of the meetings I find a schoolroom packed with people
who find an election meeting cheaper and funnier than a theatre.
On the platform sit one or two poor men who have worked hard
to keep party politics alive in the constituency. They ought to be
the candidates; but they have no more chance of such eminence
than they have of possessing a Rolls-Royce car. They move votes
of confidence in the candidate, though as the candidate is a
stranger to them and to everybody else present nobody can possibly
feel any such confidence. They lead the applause for him; they
prompt him when questions are asked; and when he is completely
floored they jump up and cry 'Let me answer that, Mr Chairman!'
and then pretend that he has answered it. The old shibboleths are
droned over; and nothing has any sense or reality in it except the
vituperation of the opposition party, which is received with shouts
of relief by the audience. Yet it is nothing but an exhibition of bad

manners. If I vote for one of these candidates, and he or she is elected, I am supposed to be enjoying a democratic control of the government—to be exercising government *of* myself, *for* myself, *by* myself. Do you wonder that the Dean cannot believe such nonsense? If I believed it I should not be fit to vote at all. If this is Democracy, who can blame Signor Mussolini for describing it as a putrefying corpse?

The candidates may ask me what more they can do for me but present themselves and answer any questions I may put to them. I quite admit that they can do nothing; but that does not mend matters. What I should like is a real test of their capacity. Shortly before the war a doctor in San Francisco discovered that if a drop of a candidate's blood can be obtained on a piece of blotting paper it is possible to discover within half an hour what is wrong with him physically. What I am waiting for is the discovery of a process by which on delivery of a drop of his blood or a lock of his hair we can ascertain what is right with him mentally. We could then have a graded series of panels of capable persons for all employments, public or private, and not allow any person, however popular, to undertake the employment of governing us unless he or she were on the appropriate panel. At the lower end of the scale there would be a panel of persons qualified to take part in a parish meeting; at the higher end a panel of persons qualified to act as Secretaries of State for Foreign Affairs or Finance Ministers. At present not more than two per thousand of the population would be available for the highest panel. I should then be in no danger of electing a postman and finding that he could neither read nor write. My choice of candidates would be perhaps more restricted than at present; but I do not desire liberty to choose windbags and nincompoops to represent me in parliament; and my power to choose between one qualified candidate and another would give as much control as is either possible or desirable. The voting and counting would be done by machinery: I should connect my telephone with the proper office; touch a button; and the machinery would do the rest.

Pending such a completion of the American doctor's discovery, how are we to go on? Well, as best we can, with the sort of government that our present system produces. Several reforms are possible without any new discovery. Our present parliament is obsolete: it can no more do the work of a modern State than Julius

Caesar's galley could do the work of an Atlantic liner. We need in these islands two or three additional federal legislatures, working on our municipal committee system instead of our parliamentary party system. We need a central authority to co-ordinate the federal work. Our obsolete little internal frontiers must be obliterated, and our units of local government enlarged to dimensions compatible with the recent prodigious advances in facility of communication and co-operation. Commonwealth affairs and supernational activities through the League of Nations or otherwise will have to be provided for, and Cabinet function to be transformed. All the pseudo-democratic obstructive functions of our political machinery must be ruthlessly scrapped, and the general problem of government approached from a positive viewpoint at which mere anarchic national sovereignty as distinguished from self-government will have no meaning.

I must conclude by warning you that when everything has been done that can be done, civilization will still be dependent on the consciences of the governors and the governed. Our natural dispositions may be good; but we have been badly brought up, and are full of anti-social personal ambitions and prejudices and snobberies. Had we not better teach our children to be better citizens than ourselves? We are not doing that at present. The Russians *are*. That is my last word. Think over it.

NOTES AND COMMENTS

Shaw always sought to cut through the fog of illusions, accepted theories, and unquestioned traditions which, he contended, envelop us. In this preface he attacks our assumptions about democracy. Does his failure to offer alternatives weaken the impact of his criticism?

One of Shaw's favorite techniques is the *homely analogy*, carefully carried beyond obvious similarities. Here, for instance, he compares a politician to a postman, and democracy to the sea. Does immediacy of understanding compensate for exaggeration? Compare Shaw's analogies with those used by Russell in describing complex physical processes in *The ABC of Relativity* (page 381). Contrast the always good-natured, but no less dogmatic, tone of Shaw's shocking reversals of accepted truisms with Mencken's more contemptuous debunking in "The Poetry of Christianity" (page 373) or with Dwight Macdonald's direct, expository style in "The Responsibility of Peoples" (page 4). Which succeeds best in making the reader consider the author's argument seriously?

EDMUND BURKE

1729-1797

Though Edmund Burke is considered the fountainhead of contemporary political conservatism, he was disconcertingly liberal in the eyes of men of his own day. As a Member of Parliament, he not only supported the demands of the American colonists before the Revolution, but also advocated advanced and enlightened policies toward India. Though he was himself a Protestant, he favored mitigating the Penal Laws against Catholics. And his attempt to secure for Ireland the trade rights she needed for survival lost him the support of his constituents in Bristol.

But the same political principles that led Burke to support the American Revolution set him firmly against the French. He was convinced that in politics wisdom is not achieved *a priori* on the basis of abstract ideas, for "circumstances are what render every civil and political scheme beneficial or noxious to mankind," and "circumstances" for him included not only material and moral considerations but also the history, habits, and temperament of the people involved. The Americans, as Burke saw it, wanted only the political institutions which were theirs by right of inheritance since they too were Englishmen. The French, in overturning a tradition, denied history and destroyed their patrimony. In seeking to innovate, to institute on metaphysical principles a totally new form of government, the French experiment was not creative, but destructive.

Burke's long essay, *Reflections on the Revolution in France* (1790), from which the present selection is taken, began as a letter to a young Parisian who had asked his opinion of the French situation. It also expresses Burke's distress at the growing number of English radicals who wanted to emulate the Jacobins.

FROM *Reflections on the Revolution in France*

. . . YOU WILL OBSERVE, that from Magna Charta to the Declaration of Right, it has been the uniform policy of our constitution to claim and assert our liberties, as an *entailed inheritance* derived to us from our forefathers, and to be transmitted to our posterity; as an estate specially belonging to the people of this kingdom, without any reference whatever to any other more general or prior right. By this means our constitution preserves a unity in so great a diversity of its parts. We have an inheritable crown; an inheritable peerage; and a House of Commons and a people inheriting privileges, franchises, and liberties, from a long line of ancestors.

This policy appears to me to be the result of profound reflection; or rather the happy effect of following nature, which is wisdom without reflection, and above it. A spirit of innovation is generally the result of a selfish temper, and confined views. People will not look forward to posterity, who never look backward to their ancestors. Besides, the people of England well know, that the idea of inheritance furnishes a sure principle of conservation, and a sure principle of transmission; without at all excluding a principle of improvement. It leaves acquisition free; but it secures what it acquires. Whatever advantages are obtained by a state proceeding on these maxims, are locked fast as in a sort of family settlement; grasped as in a kind of mortmain for ever. By a constitutional policy, working after the pattern of nature, we receive, we hold, we transmit our government and our privileges, in the same manner in which we enjoy and transmit our property and our lives. The institutions of policy, the goods of fortune, the gifts of providence, are handed down to us, and from us, in the same course and order. Our political system is placed in a just correspondence and symmetry with the order of the world, and with the mode of existence decreed to a permanent body composed of transitory parts; wherein, by the disposition of a stupendous wisdom, moulding together the great mysterious incorporation of the human race, the whole, at one time, is never old, or middle-aged, or young, but, in a condition of unchangeable constancy, moves on through the varied tenor of perpetual decay, fall, renovation, and progression. Thus, by preserving the method of nature in the conduct of the state, in what we improve, we are never wholly new; in what we retain, we are never wholly obsolete. By adhering in this manner and on those principles to our forefathers, we are guided not by the superstition of antiquarians, but by the spirit of philosophic analogy. In this choice of inheritance we have given to our frame of policy the image of a relation in blood; binding up the constitution of our country with our dearest domestic ties; adopting our fundamental laws into the bosom of our family affections; keeping inseparable, and cherishing with the warmth of all their combined and mutually reflected charities, our state, our hearths, our sepulchres, and our altars.

Through the same plan of a conformity to nature in our artificial institutions, and by calling in the aid of her unerring and powerful instincts, to fortify the fallible and feeble contrivances of our reason, we have derived several other, and those no small benefits, from considering our liberties in the light of an inheritance. Always acting as if in the presence of canonized forefathers, the spirit of freedom, leading in itself to misrule and excess, is tempered with an awful gravity. This idea of a liberal descent inspires us with a sense of habitual native dignity, which prevents that upstart insolence almost inevitably adhering to and disgracing those who are the first acquirers of any distinction. By this means our liberty becomes a noble freedom. It carries an imposing and majestic aspect. It has a pedigree and illustrating ancestors. It has its bearings and its ensigns armorial. It has its gallery of portraits; its monumental inscriptions; its records, evidences, and titles. We procure reverence to our civil institutions on the principle upon which nature teaches us to revere individual men; on account of their age, and on account of those from whom they are descended. All your sophisters cannot produce anything better adapted to preserve a rational and manly freedom than the course that we have pursued, who have chosen our nature rather than our speculations, our breasts rather than our inventions, for the great conservatories and magazines of our rights and privileges.

You might, if you pleased, have profited of our example, and have given to your recovered freedom a correspondent dignity. Your privileges, though discontinued, were not lost to memory. Your constitution, it is true, whilst you were out of possession,

suffered waste and dilapidation; but you possessed in some parts
the walls, and, in all, the foundations, of a noble and venerable
castle. You might have repaired those walls; you might have built
on those old foundations. Your constitution was suspended before
it was perfected; but you had the elements of a constitution very
nearly as good as could be wished. In your old states[1] you possessed that variety of parts corresponding with the various descriptions of which your community was happily composed; you had all
that combination, and all that opposition of interests, you had
that action and counteraction, which, in the natural and in the
political world, from the reciprocal struggle of discordant powers,
draws out the harmony of the universe. These opposed and conflicting interests, which you considered as so great a blemish in
your old and in our present constitution, interpose a salutary
check to all precipitate resolutions. They render deliberation a
matter not of choice, but of necessity; they make all change a
subject of *compromise*, which naturally begets moderation; they
produce *temperaments* preventing the sore evil of harsh, crude,
unqualified reformations; and rendering all the headlong exertions
of arbitrary power, in the few or in the many, for ever impractica-
ble. Through that diversity of members and interests, general liberty had as many securities as there were separate views in the
several orders; whilst by pressing down the whole by the weight of
a real monarchy, the separate parts would have been prevented
from warping, and starting from their allotted places.

You had all these advantages in your ancient states; but you
chose to act as if you had never been moulded into civil society,
and had everything to begin anew. You began ill, because you
began by despising everything that belonged to you. You set up
your trade without a capital. If the last generations of your country appeared without much lustre in your eyes, you might have
passed them by, and derived your claims from a more early race
of ancestors. Under a pious predilection for those ancestors, your
imaginations would have realized in them a standard of virtue and
wisdom, beyond the vulgar practice of the hour: and you would
have risen with the example to whose imitation you aspired. Respecting your forefathers, you would have been taught to respect
yourselves. You would not have chosen to consider the French as

---

[1] The Estates General, the French parliament.—*Ed.*]

a people of yesterday, as a nation of low-born servile wretches until the emancipating year of 1789. In order to furnish, at the expense of your honour, an excuse to your apologists here for several enormities of yours, you would not have been content to be repre sented as a gang of Maroon slaves, suddenly broke loose from the house of bondage, and therefore to be pardoned for your abuse of the liberty to which you were not accustomed, and ill fitted. Would it not, my worthy friend, have been wiser to have you thought, what I, for one, always thought you, a generous and gallant nation, long misled to your disadvantage by your high and romantic sentiments of fidelity, honour, and loyalty; that events had been unfavourable to you, but that you were not enslaved through any illiberal or servile disposition; that in your most devoted submission, you were actuated by a principle of public spirit, and that it was your country you worshipped, in the person of your king? Had you made it to be understood, that in the delusion of this amiable error you had gone further than your wise ancestors; that you were resolved to resume your ancient privileges, whilst you preserved the spirit of your ancient and your recent loyalty and honour; or if, diffident of yourselves, and not clearly discerning the almost obliterated constitution of your ancestors, you had looked to your neighbours in this land, who had kept alive the ancient principles and models of the old common law of Europe meliorated and adapted to its present state—by following wise examples you would have given new examples of wisdom to the world. You would have rendered the cause of liberty venerable in the eyes of every worthy mind in every nation. You would have shamed despotism from the earth, by showing that freedom was not only reconcilable. but, as when well disciplined it is, auxiliary to law. You would have had an unoppressive but a productive revenue. You would have had a flourishing commerce to feed it. You would have had a free constitution; a potent monarchy; a disciplined army; a reformed and venerated clergy; a mitigated but spirited nobility, to lead your virtue, not to overlay it; you would have had a liberal order of commons, to emulate and to recruit that nobility; you would have had a protected, satisfied, laborious, and obedient people, taught to seek and to recognise the happiness that is to be found by virtue in all conditions; in which consists the true moral equality of mankind, and not in that monstrous fiction, which, by inspiring false ideas and vain expectations into men destined to travel in the obscure walk of laborious life, serves only to aggravate and embitter that real inequality, which it never can remove; and which the order of civil life establishes as much for the benefit of those whom it must leave in an humble state, as those whom it is able to exalt to a condition more splendid, but not more happy. You had a smooth and easy career of felicity and glory laid open to you, beyond anything recorded in the history of the world; but you have shown that difficulty is good for man.

Compute your gains: see what is got by those extravagant and presumptuous speculations which have taught your leaders to despise all their predecessors, and all their contemporaries, and even to despise themselves, until the moment in which they became truly despicable. By following those false lights, France has bought undisguised calamities at a higher price than any nation has purchased the most unequivocal blessings! France has bought poverty by crime! France has not sacrificed her virtue to her interest, but she has abandoned her interest, that she might prostitute her virtue. All other nations have begun the fabric of a new government, or the reformation of an old, by establishing originally, or by enforcing with greater exactness, some rites or other of religion. All other people have laid the foundations of civil freedom in severer manners, and a system of a more austere and masculine morality. France, when she let loose the reins of regal authority, doubled the license of a ferocious dissoluteness in manners, and of an insolent irreligion in opinions and practices; and has extended through all ranks of life, as if she were communicating some privilege, or laying open some secluded benefit, all the unhappy corruptions that usually were the disease of wealth and power. This is one of the new principles of equality in France.

France, by the perfidy of her leaders, has utterly disgraced the tone of lenient council in the cabinets of princes, and disarmed it of its most potent topics. She has sanctified the dark, suspicious maxims of tyrannous distrust; and taught kings to tremble at (what will hereafter be called) the delusive plausibilities of moral politicians. Sovereigns will consider those, who advise them to place an unlimited confidence in their people, as subverters of their thrones; as traitors who aim at their destruction, by leading their easy good-nature, under specious pretences, to admit combinations of bold and faithless men into a participation of their power. This alone (if there were nothing else) is an irreparable calamity to you and to mankind. Remember that your parliament of Paris told your king, that, in calling the states together, he had nothing to fear but the prodigal excess of their zeal in providing for the support of the throne. It is right that these men should hide their heads. It is right that they should bear their part in the ruin which their counsel has brought on their sovereign and their country. Such sanguine declarations tend to lull authority asleep; to encourage it rashly to engage in perilous adventures of untried policy; to neglect those provisions, preparations, and precautions, which distinguished benevolence from imbecility; and without which no man can answer for the salutary effect of any abstract plan of government or of freedom. For want of these, they have seen the medicine of the state corrupted into its poison. They have seen the French rebel against a mild and lawful monarch, with more fury, outrage, and insult, than ever any people has been known to rise against the most illegal usurper, or the most sanguinary tyrant. Their resistance was made to concession; their revolt was from protection; their blow was aimed at a hand holding out graces, favours, and immunities.

This was unnatural. The rest is in order. They have found their punishment in their success. Laws overturned; tribunals subverted; industry without vigour; commerce expiring; the revenue unpaid, yet the people impoverished; a church pillaged, and a state not relieved; civil and military anarchy made the constitution of the kingdom; everything human and divine sacrificed to the idol of public credit, and national bankruptcy the consequence; and, to crown all, the paper securities of new, precarious, tottering power, the discredited paper securities of impoverished fraud and beggared rapine, held out as a currency for the support of an empire, in lieu of the two great recognised species that represent the lasting, conventional credit of mankind, which disappeared and hid themselves in the earth from whence they came, when the principle of property, whose creatures and representatives they are, was systematically subverted.

Were all these dreadful things necessary? Were they the inevitable results of the desperate struggle of determined patriots, compelled to wade through blood and tumult, to the quiet shore of a tranquil and prosperous liberty? No! nothing like it. The fresh ruins of France, which shock our feelings wherever we can turn our eyes, are not the devastation of civil war; they are the sad but instructive monuments of rash and ignorant counsel in time of profound peace. They are the display of inconsiderate and presumptuous, because unresisted and irresistible, authority. The persons who have thus squandered away the precious treasure of their crimes, the persons who have made this prodigal and wild waste of public evils, (the last stake reserved for the ultimate ransom of the state,) have met in their progress with little, or rather with no opposition at all. Their whole march was more like a triumphal procession, than the progress of a war. Their pioneers have gone before them, and demolished and laid everything level at their feet. Not one drop of *their* blood have they shed in the cause of the country they have ruined. They have made no sacrifices to their projects of greater consequence than their shoe-buckles, whilst they were imprisoning their king, murdering their fellow-citizens, and bathing in tears, and plunging in poverty and distress, thousands of worthy men and worthy families. Their cruelty has not ever been the base result of fear. It has been the effect of their sense of perfect safety, in authorizing treasons, robberies, rapes, assassinations, slaughters, and burnings, throughout their harassed land. But the cause of all was plain from the beginning.

This unforced choice, this fond election of evil, would appear perfectly unaccountable, if we did not consider the composition of the National Assembly: I do not mean its formal constitution, which, as it now stands, is exceptionable enough, but the materials of which, in a great measure, it is composed, which is of ten thousand times greater consequence than all the formalities in the world. If we were to know nothing of this assembly but by its title and function, no colours could paint to the imagination anything more venerable. In that light the mind of an inquirer, subdued by such an awful image as that of the virtue and wisdom of a whole people collected into a focus, would pause and hesitate in condemning things even of the very worst aspect. Instead of blameable, they would appear only mysterious. But no name, no power, no function, no artificial institution whatsoever, can make the men of whom any system of authority is composed, any other than God, and nature, and education, and their habits of life have made them. Capacities beyond these the people have not to give. Virtue and wisdom may be the objects of their choice; but their choice confers neither the one nor the other on those upon whom they lay their ordaining hands. They have not the engagement of nature, they have not the promise of revelation, for any such powers. . . .

I see that your example is held out to shame us. I know that we are supposed a dull, sluggish race, rendered passive by finding our situation tolerable, and prevented by a mediocrity of freedom from ever attaining to its full perfection. Your leaders in France began by affecting to admire, almost to adore, the British constitution; but as they advanced, they came to look upon it with a sovereign contempt. The friends of your National Assembly amongst us have full as mean an opinion of what was formerly thought the glory of their country. The Revolution Society has discovered that the English nation is not free. They are convinced that the inequality in our representation is a "defect in our constitution *so gross and palpable,* as to make it excellent chiefly in *form* and *theory.*" That a representation in the legislature of a kingdom is not only the basis of all constitutional liberty in it, but of *"all legitimate government;* that without it a *government* is nothing but an *usurpation;"*—that "when the representation is *partial,* the kingdom possesses liberty only *partially;* and if extremely partial, it gives only a *semblance;* and if not only extremely partial, but corruptly chosen, it becomes a *nuisance.*" Dr. Price[1] considers this inadequacy of representation as our *fundamental grievance;* and though, as to the corruption of this semblance of representation, he hopes it is not yet arrived to its full perfection of depravity, he fears that "nothing will be done towards gaining for us this *essential blessing,* until some *great abuse of power* again provokes our resentment, or some *great calamity* again alarms our fears, or perhaps till the acquisition of a *pure and equal representation by other countries,* whilst we are *mocked* with the *shadow,* kindles our shame." To this he subjoins a note in these words: "A representation chosen chiefly by the treasury, and a *few* thousands of the *dregs* of the people, who are generally paid for their votes."

You will smile here at the consistency of those democratists,

---

[1 Richard Price, a dissenting clergyman, who in November, 1789, had preached a sermon urging that the British Constitution be overthrown, by force if necessary, because it was not fully in accord with the Rights of Man. —*Ed.*]

who, when they are not on their guard, treat the humbler part of the community with the greatest contempt, whilst, at the same time, they pretend to make them the depositories of all power. It would require a long discourse to point out to you the many fallacies that lurk in the generality and equivocal nature of the terms "inadequate representation." I shall only say here, in justice to that old-fashioned constitution, under which we have long prospered, that our representation has been found perfectly adequate to all the purposes for which a representation of the people can be desired or devised. I defy the enemies of our constitution to show the contrary. To detail the particulars in which it is found so well to promote its ends, would demand a treatise on our practical constitution. I state here the doctrine of the Revolutionists, only that you and others may see what an opinion these gentlemen entertain of the constitution of their country, and why they seem to think that some great abuse of power, or some great calamity, as giving a chance for the blessing of a constitution according to their ideas, would be much palliated to their feelings; you see *why they* are so much enamoured of your fair and equal representation, which being once obtained, the same effects might follow. You see they consider our House of Commons as only "a semblance," "a form," a theory," "a shadow," "a mockery," perhaps "a nuisance."

These gentlemen value themselves on being systematic; and not without reason. They must therefore look on this gross and palpable defect of representation, this fundamental grievance (so they call it), as a thing not only vicious in itself, but as rendering our whole government absolutely *illegitimate,* and not at all better than a downright *usurpation.* Another revolution, to get rid of this illegitimate and usurped government, would of course be perfectly justifiable, if not absolutely necessary. Indeed their principle, if you observe it with any attention, goes much further than to an alteration in the election of the House of Commons; for, if popular representation, or choice, is necessary to the *legitimacy* of all government, the House of Lords is, at one stroke, bastardized and corrupted in blood. That House is no representative of the people at all, even in "semblance or in form." The case of the crown is altogether as bad. In vain the crown may endeavour to screen itself against these gentlemen by the authority of the establishment made on the Revolution.[1] The Revolution which is resorted to for a title, on their system, wants a title itself. The Revolution is built, according to their theory, upon a basis not more solid than our present formalities, as it was made by a House of Lords, not representing any one but themselves; and by a House of Commons exactly such as the present, that is, as they term it, by a mere "shadow and mockery" of representation.

Something they must destroy, or they seem to themselves to exist for no purpose. One set is for destroying the civil power through the ecclesiastical; another, for demolishing the ecclesiastic through the civil. They are aware that the worst consequences might happen to the public in accomplishing this double ruin of church and state; but they are so heated with their theories, that they give more than hints, that this ruin, with all the mischiefs that must lead to it and attend it, and which to themselves appear quite certain, would not be unacceptable to them, or very remote from their wishes. A man amongst them of great authority, and certainly of great talents, speaking of a supposed alliance between church and state, says, "perhaps *we must wait for the fall of the civil powers* before this most unnatural alliance be broken. Calamitous no doubt will that time be. But what convulsion in the political world ought to be a subject of lamentation, if it be attended with so desirable an effect?" You see with what a steady eye these gentlemen are prepared to view the greatest calamities which can befall their country.

It is no wonder therefore, that with these ideas of everything in their constitution and government at home, either in church or state, as illegitimate and usurped, or at best as a vain mockery, they look abroad with an eager and passionate enthusiasm. Whilst they are possessed by these notions, it is vain to talk to them of the practice of their ancestors, the fundamental laws of their country, the fixed form of a constitution, whose merits are confirmed by the solid test of long experience, and an increasing public strength and national prosperity. They despise experience

---

[1 The "Glorious Revolution" of 1688, which established the Protestant Succession. The throne passed from William and Mary to Anne, the last of the Stuarts, and then to the House of Hanover, of which George III, who reigned when Burke wrote, was a member.—*Ed.*]

as the wisdom of unlettered men; and as for the rest, they have
wrought under-ground a mine that will blow up, at one grand
explosion, all examples of antiquity, all precedents, charters, and
acts of parliament. They have "the rights of men." Against these
there can be no prescription; against these no agreement is binding: these admit no temperament, and no compromise: anything
withheld from their full demand is so much of fraud and injustice.
Against these their rights of men let no government look for
security in the length of its continuance, or in the justice and
lenity of its administration. The objections of these speculatists,
if its forms do not quadrate with their theories, are as valid
against such an old and beneficent government, as against the
most violent tyranny, or the greenest usurpation. They are always
at issue with governments, not on a question of abuse, but a
question of competency, and a question of title. I have nothing to
say to the clumsy subtilty of their political metaphysics. Let
them be their amusement in the schools.—*"Illa se jactat in aula
—Æolus, et clauso ventorum carcere regnet."* [1]—But let them not
break prison to burst like a *Levanter*, to sweep the earth with their
hurricane, and to break up the fountains of the great deep to
overwhelm us.

Far am I from denying in theory, full as far is my heart from
withholding in practice, (if I were of power to give or to with-
hold,) the *real* rights of men. In denying their false claims of
right, I do not mean to injure those which are real, and are such
as their pretended rights would totally destroy. If civil society be
made for the advantage of man, all the advantages for which it is
made become his right. It is an institution of beneficence; and
law itself is only beneficence acting by a rule. Men have a right
to live by that rule; they have a right to do justice, as between
their fellows, whether their fellows are in public function or in
ordinary occupation. They have a right to the fruits of their industry; and to the means of making their industry fruitful. They have
a right to the acquisitions of their parents; to the nourishment
and improvement of their offspring; to instruction in life, and to
consolation in death. Whatever each man can separately do, without trespassing upon others, he has a right to do for himself; and
he has a right to a fair portion of all which society, with all its

---

[1] Virgil, *Aeneid*, I. 140. [Let Æolus strut about in his hall, and reign in
the closed prison of the winds.—*Ed.*]

combinations of skill and force, can do in his favour. In this partnership all men have equal rights; but not to equal things. He that has but five shillings in the partnership, has as good a right to it, as he that has five hundred pounds has to his larger proportion. But he has not a right to an equal dividend in the product of the joint stock; and as to the share of power, authority, and direction which each individual ought to have in the management of the state, that I must deny to be amongst the direct original rights of man in civil society; for I have in my contemplation the civil social man, and no other. It is a thing to be settled by convention.

If civil society be the offspring of convention, that convention must be its law. That convention must limit and modify all the descriptions of constitution which are formed under it. Every sort of legislative, judicial, or executory power are its creatures. They can have no being in any other state of things; and how can any man claim under the conventions of civil society, rights which do not so much as suppose its existence? rights which are absolutely repugnant to it? One of the first motives to civil society, and which becomes one of its fundamental rules, is, *that no man should be judge in his own cause.* By this each person has at once divested himself of the first fundamental right of uncovenanted man, that is, to judge for himself, and to assert his own cause. He abdicates all rights to be his own governor. He inclusively, in a great measure, abandons the right of self-defence, the first law of nature. Men cannot enjoy the rights of an uncivil and of a civil state together. That he may obtain justice, he gives up his right of determining what it is in points the most essential to him. That he may secure some liberty, he makes a surrender in trust of the whole of it.

Government is not made in virtue of natural rights, which may and do exist in total independence of it; and exist in much greater clearness, and in a much greater degree of abstract perfection: but their abstract perfection is their practical defect. By having a right to everything they want everything. Government is a contrivance of human wisdom to provide for human *wants.* Men have a right that these wants should be provided for by this wisdom. Among these wants is to be reckoned the want, out of civil society, of a sufficient restraint upon their passions. Society requires not only that the passions of individuals should be subjected, but that even in the mass and body, as well as in the individuals, the inclinations of men should frequently be thwarted, their will controlled, and their passions brought into subjection. This can only be done *by a power out of themselves*; and not, in the exercise of its function, subject to that will and to those passions which it is its office to bridle and subdue. In this sense the restraints on men, as well as their liberties, are to be reckoned among their rights. But as the liberties and the restrictions vary with times and circumstances, and admit of infinite modifications, they cannot be settled upon any abstract rule; and nothing is so foolish as to discuss them upon that principle.

The moment you abate anything from the full rights of men, each to govern himself, and suffer any artificial, positive limitation upon these rights, from that moment the whole organization of government becomes a consideration of convenience. This it is which makes the constitution of a state, and the due distribution of its powers, a matter of the most delicate and complicated skill. It requires a deep knowledge of human nature and human necessities, and of the things which facilitate or obstruct the various ends, which are to be pursued by the mechanism of civil institutions. The state is to have recruits to its strength, and remedies to its distempers. What is the use of discussing a man's abstract right to food or medicine? The question is upon the method of procuring and administering them. In that deliberation I shall always advise to call in the aid of the farmer and the physician, rather than the professor of metaphysics.

The science of constructing a commonwealth, or renovating it, or reforming it, is, like every other experimental science, not to be taught *à priori*. Nor is it a short experience that can instruct us in that practical science; because the real effects of moral causes are not always immediate; but that which in the first instance is prejudicial may be excellent in its remoter operation; and its excellence may arise even from the ill effects it produces in the beginning. The reverse also happens: and very plausible schemes, with very pleasing commencements, have often shameful and lamentable conclusions. In states there are often some obscure and almost latent causes, things which appear at first view of little moment, on which a very great part of its prosperity or adversity may most essentially depend. The science of government being therefore so practical in itself, and intended for such practical purposes, a matter which requires experience, and even more experience than any person can gain in his whole life, however sagacious and observing he may be, it is with infinite caution that any man ought to venture upon pulling down an edifice, which has answered in any tolerable degree for ages the common purposes of society, or on building it up again, without having models and patterns of approved utility before his eyes.

These metaphysic rights entering into common life, like rays of light which pierce into a dense medium, are, by the laws of nature, refracted from their straight line. Indeed in the gross and complicated mass of human passions and concerns, the primitive rights of men undergo such a variety of refractions and reflections, that it becomes absurd to talk of them as if they continued in the simplicity of their original direction. The nature of man is intricate; the objects of society are of the greatest possible complexity: and therefore no simple disposition or direction of power can be suitable either to man's nature, or to the quality of his affairs. When I hear the simplicity of contrivance aimed at and boasted of in any new political constitutions, I am at no loss to decide that the artificers are grossly ignorant of their trade, or totally negligent of their duty. The simple governments are fundamentally defective, to say no worse of them. If you were to contemplate society in but one point of view, all these simple models of polity are infinitely captivating. In effect each would answer its single end much more perfectly than the more complex is able to attain all its complex purposes. But it is better that the whole should be imperfectly and anomalously answered, than that, while some parts are provided for with great exactness, others might be totally neglected, or perhaps materially injured, by the over-care of a favourite member.

The pretended rights of these theorists are all extremes: and in proportion as they are metaphysically true, they are morally and politically false. The rights of men are in a sort of *middle*, incapable of definition, but not impossible to be discerned. The rights of men in governments are their advantages; and these are often in balances between differences of good; in compromises sometimes between good and evil, and sometimes between evil and evil. Political reason is a computing principle; adding, subtracting, multiplying, and dividing, morally and not metaphysically, or mathematically, true moral denominations.

By these theorists the right of the people is almost always sophistically confounded with their power. The body of the community, whenever it can come to act, can meet with no effectual resistance; but till power and right are the same, the whole body of them has no right inconsistent with virtue, and the first of all virtues, prudence. Men have no right to what is not reasonable, and to what is not for their benefit; for though a pleasant writer said, *Liceat perire poetis,*[1] when one of them, in cold blood, is said to have leaped into the flames of a volcanic revolution, *Ardentem frigidus Ætnam insiluit,*[2] I consider such a frolic rather as an unjustifiable poetic license, than as one of the franchises of Parnassus; and whether he were poet, or divine, or politician, that chose to exercise this kind of right, I think that more wise, because more charitable, thoughts would urge me rather to save the man, than to preserve his brazen slippers as the monuments of his folly. . . .

NOTES AND COMMENTS

Because of his conviction that nations get their character less from formally written constitutions than from a growth and development that parallels growth in the natural order, Burke's view of the state has been called "organic." Dwight Macdonald's essay (page 4) has as its central thesis a denial of the concept of the organic state. Is there a difference in the term as he uses it and as it is applied to Burke? Compare, for instance, Macdonald's comments on Hegel with Burke's criticism of Dr. Price. Is there a parallel between the Jacobin approval of a calamity that would lead to revolution and the Communist agricultural policy, with its "State-induced famine," which Macdonald discusses?

Since we live under a constitution which speaks of the inalienable rights of man, we are predisposed to reject Burke's notion that we hold our political rights by convention. Does his dictum that "political reason is a computing principle" functioning not mathematically but morally—in other words not in the abstract but in the real world of living men—make his opinion more acceptable? Does he see convention as an absolute good or as a tool by which extreme political opinions can be modified and kept in check?

[1 Let poets perish.—*Ed.*]
[2] Horace, *Art of Poetry*, 11. 465-66. [In cold blood he leaped into burning Etna.—*Ed.*]

Many modern American conservatives claim Burke as their inspiration. Examine some issues of the conservative magazine, *National Review,* or look into the writings of such conservatives as Russell Kirk and Peter Viereck to see if the principles they uphold are indeed Burke's.

JOSÉ ORTEGA Y GASSET

1883-1955

José Ortega y Gasset, Spanish essayist, philosopher, and editor, came from a family of journalists. He was first educated by tutors and later at a Jesuit school. He began his career as a teacher, but he early became active in Spanish journalism and political life. He was one of the founders of the liberal newspaper *El Sol*; many of his own essays first published in that paper appeared in English in *The Modern Theme* and *Invertebrate Spain*. From 1923 to 1935 he introduced Spanish readers to the greatest writers of Europe through his literary periodical, *La Revista de Occidente*.

In 1931, Ortega was elected deputy from the province of León and took an active political role in the overthrow of the monarchy. The republican movement went too far to the left to be congenial to his political sympathies, however, and when civil war broke out, he fled to France. But when Franco later offered to make him Spain's "official philosopher" and to publish de luxe editions of his writings if he would delete politically dangerous passages, he staunchly refused. No leftist, he was even less a fascist; he preferred voluntary exile in Argentina.

In the United States Ortega y Gasset is known chiefly as the author of *The Dehumanization of Art* and *The Revolt of the Masses*. The following essay, the opening chapter of *The Revolt of the Masses*, analyzes the "inversion of values" in European culture due to the emergence of the "mass man."

The Coming of the Masses

THERE IS ONE fact which, whether for good or ill, is of utmost importance in the public life of Europe at the present moment. This fact is the accession of the masses to complete social power. As the masses, by definition, neither should nor can direct their own personal existence, and still less rule society in general, this fact means that actually Europe is suffering from the greatest crisis that can afflict peoples, nations, and civilisation. Such a crisis has occurred more than once in history. Its characteristics and its consequences are well known. So also is its name. It is called the rebellion of the masses. In order to understand this formidable fact, it is important from the start to avoid giving to the words "rebellion," "masses," and "social power" a meaning exclusively or primarily political. Public life is not solely political, but equally, and even primarily, intellectual, moral, economic, religious; it comprises all our collective habits, including our fashions both of dress and of amusement.

Perhaps the best line of approach to this historical phenomenon may be found by turning our attention to a visual experience, stressing one aspect of our epoch which is plain to our very eyes. This fact is quite simple to enunciate, though not so to analyse. I shall call it the fact of agglomeration, of "plentitude." Towns are full of people, houses full of tenants, hotels full of guests, trains full of travellers, cafés full of customers, parks full of promenaders, consulting-rooms of famous doctors full of patients, theatres full of spectators, and beaches full of bathers. What previously was, in general, no problem, now begins to be an everyday one, namely, to find room.

That is all. Can there be any fact simpler, more patent, more constant in actual life? Let us now pierce the plain surface of this observation and we shall be surprised to see how there wells forth an unexpected spring in which the white light of day, of our actual day, is broken up into its rich chromatic content. What is it that we see, and the sight of which causes us so much surprise? We see the multitude, as such, in possession of the places and the instruments created by civilisation. The slightest reflection will then make us surprised at our own surprise. What about it? Is this not the ideal state of things? The theatre has seats to be occupied—in other words, so that the house may be full—and now they are overflowing; people anxious to use them are left standing outside. Though the fact be quite logical and natural, we cannot but recognise that this did not happen before and that now it does; consequently, there has been a change, an innovation, which justifies, at least for the first moment, our surprise.

To be surprised, to wonder, is to begin to understand. This is the sport, the luxury, special to the intellectual man. The gesture characteristic of his tribe consists in looking at the world with eyes wide open in wonder. Everything in the world is strange and marvellous to well-open eyes. The faculty of wonder is the delight refused to your football "fan," and, on the other hand, is the one which leads the intellectual man through life in the perpetual ecstasy of the visionary. His special attribute is the wonder of the eyes. Hence it was that the ancients gave Minerva her owl, the bird with ever-dazzled eyes.

Agglomeration, fullness, was not frequent before. Why then is it now? The components of the multitudes around us have not sprung from nothing. Approximately the same number of people existed fifteen years ago. Indeed, after the war it might seem natural that their number should be less. Nevertheless, it is here we come up against the first important point. The individuals who made up these multitudes existed, but not *qua* multitude. Scattered about the world in small groups, or solitary, they lived a life, to all appearances, divergent, dissociate, apart. Each individual or small group occupied a place, its own, in country, village, or quarter of the great city. Now, suddenly, they appear as an agglomeration, and looking in any direction our eyes meet with the multitudes. Not only in any direction, but precisely in the best places, the relatively refined creation of human culture, previously reserved to lesser groups, in a word, to minorities. The multitude has suddenly become visible, installing itself in the preferential positions in society. Before, if it existed, it passed unnoticed, occupying the background of the social stage; now it has advanced to the footlights and is the principal character. There are no longer protagonists; there is only the chorus.

The concept of the multitude is quantitative and visual. Without changing its nature, let us translate it into terms of sociology. We then meet with the notion of the "social mass." Society is always a dynamic unity of two component factors: minorities and masses. The minorities are individuals or groups of individuals which are specially qualified. The mass is the assemblage of persons not specially qualified. By masses, then, is not to be understood, solely or mainly, "the working masses." The mass is the average man. In this way what was mere quantity—the multitude—is converted into a qualitative determination: it becomes the common social quality, man as undifferentiated from other men, but as repeating in himself a generic type. What have we gained by this conversion of quantity into quality? Simply this: by means of the latter we understand the genesis of the former. It is evident to the verge of platitude that the normal formation of a multitude implies the coincidence of desires, ideas, ways of life, in the individuals who constitute it. It will be objected that this is just what happens with every social group, however select it may strive to be. This is true; but there is an essential difference. In those groups which are characterised by not being multitude and mass, the effective coincidence of its members is based on some desire, idea, or ideal, which of itself excludes the great number. To form a minority, of whatever kind, it is necessary beforehand that each member separate himself from the multitude for special, relatively personal, reasons. Their coincidence with the others who form the minority is, then, secondary, posterior to their having each adopted an attitude of singularity, and is consequently, to a large extent, a coincidence in not coinciding. There are cases in which this singularising character of the group appears in the light of day: those English groups, which style themselves "nonconformists," where we have the grouping together of those who agree only in their disagreement in regard to the limitless multitude. This coming together of the minority precisely in order to separate themselves from the majority is a necessary ingredient in the formation of every minority. Speaking of the limited public which listened to a musician of refinement, Mallarmé wittily says that this public by its presence in small numbers stressed the absence of the multitude.

Strictly speaking, the mass, as a psychological fact, can be defined without waiting for individuals to appear in mass formation. In the presence of one individual we can decide whether he is "mass" or not. The mass is all that which sets no value on itself —good or ill—based on specific grounds, but which feels itself "just like everybody," and nevertheless is not concerned about it; is, in fact, quite happy to feel itself as one with everybody else. Imagine a humble-minded man who, having tried to estimate his own worth on specific grounds—asking himself if he has any talent for this or that, if he excels in any direction—realises that he possesses no quality of excellence. Such a man will feel that he is mediocre and common-place, ill-gifted, but will not feel himself "mass."

When one speaks of "select minorities" it is usual for the evil-minded to twist the sense of this expression, pretending to be unaware that the select man is not the petulant person who thinks himself superior to the rest, but the man who demands more of himself than the rest, even though he may not fulfil in his person those higher exigencies. For there is no doubt that the most radical division that it is possible to make of humanity is that which splits it into two classes of creatures: those who make great demands on themselves, piling up difficulties and duties; and those who demand nothing special of themselves, but for whom to live is to be every moment what they already are, without imposing on themselves any efforts towards perfection; mere buoys that float on the waves. This reminds me that orthodox Buddhism is composed of two distinct religions: one, more rigorous and difficult, the other easier and more trivial: the Mahayana—"great vehicle" or "great path"—and the Hinayana—"lesser vehicle" or "lesser path." The decisive matter is whether we attach our life to one or the other vehicle, to a maximum or a minimum of demands upon ourselves.

The division of society into masses and select minorities is, then, not a division into social classes, but into classes of men, and cannot coincide with the hierarchic separation of "upper" and "lower" classes. It is, of course, plain that in these "upper" classes, when and as long as they really are so, there is much more likelihood of finding men who adopt the "great vehicle," whereas the "lower" classes normally comprise individuals of minus quality. But, strictly speaking, within both these social classes, there are to be found mass and genuine minority. As we shall see, a characteristic of our times is the predominance, even in groups traditionally selective, of the mass and the vulgar. Thus, in the intellectual life, which of its essence requires and presupposes qualification, one can note the progressive triumph of the pseudo-intellectual, unqualified, unqualifiable, and, by their very mental texture, disqualified. Similarly, in the surviving groups of the "nobility," male and female. On the other hand, it is not rare to find to-day amongst working men, who before might be taken as the best example of what we are calling "mass," nobly disciplined minds.

There exist, then, in society, operations, activities, and functions of the most diverse order, which are of their very nature special, and which consequently cannot be properly carried out without special gifts. For example: certain pleasures of an artistic and refined character, or again the functions of government and of political judgment in public affairs. Previously these special activities were exercised by qualified minorities, or at least by those who claimed such qualification. The mass asserted no right to intervene in them; they realised that if they wished to intervene they would necessarily have to acquire those special qualities and cease being mere mass. They recognised their place in a healthy dynamic social system.

If we now revert to the facts indicated at the start, they will appear clearly as the heralds of a changed attitude in the mass. They all indicate that the mass has decided to advance to the foreground of social life, to occupy the places, to use the instruments and to enjoy the pleasures hitherto reserved to the few. It is evident, for example, that the places were never intended for the multitude, for their dimensions are too limited, and the crowd is continuously overflowing; thus manifesting to our eyes and in the clearest manner the new phenomenon: the mass, without ceasing to be mass, is supplanting the minorities.

No one, I believe, will regret that people are to-day enjoying themselves in greater measure and numbers than before, since they have now both the desire and the means of satisfying it. The evil lies in the fact that this decision taken by the masses to assume the activities proper to the minorities is not, and cannot be, manifested solely in the domain of pleasure, but that it is a general feature of our time. Thus—to anticipate what we shall see later —I believe that the political innovations of recent times signify nothing less than the political domination of the masses. The old democracy was tempered by a generous dose of liberalism and of enthusiasm for law. By serving these principles the individual bound himself to maintain a severe discipline over himself. Under the shelter of liberal principles and the rule of law, minorities could live and act. Democracy and law—life in common under the law—were synonymous. To-day we are witnessing the triumphs of a hyperdemocracy in which the mass acts directly, outside the law, imposing its aspirations and its desires by means of material pressure. It is a false interpretation of the new situation to say that the mass has grown tired of politics and handed over the exercise of it to specialised persons. Quite the contrary. That was what happened previously; that was democracy. The mass took it for granted that after all, in spite of their defects and weaknesses, the minorities understood a little more of public problems than it did itself. Now, on the other hand, the mass believes that it has the right to impose and to give force of law to notions born in the café. I doubt whether there have been other periods of history in which the multitude has come to govern more directly than in our own. That is why I speak of hyperdemocracy.

The same thing is happening in other orders, particularly in the intellectual. I may be mistaken, but the present-day writer, when he takes his pen in hand to treat a subject which he has studied deeply, has to bear in mind that the average reader, who has never concerned himself with this subject, if he reads does so with the view, not of learning something from the writer, but rather, of pronouncing judgment on him when he is not in agreement with the commonplaces that the said reader carries in his head. If the individuals who make up the mass believed themselves specially qualified, it would be a case merely of personal error, not a sociological subversion. *The characteristic of the hour is that the commonplace mind, knowing itself to be commonplace, has the assurance to proclaim the rights of the commonplace and to impose them wherever it will.* As they say in the United States: "to be different is to be indecent." The mass crushes beneath it everything that is different, everything that is excellent, individual, qualified and select. Anybody who is not like everybody, who does not think like everybody, runs the risk of being eliminated. And it is clear, of course, that this "everybody" is not "everybody." "Everybody" was normally the complex unity of the mass and the divergent, specialised minorities. Nowadays, "everybody" is the mass alone. Here we have the formidable fact of our times, described without any concealment of the brutality of its features.

NOTES AND COMMENTS

Ortega y Gasset claims that the masses are no longer merely the majority in Western civilization: their view of life—social, economic, religious, and political—predominates because social power is in their hands. Why does he find this phenomenon so dangerous? William Barrett once said, "Ortega remains above all a passionate and unreconstructed aristocrat." In what sense is Ortega an aristocrat? How do his values keep him from being a modern liberal? Are his values the same as Shaw's, Macdonald's, or Freud's? Do you feel he has more in common with Burke?

Ortega y Gasset is a sociologist as well as a philosopher. He divides society into groups and discusses these groups as if they were individuals. Does his invention of his own sociological vocabulary confuse his meaning or does it enable us to look at society from a fresh, enlightening point of view?

The Lonely Crowd, by David Riesman, is a more recent study of mass culture. It would be interesting to compare Riesman's conclusions with Ortega's.

SIGMUND FREUD

1856-1939

Sigmund Freud revolutionized our understanding of the human mind by his development of psychoanalysis, a scientific technique to uncover the unconscious elements in our thoughts and feelings. As a doctor, he used this method to treat mental illness; as a man of wide cultural interests, he found it valuable to apply his psychoanalytic knowledge in his studies of history, anthropology, and religion. These concerns dominated his thinking at the end of his career, and he brought his clinical observations to bear in writing about them. His cultural works can be viewed as epilogues to his books on psychology written during fifty years of his professional life, for his method was not so much to give up an idea as to add to it, to develop it. This is true of books like *Future of an Illusion* (1927), *Civilization and Its Discontents* (1929), and *Moses and Monotheism* (1939). It is also true of the present essay, "Why War?"

This essay was written in accordance with a recommendation of the League of Nations. The League wished "to encourage an exchange of letters between leaders of thought" and asked them "to select [subjects] best calculated to serve the common interest of the League of Nations and of the intellectual life of mankind. . . ." In July, 1932, Albert Einstein wrote to Freud about a subject which deeply concerned him—war. He asked Freud if there was "any way of delivering mankind from the menace of war," saying, "It is common knowledge that, with the advance of modern science, this issue has come to mean a matter of life and death for civilization as we know it; nevertheless, for all the zeal displayed, every attempt at its solution has ended in a lamentable breakdown." He hoped that Freud, with his knowledge of the human psyche, could "blaze the trail" toward a solution of this deadly impasse. Freud's response in September 1932 was pessimistic.

Why War?

VIENNA, September, 1932.

DEAR PROFESSOR EINSTEIN,

When I heard that you intended to invite me to an exchange of views on some subject that interested you and that seemed to deserve the interest of others besides yourself, I readily agreed. I expected you to choose a problem on the frontiers of what is knowable to-day, a problem to which each of us, a physicist and a psychologist, might have our own particular angle of approach and where we might come together from different directions upon the same ground. You have taken me by surprise, however, by posing the question of what can be done to protect mankind from the curse of war. I was scared at first by the thought of my—I had almost written "our"—incapacity for dealing with what seemed to be a practical problem, a concern for statesmen. But I then realized that you had raised the question not as a natural scientist and physicist but as a philanthropist: you were following the promptings of the League of Nations just as Fridtjof Nansen, the polar explorer, took on the work of bringing help to the starving and homeless victims of the World War. I reflected, moreover, that I was not being asked to make practical proposals but only to set out the problem of avoiding war as it appears to a psychological observer. Here again you yourself have said almost all there is to say on the subject. But though you have taken the wind out of my sails I shall be glad to follow in your wake and content myself with confirming all you have said by amplifying it to the best of my knowledge—or conjecture.

You begin with the relation between Right and Might.[1] There can be no doubt that this is the correct starting-point for our investigation. But may I replace the word "might" by the

---

Reprinted from *Collected Papers*, Vol. 5, by Sigmund Freud, edited and translated by James Strachey. By permission of The Hogarth Press Ltd., London.

[1] [In the original the words *Recht* and *Macht* are used throughout the essay. It has unfortunately been necessary to sacrifice this stylistic unity in the translation. *Recht* has been rendered indifferently by "right," "law," and "justice"; and *Macht* by "might," "force," and "power."—*Trans.*]

balder and harsher word "violence"? To-day right and violence
appear to us as antitheses. It can easily be shown, however, that
the one has developed out of the other; and if we go back to the
earliest beginnings and see how that first came about, the problem
is easily solved. You must forgive me if in what follows I go over
familiar and commonly accepted ground as though it were new,
but the thread of my argument requires it.

It is a general principle, then, that conflicts of interest between men are settled by the use of violence. This is true of the
whole animal kingdom, from which men have no business to
exclude themselves. In the case of men, no doubt, conflicts of
opinion occur as well which may reach the highest pitch of
abstraction and which seem to demand some other technique for
their settlement. That, however, is a later complication. To begin
with, in a small human horde,[1] it was superior muscular strength
which decided who owned things or whose will should prevail.
Muscular strength was soon supplemented and replaced by the
use of tools: the winner was the one who had the better weapons
or who used them the more skilfully. From the moment at which
weapons were introduced, intellectual superiority already began
to replace brute muscular strength; but the final purpose of the
fight remained the same—one side or the other was to be compelled to abandon his claim or his objection by the damage in-
flicted on him and by the crippling of his strength. That purpose
was most completely achieved if the victor's violence eliminated
his opponent permanently, that is to say, killed him. This had two
advantages: he could not renew his opposition and his fate
deterred others from following his example. In addition to this,
killing an enemy satisfied an instinctual inclination which I shall
have to mention later. The intention to kill might be countered
by a reflection that the enemy could be employed in performing
useful services if he were left alive in an intimidated condition.
In that case the victor's violence was content to subjugate him
instead of killing him. This was a first beginning of the idea of
sparing an enemy's life, but thereafter the victor had to reckon
with his defeated opponent's lurking thirst for revenge and
sacrificed some of his own security.

Such, then, was the original state of things: domination by

---

[1] [Freud uses the word "horde" to denote a comparatively small group.—
Trans.]

whoever had the greater might—domination by brute violence or by violence supported by intellect. As we know, this regime was altered in the course of evolution. There was a path that led from violence to right or law. What was that path? It is my belief that there was only one: the path which led by way of the fact that the superior strength of a single individual could be rivalled by the union of several weak ones. *"L'union fait la force."* Violence could be broken by union, and the power of those who were united now represented law in contrast to the violence of the single individual. Thus we see that right is the might of a community. It is still violence, ready to be directed against any individual who resists it; it works by the same methods and follows the same purposes. The only real difference lies in the fact that what prevails is no longer the violence of an individual but that of a community. But in order that the transition from violence to this new right or justice may be effected, one psychological condition must be fulfilled. The union of the majority must be a stable and lasting one. If it were only brought about for the purpose of combating a single domineering individual and were dissolved after his defeat, nothing would have been accomplished. The next person who found himself superior in strength would once more seek to set up a dominion by violence and the game would be repeated *ad infinitum*. The community must be maintained permanently, must be organized, must draw up regulations to anticipate the risk of rebellion and must institute authorities to see that those regulations—the laws—are respected and to superintend the execution of legal acts of violence. The recognition of a community of interests such as these leads to the growth of emotional ties between the members of a united group of people—feelings of unity which are the true source of its strength.

Here, I believe, we already have all the essentials: violence overcome by the transference of power to a larger unity, which is held together by emotional ties between its members. What remains to be said is no more than an expansion and a repetition of this.

The situation is simple so long as the community consists only of a number of equally strong individuals. The laws of such an association will determine the extent to which, if the security of communal life is to be guaranteed, each individual must surrender his personal liberty to turn his strength to violent uses. But a state of rest of that kind is only theoretically conceivable. In actuality the position is complicated by the fact that from its very beginning the community comprises elements of unequal strength —men and women, parents and children—and soon, as a result of war and conquest, it also comes to include victors and vanquished, who turn into masters and slaves. The justice of the community then becomes an expression of the unequal degrees of power obtaining within it; the laws are made by and for the ruling members and find little room for the rights of those in subjection. From that time forward there are two factors at work in the community which are sources of unrest over matters of law but tend at the same time to a further growth of law. First, attempts are made by certain of the rulers to set themselves above the prohibitions which apply to everyone—they seek, that is, to go back from a dominion of law to a dominion of violence. Secondly, the oppressed members of the group make constant efforts to obtain more power and to have any changes that are brought about in that direction recognized in the laws—they press forward, that is, from unequal justice to equal justice for all. This second tendency becomes especially important if a real shift of power occurs within a community, as may happen as a result of a number of historical factors. In that case right may gradually adapt itself to the new distribution of power or, as is more frequent, the ruling class is unwilling to recognize the change, and rebellion and civil war follow, with a temporary suspension of law and new attempts at a solution by violence, ending in the establishment of a fresh rule of law. There is yet another source from which modifications of law may arise, and one of which the expression is invariably peaceful: it lies in the cultural transformation of the members of the community. This, however, belongs properly in another connection and must be considered later.

Thus we see that the violent solution of conflicts of interest is not avoided even inside a community. But the everyday necessities and common concerns that are inevitable where people live together in one place tend to bring such struggles to a swift conclusion and under such conditions there is an increasing probability that a peaceful solution will be found. But a glance at the history of the human race reveals an endless series of conflicts between one community and another or several others, between larger and

smaller units—between cities, provinces, races, nations, empires
—which have almost always been settled by force of arms. Wars
of this kind end either in the spoliation or in the complete overthrow and conquest of one of the parties. It is impossible to make
any sweeping judgement upon wars of conquest. Some, such as
those waged by the Mongols and Turks, have brought nothing
but evil. Others, on the contrary, have contributed to the transformation of violence into law by establishing larger units within
which the use of violence was made impossible and in which a
fresh system of law led to the solution of conflicts. In this way the
conquests of the Romans gave the countries round the Mediter-
ranean the priceless *pax Romana*, and the greed of the French
kings to extend their dominions created a peacefully united and
flourishing France. Paradoxical as it may sound, it must be admitted that war might be a far from inappropriate means of
establishing the eagerly desired reign of "everlasting" peace, since
it is in a position to create the large units within which a powerful
central government makes further wars impossible. Nevertheless
it fails in this purpose, for the results of conquest are as a rule
short-lived: the newly created units fall apart once again, usually
owing to a lack of cohesion between the portions that have been
united by violence. Hitherto, moreover, the unifications created
by conquest, though of considerable extent, have only been
partial, and the conflicts between these have cried out for violent
solution. Thus the result of all these warlike efforts has only been
that the human race has exchanged numerous, and indeed unend-
ing, minor wars for wars on a grand scale that are rare but all the
more destructive.

If we turn to our own times, we arrive at the same conclusion
which you have reached by a shorter path. Wars will only be
prevented with certainty if mankind unites in setting up a central
authority to which the right of giving judgement upon all conflicts
of interest shall be handed over. There are clearly two separate
requirements involved in this: the creation of a supreme authority
and its endowment with the necessary power. One without the
other would be useless. The League of Nations is designed as an
authority of this kind, but the second condition has not been fulfilled: the League of Nations has no power of its own and can
only acquire it if the members of the new union, the separate
States, are ready to resign it. And at the moment there seems very

little prospect of this. The institution of the League of Nations would, however, be wholly unintelligible if one ignored the fact that here was a bold attempt such as has seldom (perhaps, indeed, never on such a scale) been made before. It is an attempt to base upon an appeal to certain idealistic attitudes of mind the authority (that is, the coercive influence) which otherwise rests on the possession of power. We have heard that a community is held together by two things: the compelling force of violence and the emotional ties (identifications is the technical name) between its members. If one of the factors is absent, the community may possibly be held together by the other. The ideas that are appealed to can, of course, only have any significance if they give expression to important concerns that are common to the members, and the question arises of how much strength they can exert. History teaches us that they have been to some extent effective. For instance, the Panhellenic idea, the sense of being superior to the surrounding barbarians—an idea which was so powerfully expressed in the Amphictyonies, the Oracles and the Games—was sufficiently strong to mitigate the customs of war among Greeks, though evidently not sufficiently strong to prevent warlike disputes between different sections of the Greek nation or even to restrain a city or confederation of cities from allying itself with the Persian foe in order to gain an advantage over a rival. In the same way, the community of feeling among Christians, powerful though it was, was equally unable at the time of the Renaissance to deter Christian States, whether large or small, from seeking the Sultan's aid in their wars with one another. Nor does any idea exist to-day which could be expected to exert a unifying authority of the sort. Indeed it is all too clear that the national ideals by which nations are at present swayed operate in a contrary direction. Some people are inclined to prophesy that it will not be possible to make an end of war until Communist ways of thinking have found universal acceptance. But that aim is in any case a very remote one to-day, and perhaps it could only be reached after the most fearful civil wars. Thus the attempt to replace actual force by the force of ideas seems at present to be doomed to failure. We shall be making a false calculation if we disregard the fact that law was originally brute violence and that even to-day it cannot do without the support of violence.

I can now proceed to add a gloss to another of your remarks. You express astonishment at the fact that it is so easy to make men enthusiastic about a war and add your suspicion that there is something at work in them—an instinct for hatred and destruction —which goes halfway to meet the efforts of the warmongers. Once again, I can only express my entire agreement. We believe in the existence of an instinct of that kind and have in fact been occupied during the last few years in studying its manifestations. Will you allow me to take this opportunity of putting before you a portion of the theory of the instincts which, after much tentative groping and many fluctuations of opinion, has been reached by workers in the field of psycho-analysis?

According to our hypothesis human instincts are of only two kinds: those which seek to preserve and unite—which we call "erotic," exactly in the sense in which Plato uses the word "Eros" in his *Symposium*, or "sexual," with a deliberate extension of the popular conception of "sexuality"—and those which seek to destroy and kill and which we class together as the aggressive or destructive instinct. As you see, this is in fact no more than a theoretical clarification of the universally familiar opposition between Love and Hate which may perhaps have some fundamental relation to the popularity of attraction and repulsion that plays a part in your own field of knowledge. We must not be too hasty in introducing ethical judgments of good and evil. Neither of these instincts is any less essential than the other; the phenomena of life arise from the operation of both together, whether acting in concert or in opposition. It seems as though an instinct of the one sort can scarcely ever operate in isolation; it is always accompanied—or, as we say, alloyed—with an element from the other side, which modifies its aim or is, in some cases, what enables it to achieve that aim. Thus, for instance, the instinct of self-preservation is certainly of an erotic kind, but it must nevertheless have aggressiveness at its disposal if it is to fulfil its purpose. So, too, the instinct of love, when it is directed towards an object, stands in need of some contribution from the instinct of mastery if it is in any way to possess that object. The difficulty of isolating the two classes of instinct in their actual manifestations is indeed what has so long prevented us from recognizing them.

If you will follow me a little further, you will see that human actions are subject to another complication of a different kind. It is very rarely that an action is the work of a *single* instinctual impulse (which must in itself be compounded of Eros and destructiveness). In order to make an action possible there must be as a rule a *combination* of such compounded motives. This was perceived long ago by a specialist in your own subject, a Professor G. C. Lichtenberg who taught physics at Göttingen during our classical age—though perhaps he was even more remarkable as a psychologist than as a physicist. He invented a Compass of Motives, for he wrote: "The motives that lead us to do anything might be arranged like the thirty-two winds and might be given names on the same pattern: for instance, 'food-food-fame' or 'fame-fame-food.'" So that when human beings are incited to war they may have a whole number of motives for assenting—some noble and some base, some of which they speak openly and others on which they are silent. There is no need to enumerate them all. A lust for aggression and destruction is certainly among them: the countless cruelties in history and in our everyday lives vouch for its existence and its strength. The gratification of these destructive impulses is of course facilitated by their admixture with others of an erotic and idealistic kind. When we read of the atrocities of the past, it sometimes seems as though the idealistic motives served only as an excuse for the destructive appetites; and sometimes—in the case, for instance, of the cruelties of the Inquisition—it seems as though the idealistic motives had pushed themselves forward in consciousness, while the destructive ones lent them an unconscious reinforcement. Both may be true.

I fear I may be abusing your interest, which is after all concerned with the prevention of war and not with our theories. Nevertheless I should like to linger for a moment over our destructive instinct, whose popularity is by no means equal to its importance. As a result of a little speculation, we have come to suppose that this instinct is at work in every living being and is striving to bring it to ruin and to reduce life to its original condition of inanimate matter. Thus it quite seriously deserves to be called a death instinct, while the erotic instincts represent the effort to live. The death instinct turns into the destructive instinct if, with the help of special organs, it is directed outwards, on to objects. The living creature preserves its own life, so to say, by destroying an extraneous one. Some portion of the death instinct, however, remains operative *within* the living being, and we have sought to trace quite a number of normal and pathological phenomena to this internalization of the destructive instinct. We have been guilty of the heresy of attributing the origin of conscience to this diversion inwards of aggressiveness. You will notice that it is by no means a trivial matter if this process is carried too far: it is positively unhealthy. On the other hand if these forces are turned to destruction in the external world, the living creature will be relieved and the effect must be beneficial. This would serve as a biological justification for all the ugly and dangerous impulses against which we are struggling. It must be admitted that they stand nearer to Nature than does our resistance to them, for which an explanation also needs to be found. It may perhaps seem to you as though our theories are a kind of mythology and, in the present case, not even an agreeable one. But does not every science come in the end to a kind of mythology like this? Cannot the same be said to-day of your own Physics?

For our immediate purpose then, this much follows from what has been said: there is no use in trying to get rid of men's aggressive inclinations. We are told that in certain happy regions of the earth, where nature provides in abundance everything that man requires, there are races whose life is passed in tranquillity and who know neither compulsion nor aggressiveness. I can scarcely believe it and I should be glad to hear more of these fortunate beings. The Russian Communists, too, hope to be able to cause human aggressiveness to disappear by guaranteeing the satisfaction of all material needs and by establishing equality in other respects among all the members of the community. That, in my opinion, is an illusion. They themselves are armed to-day with the most scrupulous care and not the least important of the methods by which they keep their supporters together is hatred of everyone beyond their frontiers. In any case, as you yourself have remarked, there is no question of getting rid entirely of human aggressive impulses; it is enough to try to divert them to such an extent that they need not find expression in war.

Our mythological theory of instincts makes it easy for us to find a formula for *indirect* methods of combating war. If willingness to engage in war is an effect of the destructive instinct, the most obvious plan will be to bring Eros, its antagonist, into play against it. Anything that encourages the growth of emotional ties between men must operate against war. These ties may be of two kinds. In the first place they may be relations resembling those towards a loved object, though without having a sexual aim. There is no need for psychoanalysis to be ashamed to speak of love in this connection, for religion itself uses the same words: "Thou shalt love thy neighbor as thyself." This, however, is more easily said than done. The second kind of emotional tie is by means of identification. Whatever leads men to share important interests produces this community of feeling, these identifications. And the structure of human society is to a large extent based on them.

A complaint which you make about the abuse of authority brings me to another suggestion for the indirect combating of the propensity to war. One instance of the innate and ineradicable inequality of men is their tendency to fall into the two classes of leaders and followers. The latter constitute the vast majority; they stand in need of an authority which will make decisions for them and to which they for the most part offer an unqualified submission. This suggests that more care should be taken than hitherto to educate an upper stratum of men with independent minds, not open to intimidation and eager in the pursuit of truth, whose business it would be to give direction to the dependent masses. It goes without saying that the encroachments made by the executive power of the State and the prohibition laid by the Church upon freedom of thought are far from propitious for the production of a class of this kind. The ideal condition of things would of course be a community of men who had subordinated their instinctual life to the dictatorship of reason. Nothing else could unite men so completely and so tenaciously, even if there were no emotional ties between them. But in all probability that is a Utopian expectation. No doubt the other indirect methods of preventing war are more practicable, though they promise no rapid success. An unpleasant picture comes to one's mind of mills that grind so slowly that people may starve before they get their flour.

The result, as you see, is not very fruitful when an unworldly theoretician is called in to advise on an urgent practical problem. It is a better plan to devote oneself in every particular case to meeting the danger with whatever weapons lie to hand. I should like, however, to discuss one more question, which you do not mention in your letter but which specially interests me. Why do you and I and so many other people rebel so violently against war? Why do we not accept it as another of the many painful calamities of life? After all, it seems quite a natural thing, no doubt it has a good biological basis and in practice it is scarcely avoidable. There is no need to be shocked at my raising this question. For the purpose of an investigation such as this, one may perhaps be allowed to wear a mask of assumed detachment. The answer to my question will be that we react to war in this way because everyone has a right to his own life, because war puts an end to human lives that are full of hope, because it brings individual men into humiliating situations, because it compels them against their will to murder other men, and because it destroys precious material objects which have been produced by the labours of humanity. Other reasons besides might be given, such as that in its present-day form war is no longer an opportunity for achieving the old ideals of heroism and that owing to the perfection of instruments of destruction a future war might involve the extermination of one or perhaps both of the antagonists. All this is true, and so incontestably true that one can only feel astonished that the waging of war has not yet been unanimously repudiated. No doubt debate is possible upon one or two of these points. It may be questioned whether a community ought not to have a right to dispose of individual lives; every war is not open to condemnation to an equal degree; so long as there exist countries and nations that are prepared for the ruthless destruction of others, those others must be armed for war. But I will not linger over any of these issues; they are not what you want to discuss with me, and I have something different in mind. It is my opinion that the main reason why we rebel against war is that we cannot help doing so. We are pacifists because we are obliged to be for organic reasons. And we then find no difficulty in producing arguments to justify our attitude.

No doubt this requires some explanation. My belief is this. For incalculable ages mankind has been passing through a process of evolution of culture. (Some people, I know, prefer to use the term "civilization.") We owe to that process the best of what we have become, as well as a good part of what we suffer from. Though its causes and beginnings are obscure and its outcome uncertain, some of its characteristics are easy to perceive. It may perhaps be leading to the extinction of the human race, for in more than one way it impairs the sexual function; uncultivated races and backward strata of the population are already multiplying more rapidly than highly cultivated ones. The process is perhaps comparable to the domestication of certain species of animals and it is undoubtedly accompanied by physical alterations; but we are still unfamiliar with the notion that the evolution of culture is an organic process of this kind. The psychical modifications that go along with the cultural process are striking and unambiguous. They consist in a progressive displacement of instinctual aims and a restriction of instinctual impulses. Sensations which were pleasurable to our ancestors have become indifferent or even intolerable to ourselves; there are organic grounds for the changes in our ethical and aesthetic ideals. Of the psychological characteristics of culture two appear to be the most important: a strengthening of the intellect, which is beginning to govern instinctual life, and an internalization of the aggressive impulses, with all its consequent advantages and perils. Now war is in the crassest opposition to the psychical attitude imposed on us by the cultural process, and for that reason we are bound to rebel against it; we simply cannot any longer put up with it. This is not merely an intellectual and emotional repudiation; we pacifists have a constitutional intolerance of war, an idiosyncracy magnified, as it were, to the highest degree. It seems, indeed, as though the lowering of aesthetic standards in war plays a scarcely smaller part in our rebellion than do its cruelties.

And how long shall we have to wait before the rest of mankind become pacifists too? There is no telling. But it may not be Utopian to hope that these two factors, the cultural attitude and the justified dread of the consequences of a future war, may result within a measurable time in putting an end to the waging of war. By what paths or by what side-tracks this will come about we cannot guess. But one thing we can say: whatever fosters the growth of culture works at the same time against war.

I trust you will forgive me if what I have said has disappointed you, and I remain, with kindest regards,

Yours sincerely,

SIGM. FREUD

NOTES AND COMMENTS

Consider Freud's letter as prophecy: it was written before World War II, the "cold war," Korea, the world-wide struggle for self-assertion by small nations, and unforeseen and unprecedented outbreaks of mass brutality. Ironically, the very man to whom this letter was addressed made possible the atom bomb and all the weapons of total destruction that have followed. We can go no farther: the weapons of any future war threaten to annihilate even their users. Is this why "right and violence appear to us as antitheses"? Freud suggests, however, that a knowledge of history, current events, and especially of one's own instincts shows that man's "erotic" impulses (those "which seek to preserve and unite mankind") are not so strong as his "aggressive" or "destructive" impulses. Do you agree? If so, what do you feel the outcome can be?

Does Rebecca West's essay, which follows, supply solutions which Freud does not consider? It would be interesting to discuss Joseph Conrad's *Heart of Darkness* and George Orwell's *1984* in connection with Freud's theories about our destructive instinct.

The only hope Freud offers lies in his contention that civilized men, men of reason, oppose war. Is this necessarily true? Do you think the "men of politics," who guide our destinies, are civilized men, in Freud's sense of the term?

REBECCA WEST

1892-

"Rebecca West" is the pseudonym, taken from the name of one of Ibsen's heroines, of Cecily Isabel Fairfield, the English novelist, critic, and journalist. She began her career as a journalist in 1911; her chief interest at the time was feminism, and she ardently engaged in the fight for woman suffrage. Her political essays and literary criticism appeared in American periodicals like *Bookman* and *New Republic* as well as in English publications.

Her first book was a perceptive critical biography of Henry James (1916). She has also written distinguished novels; two of the best are *The Thinking Reed* and *The Fountain Overflows*. The hallmark of all her novels, disparate as they are in mood and setting, is the psychological probing of motivation, not surprising from a serious student of Proust.

But her devotion to journalism has never flagged; she has been called "the best reporter in the world." Early in 1941 she published her magnum opus, *Black Lamb and Grey Falcon*, a two-volume travel diary, written in her best reportorial style, about a trip to Yugoslavia. After the war came her notable articles on the treason trials of "Lord Haw-Haw" and others who had collaborated with the Nazis. The following essay, "The Meaning of Treason," first appeared in *Harper's Magazine* and later, in a condensed version, as the epilogue of the book of the same title.

The Meaning of Treason

FROM TIME to time during my career as a journalist I have reported notable law cases, and I know that it is not only mor-

Reprinted from *The Meaning of Treason* by Rebecca West. Copyright 1947 by Rebecca West. By permission of the Viking Press, Inc.

bidity which makes the public enjoy following the trial of a serious crime. It is very difficult for those who study life to find a story that comes to its end under their eyes. When we select an individual whose course we want to trace, it is as likely as not that he covers his tracks with secrecy, or moves to a field outside our view, or delays his end until we ourselves have ended. That is why classical history is a valuable study; we can see the whole story, the beginning, the middle, and the end of Greece and Rome, Egypt and Persia. That is why the lives of great men in the past teach us more than knowledge of great men in the present; we know their remote consequences. The dock brings a like illumination.

Here an individual story comes to its end in a collision with the community. Every case has its unique intellectual and spiritual significance. The appearance of the accused person, the changes in his face and voice, his agreement with society as disclosed by the witnesses who approve of him, his conflict with society as disclosed by the witnesses who disapprove of him, his relation to the crime of which he is truly or falsely accused, always reveal a special case. But the crime which he committed, if he was justly accused, or the other crime which was committed by the representatives of society if he was falsely accused, has always the same cause: refusal to respect the individuality of another or others. A world in which each man respected the soul of all other men, no matter how little they seemed to merit respect, would be crimeless.

There is an obvious political implication to be drawn from this. The authoritarian state is *ipso facto* criminal. When I covered the trial of William Joyce ("Lord Haw-Haw")[1] for the *New Yorker* I saw a man in the dock who was doubly criminal. He had committed crimes against the law out of his desires to substitute a criminal state for a state which, if not completely innocent, aimed at the innocence of freedom. It was obviously doubtful if he would ever have been guilty of any offense had he not been tainted by this political guilt. But when his actual offense against the law was examined it was seen that he had acted in a manner which had long been extolled by many who were in theory pure of that guilt and firmly opposed to the authoritarian state.

Almost all contemporary left-wing writers of this generation

[1 Who tried to weaken the morale of the British during World War II by broadcasting Nazi propaganda to them.—*Ed.*]

and the last attacked the idea of nationalism. It was true that
many of these attacks were made under the delusion that the
words nationalism and imperialism mean the same thing, whereas
nationalism—which means simply a special devotion of a people
to its own material and spiritual achievements—implies no desire
for the annexation of other territories and enslavement of other
peoples. But a great many of these attacks were made under no
such apprehension. It was genuinely felt that it was pure superstition which required a man to feel any warmer emotion about
his own land, race, and people than about any other. Why then
should any man feel a lump in his throat when he saw his flag
or the statue at the harbor gate of his native land, or feel that in
a dispute between his people and another he must obey the will
of his kin and not aid their enemy?

I watched the trial of William Joyce, and of all traitors who
were charged in courts which I could conveniently attend. They
had all cleared their throats of that lump, they had all made that
transit of frontiers recommended by the nationalists; and this had
landed them in the service of the persecutors of reason, the fanatical believers in frontiers as the demarcation lines between the
saved and the damned. But as their lives were unfolded it appeared
that none of them had cast off their nationalist prejudice because
of their strength, but had been divested of it by maladjusted ambition, by madness, by cowardice, by weakness. It seemed as if
contemporary nationalists had been wrong, and I remembered that
the trouble about man is twofold. He cannot learn truths which
are too complicated; he forgets truths which are too simple. After
I had seen twenty traitors tried it seemed to me that the reason
why they were in the dock, why intellectuals preach against nationalism, is that we have forgotten certain simple truths.

We have forgotten that we live outward from the center of a
circle and that what is nearest to the center is most real to us. If
a man cut his hand, it hurts him more than if he cuts some other
man's hand; therefore he is more careful to guard his own. Even
if he spend his whole life in teaching himself that we are all of one
body, and that therefore his neighbor's pain is his also, he will still
suffer more when his own hand is hurt, for the message then runs
straight from his palm and fingers to his brain, traveling at a speed
faster than light or sound, which bear the news of others' accidents.
Throughout his life it remains true that what is nearest to his body

is of greatest interest to his mind. When a baby is given food and held warmly by a certain woman, he grows up to feel a closer concern for her than for other women of her generation, and at her death will feel greatly disturbed. Should he be institution-bred and have no woman as his particular slave and tyrant, grievance will sour him till his last day.

If in his maturity he should live with a woman for any considerable period of time, he and she are apt, unless they are overtaken by certain obviously disagreeable circumstances, to behave as though there were a complete community of interest between them. There must have been some instinctive liking between them or they would never have been drawn together in the first place; they became involved in each other's prosperity; experience has taught each how the other will behave in most eventualities. Therefore they do better by one another than strangers would. Should he have children by this or any other woman, they will have great power over him, while other children will have little or none. He will know so much more about them. The veiled moment of their conception is his secret, and resemblances to him, to a familiar woman, or to his kin enable him to trace their inner lives, disguised though they be first by their inarticulateness and then by their articulateness. He can read them by the light of his own nature, and read his own nature by their light, and will have a sense of fusion between himself and those who are so inextricably tangled with that self.

If that man live in a house during the days of his childhood, he will know it better than any house he lives in later, though it shelter him forty years longer; and though the staircase wind as deviously as any in the world he will find his way down it in the darkness as surely as if it were straight. All his life long, when he hears talk of woods, he shall see beechwoods, if he come from a Buckinghamshire village, and a castle to him shall stand on Castle Rock, if Edinburgh was his home, and in the one case he shall know Southern English country folk, and in the other Lowland Scottish townsfolk, better than other Britons. Born and bred in England, he will find it easier to understand the English than the rest of men, not for any mystical reason, but because their language is his, because he is fully acquainted with their customs, and because he is the product of their common history. So also each continent enjoys a vague unity of self-comprehension, and is divided from the others by a sharp disunity; and even those who profess the closest familiarity with the next world speak with more robust certainty of this world and seem not to want to leave it.

This is not to say that a man loves what is nearest to him. He may hate his parents, his wife, and his children. Millions have done so. On the tables of the Law it was written "Honor thy father and thy mother, as the Lord God hath commanded thee; that thy days may be prolonged, and that it may go well with thee in the land which the Lord thy God giveth thee," and it is advice of almost gross practicality aimed at preventing the faithful from abandoning themselves to their natural impulses and wasting all their force on family rows. St. Paul, that great artist who perpetually betrayed his art because he was also a great man of action, and constantly abandoned the search for truth to seek instead a myth to inspire vigorous action, tried to gild the bondage of man to the familiar. "So ought men to love their own wives as their own body," he says. "He that loveth his wife loveth himself. For no man ever yet hated his own flesh, but nourished it and cherisheth it, even as the Lord the Church." But countless men have hated their own flesh. Everywhere and at all times men have carried such hatred to the point of slaying it, and still more have persecuted it by abstinence and mortification and debauchery. It has a value to them far above their loathing or their liking. It is their own flesh and they can have no direct experience of any other. Not with all the gold in the world or by incessant prayer can we obtain another instrument-case, packed with these our only instruments, the five senses, by which alone we can irradiate the universe that is a black void around us, and build a small irradiated platform in that darkness. A wife is someone who has stood on that irradiated platform long enough to be fully examined and to add the testimony of her own sense as to the nature of that encircling mystery. She may be loved or hated, or loved and hated, and serve in that research.

A child knows that what is near is easier for him to handle than what is far. All men took it for granted till recent times, when it was challenged, together with some other traditional assumptions, not because they had proved unsound, but because a number of urbanized populations from which the intellectual classes were largely drawn had lost their sense of spiritual as well as material process. They had lost their sense of material process owing to the development of the machine; goods which had formerly been produced by simple and comprehensible processes, often carried on where they could be witnessed by the consumer, were now produced by elaborate processes, not to be grasped by people without mechanical training, and carried on in the privacy of the large factories.

The reason for their ignorance of spiritual process was the urban lack of the long memory and the omniscient gossip enjoyed by the village. The townsman is surrounded by people whose circumstances he does not know and whose heredities are the secrets of other districts; and he is apt to take their dissimulating faces and their clothed bodies as the sum of them. People began to think of each other in a new way; as simple with a simplicity in fact unknown in organic life. They ignored the metabolism of human nature, by which experiences are absorbed into the mind and magically converted into personality, which rejects much of the material life brings to it and handles the rest to serve the interests of love or hate, good or evil, life or death, according to an inhabiting daemon, whose reasons are never given. Man conceived himself as living reasonably under the instruction of the five senses, which tell him to seek pleasure and avoid pain.

The first effect of this rational conception of life was cheerful vulgarity; and there are worse things than that. Man might well have felt this view of his destiny as a relief after the Christian philosophy, which abased his origin to criminality, and started him so low only to elevate him to the height, most disagreeable to most people, of company with godhead, after dragging him through all sorts of unpalatable experiences, including participation in a violent and apparently unnecessary death. In so far as a man adopted the new and rationalist philosophy he could be compared to an actor who, after spending a lifetime playing Hamlet and Othello and King Lear, retires to keep a country pub. All was thenceforward to go at a peaceable jog-trot. Children were to grow up straight striplings of light, undeformed by repression, unscarred by conflicts, because their parents would hand them over in their earliest years to the care of pedagogic experts. Divorce was not to be reckoned as a disgrace nor as tragedy nor even as a failure, but as a pleasurable extension of experience, like travel. Furthermore— and this was considered as the sanest adjustment of all—the ardors of patriotism were to be abandoned, and replaced by a cool resolution to place one's country on a level with all others in one's af-

fections, and to hand it over without concern to the dominion of
any other power which could offer it greater material benefits. It
was not out of cynicism that the benefits demanded were material:
it was believed that the material automatically produced the intellectual and the spiritual. These reasonable steps having been
taken, there was to follow harmony. The only peril was that it
might become too sweet.

But the five senses had evidently not been rightly understood.
Such children as were surrendered by their parents to expert treatment, complained against that surrender as if it had been any other
kind of abandonment. They quarreled with the pedagogues as
much as they would have quarreled with their parents; but, the
bond of the flesh being absent, there was something sapless in
their quarrels, and there was less energy engendered. Sexual life was
not noticeably smoother than it had been. The epic love of marriage and the lyric love-song of the encounter both lost much by
the pretense that they were the same. Nor, as patriotism was discredited, did peace come nearer. Indeed, the certainty of war now
arched over the earth like a second sky, inimical to the first. If
harmony had been our peril, we were preserved from it, both
within and without. For it was plain that, as Christian philosophy
had so harshly averred, the world was a stage on which an extraordinary drama, not yet fully comprehended by the intellect, was
being performed; and its action was now an agony. But, owing
to the adoption of the rationalist philosophy, some of the actors
filling the most important parts were now incapable of speaking
their lines. It appeared that *Hamlet* and *Othello* and *King Lear*
would be no longer cathartic tragedies but repellent and distressing farces if the leading characters had, in the climactic scenes,
been overtaken by the delusion that they had retired and were
keeping country pubs.

So the evil moment came and was clear: not surpassed in evil
since the days of the barbarian invasions. The devil of nationalism
had been driven out of man, but he had not become the headquarters of the dove. Instead there had entered into him the seven
devils of internationalism, and he was torn by their frenzies. Then
what is against all devils came to his aid. The achievement (which,
as yet, is unfinished, since peace does not reign) was accomplished
by a continuance of the drama in spite of the difficulties created
by the rationalist philosophy. Since the actors cast to play the

leading parts would not speak, the action was carried on by the peoples who used to walk to and fro at the back of the scene, softly laughing or softly weeping, or simply quietly being. Now these people streamed across the continents, inscribing their beliefs on the surface of the earth by the course of their flights, and on the sites of their martyrdoms. They defeated fascism by not being fascist. They showed the contrast between fascism and nonfascism so clearly that the world, wishing to live, defended their side because it could be seen that they were the representatives of life. As they exorcised the devils from the body of Europe they seemed to affirm certain values. It was perhaps true that the origin of man was in criminality, for once a community refused to make the effort of seeking the company of godhead it certainly became criminal. It was perhaps true that hedonism is an impotent gospel, for now it could be seen that pleasure means nothing to many men. As fast as those who ran to save their lives ran those who ran to slay them, even if their pursuit, pressed too hard, might change them into fugitives, whose own lives were in danger. Now the scorned bonds of the flesh asserted their validity. It was the final and unbearable misery of these flights that husbands were separated from their wives, and parents lost sight of their children. The men who performed the cruelest surgery on these families, who threw the husband and wife into the gas chamber while the children traveled by train to an unknown destination, had themselves been brought up to condemn their own ties of blood. The anguish of the divided was obviously holy. The contentment of those who felt no reluctance to divide was plainly damned.

In this day of exposition those who made the other sacrifice of the near for the far, and preferred other countries to their own, proved also to be unholy. The relationship between a man and a fatherland is always disturbed by conflict, if either man or fatherland is highly developed. A man's demands for liberty must at some point challenge the limitations the state imposes on the individual for the sake of the mass. If he is to carry on the national tradition he must wrestle with those who, speaking in its name, desire to crystallize it at the point reached by the previous generation. In any case national life itself must frequently exasperate him, because it is the medium in which he is expressing himself, and every craftsman or artist is repelled by the resistance of his medium to his will. All men should have a drop or two of treason in their veins, if the nations are not to go soft like so many sleepy pears.

Yet to be a traitor is most miserable. All the men I saw in the prisoner's dock were sad as they stood their trials, not only because they were going to be punished. They would have been sad even if they had never been brought to justice. They had forsaken the familiar medium; they had trusted themselves to the mercies of those who had no reason to care for them; knowing their custodians' indifference they had lived for long in fear; and they were aware that they had thrown away their claim on those who might naturally have felt affection for them. Strangers, as King Solomon put it, were filled with their wealth, and their labors were in the house of a stranger, and they mourned at the last when their flesh and body were consumed. As a divorce sharply recalls what a happy marriage should be, so the treachery of these men recalled what a nation should be; a shelter where all talents are generously recognized, all forgivable oddities forgiven, all viciousness quietly frustrated, and those who lack talent honored for equivalent contributions of graciousness. Each of these men was as dependent on the good opinion of others as one is oneself; they needed a nation which was also a hearth, and their capacity for suffering made it tragic that they had gone out from their own hearth to suffer among strangers, because the intellectual leaders of their time had professed a philosophy which was scarcely more than a lapse of memory, and had forgotten that a hearth gives out warmth.

NOTES AND COMMENTS

Rebecca West claims there is nothing treasonous to the human race about loving your own—your home, your family, your very hand —better than someone else's. Unlike Shaw, she defends sentiment against cold reason, feeling against logic. Why does she consider treason an especially reprehensible crime? Why did pre-war intellectuals and internationalists often claim it was not a crime at all? Does Dwight Macdonald's definition of responsibility conflict with Miss West's definition of nationalism? Perhaps Freud would have approved her studies of traitors—but he certainly might have suggested that nationalism is also a kind of crime. Would her argument answer this charge?

Like Orwell, Rebecca West elevates journalism to a literary art.

In what ways does her technique seem as appropriate to fiction as to journalism? Compare her *approach* to that of most newspaper and magazine writers. Does her essay have anything in common stylistically with Virginia Woolf's "Mary Wollstonecraft"? (Remember that both authors are women and both are novelists.)

GEORGE ORWELL

1903-1950

George Orwell, whose real name was Eric Blair, was born into an English family living in India. For several years he served with the Indian Imperial Police in Burma, but left because he had come to look upon imperialism as "very largely a racket." He moved to Europe where he worked as a dishwasher in Paris and lived like a tramp in England. From these experiences came his first book, *Down and Out in Paris and London*, a minor triumph of realism.

Orwell had an exceptional capacity for seeing political events in historical perspective. He was a socialist who did not hesitate to uncover flaws in socialist practice at a time when other liberals were defending it uncritically. Certainly no English writer had ever before written with such directness about the shabby motives of middle-class socialists who enjoyed their comfortable status during the depression while deluding themselves that they and the working class were "really in the same boat." Orwell also fought with the Loyalists in Spain during the Civil War. But in his *Homage to Catalonia* (1938) he was the first intellectual sympathetic to the Loyalists who was honest enough to describe how the Russian-led Spanish Communists had perverted and destroyed their own cause.

Orwell's best-known works are two fantasy novels, *Animal Farm* and *1984*, which depict vividly the intolerableness of life under totalitarianism—the first, by parodying Soviet history; the second, by painting a picture of the whole world under a totalitarian regime. Orwell's novels are more concerned with events than with characters; his interests were political, although in his hands the discussion of politics becomes a literary art. What still impresses us about Orwell is his unflinching honesty about the catastrophe of Russian communism and the failures of socialism in Europe. He could also see value in people and ideas he did not necessarily admire; this quality is evident in the present essay, "Reflections on Gandhi."

Reflections on Gandhi

SAINTS SHOULD always be judged guilty until they are proved innocent, but the tests that have to be applied to them are not, of course, the same in all cases. In Gandhi's case the questions one feels inclined to ask are: to what extent was Gandhi moved by vanity—by the consciousness of himself as a humble, naked old man, sitting on a praying mat and shaking empires by sheer spiritual power—and to what extent did he compromise his own principles by entering politics, which of their nature are inseparable from coercion and fraud? To give a definite answer one would have to study Gandhi's acts and writings in immense detail, for his whole life was a sort of pilgrimage in which every act was significant. But this partial autobiography,[1] which ends in the nineteen-twenties, is strong evidence in his favor, all the more because it covers what he would have called the unregenerate part of his life and reminds one that inside the saint, or near-saint, there was a very shrewd, able person who could, if he had chosen, have been a brilliant success as a lawyer, an administrator or perhaps even a businessman.

At about the time when the autobiography first appeared I remember reading its opening chapters in the ill-printed pages of some Indian newspaper. They made a good impression on me, which Gandhi himself at that time did not. The things that one associated with him—home-spun cloth, "soul forces" and vegetarianism—were unappealing, and his medievalist program was obviously not viable in a backward, starving, over-populated country. It was also apparent that the British were making use of him, or thought they were making use of him. Strictly speaking, as a Nationalist, he was an enemy, but since in every crisis he would exert himself to prevent violence—which, from the British point of view, meant preventing any effective action whatever—he could be re-

Reprinted from *Shooting An Elephant and Other Essays* by George Orwell. Copyright, 1945, 1946, 1949, 1950, by Sonia Brownell Orwell. By permission of Harcourt, Brace & World, Inc., and Martin Secker & Warburg, Ltd., London.

[1] *The Story of my Experiments with Truth.* By M. K. Gandhi.

garded as "our man." In private this was sometimes cynically admitted. The attitude of the Indian millionaires was similar. Gandhi called upon them to repent, and naturally they preferred him to the Socialists and Communists who, given the chance, would actually have taken their money away. How reliable such calculations are in the long run is doubtful; as Gandhi himself says, "in the end deceivers deceive only themselves"; but at any rate the gentleness with which he was nearly always handled was due partly to the feeling that he was useful. The British Conservatives only became really angry with him when, as in 1942, he was in effect turning his non-violence against a different conqueror.

But I could see even then that the British officials who spoke of him with a mixture of amusement and disapproval also genuinely liked and admired him, after a fashion. Nobody ever suggested that he was corrupt, or ambitious in any vulgar way, or that anything he did was actuated by fear or malice. In judging a man like Gandhi one seems instinctively to apply high standards, so that some of his virtues have passed almost unnoticed. For instance, it is clear even from the autobiography that his natural physical courage was quite outstanding: the manner of his death was a later illustration of this, for a public man who attached any value to his own skin would have been more adequately guarded. Again, he seems to have been quite free from that maniacal suspiciousness which, as E. M. Forster rightly says in *A Passage to India*, is the besetting Indian vice, as hypocrisy is the British vice. Although no doubt he was shrewd enough in detecting dishonesty, he seems wherever possible to have believed that other people were acting in good faith and had a better nature through which they could be approached. And though he came of a poor middle-class family, started life rather unfavorably, and was probably of unimpressive physical appearance, he was not afflicted by envy or by the feeling of inferiority. Color feeling when he first met it in its worst form in South Africa, seems rather to have astonished him. Even when he was fighting what was in effect a color war, he did not think of people in terms of race or status. The governor of a province, a cotton millionaire, a half-starved Dravidian coolie, a British private soldier were all equally human beings, to be approached in much the same way. It is noticeable that even in the worst possible circumstances, as in South Africa when he was making himself unpopular as the champion of the Indian community, he did not lack European friends.

Written in short lengths for newspaper serialization, the autobiography is not a literary masterpiece, but it is the more impressive because of the commonplaceness of much of its material. It is well to be reminded that Gandhi started out with the normal ambitions of a young Indian student and only adopted his extremist opinions by degrees and, in some cases, rather unwillingly. There was a time, it is interesting to learn, when he wore a top hat, took dancing lessons, studied French and Latin, went up the Eiffel Tower and even tried to learn the violin—all this was the idea of assimilating European civilization as thoroughly as possible. He was not one of those saints who are marked out by their phenomenal piety from childhood onwards, nor one of the other kind who forsake the world after sensational debaucheries. He makes full confession of the misdeeds of his youth, but in fact there is not much to confess. As a frontispiece to the book there is a photograph of Gandhi's possessions at the time of his death. The whole outfit could be purchased for about £5, and Gandhi's sins, at least his fleshly sins, would make the same sort of appearance if placed all in one heap. A few cigarettes, a few mouthfuls of meat, a few annas pilfered in childhood from the maidservant, two visits to a brothel (on each occasion he got away without "doing anything"), one narrowly escaped lapse with his landlady in Plymouth, one outburst of temper—that is about the whole collection. Almost from childhood onwards he had a deep earnestness, an attitude ethical rather than religious, but, until he was about thirty, no very definite sense of direction. His first entry into anything describable as public life was made by way of vegetarianism. Underneath his less ordinary qualities one feels all the time the solid middle-class businessmen who were his ancestors. One feels that even after he had abandoned personal ambition he must have been a resourceful, energetic lawyer and a hard-headed political organizer, careful in keeping down expenses, an adroit handler of committees and an indefatigable chaser of subscriptions. His character was an extraordinarily mixed one, but there was almost nothing in it that you can put your finger on and call bad, and I believe that even Gandhi's worst enemies would admit that he was an interesting and unusual man who enriched the world simply by being alive. Whether he was also a lovable man, and whether his teachings can have much value for those who do not accept the religious beliefs on which they are founded, I have never felt fully certain.

Of late years it has been the fashion to talk about Gandhi as though he were not only sympathetic to the Western Left-wing movement, but were integrally part of it. Anarchists and pacifists, in particular, have claimed him for their own, noticing only that he was opposed to centralism and State violence and ignoring the other-worldly, anti-humanist tendency of his doctrines. But one should, I think, realize that Gandhi's teachings cannot be squared with the belief that Man is the measure of all things and that our job is to make life worth living on this earth, which is the only earth we have. They make sense only on the assumption that God exists and that the world of solid objects is an illusion to be escaped from. It is worth considering the disciplines which Gandhi imposed on himself and which—though he might not insist on every one of his followers observing every detail—he considered indispensable if one wanted to serve either God or humanity. First of all, no meat-eating, and if possible no animal food in any form. (Gandhi himself, for the sake of his health, had to compromise on milk, but seems to have felt this to be a backsliding.) No alcohol or tobacco, and no spices or condiments even of a vegetable kind, since food should be taken not for its own sake but solely in order to preserve one's strength. Secondly, if possible, no sexual intercourse. If sexual intercourse must happen, then it should be for the sole purpose of begetting children and presumably at long intervals. Gandhi himself, in his middle thirties, took the vow of *brahmacharya*, which means not only complete chastity but the elimination of sexual desire. This condition, it seems, is difficult to attain without a special diet and frequent fasting. One of the dangers of milk-drinking is that it is apt to arouse sexual desire. And finally—this is the cardinal point—for the seeker after goodness there must be no close friendships and no exclusive loves whatever.

Close friendships, Gandhi says, are dangerous, because "friends react on one another" and through loyalty to a friend one can be led into wrong-doing. This is unquestionably true. Moreover, if one is to love God, or to love humanity as a whole, one cannot give one's preference to any individual person. This again is true, and it marks the point at which the humanistic and the religious attitude cease to be reconcilable. To an ordinary human being, love means nothing if it does not mean loving some people more than others. The autobiography leaves it uncertain whether Gandhi behaved in an inconsiderate way to his wife and children, but at any rate it makes clear that on three occasions he was willing to let his wife or a child die rather than administer the animal food prescribed by the doctor. It is true that the threatened death never actually occurred, and also that Gandhi—with, one gathers, a good deal of moral pressure in the opposite direction—always gave the patient the choice of staying alive at the price of committing a sin: still, if the decision had been solely his own, he would have forbidden the animal food, whatever the risks might be. There must, he says, be some limit to what we will do in order to remain alive, and the limit is well on this side of chicken broth. This attitude is perhaps a noble one, but, in the sense which—I think—most people would give to the word, it is inhuman. The essence of being human is that one does not seek perfection, that one *is* sometimes willing to commit sins for the sake of loyalty, that one does not push asceticism to the point where it makes friendly intercourse impossible, and that one is prepared in the end to be defeated and broken up by life, which is the inevitable price of fastening one's love upon other human individuals. No doubt alcohol, tobacco, and so forth, are things that a saint must avoid, but sainthood is also a thing that human beings must avoid. There is an obvious retort to this, but one should be wary about making it. In this yogi-ridden age, it is too readily assumed that "non-attachment" is not only better than a full acceptance of earthly life, but that the ordinary man only rejects it because it is too difficult: in other words, that the average human being is a failed saint. It is doubtful whether this is true. Many people genuinely do not wish to be saints, and it is probable that some who achieve or aspire to sainthood have never felt much temptation to be human beings. If one could follow it to its psychological roots, one would, I believe, find that the main motive for "non-attachment" is a desire to escape from the pain of living, and above all from love, which, sexual or non-sexual, is hard work. But it is not necessary here to argue whether the other-worldly or the humanistic ideal is "higher." The point is that they are incompatible. One must choose between God and Man, and all "radicals" and "progressives," from the mildest Liberal to the most extreme Anarchist, have in effect chosen Man.

However, Gandhi's pacifism can be separated to some extent from his other teachings. Its motive was religious, but he claimed also for it that it was a definite technique, a method, capable of producing desired political results. Gandhi's attitude was not that of most Western pacifists. *Satyagraha*, first evolved in South Africa, was a sort of non-violent warfare, a way of defeating the enemy without hurting him and without feeling or arousing hatred. It entailed such things as civil disobedience, strikes, lying down in front of railway trains, enduring police charges without running away and without hitting back, and the like. Gandhi objected to "passive resistance" as a translation of *Satyagraha*: in Gujarati, it seems, the world means "firmness in the truth." In his early days Gandhi served as a stretcher-bearer on the British side in the Boer War, and he was prepared to do the same again in the war of 1914-18. Even after he had completely abjured violence he was honest enough to see that in war it is usually necessary to take sides. He did not—indeed, since his whole political life centred round a struggle for national independence, he could not—take the sterile and dishonest line of pretending that in every war both sides are exactly the same and it makes no difference who wins. Nor did he, like most Western pacifists, specialize in avoiding awkward questions. In relation to the late war, one question that every pacifist had a clear obligation to answer was: "What about the Jews? Are you prepared to see them exterminated? If not, how do you propose to save them without resorting to war?" I must say that I have never heard, from any Western pacifist, an honest answer to this question, though I have heard plenty of evasions, usually of the "you're another" type. But it so happens that Gandhi was asked a somewhat similar question in 1938 and that his answer is on record in Mr. Louis Fischer's *Gandhi and Stalin*. According to Mr. Fischer, Gandhi's view was that the German Jews ought to commit collective suicide, which "would have aroused the world and the people of Germany to Hitler's violence." After the war he justified himself: the Jews had been killed anyway, and might as well have died significantly. One has the impression that this attitude staggered even so warm an admirer as Mr. Fischer, but Gandhi was merely being honest. If you are not prepared to take life, you must often be prepared for lives to be lost in some other way. When, in 1942, he urged non-violent resistance against a Japanese invasion, he was ready to admit that it might cost several million deaths.

At the same time there is reason to think that Gandhi, who after all was born in 1869, did not understand the nature of totalitarianism and saw everything in terms of his own struggle against the British government. The important point here is not so much that the British treated him forbearingly as that he was always able to command publicity. As can be seen from the phrase quoted above, he believed in "arousing the world," which is only possible if the world gets a chance to hear what you are doing. It is difficult to see how Gandhi's methods could be applied in a country where opponents of the régime disappear in the middle of the night and are never heard of again. Without a free press and the right of assembly, it is impossible not merely to appeal to outside opinion, but to bring a mass movement into being, or even to make your intentions known to your adversary. Is there a Gandhi in Russia at this moment? And if there is, what is he accomplishing? The Russian masses could only practice civil disobedience if the same idea happened to occur to all of them simultaneously, and even then, to judge by the history of the Ukraine famine, it would make no difference. But let it be granted that non-violent resistance can be effective against one's own government, or against an occupying power: even so, how does one put it into practice internationally? Gandhi's various conflicting statements on the late war seem to show that he felt the difficulty of this. Applied to foreign politics, pacifism either stops being pacifist or becomes appeasement. Moreover the assumption, which served Gandhi so well in dealing with individuals, that all human beings are more or less approachable and will respond to a generous gesture, needs to be seriously questioned. It is not necessarily true, for example, when you are dealing with lunatics. Then the question becomes: Who is sane? Was Hitler sane? And is it not possible for one whole culture to be insane by the standards of another? And, so far as one can gauge the feelings of whole nations, is there any apparent connection between a generous deed and a friendly response? Is gratitude a factor in international politics?

These and kindred questions need discussion, and need it urgently, in the few years left to us before somebody presses the button and the rockets begin to fly. It seems doubtful whether civilization can stand another major war, and it is at least thinkable that the way out lies through non-violence. It is Gandhi's virtue that he would have been ready to give honest consideration to the kind of question that I have raised above; and, indeed, he probably did discuss most of these questions somewhere or other in his innumerable newspaper articles. One feels of him that there was much that he did not understand, but not that there was anything that he was frightened of saying or thinking. I have never been able to feel much liking for Gandhi, but I do not feel sure that as a political thinker he was wrong in the main, nor do I believe that his life was a failure. It is curious that when he was assassinated, many of his warmest admirers exclaimed sorrowfully that he had lived just long enough to see his life work in ruins, because India was engaged in a civil war which had always been foreseen as one of the by-products of the transfer of power. But it was not in trying to smooth down Hindu-Moslem rivalry that Gandhi had spent his life. His main political objective, the peaceful ending of British rule, had after all been attained. As usual the relevant facts cut across one another. On the other hand, the British did get out of India without fighting, an event which very few observers indeed would have predicted until about a year before it happened. On the other hand, this was done by a Labour government, and it is certain that a Conservative government, especially a government headed by Churchill, would have acted differently. But if, by 1945, there had grown up in Britain a large body of opinion sympathetic to Indian independence, how far was this due to Gandhi's personal influence? And if, as may happen, India and Britain finally settle down into a decent and friendly relationship, will this be partly because Gandhi, by keeping up his struggle obstinately and without hatred, disinfected the political air? That one even thinks of asking such questions indicates his stature. One may feel, as I do, a sort of aesthetic distaste for Gandhi, one may reject the claims of sainthood made on his behalf (he never made any such claim himself, by the way), one may also reject sainthood as an ideal and therefore feel that Gandhi's basic aims were anti-human and reactionary: but regarded simply as a politician, and compared with the other leading political figures of our time, how clean a smell he has managed to leave behind!

NOTES AND COMMENTS

Orwell's view of Gandhi (the essay was written in 1949) differed from most people's. Admirers regarded Gandhi as a saint; detractors looked upon him as a religious fanatic whose belief in passive resistance made him politically dangerous. Orwell, who makes his personal distaste for sainthood quite clear, nevertheless respects Gandhi. Why?

Orwell's contempt for political figures is a widely shared attitude in the twentieth century. How does this attitude toward statesmen and politics contrast with Burke's eighteenth-century ideals? In what ways is Orwell's view closer to Macdonald's idea of the state, or Shaw's opinion of "representatives"? Macdonald's essay, "Gandhi" (1948), makes a good contrast to Orwell's.

Orwell's style differs from Belloc's and Virginia Woolf's. Theirs are personal, biased, hyper-literary. Do you prefer any one of the three? As an experiment, write an essay on Gandhi or Mary Wollstonecraft in a style different from Orwell's or Virginia Woolf's.

HILAIRE BELLOC

1870-1953

Hilaire Belloc, though a novelist and poet as well, was most completely at home in the essay. A devout Catholic and a staunch conservative, he devoted much of his work, especially in the realm of history, to defense of unorthodox and highly controversial positions. Such books as *Characters of the Reformation* and *The Servile State* are especially provocative in their vigorous logic, lucid style, and unabashed partisanship.

Belloc's many biographies—including *Danton, Marie Antoinette, Wolsey,* and *Henry VIII*—attest to his belief that history can be understood through insight into the leading figures who shape it. The present selection, from *The Eyewitness*, modifies this approach. In it the beheading of Charles I is presented in terms of its impact upon an ordinary Londoner who could not influence effectively the events which shaped his life.

The Apprentice

29TH JANUARY (OR, AS WE SHOULD SAY, 10TH FEBRUARY), 1649
Charles I was executed on this day, upon a scaffold outside the second window on the north of Whitehall Banqueting Hall, at four in the afternoon.

Men were well into the working week; it was a Tuesday and apprentices were under the hard eyes of their masters throughout the City of London and in the rarer business places that elbowed

Reprinted from *The Eyewitness* by Hilaire Belloc, published by J. M. Dent & Sons Ltd., London. By permission of A. D. Peters, agents for the Author's estate.

the great palaces along the Strand. The sky was overcast and the air distastefully cold, nor did anything in the landscape seem colder than the dark bank of the river under those colourless and lifeless January clouds.

Whether it were an illusion or a reality, one could have sworn that there was a sort of silence over the houses and on the families of the people; one could have sworn that men spoke in lower tones than was their custom, and that the streets were emptier. The trial and the sentence of the king had put all that great concourse of men into the very presence of Death.

The day wore on; the noise of the workmen could be heard at the scaffold by Whitehall; one hour was guessed at and then another; rumours and flat assertions were busy everywhere, especially among the young, and an apprentice to a harness-maker in the Water Lane, near Essex House, knew not what to believe. But he was determined to choose his moment and to slip away lest he should miss so great a sight. The tyranny of the army kept all the city in doubt all day long, and allowed no news; none the less, from before noon there had begun a little gathering of people in Whitehall, round the scaffold at which men were still giving the last strokes of the hammer. Somewhat after noon a horseshoe of cavalry assembled in their long cloaks and curious tall civilian hats; they stood ranked, with swords drawn, all round the platform. Their horses shifted uneasily in the cold.

The harness-maker's apprentice found his opportunity; his master was called to the door for an order from Arundel House, and the lad left his bench quickly, just as he was, without hat or coat, in the bitter weather, and darting through the side door ran down through the Water Gate and down its steps to the river. The tide was at the flood and his master's boat lay moored. He cast her off and pulled rapidly up the line of gardens, backing water when he came to the public stairs just beyond Whitehall. Here he quickly tied the painter and ran up breathless to Whitehall Gate, fearing he might have missed his great expectation. He was in ample time.

It was perhaps half-past three o'clock when he got through the gate and found himself in the press of people. Far off to the left, among the soldiery that lined the avenue from the park to the Mall, and so to St. James's, a continuous roll of drums burdened the still air.

The crowd was not very large, but it filled the space from the gate to the scaffold and a little beyond, save where it was pressed outward by the ring of cavalry. It did not overflow into the wide spaces of the park, though these lay open to Whitehall, nor did it run up towards Charing Cross beyond the Banqueting Hall.

The apprentice was not so tall as the men about him; he strained and elbowed a little to see, and he was sworn at. He could make out the low scaffold, a large platform all draped in black, with iron staples, and a railing round it; it covered the last three blank windows of Whitehall, running from the central casement until it met the brick house at the north end of the stonework; there the brickwork beneath one of the windows had been taken out so as to give access through it from the floor within to the scaffold on the same level without; and whispers round told the apprentice, though he did not know how much to trust them, that it was through this hasty egress that the king would appear. Upon the scaffold itself stood a group of men, two of them masked, and one of the masked ones, of great stature and strong, leant upon the axe with his arm crossed upon the haft of it. A little block, barely raised above the floor of the platform, he could only see by leaping on tip-toe, catching it by glimpses between the heads of his neighbours or the shoulders of the cavalry guard; but he noticed in those glimpses how very low it was, and saw, ominous upon it, two staples driven as though to contain the struggler. Before it, so that one kneeling would have his face toward the palace and away from the crowd, was a broad footstool covered with red velvet, and making a startling patch upon all that expanse of black baize.

It was cold waiting; the motionless twigs of the small bare trees in the park made it seem colder still. The three-quarters struck in the new clock behind him upon Whitehall Gate, but as yet no one had appeared.

In a few moments, however, there was a movement in the crowd, heads turning to the right, and a corresponding backing of the mounted men to contain the first beginnings of a rush, for the commanders of the army feared, while they despised, the popular majority of London; and the wealthy merchants, the allies of the army, had not joined this common lot. This turning of faces towards the great blank stone wall of the palace was caused by a sound of many footsteps within. The only window not masked with stone, the middle window, was that upon which their gaze universally turned. They saw, passing it very rapidly, a group of men within; they were walking very sharply along the floor (which was here raised above the level of the window itself and cut the lower panes of it); they were hurrying towards the northern end of the great Banqueting Hall. It was but a moment's vision, and again they appeared in the open air through the broken brickwork at the far end of the stone façade.

For a moment the apprentice saw clearly the tall king, his face grown old, his pointed beard left full, his long features not moved. The great cloak that covered him with the Great Star of the Garter upon the left shoulder, he drew off quickly and let fall into the hands of Herbert. He wore no hat; he stepped forward with precision towards the group of executioners, and a little murmur ran through the crowd.

The old bishop, moving his limbs with difficulty, but suppliant and attendant upon his friend, stood by in agony. He helped the king to pull off his inner coat until he stood conspicuous in the sky-blue vest beneath it, and round his neck a ribbon and one ornament upon it, a George carved in onyx. This also he removed and gave to the bishop, while he took from his hands a little white silken cap and fixed it firmly upon his long and beautiful hair. From beneath the sky-blue of his garment, at the neck and at the wrists, appeared frills of exquisite linen and the adornment of lace. He stood for a few moments praying, then turned and spoke as though he were addressing them all. But the apprentice, though he held his breath, and strained to hear, as did all others about him, could catch no separate word, but only the general sound of the king's voice speaking. The movement of the horses, the occasional striking of a hoof upon the setts of the street, the distance, covered that voice. Next, Charles was saying something to the masked man, and a moment later he was kneeling upon the footstool. The apprentice saw him turn a moment and spread his arms out as an example of what he next should do; he bent him toward the block—it was too low; he lay at full length, and the crowd lifted and craned to see him in this posture.

The four heavy strokes of the hour struck and boomed in silence. The hands of the lying figure were stretched out again, this time as a final signal, and right up in the air above them all the axe swung, white against the grey sky, flashed and fell.

In a moment the group upon the scaffold had closed round, a
cloth was thrown, the body was raised, and among the hands
stretched out to it were the eager and enfeebled hands of the
bishop, trembling and still grasping the George.

A long moan or wail, very strange and dreadful, not very
loud, rose from the people now that their tension was slackened by
the accomplishment of the deed. And at once from the north and
from the south, with such ceremony as is used to the conquered,
the cavalry charged right through, hacking and dispersing these
Londoners and driving them every way.

.   .   .

The apprentice dodged and ran, his head full of the tragedy
and bewildered, his body in active fear of the horses that pursued
flying packets of the crowd down the alley-ways of the offices and
palace buildings.

He went off by a circuitous way to find, not his master's house
after such an escapade, but his mother's, where she lived beyond
St. Martin's.

The dusk did not long tarry; as it gathered and turned to
night small flakes of snow began to fall and lie upon the frozen
ground.

NOTES AND COMMENTS

Since the events Belloc presents come to the reader through the
eyes of the apprentice, the boy assumes major importance in the
piece. Why Belloc presented the situation dramatically is easy to
understand. Why, however, did he choose the apprentice as his chief
observer?

Is Belloc the controversialist at work in this essay or are we
listening simply to Belloc the historian? To what extent is it possible
to be interesting and stimulating in the writing of history without
becoming involved in controversy?

For Belloc in a less somber relationship to the young, try *Cau-
tionary Tales for Children, The Bad Child's Book of Beasts,* or *More
Beasts for Worse Children.*

VIRGINIA WOOLF

1882-1941

Virginia Woolf was born into the center of Victorian intellectual life: her father was Sir Leslie Stephen, a pre-eminent critic and the editor of the English Men of Letters Series. But she herself has a foremost place in the literature we know as modern. Her novels—among them *Mrs. Dalloway, To the Lighthouse,* and *Orlando*—are considered classics of the twentieth century. Through her development of the stream-of-consciousness technique and her exploitation of the difference between psychological time and external time, she has wielded considerable influence on succeeding novelists.

Mrs. Woolf was, as well, her own kind of critic, the kind she called, borrowing a phrase from Samuel Johnson, "the Common Reader." The term to her meant one who reads "for his own pleasure . . . is guided by instinct to create for himself, out of whatever odds and ends he can come by, some kind of whole—a portrait of a man, a sketch of an age, a theory of the art of writing." The essay which follows portrays intuitively rather than in scholarly fashion one of the famous women of the eighteenth century, and suggests as well the feeling of the times in which she lived.

Mary Wollstonecraft

GREAT WARS are strangely intermittent in their effects. The French Revolution took some people and tore them asunder; others it passed over without disturbing a hair of their heads. Jane Austen, it is said, never mentioned it; Charles Lamb ignored it;

Beau Brummell never gave the matter a thought. But to Wordsworth and to Godwin it was the dawn; unmistakably they saw

> France standing on the top of golden hours,
> And human nature seeming born again.

Thus it would be easy for a picturesque historian to lay side by
side the most glaring contrasts—here in Chesterfield Street was
Beau Brummell letting his chin fall carefully upon his cravat and
discussing in a tone studiously free from vulgar emphasis the
proper cut of the lapel of a coat; and here in Somers Town was a
party of ill-dressed, excited young men, one with a head too big for
his body and a nose too long for his face, holding forth day by day
over the tea-cups upon human perfectibility, ideal unity, and the
rights of man. There was also a woman present with very bright
eyes and a very eager tongue, and the young men, who had middle-
class names, like Barlow and Holcroft and Godwin, called her
simply "Wollstonecraft," as if it did not matter whether she were
married or unmarried, as if she were a young man like themselves.

Such glaring discords among intelligent people—for Charles
Lamb and Godwin, Jane Austen and Mary Wollstonecraft were all
highly intelligent—suggest how much influence circumstances have
upon opinions. If Godwin had been brought up in the precincts of
the Temple and had drunk deep of antiquity and old letters at
Christ's Hospital, he might never have cared a straw for the future
of man and his rights in general. If Jane Austen had lain as a
child on the landing to prevent her father from thrashing her
mother, her soul might have burnt with such a passion against
tyranny that all her novels might have been consumed in one cry
for justice.

Such had been Mary Wollstonecraft's first experience of the
joys of married life. And then her sister Everina had been married
miserably and had bitten her wedding ring to pieces in the coach.
Her brother had been a burden on her; her father's farm had failed,
and in order to start that disreputable man with the red face and
the violent temper and the dirty hair in life again she had gone
into bondage among the aristocracy as a governess—in short, she
had never known what happiness was, and, in its default, had
fabricated a creed fitted to meet the sordid misery of real human
life. The staple of her doctrine was that nothing mattered save
independence. "Every obligation we receive from our fellow-

creatures is a new shackle, takes from our native freedom, and debases the mind." Independence was the first necessity for a woman; not grace or charm, but energy and courage and the power to put her will into effect were her necessary qualities. It was her highest boast to be able to say, "I never yet resolved to do anything of consequence that I did not adhere readily to it." Certainly Mary could say this with truth. When she was a little more than thirty she could look back upon a series of actions which she had carried out in the teeth of opposition. She had taken a house by prodigious efforts for her friend Fanny, only to find that Fanny's mind was changed and she did not want a house after all. She had started a school. She had persuaded Fanny into marrying Mr. Skeys. She had thrown up her school and gone to Lisbon alone to nurse Fanny when she died. On the voyage back she had forced the captain of the ship to rescue a wrecked French vessel by threatening to expose him if he refused. And when, overcome by a passion for Fuseli, she declared her wish to live with him and was refused flatly by his wife, she had put her principle of decisive action instantly into effect, and had gone to Paris determined to make her living by her pen.

The Revolution thus was not merely an event that had happened outside her; it was an active agent in her own blood. She had been in revolt all her life—against tyranny, against law, against convention. The reformer's love of humanity, which has so much of hatred in it as well as love, fermented within her. The outbreak of revolution in France expressed some of her deepest theories and convictions, and she dashed off in the heat of that extraordinary moment those two eloquent and daring books—the *Reply to Burke* and the *Vindication of the Rights of Woman,* which are so true that they seem now to contain nothing new in them—their originality has become our commonplace. But when she was in Paris lodging by herself in a great house, and saw with her own eyes the King whom she despised driving past surrounded by National Guards and holding himself with greater dignity than she expected, then, "I can scarcely tell you why," the tears came to her eyes. "I am going to bed," the letter ended, "and, for the first time in my life, I cannot put out the candle." Things were not so simple after all. She could not understand even her own feelings. She saw the most cherished of her convictions put into practice—and her eyes filled with tears. She had won fame and independence and the right to live her own life—and she wanted something different. "I do not want to be loved like a goddess," she wrote, "but I wish to be necessary to you." For Imlay, the fascinating American to whom her letter was addressed, had been very good to her. Indeed, she had fallen passionately in love with him. But it was one of her theories that love should be free—"that mutual affection was marriage and that the marriage tie should not bind after the death of love, if love should die." And yet at the same time that she wanted freedom she wanted certainty. "I like the word affection," she wrote, "because it signifies something habitual."

The conflict of all these contradictions shows itself in her face, at once so resolute and so dreamy, so sensual and so intelligent, and beautiful into the bargain with its great coils of hair and the large bright eyes that Southey thought the most expressive he had ever seen. The life of such a woman was bound to be tempestuous. Every day she made theories by which life should be lived; and every day she came smack against the rock of other people's prejudices. Every day too—for she was no pedant, no cold-blooded theorist—something was born in her that thrust aside her theories and forced her to model them afresh. She acted upon her theory that she had no legal claim upon Imlay; she refused to marry him; but when he left her alone week after week with the child she had borne him her agony was unendurable.

Thus distracted, thus puzzling even to herself, the plausible and treacherous Imlay cannot be altogether blamed for failing to follow the rapidity of her changes and the alternate reason and unreason of her moods. Even friends whose liking was impartial were disturbed by her discrepancies. Mary had a passionate, an exuberant, love of Nature, and yet one night when the colours in the sky were so exquisite that Madeleine Schweizer could not help saying to her, "Come, Mary—come, nature lover—and enjoy this wonderful spectacle—this constant transition from colour to colour." Mary never took her eyes off the Baron de Wolzogen. "I must confess," wrote Madame Schweizer, "that this erotic absorption made such a disagreeable impression on me, that all my pleasure vanished." But if the sentimental Swiss was disconcerted by Mary's sensuality, Imlay, the shrewd man of business, was exasperated by her intelligence. Whenever he saw her he yielded to her charm, but then her quickness, her penetration, her uncompromising idealism harassed him. She saw through his excuses; she met all his reasons; she was even capable of managing his business. There was no peace with her—he must be off again. And then her letters followed him, torturing him with their sincerity and their insight. They were so outspoken; they pleaded so passionately to be told the truth; they showed such a contempt for soap and alum and wealth and comfort; they repeated, as he suspected, so truthfully that he had only to say the word, "and you shall never hear of me more," that he could not endure it. Tickling minnows he had hooked a dolphin, and the creature rushed him through the waters till he was dizzy and only wanted to escape. After all, though he had played at theory-making too, he was a business man, he depended upon soap and alum; "the secondary pleasures of life," he had to admit, "are very necessary to my comfort." And among them was one that for ever evaded Mary's jealous scrutiny. Was it business, was it politics, was it a woman that perpetually took him away from her? He shillied and shallied; he was very charming when they met; then he disappeared again. Exasperated at last, and half insane with suspicion, she forced the truth from the cook. A little actress in a strolling company was his mistress, she learnt. True to her own creed of decisive action, Mary at once soaked her skirts so that she might sink unfailingly, and threw herself from Putney Bridge. But she was rescued; after unspeakable agony she recovered, and then her "unconquerable greatness of mind," her girlish creed of independence, asserted itself again, and she determined to make another bid for happiness and to earn her living without taking a penny from Imlay for herself or their child.

It was in this crisis that she again saw Godwin, the little man with the big head, whom she had met when the French Revolution was making the young men in Somers Town think that a new world was being born. She met him—but that is a euphemism, for in fact Mary Wollstonecraft actually visited him in his own house. Was it the effect of the French Revolution? Was it the blood she had seen spilt on the pavement and the cries of the furious crowd that had run in her ears that made it seem a matter of no importance whether she put on her cloak and went to visit Godwin in Somers Town, or waited in Judd Street West for Godwin to come to her? And what strange upheaval of human life was it that inspired that curious man, who was so queer a mixture of meanness and magnanimity, of coldness and deep feeling—for the memoir of his wife could not have been written without unusual depth of

heart—to hold the view that she did right—that he respected Mary
for trampling upon the idiotic convention by which women's lives
were tied down? He held the most extraordinary views on many
subjects, and upon the relations of the sexes in particular. He
thought that reason should influence even the love between men
and women. He thought that there was something spiritual in
their relationship. He had written that "marriage is a law, and the
worst of all laws . . . marriage is an affair of property, and the
worst of all properties." He held the belief that if two people of the
opposite sex like each other, they should live together without any
ceremony, or, for living together is apt to blunt love, twenty doors
off, say, in the same street. And he went further; he said that if
another man liked your wife "this will create no difficulty. We may
all enjoy her conversation, and we shall all be wise enough to consider the sensual intercourse a very trivial object." True, when he
wrote those words he had never been in love; now for the first time
he was to experience that sensation. It came very quietly and
naturally, growing "with equal advances in the mind of each" from
those talks in Somers Town, from those discussions upon everything under the sun which they held so improperly alone in his
rooms. "It was friendship melting into love . . . ," he wrote.
"When, in the course of things, the disclosure came, there was
nothing in a manner for either party to disclose to the other."
Certainly they were in agreement upon the most essential points;
they were both of opinion, for instance, that marriage was unnecessary. They would continue to live apart. Only when Nature again
intervened, and Mary found herself with child, was it worth while
to lose valued friends, she asked, for the sake of a theory? She
thought not, and they were married. And then that other theory—
that it is best for husband and wife to live apart—was not that also
incompatible with other feelings that were coming to birth in her?
"A husband is a convenient part of the furniture of the house," she
wrote. Indeed, she discovered that she was passionately domestic.
Why not, then, revise that theory too, and share the same roof?
Godwin should have a room some doors off to work in; and they
should dine out separately if they liked—their work, their friends,
should be separate. Thus they settled it, and the plan worked admirably. The arrangement combined "the novelty and lively sensation of a visit with the more delicious and heartfelt pleasures of
domestic life." Mary admitted that she was happy; Godwin con-

fessed that, after all one's philosophy, it was "extremely gratifying" to find that "there is some one who takes an interest in one's happiness." All sorts of powers and emotions were liberated in Mary by her new satisfaction. Trifles gave her an exquisite pleasure—the sight of Godwin and Imlay's child playing together; the thought of their own child who was to be born; a day's jaunt into the country. One day, meeting Imlay in the New Road, she greeted him without bitterness. But, as Godwin wrote, "Ours is not an idle happiness, a paradise of selfish and transitory pleasures." No, it too was an experiment, as Mary's life had been an experiment from the start, an attempt to make human conventions conform more closely to human needs. And their marriage was only a beginning; all sorts of things were to follow after. Mary was going to have a child. She was going to write a book to be called *The Wrongs of Women*. She was going to reform education. She was going to come down to dinner the day after her child was born. She was going to employ a midwife and not a doctor at her confinement—but that experiment was her last. She died in child-birth. She whose sense of her own existence was so intense, who had cried out even in her misery, "I cannot bear to think of being no more—of losing myself—nay, it appears to me impossible that I should cease to exist," died at the age of thirty-six. But she has her revenge. Many millions have died and been forgotten in the hundred and thirty years that have passed since she was buried; and yet as we read her letters and listen to her arguments and consider her experiments, above all that most fruitful experiment, her relation with Godwin, and realise the high-handed and hot-blooded manner in which she cut her way to the quick of life, one form of immortality is hers undoubtedly: she is alive and active, she argues and experiments, we hear her voice and trace her influence even now among the living.

NOTES AND COMMENTS

Mary Wollstonecraft enters Mrs. Woolf's sketch not so much as people do in a biography but as they do in a novel. She comes upon a stage artistically prepared for her. When she does, she acts, and we come to know her through her actions, not through the author's abstract analysis of her character. Similarly her unfolding personality, her point of view, determine the way in which we come to know the other people in her life. Perhaps the most distinctive mark of the piece is the sympathy the author feels and asks her reader to feel for Mary. Try to decide how much of the tone is due to a novelist's technique by re-writing the essay in a more directly expository style.

More of Mrs. Woolf's impressionistic comments upon literature and literary history may be found in the two volumes of *The Common Reader*, and in *The Death of the Moth*.

ART AND
THE ARTIST

◄§ This section brings together a group of essays about art, artists, and the creative process—and the audience that reads or looks at or listens to works of art. It opens with a famous essay by Thomas De Quincey that seeks, with the urgent intensity typical of this English Romantic, to define what it is that makes a piece of writing *literature* and makes it endure. It includes two other classic pieces of English criticism, the "Preface to Shakespeare," by Samuel Johnson, and Henry James's "The Art of Fiction"—both of them, by their qualities of soundness, interest, and style, as relevant to the study of literature now as when they first were written.

Freud's essay on creative writing and day-dreaming and the selection from Bergson's *Laughter* are classic pieces of a different sort: studies by two of the most influential thinkers in modern psychology, both concerned with isolating basic elements of human creativity. Of the more recent essayists, several are concerned with poetry. Mark Van Doren's careful analyses of some famous lyrics constitute a lesson in the reading, understanding, and appreciation of great verse. John Ciardi, a poet himself, discusses the problem of poetry (particularly modern poetry) and the people who read it—as indeed does William Edward Wilson in his hilarious account of teaching Keats at Annapolis. Bernard Grebanier compares modern notions of the nature of tragedy with the traditional view based on Aristotle's celebrated theory. The final two essays, those by Aldous Huxley and Clement Greenberg, are concerned with certain twentieth-century developments in music and painting.

THOMAS DE QUINCEY

1785-1859

Thomas De Quincey is one of the most interesting of the English Romantic essayists. His psychological penetration into works of literature and his ability to convey emotional states (either his own, or those created by other authors) make him especially fascinating to modern readers. In his most memorable essay, "On the Knocking at the Gate in Macbeth," he begins by warning us that human emotions cannot be explained by "mere understanding" or reason. He was an advocate of unreason and intuition, an exploiter of dreams fifty years before Freud. His prose is discursive, overwrought and metaphoric, and since he was more interested in "moving" people than in "teaching" them (to borrow terms he uses in the following essay), his style is free, energetic, digressive, and irregular.

"Literature of Knowledge and Literature of Power" is a section of a long essay on the poetry of Pope.

Literature of Knowledge and Literature of Power

WHAT IS IT that we mean by *literature?* Popularly, and amongst the thoughtless, it is held to include everything that is printed in a book. Little logic is required to disturb *that* definition. The most thoughtless person is easily made aware that in the idea of *literature* one essential element is,—some relation to a general and common interest of man, so that what applies only to a local or professional or merely personal interest, even though presenting itself in the shape of a book, will not belong to literature. So far the definition is easily narrowed; and it is as easily expanded. For not only is much that takes a station in books not literature, but, inversely, much that really *is* literature never reaches a station in books. The weekly sermons of Christendom, that vast pulpit literature which acts so extensively upon the popular mind—to warn, to uphold, to renew, to comfort, to alarm—does not attain the sanctuary of libraries in the ten-thousandth part of its extent. The drama, again, as for instance the finest of Shakespeare's plays in England and all leading Athenian plays in the noontide of the Attic stage, operated as a literature on the public mind, and were (according to the strictest letter of that term) *published* through the audiences that witnessed[1] their representation, some time before they were published as things to be read; and they were published in this scenical mode of publication with much more effect than they could have had as books during ages of costly copying or of costly printing.

Books, therefore, do not suggest an idea co-extensive and interchangeable with the idea of literature, since much literature, scenic, forensic, or didactic (as from lectures and public orators), may never come into books, and much that *does* come into books may connect itself with no literary interest. But a far more important correction, applicable to the common vague idea of literature, is to be sought, not so much in a better definition of literature, as in a sharper distinction of the two functions which it fulfils. In that great social organ which, collectively, we call literature, there may be distinguished two separate offices, that may blend and often *do* so, but capable, severally, of a severe insulation, and naturally fitted for reciprocal repulsion. There is, first, the literature of *knowledge,* and, secondly, the literature of *power.* The function of the first is to *teach;* the function of the second is to *move:* the first is a rudder; the second an oar or a sail. The first speaks to the *mere* discursive understanding; the second speaks ultimately, it may happen, to the higher understanding, or reason, but always *through* affections of pleasure and sympathy. Remotely it may travel towards an object seated in

---

[1] "Charles I, for example, when Prince of Wales, and many others in his father's court, gained their known familiarity with Shakespeare—not through the original quartos, so slenderly diffused, nor through the first folio of 1623, but through the court representations of his chief dramas at Whitehall."—De Quincey.

what Lord Bacon calls *dry* light;[1] but proximately it does and must operate—else it ceases to be a literature of *power*—on and through that *humid* light which clothes itself in the mists and glittering *iris*[2] of human passions, desires, and genial emotions. Men have so little reflected on the higher functions of literature as to find it a paradox if one should describe it as a mean or subordinate purpose of books to give information. But this is a paradox only in the sense which makes it honorable to be paradoxical. Whenever we talk in ordinary language of seeking information or gaining knowledge, we understand the words as connected with something of absolute novelty. But it is the grandeur of all truth which *can* occupy a very high place in human interests that it is never absolutely novel to the meanest of minds: it exists eternally, by way of germ or latent principle, in the lowest as in the highest, needing to be developed but never to be planted. To be capable of transplantation is the immediate criterion of a truth that ranges on a lower scale. Besides which, there is a rarer thing than truth, namely, *power*, or deep sympathy with truth. What is the effect, for instance, upon society, of children? By the pity, by the tenderness, and by the peculiar modes of admiration, which connect themselves with the helplessness, with the innocence, and with the simplicity of children, not only are the primal affections strengthened and continually renewed, but the qualities which are dearest in the sight of heaven—the frailty, for instance, which appeals to forbearance, the innocence which symbolizes the heavenly, and the simplicity which is most alien from the worldly —are kept up in perpetual remembrance, and their ideals are continually refreshed. A purpose of the same nature is answered by the higher literature, *viz.*, the literature of power. What do you learn from *Paradise Lost*? Nothing at all. What do you learn from a cookery-book? Something new, something that you did not know before, in every paragraph. But would you therefore put the wretched cookery-book on a higher level of estimation than the divine poem? What you owe to Milton is not any knowledge, of which a million separate items are still but a million of advanc-

---

[1] "Heraclitus the Obscure said: *The dry light was the best soul.* Meaning, when the faculties intellectual are in vigor, not wet, nor, as it were, blooded by the affections."—Bacon, *Apophthegms New and Old*, 268 (188).

[2] Rainbow (Iris was the goddess of the rainbow).—*Ed.*]

ing steps on the same earthly level; what you owe is *power*, that is,
exercise and expansion to your own latent capacity of sympathy
with the infinite, where every pulse and each separate influx is a
step upwards, a step ascending as upon a Jacob's ladder from
earth to mysterious altitudes above the earth. *All* the steps of
knowledge, from first to last, carry you further on the same plane,
but could never raise you one foot above your ancient level of
earth; whereas the very *first* step in power is a flight, is an ascending movement into another element where earth is forgotten.

Were it not that human sensibilities are ventilated and continually called out into exercise by the great phenomena of infancy, or of real life as it moves through chance and change, or of
literature as it recombines these elements in the mimicries of
poetry, romance, etc., it is certain that, like any animal power or
muscular energy falling into disuse, all such sensibilities would
gradually droop and dwindle. It is in relation to these great *moral*
capacities of man that the literature of power, as contra-distin-
guished from that of knowledge, lives and has its field of action.
It is concerned with what is highest in man; for the Scriptures
themselves never condescended to deal by suggestion or co-operation with the mere discursive understanding: when speaking of
man in his intellectual capacity, the Scriptures speak, not of the
understanding, but of *"the understanding heart,"* [1] making the
heart—that is, the great *intuitive* (or non-discursive) organ, to be
the interchangeable formula for man in his highest state of capacity
for the infinite. Tragedy, romance, fairy tale, or epopee,[2] all alike
restore to man's mind the ideals of justice, of hope, of truth, of
mercy, of retribution, which else (left to the support of daily life
in its realities) would languish for want of sufficient illustration.
What is meant, for instance, by *poetic justice?* It does not mean
a justice that differs by its object from the ordinary justice of
human jurisprudence, for then it must be confessedly a very bad
kind of justice; but it means a justice that differs from common
forensic justice by the degree in which it *attains* its object, a justice
that is more omnipotent over its own ends, as dealing, not with
the refractory elements of earthly life, but with the elements of
its own creation and with materials flexible to its own purest

---

[1] 1 *Kings*, 3:9,12.
[2 Epic.—*Ed.*]

preconceptions. It is certain that, were it not for the literature of power, these ideals would often remain amongst us as mere arid notional forms; whereas, by the creative forces of man put forth in literature, they gain a vernal life of restoration and germinate into vital activities. The commonest novel, by moving in alliance with human fears and hopes, with human instincts of wrong and right, sustains and quickens those affections. Calling them into action, it rescues them from torpor. And hence the pre-eminency, over all authors that merely *teach*, of the meanest that moves, or that teaches, if at all, indirectly *by* moving. The very highest work that has ever existed in the literature of knowledge is but a provisional work, a book upon trial and sufferance, and *quamdiu bene se gesserit*.[1] Let its teaching be even partially revised, let it be but expanded, nay, even let its teaching be but placed in a better order, and instantly it is superseded. Whereas the feeblest works in the literature of power, surviving at all, survive as finished and unalterable among men. For instance, the *Principia* of Sir Isaac Newton was a book *militant* on earth from the first. In all stages of its progress it would have to fight for its existence: first, as regards absolute truth; secondly, when that combat was over, as regards its form, or mode of presenting the truth. And as soon as a La Place, or anybody else, builds higher upon the foundations laid by this book, effectually he throws it out of the sunshine into decay and darkness; by weapons won from this book he superannuates and destroys this book, so that soon the name of Newton remains as a mere *nominis umbra*,[2] but his book, as a living power, has transmigrated into other forms. Now, on the contrary, the *Iliad*, the *Prometheus* of Aeschylus, the *Othello* or *King Lear*, the *Hamlet* or *Macbeth*, and the *Paradise Lost* are not militant but triumphant forever, as long as the languages exist in which they speak or can be taught to speak. They never *can* transmigrate into new incarnations. To reproduce these in new forms or variations, even if in some things they should be improved, would be to plagiarize. A good steam-engine is properly superseded by a better. But one lovely pastoral valley is not superseded by another, nor a statue of Praxiteles by a statue of Michael Angelo. These things are separated, not by imparity, but by disparity. They are not thought of as unequal under the same standard, but as different in *kind*, and,

[1 As long as it bore itself well.—*Ed.*]
[2 Shadow of a name.—*Ed.*]

if otherwise equal, as equal under a different standard. Human
works of immortal beauty and works of nature in one respect
stand on the same footing: they never absolutely repeat each
other, never approach so near as not to differ; and they differ not
as better and worse, or simply by more and less; they differ by
undecipherable and incommunicable differences, that cannot be
caught by mimicries, that cannot be reflected in the mirror of
copies, that cannot become ponderable in the scales of vulgar
comparison.

Applying these principles to Pope as a representative of fine
literature in general, we would wish to remark the claim which he
has, or which any equal writer has, to the attention and jealous
winnowing of those critics in particular who watch over public
morals. Clergymen, and all organs of public criticism put in motion
by clergymen, are more especially concerned in the just appreciation of such writers, if the two canons are remembered which we
have endeavored to illustrate, viz., that all works in this class, as
opposed to those in the literature of knowledge, 1st, work by far
deeper agencies, and 2dly, are more permanent; in the strictest
sense they are κτήματα ἐς ἀεί:[1] and what evil they do, or what good
they do, is commensurate with the national language, sometimes
long after the nation has departed. At this hour, five hundred
years since their creation, the tales of Chaucer, never equaled on
this earth for their tenderness, and for life of picturesqueness, are
read familiarly by many in the charming language of their natal
day, and by others in the modernisations of Dryden, of Pope, and
Wordsworth. At this hour, one thousand eight hundred years
since their creation, the Pagan tales of Ovid, never equaled on
this earth for the gayety of their movement and the capricious
graces of their narrative, are read by all Christendom. This man's
people and their monuments are dust; but *he* is alive: he has
survived them, as he told us that he had it in his commission to
do, by a thousand years "and *shall* a thousand more."

All the literature of knowledge builds only ground-nests, that
are swept away by floods, or confounded by the plow; but the
literature of power builds nests in aërial altitudes of temples sacred
from violation, or of forests inaccessible to fraud. *This* is a great
prerogative of the *power* literature; and it is a greater which lies
in the mode of its influence. The *knowledge* literature, like the

[1 *Ktemata es aei*, permanent possessions.—*Ed.*]

fashion of this world, passeth away. An Encyclopedia is its abstract; and, in this respect, it may be taken for its speaking symbol —that before one generation has passed, an Encyclopedia is superannuated; for it speaks through the dead memory and unimpassioned understanding, which have not the repose of higher faculties, but are continually enlarging and varying their phylacteries. But all literature properly so called—literature κατέξοχην[1] —for the very same reason that it is so much more durable than the literature of knowledge, is (and by the very same proportion it is) more intense and electrically searching in its impressions. The directions in which the tragedy of this planet has trained our human feelings to play, and the combinations into which the poetry of this planet has thrown our human passions of love and hatred, of admiration and contempt, exercise a power for bad or good over human life that cannot be contemplated, when stretching through many generations, without a sentiment allied to awe. And of this let everyone be assured—that he owes to the impassioned books which he has read many a thousand more of emotions than he can consciously trace back to them. Dim by their origination, these emotions yet arise in him and mold him through life, like forgotten incidents of his childhood.

NOTES AND COMMENTS

De Quincey says that "the literature of power" provides essential exercise for human sensibilities and moral capacities which would otherwise wither away. Do you agree? In the modern world, De Quincey's belief in the effect of literature on society may appear naive. On the other hand, it seems pertinent when one considers the attempts of totalitarian states to control literary expression within their borders and to enlist the arts for propaganda purposes.

Do you think that De Quincey's definition of "power" can be applied also to the other serious arts? Notice how Bertrand Russell uses the word "power" in his essay from *The ABC of Relativity* (page 381). Try defining "power" as the word would be used by a politician, a scientist, a teacher, a theologian, and a literary man.

By "knowledge" De Quincey means information. Does his comparison of "the literature of knowledge" with a cook book make you understand what he means? Compare De Quincey's analogies with Shaw's. Do you feel they are equally successful?

[1 *Katexochen, par excellence.—Ed.*]

MARK VAN DOREN

1894-

Mark Van Doren has been Professor of English literature at Columbia University since 1942. He has written poetry, fiction, biography, and criticism, and has edited a large number of anthologies. *Introduction to Poetry* (1951) is an anthology of lyric poems. In the first section of the book, from which the present selection is taken, Van Doren analyzes thirty poems. His critical method is intended to introduce the beginning reader to poetry and poetry criticism, but it can enlighten the seasoned reader as well.

Five Critiques

1. A SONG

Ask me no more where Jove bestows,
When June is past, the fading rose;
For in your beauty's orient deep
These flowers, as in their causes, sleep.

Ask me no more whither do stray
The golden atoms of the day;
For, in pure love, heaven did prepare
Those powders to enrich your hair.

Ask me no more whither doth haste
The nightingale, when May is past;

For in your sweet dividing throat
She winters, and keeps warm her note.

Ask me no more where those stars light
That downwards fall in dead of night;
For in your eyes they sit, and there
Fixèd become, as in their sphere.

Ask me no more if east or west
The Phoenix builds her spicy nest;
For unto you at last she flies,
And in your fragrant bosom dies.
                                    —THOMAS CAREW

In the five stanzas of this formal song a lover pays five compliments to his lady. She is not named; nor does the song itself
have any name except this noncommittal one which begins,
casually enough, with the indefinite article. "A Song"—as if
any lover, anywhere or at any time, might be understood to have
seized a musical instrument of some sort and, looking into his
lady's eyes, strummed it five times as he sang five answers to five
questions which she or someone else has asked. It is not necessarily
she who has put the questions. Perhaps she is perfectly silent, smiling as she listens; or she may not be here at all; she may indeed not
exist, though we should prefer to think she does. The questions
may well be the lover's own, which he has invented for the sake
of their answers. They are rhetorical; they assist statement.

The five statements to which they lead are all, if one pleases,
extravagant. Where does Jove, the king of the universe, send roses
when they fade? Into your beauty, where they sleep. What is the
destination, if any, of the sunlight's particles? Your hair, which
they were created to adorn. Where does the nightingale fly when
she stops singing? Into your throat, where she continues to sing
until another season returns. Where do falling stars go? Into your
eyes, as into the place for which they were intended. Where does
the phoenix, that fabulous Arabian bird which lives forever by
alternately burning itself and rising newborn from the ashes, build
its nest upon which this act of immortality may be accomplished?
In your bosom, of course.

Doubtless it is the extravagance of the compliments at which
the lady smiles. Yet she is pleased, for she knows that her lover

is trying to be absolute in the expression of his love. The things he says are true for him because he loves her without qualification. If to an indifferent person they would sound exaggerated or fantastic, he trusts her not to find them so; he counts on her to understand, as of course he understands, that overstatement is adoration's natural language. Only too much love is love enough; or rather, only too strong a statement is strong at all. The exact truth about her, supposing it could be put into words, would be inadequate to his purpose, which is to suggest that this after all is the exact truth—for him, anyway. He too smiles as he sings, watching his lady's eyes for signs that she measures the playful force with which he overstates his case. Absolute eloquence is the minimum effect at which he aims. All or nothing, as with any lover in the world, is the motto of his words and music.

But whereas he is like any other lover in his feeling he is different in his art. He is formal to what might seem a fault if we did not become aware of the resources he is using. We might let the matter go with conventional terms, or hum some current song; he explores nature, science, and myth in search of symbols which will carry his meaning. And he composes his poem with the utmost care for its structure, metrically and otherwise. The five stanzas are highly regular in their rhythm, and each of them strictly honors a pattern of syntax as well as a pattern of rhyme. Each first line begins with "Ask me no more," and each third line with "For." The punctuation almost never varies. The rhyme scheme is the couplet scheme; and yet it is proper that the poem should appear as stanzas, as quatrains, for each set of four lines, with its asking and its answering couplet, is complete in itself, bringing the poem to a pause from which it will start again.

When it starts again, will it be any farther along? Is the poem aiming to be more than a series of statements—five, as it happens, and this is the number of the fingers on the hand that strokes the instrument whence the music comes—strung as stationary beads are strung, one after another on the string? Or is there movement in the whole? Does the poem climb? Does it reach a conclusion? Does it have a climax?

A progression appears if we consider the successive stanzas in terms of the activity, or the amount of activity, each describes. The first stanza, for example, contains no activity at all. Nothing could be quieter than the act, if it is an act, of sleeping in one's cause as the oak sleeps in the acorn or the rose in its seed, its root, waiting patiently to become itself. If this is an act, it must be done in a deep place out of time's reach; for cause itself is not a temporal thing. The place, indeed, is as deep as the lady's beauty, which is an "orient" deep. A famous word, sufficient in itself to have created Carew's reputation. For it suggests many things: the East, the brilliant spaces out of which suns rise, radiance itself, and the more general idea of source or origin—wells or fountains out of which come forth again whatever things have descended into them, or life which can be where death once was. Yet the tangible activity is nil. All is potentiality, and the sweet promise of more in place of less. Nor is the promise lightly stated: Jove is the agent of its fulfilment, and his name alliterates powerfully, decisively, with "June."

The second stanza, breaking the trance of the first, sets things in motion, but small things, and indeed the smallest we can conceive. Atoms of light are finer even than the motes we watch dancing in a sunbeam; yet those motes will do for an image, particularly if we think of them as golden, as gold dust floating. The irregular accents we hear in the word "whither" are in the interest of what now is to be achieved: our sense of irreducible, indivisible, and all but invisible particles of matter set free—"whither do stray"—to wander where they will. Their will, in fact, is to wander toward that place of which their creator was thinking when he ground them up so light and fine. They are to settle upon my lady's already golden hair, where they will be noticed only as perfection is noticed, gracing what once seemed, yet only seemed, to be sufficiently beautiful without it.

The third stanza follows a larger creature to its destination. The nightingale, which sounds as well as is seen—where is its song continued after music's season closes? For such a singer cannot really cease; something must keep her voice warm and sweet, ready to be heard again. And here the poet runs a risk. For his answer, which is that the bird flies into his lady's throat and remains there, could be grotesque or painful if he did not know how to manage the reader's responses. He manages them, among other ways too mysterious to understand, by the word "dividing" and by the alliteration of "winters" with "warm." "Dividing" is a musical term of Carew's century, the seventeenth, and refers to the art of descant, or singing in harmony, or performing in parts.

It is a technical term for the miracle by which the many divisions of a song melt finally into one sweet thing, the song itself. The lady's throat, like the whole body of the nightingale, is where music may be said to live, singing for its own pleasure, making sound or no sound as it chooses; wintering, or waiting, in the warmth of its own notes until it chooses to sing so that all may hear. The lady is speaking or singing now; the nightingale will sing in May; but both are the same in idea, and it is in fact idea that entertains us here, not fact, not feathers, not vocal cords, not flesh in any form, nor even any audible sound. Again it is the promise of sound, the certainty that music remains possible, which reassures us after the disappearance of the nightingale. She has not disappeared after all, any more than the flowers of Jove can be said to have died, or the atoms of day to have wandered nowhere.

The fourth stanza reaches far into the universe—a dark universe, too, for now it is the dead of night—and sees the most startling of all movements. Stars fall. And where? Into my lady's eyes, where the quietest of verbs is found for what they do. They "sit," fixed as proper stars are fixed, in the spheres which an old astronomy assumed were there to contain them. These spheres made music, too, grander than that of the nightingale; but the poem, though it lets us think of this, says nothing further about it. Our attention is upon the lady's eyes, which are bright not merely as stars are bright in the conventional comparison, but happy in their brightness because they are the home to which celestial wanderers have come. Once more the image of motion has given way to the image of rest; the moving object has plunged into the medium best fitted to receive it and henceforth to display it.

In the final stanza the mythical phoenix, more potent to our imagination than even the brightest star, plunges also to her rest. But it is not the rest of death. It is a rest after which action will commence again as life recommences in new birth. Nor does it matter where this happens. East or west is immaterial now; we remember "orient" in the third line of the poem, but we are far away from even the remotest east, as we are far away from any west. The phoenix, searching for that spicy place where she can seem to die and yet not die, speeds unerringly to my lady's fragrant bosom, whence she will spring into future flight that contrasts with the quiet power, stated itself so noiselessly in stanza one, exerted by the causes of things. The poem returns to its beginning; draws a circle back through the world of atoms, birds, and stars; and enters, so to speak, itself.

The lady, meanwhile, has not moved, nor has the rhythm of the song abandoned its stateliness, its all but monotonous march of heavy and light syllables, its iambic walk which only in the fifth, seventh, ninth, twelfth, and sixteenth lines shifts momentarily into trochaic. Nor has the singer for one instant relaxed the formality of his smile. He has never become personal. He has kept his mind among metaphysical things, letting science and philosophy do his work of praise. But it was not praise either; it was compliment, which is more intimate and fanciful a thing. The lady never deserved this much. Or did she? The music says she did, and so does the gravity which still lingers in the lover's face. She deserved all that words can say when words refer to the greatest and highest things in the world: immortal things, whose home she is. "Dies" is the last word of the poem, yet death is the last thing it suggests. If any love can last forever, this love will. If any poem can, then this one must.

2. MARY MORISON

O Mary, at thy window be,
    It is the wish'd, the trysted hour!
Those smiles and glances let me see,
    That make the miser's treasure poor:
How blythely wad I bide the stour,
    A weary slave frae sun to sun,
Could I the rich reward secure,
    The lovely Mary Morison!

Yestreen, when to the trembling string
    The dance gaed thro' the lighted ha',
To thee my fancy took its wing,
    I sat, but neither heard nor saw:
Tho' this was fair, and that was braw,
    And yon the toast of a' the town,
I sigh'd, and said amang them a',
    "Ye are na Mary Morison."

Oh, Mary, canst thou wreck his peace,
Wha for thy sake wad gladly die?
Or canst thou break that heart of his,
Whase only faut is loving thee?
If love for love thou wilt na gie,
At least be pity to me shown;
A thought ungentle canna be
The thought o' Mary Morison.

—ROBERT BURNS

In this love poem there is as much distance between the man who sings and the girl who listens as there was between the lover and the lady of Carew's more elaborate and intellectual song. Or does the girl in this case listen? She is named—three times in the refrain and twice as simply "Mary"—but it is not certain that she hears one word; whereas Carew's lady can be imagined as not only listening but looking, and doubtless smiling at the formal conceits wherewith her beauty is celebrated.

The distance now is measured by a longing for one who perhaps is unattainable. Mary Morison is not yet even at her window. She may never come there; or if she does, she may stand quietly, or sit serenely, giving only half her heed to words she has no intention of answering. Yet it is possible that she will appear, and it is even possible that she loves the singer who desires and misses her so much. Nothing less than the tenderest and sincerest words will test whether this is true. The words of the song must do all that words can do in love's extreme need; they must convince Mary Morison that she is lovable as no other girl is lovable, and they must make it clear that someone is outside her cottage who feels and understands this as no other person could. Music of course would help; but in the absence of an instrument the words must make their own sound, the lines must be their own melody, the stanzas must develop their own effect of extended and considered composition.

The words are Scots words, and there is an advantage in that. The r's are caressingly rolled, and the vowels have a deeper register than English would give them. In the first stanza it is important to note that "hour" rhymes with "poor" and "secure," and of course with the strange word "stour," which stands for the dust, the struggle, the confusion of existence. In the second stanza "hall" and "all" drop their consonant endings so that they may rhyme with "saw" and "braw" (fine, handsome). And in the third stanza "die" and "gie" (give) rhyme with "thee" and "be." It makes a great deal of difference that this is so. The voice of the singer is in consequence not only clear and strong but gentle and concerned; is soft as absolute seriousness is soft, without any suggestion of weakness.

It also makes a great deal of difference that the rhyme scheme is what it is. Each stanza begins with a quatrain, alternately rhymed; and it might be expected, since there are eight lines in each stanza, that a similar quatrain would follow. Such indeed is the case, but instead of a new set of rhymes we hear the sound of the fourth line repeated at the end of the fifth; which means that although the sixth and eighth lines are free to terminate with fresh sounds—and one of these will always be the last syllable of Mary's name—the seventh line must agree with the couplet at the center. But the main thing is that couplet at the center, upon which the stanza pivots. The second of its two lines, surprisingly continuous in sound with the one before it ("stour" with "poor," "braw" with "saw," "gie" with "thee"), has thus an opportunity to express the peculiar earnestness of the singer, who as it were is not willing to let the initial quatrain go without savoring its final note once more. The insistence of the sound is like the insistence of his love. You see, he seems to say, it is really true what I am singing; if my voice rises in this fifth line, and a new energy is heard in it, that is because my love is powerful. My love is a dramatic thing, feeding upon its own thoughts and finding climaxes in the very sounds it utters.

If the middle stanza of the three is more energetic and moving than either of its neighbors, this corresponds with what we have noted—namely, that every stanza is most energetic at its center. The poem, like any good poem, comes in waves; it rises and falls, over all and in its parts. So there is a special fitness in the fact that Burns's middle stanza is his best—his most interesting, his most dramatic, his most persuasive. Each of the three comes to its peak at the proper point, and so does the whole of which they are the parts. The first stanza contents itself with stating the wealth that would be in the singer's hands if Mary were possessed. The third stanza descends into self-pity at the thought that this may never happen—she may never permit herself to be possessed, this gentle girl whom he then implores to respect his longing anyway, to love it if she cannot love him. In the middle stanza, however, he sets his subject in motion; he steps out of the present moment and remembers last night when there was dancing in the lighted hall and he thought of Mary who was not there. As the music sounded and the figures whirled he sat in a trance, contemplating her superiority to every fashionable lady before him. One of them was fair and one of them was fine, and another was the toast of all the town, but none of them was what *she* is. None of them was Mary Morison.

The name itself is enough. To speak it is the only way at last to praise this unique person concerning whom we know nothing except that she is loved by one who when everything else fails can make himself happy by pronouncing two words. She cannot have ungentle thoughts—we know that, or know he hopes so. We know too that she has a window at which she can appear if she will, smiling and glancing. But the one thing we know with conviction and feeling is that he loves her and desires that she love him. The thought of Mary Morison is all we have. It is all *he* has—the lovely Mary Morison, about whom nothing can really be said except that no one else is she. To every other girl alive the poem says: Ye are na Mary Morison. Three times, at the conclusion of three stanzas, the name sings itself with the utmost tenderness, dwelling especially on its own final syllable which the rhythm serves to prolong. But the most telling of these three times is, properly, the second or middle one. It is the proudest, the surest, the most excited. The climax of the poem is where any climax should be: not at the close, but halfway there, with room ahead for afterthought and fullest realization; and, sobering though this may be, for possible sorrow.

3. I HAD NOT MINDED WALLS

I had not minded walls
Were Universe one rock,
And far I heard his silver call
The other side the block.

I'd tunnel until my groove
Pushed sudden through to his,

But 'tis a single hair,
A filament, a law—
A cobweb wove in adamant,
A battlement of straw—

A limit like the veil
Unto the lady's face,
But every mesh a citadel
And dragons in the crease!
                    —EMILY DICKINSON*

The beloved person of this poem is unattainable for another
reason than that which operated in Mary Morison's case. Mary
Morison was attainable whenever she chose to be; she might
never so choose, but she was free to make her lover happy; nothing
substantial separated them, no third thing outside themselves. In
Emily Dickinson's poem there is a third thing, and it will separate
two persons forever. The man who is loved can never be reached.
Something that seems slight, that indeed is all but invisible, is
there between them as big as a mountain, and more rough and
hard. It is bigger of course than any mountain; were the entire
universe one solid block of rock, this thing would still be greater.
The block of rock could be tunnelled through, but this delicate
barrier is impregnable. It is convention, it is morality. Or if it is
not that—the poem does not give it a name—it is something
equally strong. And the business of the poem is to state its
strength.

The poem is difficult perhaps. The idea that something in a
human mind—or two human minds, or all human minds—may
be harder than granite is itself difficult; or it could be to a reader
untrained in paradox. But in addition the subject as it exists here
is highly personal to the speaker. It is even a secret subject, which
she is shy in divulging—shy because it is important, and shy because she is modest. She does not hesitate to confess her own love,
but she will not confess for another. The difficulty, such as it is,
comes partly from her instinct to protect him; she leaves him
unknown to us, as she leaves the subject unknown to all save those
who will work it out.

As for him, the beloved person, the first two stanzas come near to suggesting that he is God. In a sense he *is* God, as those greatly loved seem to be. He is too remote and wonderful to possess; he is on the other side of the universe, waiting to be known; and he can be known only by heroic effort. But the last two stanzas remove the suggestion. There is no law against our loving God; the limits interposed between deity and man are not like these. It is a human situation we have, and indeed it is all the more tortuous for that. Yet Emily Dickinson has managed, in the suggestion itself, to deposit in our minds a feeling that the unattainable person is benign and blameless—is a great person, to her at any rate, and worthy of comparison with the greatest Person she knows.

Still she is concealing as much as she can, consistently with the fact that she speaks at all. She writes so tersely, and wraps her message so tightly, that we shall miss it unless we listen close. Her syntax, for example, tends toward oddity; she seems to leave out necessary words, and she ignores certain rules of grammar. She is daring us to paraphrase her poem. Yet it is her desire that we do so, and consequently we shall. A different and weaker statement will result; but then we shall know what the force of her utterance was.

"I would not have minded walls between me and the man I love. If the universe itself were one great wall, as thick as it was high, and built of solid rock; and if, far around on the other side of this obstruction, I heard his silver voice calling to me (or, simply, heard it and knew it was his), then I would cheerfully tunnel through to where he was. He would have started too; tunnels are built from both ends, and meet in the middle; suddenly, therefore, the last bit of rock between us would be gone, and I would have my reward. My reward, because the effort was chiefly mine. My tunnel reached   his. Then the reward—my opportunity to look into his eyes. But this is an idle story. Nothing of the sort ever happened or will happen. No such opportunity exists. There is no wall, no universal block between his eyes and mine. Something worse is there—something as thin as a single hair, a filament; something as unreal (yet how real!) as a human law. It is as if a cobweb had been woven out of adamant, the hardest stone; or as if a fortress, though built only with straw, turned out to be more invincible than stone. Something stands between us that looks like nothing at all—a veil, say, on a lady's face. But every part of

it is terrible in its power to resist penetration. Suppose it *is* a veil.
Well, every mesh of it is a citadel, and every fold of it contains a
dragon."

The paraphrase says less than the poem does—so much less
that we may learn from the difference what poetry is. The only
merit of the prose is that it calls attention to some of the things
Emily Dickinson is doing. It accentuates, for instance, her changes
of tense. She begins with "I had not," goes on to "I would," and
ends in the strict present: "It is." The present fact, the controlling
and only fact, is painful; so she has come to it with delays and
diversions, pretending for the while that something else was fact.
But nothing else was, whereas this *is*. Then there are the suppressed words, the units of grammar and syntax which she forces
us to supply. *If the* universe were one rock, and *if* I heard his silver
call *on* the other side *of* the block—she does not use italicized
terms, any more than she says in the next stanza: Then my face
would take recompense. Meanwhile she has written "sudden" for
"suddenly," as later on she writes "unto" for "to"—for once a
longer word, but this is because it has a more formidable sound
than the one we would use in prose, as befits the fact that the
situation itself is now absolutely formidable.

What the paraphrase does not do, however, is more significant than what it does. It gives us no sense of the nervous quickness with which Emily Dickinson moves toward the conclusion of
her tragic statement. It is not in verse, and it is not in stanzas; nor
does it rhyme. Emily Dickinson uses line, stanza, and rhyme to
give what she is saying velocity and terror; or, at the end of the
second stanza, softness and joy.

> Then my face take recompense—
> The looking in his eyes.

The absence of rhyme between "groove" and "recompense," and
the consonance rather than rhyme between "his" and "eyes"—
these are bold surprises, even if in the service of an imaginary
moment which is not bold at all: two lovers, long separated, are
quietly together at last. The failure of perfect rhyme between
"walls" and "call" in the first stanza is of another order. The silver
call is singular, as it must be, and therefore clear and slender, as
the walls are not. So, in the third stanza, the refusal of "adamant"
to rhyme with "hair" expresses its implacable hardness. So, in the

fourth stanza, "citadel" and "crease" rebel against the law that
they repeat the civil music of "veil" and "face." The sound of the
long *a* drops suddenly to the sound of short *e* in "every" and
"mesh" as well as in "citadel"; and the last line converts it altogether, in the harsh word "dragons" and in the "crease" through
which their malevolence can be imagined to hiss. The gentle alliteration in "limit," "like," and "lady" is also gone out of our ears,
along with any sense of proportion we might have had permitting
us to inquire whether a mesh could ever be a citadel, or dragons in-
habit creases.

The stanza looks like a ballad stanza, and yet is not. The first
line is short, like the second and fourth; only the third has four
feet. The third line in every case is long and full; and each time
this has a different function. The drawn-out, lucid silver call; the
leisurely taking recompense; the cobweb announcing that it is not
silk but adamant, and saying so with special emphasis on the last
syllable of that mighty word; the hoarse voice issuing from each
mesh of the veil, proclaiming itself, astonishingly and yet convincingly, to be a medieval stronghold—each of these third lines
works its own magic, assisting the poem of which it is a part to
become one of the most potent in any tongue.

4. AN ODE

The merchant, to secure his treasure,
   Conveys it in a borrowed name.
Euphelia serves to grace my measure;
   But Chloe is my real flame.

My softest verse, my darling lyre,
   Upon Euphelia's toilet lay;
When Chloe noted her desire,
   That I should sing, that I should play.

My lyre I tune, my voice I raise;
   But with my numbers mix my sighs:
And whilst I sing Euphelia's praise,
   I fix my soul on Chloe's eyes.

Fair Chloe blushed: Euphelia frowned:
   I sung and gazed: I played and trembled:

And Venus to the Loves around
Remarked, how ill we all dissembled.
                                            —MATTHEW PRIOR

Prior's famous little ode takes us back to Carew's song with
which we began. They are not the same, but they are alike at one
important point. The lover literally sings to his lady, and an instrument accompanies his words. Or so it is in Prior's case at any
rate; or so he says. He has a lyre. Carew can be imagined with
one, but he does not mention it, entirely occupied as he is with the
words he addresses to his listening lady. We do not hear the words
of Prior's song to Chloe. We are merely told the story of how he
sang them—pretending they were for Euphelia, but intending
them for his real flame; and fooling nobody, least of all Venus
and her Loves who were looking on, perhaps from the wallpaper,
perhaps from a mural which decorated this eighteenth-century
chamber, perhaps from the very air; for it was an atmosphere in
which the goddess and her Cupids might very well be suspended,
half visible, half not, half flesh, half fancy.

It was the atmosphere of gallantry, and gallantry goes by rules.
The lover conceals not only the identity of his mistress but the
intensity of his feeling for her. His formality is an attempt to
sound and look superficial. He is not superficial, but the law of his
society demands that he seem so, just as it dresses both him and his
lady in wig and ruffle, and powders them like dolls. Every phrase
and gesture must be light, and somehow at the same time stiff, as
if a dance were being danced, and its elegant figures had been in-
structed to look as little as possible like human beings.

Prior follows all the rules, and yet his poem is not the frigid
thing that each of ten thousand other such poems in its time was
then and certainly is now. It has survived its fashion and its age.
But not by trying consciously to be different. It is trying to be
altogether typical, and in fact succeeding. It is fully realizing the
possibilities of its type; and that, no doubt, is the secret of its success with us. Every poem must begin somewhere, must be some
kind of poem rather than another, or rather than all others, or
rather than none at all. And its chance for immortality may lie
in the very fidelity it achieves to its kind. If the fidelity is complete,
if the true meaning of the form is found, then the poem becomes
true as any other is, no matter what its form or kind. All good

poems are different, yet all are alike in being good. Goodness in poems, as in persons, tends to be the same everywhere.

Prior, however, seems to be unaware of this. He begins with a cynical analogy—he deals in matters of love as a merchant deals in matters of cargo and consignment. As the merchant, wishing to make sure that his treasure is safe, labels it with a cheaper name that will tempt no thief to plunder it—cotton instead of gold, or straw instead of cotton—so the hero of the poem (if hero he is) protects the secrecy of his love by pretending in public that some-one else is his mistress. Euphelia may not be cheaper than Chloe, but she is not Chloe; and so she will do as the figure he feigns to adore. He addresses his poems to her, he seizes his lyre and sings to her, he encourages people to couple their names; yet all the while it is Chloe whom he loves, as she alone knows (or so he hopes) by the fact that he gazes at her whenever he sings to Euphelia.

The rest of the poem seems to proceed on the same level. Its language is as conventional as Prior can make it. Poetry is "meas-ure" or "numbers," a mistress is a "flame," and the soul of the lover sighs. Also, there is a lyre: the most conventional of instru-ments, and in a sense the most unreal. There is in fact no lyre, as in fact there is no soul and no attending goddess. Or is this true? Is the poem not passionate, not persuasive? If it is, then the lyre somehow exists, and so does Venus. But Prior seems to be making no effort to convince us. Rather, he is strumming out the most regular tetrameters he can manage; he is keeping his meter me-chanical, as if there were no passion for it to convey; and often enough he breaks a line exactly in the middle, leaving two half-lines that bow to each other like figures in a minuet. The fifth, the eighth, the ninth, the thirteenth, and the fourteenth lines—five out of sixteen altogether—are divided in the middle by a knife-sharp caesura, and the two halves thus created are perfectly uni-form in grammatical structure. In the fifth line, for example, "softest" balances "darling," and "verse" balances "lyre." So in every case among the five with one exception. In line 13 there is no epithet before Euphelia's name to balance the "fair" before Chloe's; but there could have been none, since Euphelia's name has three syllables. The meter, as we have noted, nowhere is per-mitted to violate itself. There are precisely eight syllables in every line (ignoring the feminine endings in lines 1, 3, 14, and 16); the rhymes are perfect; the music is willing to sound monotonous.

Yet it is not monotonous; or if it is, the monotony is powerful. The ode drives on to its end as if its end were important, as indeed it is. For we cannot miss some accent of seriousness here. Perhaps it discloses itself in those five divided lines—especially in the last of them:

> I sung and gazed: I played and trembled.

Why the trembling? A cynical lover, willing to use a lady as Euphelia is being used, and in her very house, from her very toilet table, snatching up his lyre to sing a song that will deceive her if it can, and beating out its measure with his voice, his head, his foot—why is he trembling? The reason must be that he loves Chloe very much indeed; that he knows very well what he is doing; that he feels some guilt about Euphelia; that the whole situation has suddenly become tremendous for him—and for the ladies too, who understand this as well as he does, and respectively blush and frown. An artifice has confessed that it is an artifice. The tissue of convention has been torn. A poem that desired to be indistinguishable from ten thousand others has achieved uniqueness, has become comparable with any good poem anywhere. Passion has found its voice. The wigs, the ruffles, the patches, and the powder are forgotten as we realize that these are people like ourselves, trying to live in a set of conventions and—because they are people—failing.

But how has this happened? The poem is short; there would seem to have been too little time for such a development, such a reversal. The answer is not easy to give. There is mystery here as in all successful art. Yet we can remember how early in the ode the bisected line appeared—innocently then, but preparing nevertheless, through three repetitions, for the final instance:

> I sung and gazed: I played and trembled.

We can remember too how strong and decisive the accents in each line had been, as if the poem marched somewhere. And now at the end there is Venus, the goddess who hovers over all such scenes when she is deeply concerned with the actors. She must be so concerned in the present case. She has come alive out of the landscape she was in. For she knows what we know—what the verse has made us know—namely, that nobody in love ever fools anybody else. There is a game of gallantry, but its rules are toy things, easily dominated by the law of love. She seems to be saying to her Cupids: "See, dears? They tried well, but they had to fail. My power thrusts through at last. The treasure is not safe. The name was borrowed for nothing. The flame is real indeed." And even so she has not cast off the costume Prior sees her as wearing. She assists in the convention, she encourages the artifice. For she knows that all people must have their conventions, as all poems must have their styles. She can manifest herself in spite of this; or even with its help.

5. TO LUCASTA, ON GOING TO THE WARS

Tell me not, Sweet, I am unkind,
    That from the nunnery
Of thy chaste breast and quiet mind
    To war and arms I fly.

True, a new mistress now I chase,
    The first foe in the field;
And with a stronger faith embrace
    A sword, a horse, a shield.

Yet this inconstancy is such
    As thou too shalt adore;
I could not love thee, Dear, so much,
    Loved I not Honor more.
                                —RICHARD LOVELACE

Perhaps no poet has said more in twelve short lines than Lovelace says in this farewell to his mistress as he leaves her on his way to war—to honorable war, whose claims rival in his feeling, since he is a Cavalier, the claims of love. Once more we have a love poem whose subject is separation; indeed, this is the best subject love has if it will be talking; but Lovelace is not lamenting his necessity to leave. He is justifying it, even exulting in it, and he is counting on Lucasta to understand. She may have called him unkind to go, as the first line suggests; but that is only his cue to speak with all the authority verse can give his voice. The authority sounds in the imperative sentence with which the poem begins.

That it is the authority of intelligence, however, is manifest in the completeness with which the next two lines comprehend the sweetness of the person he is leaving. There may have been gentleness in the fourth word uttered at all, the "Sweet" set off with commas as if a bow or a kiss accompanied it, but lines 2 and 3 can leave no doubt in Lucasta's mind that her lover values the quality in her most opposite to the quality of the experience he now seeks. She is faithful and good, and her spirit is serene. But listen to the verse as it says this.

> That from the nunnery—

the line looks shorter than it is. The ballad stanza of which it is the second line requires that it have three iambic feet, and that it rhyme with the fourth line. It does both things, but only if we stretch out the word "nunnery" as we speak it, and gives its last light syllable a fuller emphasis than it normally receives. When we do that—and the stanza makes us do it—we perceive how reluctant the lover is to leave the nest of his happiness. He lingers over the word, which again, since the sense runs on from it into the next line, hangs in the air an instant as if it were unwilling to go the way of other words.

Its essence passes, in fact, into the next line. Without pause and yet without hurry, slowly and most reverently, we hear:

> That from the nunnery
> Of thy chaste breast and quiet mind—

from all that, what? This remains to be seen, but meanwhile the third line has made it clear why "nunnery" was used, and why it was no exaggeration. It is a slow line, mostly monosyllables; and each monosyllable must be deliberately pronounced. Only the "of" and the "and" are unimportant. "Thy chaste breast"—the reader will be aware that he is being forced to say "thy" as if its reference were gravely important, and to say "chaste breast" as if much time had been lovingly allotted to it. Indeed it is physically impossible to say "chaste breast" fast. Both words end in sounds that are unintelligible in English unless they are painstakingly articulated, and the sameness of the sound here makes this doubly true. Another sort of sameness appears in "quiet" and "mind," two words that open themselves slowly on the long *i* and remain open, poised

there as "nunnery" was poised at the end of the line before. There
is a recollection in them also of "unkind" that closed line one on
the same sound. They answer the accusation in that word, suggesting by the very vowel they use, and use so seriously, that if the
lover *is* unkind it is because he has to be, and that he has counted
the cost. He knows what he is leaving, he knows whom he is being
unfaithful to. She is a lady perfect in virtue and serenity, whose
chaste breast and quiet mind are a whole world, removed from
every other world, in which he would stay if he could.

The poem, poised then once more on "mind," flies swiftly to
the ground for the conclusion of its opening stanza.

> To war and arms I fly—

there is the long *i* again, but between it and the sounds it recalls,
for the first time in the poem thus far, there is the heavier note
of "war and arms." Heavier, not merely because war and arms are
in themselves alarming terms, but also—and Lovelace knows this
well—because their vowel is hard and alien. The nunnery is no
more, the chaste breast and quiet mind are already put far behind
as the lover goes racing away—almost literally flying—as if to a
new mistress who will make him forget this one who watches him
go. There indeed he goes, saying the rest of the poem as it were
over his shoulder, firmly, and without any further attempt to re-
capture the tone of lines 2 and 3. They have done their work, but
he must now do his.

"True, a new mistress now I chase"—he makes the confession
at once, and proceeds to describe her. The stanza in which he does
so is the cleverest of the three, and for that reason the poorest,
though it is only relatively poor. Cleverness is a fine thing even
if it is not the finest. In this case it consists in saying that the
mistress is a man—"the first foe in the field." She is the enemy.
And this enemy has a forceful front: all three of the key words in
line 6 begin with the same letter, the stout letter *f*. "True"—the
beginning word, suggestive of logic and argument, was itself a sign
that the speaker intended to make his point by any means available. These are the means; and repetition is another, for the second
pair of lines in this stanza says the same thing over: with a still
stronger faith than had been proved in lines 2 and 3 of the poem,
his embraces are now to be bestowed on a sword, a horse, a shield

—impossible things to embrace, particularly the horse, but the exaggeration is consistent with the cleverness. An idea is working now, not a feeling; which again is consistent with the tone of persuasion, that undertakes paradox if it must.

The third stanza returns to the deeper level of the first, though now there is a mixture of feeling and thought. For one thing, Lucasta is addressed again: in the third line another epithet is set off between commas—"Dear," to balance the "Sweet" with which the song began. "Thou too" and "thee"—it is clear that the poet's discourse is once more in the second person. So is it clear that Lovelace is asking Lucasta to think with him and understand him. Her quiet mind is to take in one last paradox. Such a mind is above being interested in cleverness for its own sake, so he will be very serious; still, the statement is one that must be understood by the intellect, and therefore, though with consummate tenderness, he makes it with the last breath he uses.

Yet you too, he says, must adore the inconstancy my second stanza has confessed. Only you, as a matter of fact, *could* adore it. For you are truly extraordinary in being able to comprehend that I could not love you as much as I do if I did not love something else still more than that. I love it more, and you have helped me to do so, because *you* love it as much as you do. One of the reasons I love you—indeed it is the controlling reason—is that distinction in you, that capacity to worship Honor, which has educated me. The qualities of persons are even more important than the persons themselves. Your faithfulness and quietness are still more beautiful than you, being permanent, abstract things. We compliment persons, but we praise qualities; and praise is the greater act, deserved only by the greatest persons. The greatest Person of all we never compliment—how absurd is the very thought. We praise God, and for His qualities of strength and goodness. So with you, for there is in you something still more important and lovable than yourself. It is Honor, which now I am giving every evidence that I love. Therefore you must consent, as I know you do.

The last two lines of the poem say all of that, and as much more as verse is capable of saying when a master uses it. The longest prose paraphrase would still not capture the whole meaning of these justly famous lines. They are famous precisely because they cannot *be* paraphrased.

I could not love thee, Dear, so much,
Loved I not Honor more.

There they are, and the statement is complete. So is the poem—
one of the briefest masterpieces in the world, and one of the best
proofs that poetry can say what nothing else can. A good line of
poetry, like any line well and straightly drawn, is the shortest distance between two points. And the two present points are worlds
apart: the nunnery, the battlefield.

NOTES AND COMMENTS

Van Doren's critical essays can serve as models for analyzing
poetry. Although he explains the meaning of each poem in an objective
sense, his critiques are also personal and intuitive. One has the feeling
that another critic might approach each poem from a different point
of view and come to entirely different conclusions. Do you feel that
this lessens or enhances the value of Van Doren's appraisals? Using
Van Doren's technique, analyze a short poem of your own choice.

In these essays Van Doren is a "new critic"—that is, he does not
concern himself with the historical periods in which the poems were
written, or with biographical details about the authors which might
give us insight into the meaning of the poems. Rather he deals only
with the poems themselves, as if they had organic lives quite apart
from the poets who wrote them or the circumstances in which they
were written. Do you think this method (elaborated by Cleanth Brooks
and Robert Penn Warren in their book *Understanding Poetry*) is
enlightening? Or do you feel that ultimately it leaves you suspended in
mid-air, without a real-life peg to hang the poetry on?

JOHN CIARDI

1916-

John Ciardi is well known in several capacities to the "vertical audience" of which he speaks in this essay. As poetry editor of *Saturday
Review* he has been involved in most of the recent controversies
about what constitutes good poetry. His translation of Dante's *Inferno*
is perhaps the best ever done. *Midcentury American Poets*, a book he
edited and contributed to, presents an interesting slice of modern
poetry. Among the best of his own poems are "Elegy Just in Case,"
"Ode for the Burial of a Citizen," and "In the Year of Many Con-
versions and the Private Soul."

Dialogue with the Audience

"I'M NOT exactly illiterate," says the Citizen. "I'm a pretty fair
historian. I can read Freud—at least some of him—without being
entirely in the dark. But I get nowhere with this modern poetry.
I've given up trying."

The Poet has heard it all before, but the Citizen obviously
wants to talk about it. The Poet, as a matter of fact, rather likes
the Citizen. Maybe, the Poet thinks, if I can peg the talk to something specific it won't just ramble on aimlessly and forever. Aloud
he says: "Just for the fun of it—who is the last particular poet you
gave up on?"

"It was Wallace Stevens," says the Citizen. "I read your review of the 'Collected Poems' and I shelled out $7.50 for it on
your say-so." He reaches up to a shelf and hauls down the book.

Reprinted from *Saturday Review*. By permission.

"Here it is," he says, tossing it on the table, "a big fat collection of unintelligibility."

"Sorry," says the Poet, "no refunds, if that's what you're getting at. But do me a favor: show me a specific poem that you take to be unintelligible."

The Citizen stares. "Do you mean to say you understand every poem in this book?"

The Poet shakes his head. "Far from it. I don't even understand White House news releases. But I like Stevens better."

"Without knowing what it is you like?"

"Let's keep the talk as specific as we can. I've asked you to cite a poem: turn around is fair play—find a poem called 'Asides on the Oboe.' Here, take this passage:

> The obsolete fiction of the wide river in
> An empty land; the Gods that Boucher killed;
> And the metal heroes that time granulates—
> The philosophers' man alone still walks in dew,
> Still by the sea-side mutters milky lines
> Concerning an immaculate imagery.
> If you say on the hautboy man is not enough,
> Can never stand as god, is ever wrong
> In the end, however naked, tall, there is still
> The impossible possible philosophers' man,
> The man who has had the time to think enough,
> The central man, the human globe, responsive
> As a mirror with a voice, the man of glass,
> Who in a million diamonds sums us up.

"Let me get it straight," says the Citizen. "Is this an example of a passage you do understand, or of one you don't?"

"As a matter of fact, it's an example of both," says the Poet. "Suppose I were to say I found it elusive, yet clear—would that make any sense? I can't unravel it detail by detail. I encounter areas of obscurity in it. Yet the total force of the passage is both unmistakable and moving, and just beyond every momentary obscurity I keep emerging into areas of immediate clarity."

"No, in a word. It makes no sense to me."

"Well, what do you mean by sense? Stevens does not write for factual-information sense. Why should he? He picks up a theme and orchestrates it. His 'sense' is a structure. The reader must keep that total structure in mind in order to grasp Stevens's kind of sense. He does not, moreover, 'mean' any one thing, but rather all the possibilities of all the relationships he is orchestrating."

"Clear as Navy coffee," says the Citizen. "Am I supposed to swallow it?"

"You do in music," says the Poet, glancing at the Citizen's collection of recordings, "why not in poetry?"

"Because, among other things, words have meanings."

"They have," says the Poet, "but far more meanings than anyone thinks about in reading factual prose. A word is not a meaning but a complex of meanings consisting of all its possibilities: its ability to identify something, the image it releases in making that identification, its sound, its history, its association-in-context with the other words of the passage. Good poets use *more* of the word than most readers are used to."

"Yes," says the Citizen, who is proud of being a fair-minded person, "I suppose that *is* true."

"But not only is the individual word a complex. It is used in a phrase that is itself a complex of complexes. And the phrase is in turn used in the complex of the total poem's structure."

"So a poem is a complex of complexes of complexes," says the Citizen, half-indignant now. "I'm beginning to get a complex myself."

"No," says the Poet, "that's a complex you've always had. You are used to words basically as denotations in statements intended or purporting to intend to convey facts. You have the 'practicality complex' and your basic symptom is 'why doesn't he say it straight?' "

"Well, why doesn't he?"

"As a matter of fact he does at times—even in your terms. Take the line, 'The man who has had the time to think enough.' How much 'straighter' could he make the praise of that line?"

"I can agree there," says the Citizen. "But what about 'milky lines'? Why does he have to say it on 'the hautboy'? And what's all that about a mirror with a voice?"

"One at a time," says the Poet. "The 'milky lines' is one of those details I remain unsure of. I suspect that Stevens was thinking of the sea as a kind of mother-of-life and that he used 'milky' in that connection. If my guess is right that makes 'milky lines' mean something like 'lines fed by the essential life fluid of all-mothering nature.' But that is only a guess and I have no way of verifying it. In fact, some of what follows in the poem—not in this passage—troubles my guess. That is one of the obscurities I feel in the passage. One I feel and *welcome*, may I say.

"The hautboy, on the other hand, is a straightforward Stevens signature, a part of his personal idiom, like his blue-guitar. The hautboy is the kind of detail that reveals itself immediately as you get to know more about the way the poet writes. For the time being I can only suggest that you take the hautboy to be one of the instruments of art. On that instrument of artifice, Stevens must make the 'fiction' (always a special term in his writing) that can replace the 'obsolete fiction' of the gods. In Stevens, the rituals of art constantly take the place of the rituals of religion—themselves richly obscure.

"As for the 'mirror with a voice,'—there I have to charge you with petulant mis-reading. Stevens has established the context of his statement clearly enough for any willing reader, and it is no reading at all to ignore the context. What he is saying is roughly 'that it is *as if* the responsive man were a mirror with a voice reflecting all of us in a heightened way, *as if* summing us up in the million-diamond-reflection of his artifice.' I am satisfied that the gist of it is about that, though I confess I am uncertain about it later when the poem becomes unmistakably Leibnizian. At that later point, I conclude I don't know Leibniz well enough to guess out Stevens's sense of him. I am left puzzled. But I am also left considerably richer. Certainly, I should be willing to read a much longer and much more obscure poem than this if only to meet that man 'who has had the time to think enough.' I want him in my mind."

"Yes," says the Citizen, "I can go along with some of that. Even with most of it. But why must he be so elusive about it?"

The Poet smiles. "We're back to the business of 'saying it straight' again. I suggest, first, that the thought itself is elusive. And, second, that it's a kind of thinking you're not used to, partly because you have not read enough Stevens to catch the flavor of his thinking, and partly because you're not really a reader of poetry and never have been."

The Citizen draws himself up. "Now I don't know about that," he says. "I took quite a lot of English courses in school and . . ."

"And you haven't read as many as three books of new poems a year since then."

"Well," says the Citizen slowly. "I guess you have me there. Maybe if I were a more practised reader I'd see more. But isn't some of it the poets' fault? Why do they make it so hard for a man to read them? I'm no genius, but I'm reasonably intelligent."

"And rational," suggests the Poet.

"Certainly, What's wrong with rationality?"

"Ask yourself that question as you read through an issue of the *Reader's Digest* sometime," says the Poet. "Or let me ask you how rationally you got married? Or by what sequence of syllogisms you begot your children? Or what Certified Public Accountant writes the scripts of your dream-life?"

The Poet is talking fast now, warming to his most fundamental sermon. "We all contain elements of rationality, but we're all much more than those elements. A poet thinks with his senses, his nerve endings, his whole body. He hooks at his thought physically, and he hooks from many directions at once. He *feels* what he thinks, and he feels it most in the act of making a poetic structure of it. Just as a composer feels himself into his musical structure. There is no auditing of rationalities in that process; there is, rather, the accomplishment into form of some part of a whole life."

The Citizen is being fair-minded again. "I can't grasp entirely your way of putting things," he says after a while, "but I can get a glimpse of what I think you're saying—especially when I try to feel it in terms of what a composer does inside his music." He rubs his jaw. "I don't know. There are too many ideas in it that are new to me. I suppose if you say so . . ."

"The last time you started supposing on my say-so it cost you $7.50," says the Poet. "Suppose me nothing on my say-so: I refuse to be trusted by any man who can trust himself, and I doubly refuse to be trusted by a man who can't trust himself. Make up your own mind on the basis of what makes sense in itself."

"That's just the trouble," says the Citizen. "You make it sound sensible enough, but then I turn to a poem and I just can't get my hooks into it."

"That's just what I started to ask you in the beginning. There's the book: give me a for-instance."

"I remember one queer thing called 'Bantam in Pine Woods,' " says the Citizen, thumbing the pages. "I swear I spent a day trying to make sense of the first two lines. Here they are."

> Chieftain Iffucan of Azcan in caftan
> Of tan with henna hackles, halt!

"What's the problem?" says the Poet.

"No problem," says the Citizen. "Just gibberish. What the devil is all this henna-hackled Iffucan of Azcan trashcan stuff?"

"Ah!" says the Poet, "I see. To tell you the truth I hadn't ever thought of those lines as a difficulty: they're having such fun with themselves—all those lovely exaggerated sound-sequences and that big spoofing tone."

"Is all that—whatever it is—enough excuse for writing non-sense-syllables?"

"Ask Lewis Carroll," says the Poet. "But the fact is they're not nonsense syllables. Note the title. A bantam may certainly be taken as a pretentious and pompous bird strutting around in his half-pint ego as if he owned the world, and refusing to be dwarfed even by pine woods . . ."

"I'm still lost in the Azcan ashcan. And at this point I've had enough of your symbol-threading."

"But the Azcan business is a fact from the world," says the Poet. "Have you ever looked into a pedigree book? I assume this to be a pure-bred bantam and that he is registered as Chieftain Iffucan of Azcan. Stevens begins by reporting the fact, obviously relishing its pretentiousness. 'Caftan' is his first 'poetic' addition. But note this: a caftan is a garment that hangs down just about the way the leg-feathers of a bantam do. The detail is physically right. And the sound of the word itself is exactly right for the sound-sequence Stevens builds. That's always a sign of the poet—the ability to do more than one thing at once and to have his choices come out equally right on all levels."

The Citizen sits thoughtfully, turning it over in his mind. The Poet, watching the Citizen, once more has the impression of a painful fair-mindedness at work. Somehow that sense depresses him. He has a vision of the Citizen forever laboring to be open-minded and forever lost to the real life of the poem.

"I have to conclude that you're right," says the Citizen. "But

I also know I could never have seen it that way. And I still don't understand the poem."

"Nor do I, completely," confesses the Poet. "But what of it? I don't understand 'Kubla Khan,' nor 'Tiger, Tiger.' Not in detail. But I can certainly experience them as poems. I can, to put it metaphorically, identify their emotional frequencies and the areas into which they transmit."

The Citizen is not satisfied. "I'm still thinking of this Iffucan of Azcan business. There I bogged down on a detail I did not recognize. And perhaps I'll never be any better at identifying odd details. But what about the poem that comes right after it? This one—'Anecdote of a Jar.' Now there is a poem I spent a lot of time on and although I understand every word and every sentence, I'm blessed if I know what Stevens is talking about." He reads it over:

> I place a jar in Tennessee,
> And round it was upon a hill.
> It made the slovenly wilderness
> Surround that hill.
>
> The wilderness rose up to it,
> And sprawled around, no longer wild.
> The jar was round upon the ground
> And tall and of a port in air.
>
> It took dominion everywhere.
> The jar was gray and bare.
> It did not give of bird or bush,
> Like nothing else in Tennessee.

The Citizen finishes reading and looks up. "I was bothered at first by 'Port,'" he says, "but I checked the word in the dictionary and I think I see what he's doing with it. But how am I supposed to understand 'It made the slovenly wilderness surround that hill'? How can a jar make a wilderness surround a hill? The wilderness was already surrounding the hill, and long before Stevens and his jar came along."

"In a sense, yes," says the Poet, "but only in the most usual prose-sense. Poetry constantly makes over that usual sense of things. The jar is a made-form; as such it stands for all artifice. The wilderness is nature as-it-happens, the opposite of made-form. But

to 'surround' is 'to take position around a center.' And what is
formless has no center. It is human artifice, the assertion of human
artifice, that puts a center to the wilderness. Because the wilderness is formless it still 'sprawls' but now it sprawls 'up to' the jar.
It approaches form, that is, and therefore it 'is no longer wild.' "

"Wait a minute," says the Citizen, "aren't you the one who
is doing the paraphrasing now?"

"Yes, surely. I have no quarrel with paraphrase: only with
paraphrase as a substitute for the poem. I am not trying to say
'this is what the poem comes to.' Far from it. I am trying to point
out the symbolic areas in which the poem moves. The two poles
of Stevens's thought seem clearly enough to be 'artifice' and 'formless nature.' Why shouldn't those poles be identified? But the
poles are not the poem. The poem is much better seen as those
poles plus the force-field they create."

"That does it!" says the Citizen and slams the book shut,
"symbolic areas, force-fields, artifice versus formless-nature—what
is all this jargon? Didn't you write once that a poem is an emotion
or nothing?"

"I certainly did."

"Then tell me how on earth I am supposed to get an emotion
from this sort of haywire theorizing?"

The Poet smiles sadly. "I'm about ready to grant you that all
criticism is in fact haywire, but would you grant me that criticism
is not the poem? At that, one can still rig a weathervane out of
haywire, and that vane can point to the weather. The poem is not
the vane, nor is it the haywire from which the vane is improvised:
the poem is the weather that is pointed-to.

"Stevens, as it happens, had very strong feelings about form
versus the formless. Those feelings crowd all his poems. They are
fundamental to his very sense of reality. His emotions, to be sure,
are intellectual things. If you refuse to think a sense of esthetic-
reality as opposed to some other more common ideas of reality
is worth an emotion, you are breaking no law, but Stevens is obviously not for you. And that, I find myself thinking, is your loss
rather than his."

"Maybe so," says the Citizen, but now he is sitting up as if
squared for battle. "I'll even say he is obviously not for me. Who
is he for? I'm the one who brought up Stevens, and I'll grant he
may be a special case. But Stevens is not the only one who is ob-

viously not for me. Who *are* you modern poets for? Is there no such thing as an audience?"

This charge, too, is a familiar one to the Poet. "You've fired a lot of questions," he says, "and a full answer would call for a long sermon. Let me try the short form.

"What is the idea of 'the audience'? Is it enough to argue 'I have bought this book of poems and therefore I have certain audience-rights'? I think, first, one must distinguish between two ideas of 'the audience.'

"One idea may be called the horizontal audience and the other the vertical audience. The horizontal consists of everybody who is alive at this moment. The vertical audience consists of everyone, vertically through time, who will ever read a given poem.

"Isn't it immediately obvious that Stevens can only 'be for' a tiny percentage of the horizontal audience? Even Frost, who is the most seemingly-clear and the most widely loved of our good poets, certainly does not reach more than a small percentage of the total population, or even of that part of the population that thinks of itself as literate—as at least literate enough to buy a best-seller. The fact is that no horizontal audience since the age of folk-poetry has been much interested in good poetry. And you may be sure that a few spokesmen sounding off in the name of that horizontal audience are not going to persuade the poets.

"All good poets write for the vertical audience. The vertical audience for Dante, for example, is now six centuries old. And it is growing. If the human race has any luck at all, part of Dante's audience is still thousands of years short of being born.

"Now try a flight of fancy. Imagine that you held an election tomorrow and asked the horizontal audience to vote for Dante as opposed to Eddie Guest. Guest would certainly swamp Dante in such an election. More people in the horizontal audience have read Guest and even, God save the mark, been moved by him— if only to their own inanition. But moved, nevertheless. And we're a democracy, aren't we? The majority rules: bless the majority?

"Not in art. Not horizontally at least. The verdict in art is vertical. Take the idea of majority vote a step further. Imagine that you held the same election on Judgment Day, calling for a total vote of the human race down through time. Can you fail to believe that Dante would then swamp Eddie Guest plus all the horizontalists from Robert Service to Carl Sandburg?

"The point is that the horizontal audience always outnumbers the vertical at any one moment, but that the vertical audience for good poetry always outnumbers the horizontal in time-enough. And not only for the greatest poets. Andrew Marvell is certainly a minor poet, but given time enough, more people certainly will have read 'To His Coy Mistress' than will ever have subscribed to *Time, Life,* and *Fortune.* Compared to what a good poem can do, Luce is a piker at getting circulation."

"Impressive, if true," says the Citizen, "but how does any given poet get his divine sense of this vertical audience?"

"By his own ideal projection of his own best sense of himself. It's as simple as that," says the Poet. "He may be wrong, but he has nothing else to go by. And there is one thing more—all good poets are difficult when their work is new. And their work always becomes less difficult as their total shape becomes more and more visible. As that shape impresses itself upon time, one begins to know how to relate the parts to their total. Even Keats and Shelley confounded their contemporary critics as 'too difficult' and 'not for me.'"

The Citizen throws his hands up. "All right, all right: I've been out-talked. But who *does* write for me?"

The Poet spreads his hands palms out. "Keats and Shelley—now that they have lost their first difficulty."

"And are dead enough?" says the Citizen. "Well, may be. But why is it so impossible for *you* to think about writing for me? I'm willing to give it a try."

The Poet shrugs. "The sort of try you gave Stevens? But no matter. The point is why *should* I write for you?—you're going to be dead the next time anyone looks. We all are for that matter. But not the poem. Not if it's made right. If I make it for you I have to take the chance that it will die with you. I'm not sure you're that good an investment. Besides which, I have to invest in myself. If we happen to share some of the same sense of poetry, it may work out that I do happen to write for you. But that would be a happy bonus at best. I still cannot think of you as a main investment—not till you show a better 'vertical-sense.'"

"We who are about to die," says the Citizen, "salute the poems we cannot grasp. Is that it?"

"Like nothing else in Tennessee," says the Poet bowing.

NOTES AND COMMENTS

Ciardi captures with accuracy and humor the helplessness many people feel when confronted by modern poetry. He also states the position of many modern poets (and other artists). By contrasting so directly the two viewpoints he focuses on the real issue: to understand a language you must be willing to learn it; until you *do*, you can't expect to understand it. Poetry and prose are quite different languages, according to Ciardi, even though they both use words. Does Ciardi's Poet make you feel that learning his language is either possible or worth-while?

Do you think that poets living in other centuries had as much difficulty communicating with their public? Did they try? Do you think this particular Citizen would have as much difficulty reading good fiction (the kind Henry James praises in "The Art of Fiction") as he does in reading modern poetry?

WILLIAM EDWARD WILSON

1906-

William Edward Wilson, novelist and teacher, once served on the English faculty at the United States Naval Academy—as the present essay surely reveals.

Madeline Among the Midshipmen

ONE NIGHT not long ago, I found myself remembering for the first time in years a gruff and briny old sea-dog I served under for a while in the Second World War. I had been reading the poems of Percy Bysshe Shelley, and it was the "Hymn to Intellectual Beauty" that brought my old skipper to mind.

No finer officer than this Captain, U.S.N., ever sailed the seas, I am sure, but when I knew him he was Head of the Department of English, History, and Government at the United States Naval Academy. At the Academy, the Department of E., H., and G. is appropriately known as "the Bull Department," and I was assigned to it early in the war when BuPers decided I was more expendable with a book in my hand than while conning an LST. Why the Captain was assigned to that Department I do not know, unless it was because he had once read "A Dissertation on Roast Pig."

"You ever read that thing about roast pork?" he always asked newcomers to the Department, as a test of their backgrounds in

Reprinted from *College English*, vol. 22, no. 5 (February 1961). By permission of the author.

literature. "I thought it was a pretty good yarn when I was a Midshipman."

I admired the Captain. Indeed, I was grateful that he was my first skipper on shore duty, because he gave a salty atmosphere to Mahan Hall and almost justified the Academy's ironclad rule that we must think of walls as bulkheads, floors as decks, drinking fountains as scuttlebutts, and ourselves as Naval officers. Still, with all the ribbons on his broad chest, the Captain had never fought the campaign of iambic pentameter nor the battle of the synecdoche, nor had he navigated any closer to the main current of English Literature than Charles Lamb's little eddy about roast pig. It was therefore inevitable that the day he discovered Shelley in the Plebe reading assignments he blew all his stacks at once.

When he came steaming across the gangway to the Lit Deck in Mahan Hall that day, the Lit textbook in his hand and his eyes ablaze, we officers of the Lit Detail were so startled that we knocked over a half dozen chairs coming to attention.

"Ten*shun!*" shouted the Chairman of the Lit Detail, a Lieutenant, U.S.N.R., recently surfaced from the Harvard Graduate School; but we were already standing and as stiff as *rigor mortis.*

"What is *this* doing in here?" the Captain roared; and as he spoke he pounded the Lit text so hard with his fist that he knocked it out of his own hand.

The Chairman of the Lit Detail leaped to pick the book up.

"Find that fellow Shelley for me," the Captain commanded. "That thing about beauty."

Later, the Chairman of the Lit Detail said it was like looking for hay in a haystack. But he took a long shot and returned the book to the Captain opened to "Hymn to Intellectual Beauty."

The Captain scanned the page till he found the lines he wanted.

"Now, hear this!" he bellowed, and began to read to us in a high falsetto, which he obviously intended to sound effeminate but which sounded, instead, more like a bosun with laryngitis:

"Sudden, thy shadow fell on me; I shrieked and clasped my hands with ecstasy."

Snapping the book shut, the Captain then glowered at each of us in turn, as if to ferret out any concealed admiration for the lines he had read. If there was any such admiration in that complement of men, it was not exposed. The officers of the Lit Detail, every man-jack of them—and the majority held Ph.D.'s in English —looked as if they had never before heard of Percy Bysshe Shelley.

When he was satisfied with his inspection, the Captain proceeded to a pronouncement.

"That Shelley fellow was a *sissy!* Strike the poem off the reading list."

"Aye, aye, sir!" said the Chairman of the Lit Detail.

The Captain warped his majestic hull around toward the door, but there he stopped, caught in the backwash of an afterthought.

"Belay that," he said, turning to the Chairman. "Not just that thing about beauty. Strike off everything in the book by that fellow. No Shelley. Understand?"

"But, sir—" the Chairman began.

"*All* of it!" the Captain shouted. "No Shelley! Won't do for Midshipmen. Can't have them exposed to that kind of bilge." He gave his falsetto a try again. "*Shrieking* and *clasping* his hands!" But he still sounded like a bosun in sick bay. "I might have known it when I saw the fellow's name on the list. *Percy*—!"

"Please let us keep 'Ode to the West Wind,' Captain," the Chairman of the Lit Detail pleaded. "In a way, sir, it's a nautical poem. That is, it's about the weather."

The Captain shook his head.

"Won't do!" he said. "That one too! *All* of them! After all, there's a war on. Throw them *all* out! Understand? *Shrieking* and all that bilge! *Percy*—! Percy Bysshe—! Percy *Bosh,* I say!"

So, that year at the United States Naval Academy, Nineteenth Century English Poetry was taught with no mention of Percy Bysshe Shelley. To quiet my conscience in the matter, I tried to believe that a whole class of officers in the U. S. Navy would be manlier than their comrades in Blue and Gold because they had never heard of him. At least, if they ever encountered Beauty and recognized it and *shrieked,* they would have no one to blame but themselves.

We did retain Keats in the Plebe syllabus that year, however, probably because the Captain never had the stomach for looking into "The Eve of St. Agnes" after he jettisoned Shelley. At the time, I was sure that if he had known what was going on in Madeline's bedroom on St. Agnes Eve and heard the commotion it caused in my Plebe class, John Keats would have gone over the side too.

At the Naval Academy, the teaching method is somewhat different from the method practiced in most institutions of so-called higher learning. Or so it was during the war. Every Midshipman had to have a grade in the instructor's grade book for every day, and for that reason you had very little time for shilly-shallying around with superfluous things like ideas. You got each Midshipman on his feet in the course of the fifty-minute period, asked him a question that he would find it hard to answer equivocally, jotted a numerical grade in your grade book, and proceeded to the next man. According to Academy Regs, you said, "That is well," at the end of each recitation, whether all was well or not; and it was a good idea to observe this rule because, if you didn't, your Midshipman would remain standing at attention, as solemn as a ninepin, even after you had called on someone else.

When I came to "The Eve of St. Agnes" in the Lit syllabus, I was pleased to note that there were forty-two stanzas in the poem. There were twenty-one Plebes in my Lit class. That meant two stanzas per Plebe. At the rate of a minute per stanza, I would have eight minutes left over for teaching.

We cast off to a good start with Keats's poem. I gave the class the poop about the legend of St. Agnes Eve, made sure they had the word on the rivalry between Madeline's family and Porphyro's, ran them through a drill in pronouncing Porphyro as *Porphyro* and not *Proffero*, and together we convoyed that amorous young man through the "dusky galleries" of Madeline's castle and into Madeline's bedroom, where, as Keats put it, he "took covert, pleased amain." That phrase caused a little difficulty, but I persuaded my future officers and gentlemen that Porphyro, being himself a gentleman if not a Naval officer, only hid in a corner of Madeline's room and did not take to the covers of her sack.

Then came Madeline's turn. All innocence, but eagerness too, "St. Agnes' charméd maid" climbed the marble stairs, lighting her way with a candle, and finally hove to at the door of her room, where Porphyro was hiding.

"Then what happened?" I asked the Plebe I had brought to attention to sound off on Stanzas 23 and 24.

The Plebe hesitated, and I thought he looked puzzled. But

it was hard to tell. Most Plebes looked puzzled aboard the Bull Department.

"Well, sir," he said, finally, "when Madeline opened her bedroom door, a big animal ran out."

I could not have been more startled if the Engineering Department (known as "Steam") had blown out a boiler under my classroom windows, as indeed they were in the habit of doing from time to time.

"A big *what?*" I said.

"A big animal, sir."

I tried to think of all the things cluttering Madeline's bedroom that St. Agnes Eve. There was a table covered with cloth of woven crimson, gold, and jet. There were candied apple, quince, and plum and lucent syrops, tinct with cinnamon. And of course there was Porphyro. But I could recall no animals, large or small, on the loose in the girl's chamber.

"I think you must be mistaken," I said.

"It's in the book, sir," the Plebe replied, solemnly. "May I show you?"

In the Navy, if it's in the book it's so. In my place, even the Captain would have had to give that Plebe a 4.0 for the day if he proved himself right.

"Very well," I said. "Find it in the book and read it to me."

The Plebe opened his book to Stanza 23 and read the first line.

"*Out went the taper as she hurried in.* . . . That's a large tropical animal found mainly in South America, sir," he said. "I looked it up."

Five minutes later, Steam was sending over a man to ask *us* to pipe down.

The Captain never heard about this interpretation of Keats in my classroom, and at the time I was grateful. Maybe, though, it would have been all right if he had. On second thought, I believe he would have approved of Madeline's bedroom. After all, he liked animals in literature. It was only Beauty and that sort of bilge that he disapproved of.

NOTES AND COMMENTS

Funny as this piece is, it raises several serious questions. Do you think that many American men associate poetic expression and effeminacy? Why? Does the gap between rugged men of action (like the Captain and the midshipmen aspiring to be captains) and the world of art and beauty have to be as large as this essay makes it seem? What other questions does Wilson raise by implication about the sort of teaching the Academy system typifies? About the reaction of the faculty to the Captain? About the value of "bull" subjects in modern life? Compare Wilson's view of the Academy with Thurber's picture of university life.

HENRY JAMES

1843-1916

Henry James, writer of fiction and critic, was born in New York City but preferred to live in the more cosmopolitan world of England and the Continent. His influence on literature in the twentieth century has been immense. He was a pioneer of psychological realism and master of a sensitive, almost feminine style of great richness and complexity. The present essay, "The Art of Fiction," was written in reply to a lecture on the same subject by Walter Besant, a Victorian novelist and historian, but it is far more than a mere "reply": it is a searching discussion of good fiction, and a fine statement of James's own artistic creed and the principles exemplified in his novels (such as *The Portrait of a Lady, The Bostonians, The Ambassadors*) and stories (like "The Figure in the Carpet," "The Real Thing," "The Lesson of a Master").

The Art of Fiction

I SHOULD NOT have affixed so comprehensive a title to these few remarks, necessarily wanting in any completeness upon a subject the full consideration of which would carry us far, did I not seem to discover a pretext for my temerity in the interesting pamphlet lately published under this name by Mr. Walter Besant. Mr. Besant's lecture at the Royal Institution—the original form of his pamphlet—appears to indicate that many persons are interested in the art of fiction, and are not indifferent to such remarks, as those who practice it may attempt to make about it. I am therefore anxious not to lose the benefit of this favorable association, and to edge in a few words under cover of the attention which Mr.

Besant is sure to have excited. There is something very encouraging in his having put into form certain of his ideas on the mystery of story-telling.

It is a proof of life and curiosity—curiosity on the part of the brotherhood of novelists as well as on the part of their readers. Only a short time ago it might have been supposed that the English novel was not what the French call *discutable*. It had no air of having a theory, a conviction, a consciousness of itself behind it —of being the expression of an artistic faith, the result of choice and comparison. I do not say it was necessarily the worse for that: it would take much more courage than I possess to intimate that the form of the novel as Dickens and Thackeray (for instance) saw it had any taint of incompleteness. It was, however, *naïf* (if I may help myself out with another French word); and evidently if it be destined to suffer in any way for having lost its *naïveté* it has now an idea of making sure of the corresponding advantages. During the period I have alluded to there was a comfortable, good-humored feeling abroad that a novel is a novel, as a pudding is a pudding, and that our only business with it could be to swallow it. But within a year or two, for some reason or other, there have been signs of returning animation—the era of discussion would appear to have been to a certain extent opened. Art lives upon discussion, upon experiment, upon curiosity, upon variety of attempt, upon the exchange of views and the comparison of standpoints; and there is a presumption that those times when no one has anything particular to say about it, and has no reason to give for practice or preference, though they may be times of honor, are not times of development—are times, possibly even, a little of dullness. The successful application of any art is a delightful spectacle, but the theory too is interesting; and though there is a great deal of the latter without the former I suspect there has never been a genuine success that has not had a latent core of conviction. Discussion, suggestion, formulation, these things are fertilizing when they are frank and sincere. Mr. Besant has set an excellent example in saying what he thinks, for his part, about the way in which fiction should be written, as well as about the way in which it should be published; for his view of the "art," carried on into an appendix, covers that too. Other laborers in the same field will doubtless take up the argument, they will give it the light of their experience, and the effect will surely be to make our interest in the novel a little more what it had for some time threatened to fail to be—a serious, active, inquiring interest, under protection of which this delightful study may, in moments of confidence, venture to say a little more what it thinks of itself.

It must take itself seriously for the public to take it so. The old superstition about fiction being "wicked" has doubtless died out in England; but the spirit of it lingers in a certain oblique regard directed toward any story which does not more or less admit that it is only a joke. Even the most jocular novel feels in some degree the weight of the proscription that was formerly directed against literary levity: the jocularity does not always succeed in passing for orthodoxy. It is still expected, though perhaps people are ashamed to say it, that a production which is after all only a "make-believe" (for what else is a "story"?) shall be in some degree apologetic—shall renounce the pretension of attempting really to represent life. This, of course, any sensible, wide-awake story declines to do, for it quickly perceives that the tolerance granted to it on such a condition is only an attempt to stifle it disguised in the form of generosity. The old evangelical hostility to the novel, which was as explicit as it was narrow, and which regarded it as little less favorable to our immortal part than a stage play, was in reality far less insulting. The only reason for the existence of a novel is that it does attempt to represent life. When it relinquishes this attempt, the same attempt that we see on the canvas of the painter, it will have arrived at a very strange pass. It is not expected of the picture that it will make itself humble in order to be forgiven; and the analogy between the art of the painter and the art of the novelist is, so far as I am able to see, complete. Their inspiration is the same, their process (allowing for the different quality of the vehicle) is the same, their success is the same. They may learn from each other, they may explain and sustain each other. Their cause is the same, and the honor of one is the honor of another. The Mahometans think a picture an unholy thing, but it is a long time since any Christian did, and it is therefore the more odd that in the Christian mind the traces (dissimulated though they may be) of a suspicion of the sister art should linger to this day. The only effectual way to lay it to rest is to emphasize the analogy to which I just alluded—to insist on the fact that as the picture is reality, so the novel is history. That is the only general description (which does it justice) that we may give of the novel.

But history also is allowed to represent life; it is not, any more than painting, expected to apologize. The subject-matter of fiction is stored up likewise in documents and records, and if it will not give itself away, as they say in California, it must speak with assurance, with the tone of the historian. Certain accomplished novelists have a habit of giving themselves away which must often bring tears to the eyes of people who take their fiction seriously. I was lately struck, in reading over many pages of Anthony Trollope, with his want of discretion in this particular. In a digression, a parenthesis or an aside, he concedes to the reader that he and this trusting friend are only "making believe." He admits that the events he narrates have not really happened, and that he can give his narrative any turn the reader may like best. Such a betrayal of a sacred office seems to me, I confess, a terrible crime; it is what I mean by the attitude of apology, and it shocks me every whit as much in Trollope as it would have shocked me in Gibbon or Macaulay. It implies that the novelist is less occupied in looking for the truth (the truth, of course I mean, that he assumes, the premises that we grant him, whatever they may be) than the historian, and in doing so it deprives him at a stroke of all his standing room. To represent and illustrate the past, the actions of men, is the task of either writer, and the only difference that I can see is, in proportion as he succeeds, to the honor of the novelist, consisting as it does in his having more difficulty in collecting his evidence, which is so far from being purely literary. It seems to me to give him a great character, the fact that he has at once so much in common with the philosopher and the painter; this double analogy is a magnificent heritage.

It is of all this evidently that Mr. Besant is full when he insists upon the fact that fiction is one of the *fine* arts, deserving in its turn of all the honors and emoluments that have hitherto been reserved for the successful profession of music, poetry, painting, architecture. It is impossible to insist too much on so important a truth, and the place that Mr. Besant demands for the work of the novelist may be represented, a trifle less abstractly, by saying that he demands not only that it shall be reputed artistic, but that it shall be reputed very artistic indeed. It is excellent that he should have struck this note, for his doing so indicates that there was need of it, that his proposition may be to many people a novelty. One rubs one's eyes at the thought; but the rest of Mr.

Besant's essay confirms the revelation. I suspect in truth that it would be possible to confirm it still further, and that one would not be far wrong in saying that in addition to the people to whom it has never occurred that a novel ought to be artistic, there are a great many others who, if this principle were urged upon them, would be filled with an indefinable mistrust. They would find it difficult to explain their repugnance, but it would operate strongly to put them on their guard. "Art," in our Protestant communities, where so many things have got so strangely twisted about, is supposed in certain circles to have some vaguely injurious effect upon those who make it an important consideration, who let it weigh in the balance. It is assumed to be opposed in some mysterious manner to morality, to amusement, to instruction. When it is embodied in the work of the painter (the sculptor is another affair!) you know what it is: it stands there before you, in the honesty of pink and green and a gilt frame; you can see the worst of it at a glance, and you can be on your guard. But when it is introduced into literature it becomes more insidious—there is danger of its hurting you before you know it. Literature should be either instructive or amusing, and there is in many minds an impression that these artistic preoccupations, the search for form, contribute to neither end, interfere indeed with both. They are too frivolous to be edifying, and too serious to be diverting; and they are moreover priggish and paradoxical and superfluous. That, I think, represents the manner in which the latent thought of many people who read novels as an exercise in skipping would explain itself if it were to become articulate. They would argue, of course, that a novel ought to be "good," but they would interpret this term in a fashion of their own, which indeed would vary considerably from one critic to another. One would say that being good means representing virtuous and aspiring characters, placed in prominent positions; another would say that it depends on a "happy ending," on a distribution at the last of prizes, pensions, husbands, wives, babies, millions, appended paragraphs, and cheerful remarks. Another still would say that it means being full of incident and movement, so that we shall wish to jump ahead, to see who was the mysterious stranger, and if the stolen will was ever found, and shall not be distracted from this pleasure by any tiresome analysis or "description." But they would all agree that the "artistic" idea would spoil some of their fun. One would hold

it accountable for all the description, another would see it revealed in the absence of sympathy. Its hostility to a happy ending
would be evident, and it might even in some cases render any
ending at all impossible. The "ending" of a novel is, for many
persons, like that of a good dinner, a course of dessert and ices,
and the artist in fiction is regarded as a sort of meddlesome doctor
who forbids agreeable aftertastes. It is therefore true that this
conception of Mr. Besant's of the novel as a superior form encounters not only a negative but a positive indifference. It matters
little that as a work of art it should really be as little or as much
of its essence to supply happy endings, sympathetic characters,
and an objective tone, as if it were a work of mechanics: the association of ideas, however incongruous, might easily be too much
for it if an eloquent voice were not sometimes raised to call
attention to the fact that it is at once as free and as serious a
branch of literature as any other.

Certainly this might sometimes be doubted in presence of
the enormous number of works of fiction that appeal to the
credulity of our generation, for it might easily seem that there
could be no great character in a commodity so quickly and easily
produced. It must be admitted that good novels are much compromised by bad ones, and that the field at large suffers discredit
from overcrowding. I think, however, that this injury is only
superficial, and that the superabundance of written fiction proves
nothing against the principle itself. It has been vulgarized, like all
other kinds of literature, like everything else today, and it has
proved more than some kinds accessible to vulgarization. But there
is as much difference as there ever was between a good novel and
a bad one: the bad is swept with all the daubed canvases and
spoiled marble into some unvisited limbo, or infinite rubbish-yard
beneath the back-windows of the world, and the good subsists and
emits its light and stimulates our desire for perfection. As I
shall take the liberty of making but a single criticism of Mr.
Besant, whose tone is so full of the love of his art, I may as well
have done with it at once. He seems to me to mistake in attempting to say so definitely beforehand what sort of an affair the good
novel will be. To indicate the danger of such an error as that has
been the purpose of these few pages; to suggest that certain traditions on the subject, applied *a priori*, have already had much to
answer for, and that the good health of an art which undertakes

so immediately to reproduce life must demand that it be perfectly
free. It lives upon exercise, and the very meaning of exercise is
freedom. The only obligation to which in advance we may hold
a novel, without incurring the accusation of being arbitrary, is that
it be interesting. That general responsibility rests upon it, but it is
the only one I can think of. The ways in which it is at liberty to
accomplish this result (of interesting us) strike me as innumerable,
and such as can only suffer from being marked out or fenced in by
prescription. They are as various as the temperament of man, and
they are successful in proportion as they reveal a particular mind,
different from others. A novel is in its broadest definition a personal, a direct impression of life: that, to begin with, constitutes
its value, which is greater or less according to the intensity of the
impression. But there will be no intensity at all, and therefore no
value, unless there is freedom to feel and say. The tracing of a
line to be followed, of a tone to be taken, of a form to be filled
out, is a limitation of that freedom and a suppression of the
very thing that we are most curious about. The form, it seems to
me, is to be appreciated after the fact: then the author's choice
has been made, his standard has been indicated; then we can
follow lines and directions and compare tones and resemblances.
Then in a word we can enjoy one of the most charming of pleasures, we can estimate quality, we can apply the test of execution.
The execution belongs to the author alone; it is what is most
personal to him, and we measure him by that. The advantage, the
luxury, as well as the torment and responsibility of the novelist,
is that there is no limit to what he may attempt as an executant
—no limit to his possible experiments, efforts, discoveries, successes. Here it is especially that he works, step by step, like his
brother of the brush, of whom we may always say that he has
painted his picture in a manner best known to himself. His
manner is his secret, not necessarily a jealous one. He cannot
disclose it as a general thing if he would; he would be at a loss to
teach it to others. I say this with a due recollection of having
insisted on the community of method of the artist who paints a
picture and the artist who writes a novel. The painter *is* able to
teach the rudiments of his practice, and it is possible, from the
study of good work (granted the aptitude), both to learn how to
paint and to learn how to write. Yet it remains true, without
injury to the *rapprochement*, that the literary artist would be

obliged to say to his pupil much more than the other, "Ah, well, you must do it as you can!" It is a question of degree, a matter of delicacy. If there are exact sciences, there are also exact arts, and the grammar of painting is so much more definite that it makes the difference.

I ought to add, however, that if Mr. Besant says at the beginning of his essay that the "laws of fiction may be laid down and taught with as much precision and exactness as the laws of harmony, perspective, and proportion," he mitigates what might appear to be an extravagance by applying his remark to "general" laws, and by expressing most of these rules in a manner with which it would certainly be unaccommodating to disagree. That the novelist must write from his experience, that his "characters must be real and such as might be met with in actual life"; that "a young lady brought up in a quiet country village should avoid descriptions of garrison life," and "a writer whose friends and personal experiences belong to the lower middle-class should carefully avoid introducing his characters into society"; that one should enter one's notes in a common-place book; that one's figures should be clear in outline; that making them clear by some trick of speech or of carriage is a bad method, and "describing them at length" is a worse one; that English Fiction should have a "conscious moral purpose"; that "it is almost impossible to estimate too highly the value of careful workmanship—that is, of style"; that "the most important point of all is the story," that "the story is everything": these are principles with most of which it is surely impossible not to sympathize. That remark about the lower middle-class writer and his knowing his place is perhaps rather chilling; but for the rest I should find it difficult to dissent from any one of these recommendations. At the same time, I should find it difficult positively to assent to them, with the exception, perhaps, of the injunction as to entering one's notes in a common-place book. They scarcely seem to me to have the quality that Mr. Besant attributes to the rules of the novelist—the "precision and exactness" of "the laws of harmony, perspective, and proportion." They are suggestive, they are even inspiring, but they are not exact, though they are doubtless as much so as the case admits of: which is a proof of that liberty of interpretation for which I just contended. For the value of these different injunctions—so beautiful and so vague—is wholly in the meaning one attaches to them.

The characters, the situation, which strike one as real will be those that touch and interest one most, but the measure of reality is very difficult to fix. The reality of Don Quixote or of Mr. Micawber is a very delicate shade; it is a reality so colored by the author's vision that, vivid as it may be, one would hesitate to propose it as a model; one would expose one's self to some very embarrassing questions on the part of a pupil. It goes without saying that you will not write a good novel unless you possess the sense of reality; but it will be difficult to give you a recipe for calling that sense into being. Humanity is immense, and reality has a myriad forms; the most one can affirm is that some of the flowers of fiction have the odor of it, and others have not; as for telling you in advance how your nosegay should be composed, that is another affair. It is equally excellent and inconclusive to say that one must write from experience; to our supposititious aspirant such a declaration might savor of mockery. What kind of experience is intended, and where does it begin and end? Experience is never limited, and it is never complete; it is an immense sensibility, a kind of huge spider-web of the finest silken threads suspended in the chamber of consciousness, and catching every air-borne particle in its tissue. It is the very atmosphere of the mind; and when the mind is imaginative—much more when it happens to be that of a man of genius—it takes to itself the faintest hints of life, it converts the very pulses of the air into revelations. The young lady living in a village has only to be a damsel upon whom nothing is lost to make it quite unfair (as it seems to me) to declare to her that she shall have nothing to say about the military. Greater miracles have been seen than that, imagination assisting, she should speak the truth about some of these gentlemen. I remember an English novelist, a woman of genius,[1] telling me that she was much commended for the impression she had managed to give in one of her tales of the nature and way of life of the French Protestant youth. She had been asked where she learned so much about this recondite being, she had been congratulated on her peculiar opportunities. These opportunities consisted in her having once, in Paris, as she ascended a staircase, passed an open door where, in the household of a

---

[1 This probably refers to Anne Thackeray, Lady Ritchie, daughter of Thackeray, whose first novel *The Story of Elizabeth* resembles James's description.—Ed.]

pasteur, some of the young Protestants were seated at table round a finished meal. The glimpse made a picture; it lasted only a moment, but that moment was experience. She had got her direct personal impression, and she turned out her type. She knew what youth was, and what Protestantism; she also had the advantage of having seen what it was to be French, so that she converted these ideas into a concrete image and produced a reality. Above all, however, she was blessed with the faculty which when you give it an inch takes an ell, and which for the artist is a much greater source of strength than any accident of residence or of place in the social scale. The power to guess the unseen from the seen, to trace the implication of things, to judge the whole piece by the pattern, the condition of feeling life in general so completely that you are well on your way to knowing any particular corner of it —this cluster of gifts may almost be said to constitute experience, and they occur in country and in town, and in the most differing stages of education. If experience consists of impressions, it may be said that impressions *are* experience, just as (have we not seen it?) they are the very air we breathe. Therefore, if I should certainly say to a novice, "Write from experience and experience only," I should feel that this was rather a tantalizing monition if I were not careful immediately to add, "Try to be one of the people on whom nothing is lost!"

I am far from intending by this to minimize the importance of exactness—of truth of detail. One can speak best from one's own taste, and I may therefore venture to say that the air of reality (solidity of specification) seems to me to be the supreme virtue of a novel—the merit on which all its other merits (including that conscious moral purpose of which Mr. Besant speaks) helplessly and submissively depend. If it be not there they are all as nothing, and if these be there, they owe their effect to the success with which the author has produced the illusion of life. The cultivation of this success, the study of this exquisite process, form, to my taste, the beginning and the end of the art of the novelist. They are his inspiration, his despair, his reward, his torment, his delight. It is here in very truth that he competes with life; it is here that he competes with his brother the painter in *his* attempt to render the look of things, the look that conveys their meaning, to catch the color, the relief, the expression, the surface, the substance of the human spectacle. It is in regard to this that Mr.

Besant is well inspired when he bids him take notes. He cannot
possibly take too many, he cannot possibly take enough. All life
solicits him, and to "render" the simplest surface, to produce the
most momentary illusion, is a very complicated business. His case
would be easier, and the rule would be more exact, if Mr. Besant
had been able to tell him what notes to take. But this, I fear, he
can never learn in any manual; it is the business of his life. He has
to take a great many in order to select a few, he has to work them
up as he can, and even the guides and philosophers who might
have most to say to him must leave him alone when it comes to
the application of precepts, as we leave the painter in communion
with his palette. That his characters "must be clear in outline,"
as Mr. Besant says—he feels that down to his boots; but how he
shall make them so is a secret between his good angel and himself. It would be absurdly simple if he could be taught that a great
deal of "description" would make them so, or that on the contrary
the absence of description and the cultivation of dialogue, or the
absence of dialogue and the multiplication of "incident," would
rescue him from his difficulties. Nothing, for instance, is more
possible than that he be of a turn of mind for which this odd,
literal opposition of description and dialogue, incident and description, has little meaning and light. People often talk of these things
as if they had a kind of internecine distinctness, instead of melting
into each other at every breath, and being intimately associated
parts of one general effort of expression. I cannot imagine composition existing in a series of blocks, nor conceive, in any novel
worth discussing at all, of a passage of description that is not in its
intention narrative, a passage of dialogue that is not in its intention descriptive, a touch of truth of any sort that does not partake
of the nature of incident, or an incident that derives its interest
from any other source than the general and only source of the
success of a work of art—that of being illustrative. A novel is a
living thing, all one and continuous, like any other organism, and
in proportion as it lives will it be found, I think, that in each of
the parts there is something of each of the other parts. The critic
who over the close texture of a finished work shall pretend to
trace a geography of items will mark some frontiers as artificial, I
fear, as any that have been known to history. There is an old-
fashioned distinction between the novel of character and the novel
of incident which must have cost many a smile to the intending

fabulist who was keen about his work. It appears to me as little to the point as the equally celebrated distinction between the novel and the romance—to answer as little to any reality. There are bad novels and good novels, as there are bad pictures and good pictures; but that is the only distinction in which I see any meaning, and I can as little imagine speaking of a novel of character as I can imagine speaking of a picture of character. When one says picture one says of character, when one says novel one says of incident, and the terms may be transposed at will. What is character but the determination of incident? What is incident but the illustration of character? What is either a picture or a novel that is *not* of character? What else do we seek in it and find in it? It is an incident for a woman to stand up with her hand resting on a table and look out at you in a certain way; or if it be not an incident I think it will be hard to say what it is. At the same time it is an expression of character. If you say you don't see it (character in *that*—*allons donc!*), this is exactly what the artist who has reasons of his own for thinking he *does* see it undertakes to show you. When a young man makes up his mind that he has not faith enough after all to enter the church as he intended, that is an incident, though you may not hurry to the end of the chapter to see whether perhaps he doesn't change once more. I do not say that these are extraordinary or startling incidents. I do not pretend to estimate the degree of interest proceeding from them, for this will depend upon the skill of the painter. It sounds almost puerile to say that some incidents are intrinsically much more important than others, and I need not take this precaution after having professed my sympathy for the major ones in remarking that the only classification of the novel that I can understand is into that which has life and that which has it not.

The novel and the romance, the novel of incident and that of character—these clumsy separations appear to me to have been made by critics and readers for their own convenience, and to help them out of some of their occasional queer predicaments, but to have little reality or interest for the producer, from whose point of view it is of course that we are attempting to consider the art of fiction. The case is the same with another shadowy category which Mr. Besant apparently is disposed to set up—that of the "modern English novel"; unless indeed it be that in this matter he has fallen into an accidental confusion of standpoints. It is not quite clear whether he intends the remarks in which he alludes to it to be didactic or historical. It is as difficult to suppose a person intending to write a modern English as to suppose him writing an ancient English novel: that is a label which begs the question. One writes the novel, one paints the picture, of one's language and of one's time, and calling it modern English will not, alas! make the difficult task any easier. No more, unfortunately, will calling this or that work of one's fellow-artist a romance— unless it be, of course, simply for the pleasantness of the thing, as for instance when Hawthorne gave this heading to his story of *Blithedale*. The French, who have brought the theory of fiction to remarkable completeness, have but one name for the novel, and have not attempted smaller things in it, that I can see, for that. I can think of no obligation to which the "romancer" would not be held equally with the novelist; the standard of execution is equally high for each. Of course it is of execution that we are talking— that being the only point of a novel that is open to contention. This is perhaps too often lost sight of, only to produce interminable confusions and cross-purposes. We must grant the artist his subject, his idea, his *donnée*: our criticism is applied only to what he makes of it. Naturally I do not mean that we are bound to like it or find it interesting: in case we do not our course is perfectly simple—to let it alone. We may believe that of a certain idea even the most sincere novelist can make nothing at all, and the event may perfectly justify our belief; but the failure will have been a failure to execute, and it is in the execution that the fatal weakness is recorded. If we pretend to respect the artist at all, we must allow him his freedom of choice, in the face, in particular cases, of innumerable presumptions that the choice will not fructify. Art derives a considerable part of its beneficial exercise from flying in the face of presumptions, and some of the most interesting experiments of which it is capable are hidden in the bosom of common things. Gustave Flaubert has written a story[1] about the devotion of a servant-girl to a parrot, and the production, highly finished as it is, cannot on the whole be called a success. We are perfectly free to find it flat, but I think it might have been interesting; and I, for my part, am extremely glad he should have written it; it is a contribution to our knowledge of what can be

---

[1] *Un coeur simple.*

done—or what cannot. Ivan Turgenev has written a tale about a deaf and dumb serf and a lap-dog,[1] and the thing is touching, loving, a little masterpiece. He struck the note of life where Gustave Flaubert missed it—he flew in the face of a presumption and achieved a victory.

Nothing, of course, will ever take the place of the good old fashion of "liking" a work of art or not liking it: the most improved criticism will not abolish that primitive, that ultimate test. I mention this to guard myself from the accusation of intimating that the idea, the subject, of a novel or a picture, does not matter. It matters, to my sense, in the highest degree, and if I might put up a prayer it would be that artists should select none but the richest. Some, as I have already hastened to admit, are much more remunerative than others, and it would be a world happily arranged in which persons intending to treat them should be exempt from confusions and mistakes. This fortunate condition will arrive only, I fear, on the same day that critics become purged from error. Meanwhile, I repeat, we do not judge the artist with fairness unless we say to him,

"Oh, I grant you your starting-point, because if I did not I should seem to prescribe to you, and heaven forbid I should take that responsibility. If I pretend to tell you what you must not take, you will call upon me to tell you then what you must take; in which case I shall be prettily caught. Moreover, it isn't till I have accepted your data that I can begin to measure you. I have the standard, the pitch; I have no right to tamper with your flute and then criticize your music. Of course I may not care for your idea at all; I may think it silly, or stale, or unclean; in which case I wash my hands of you altogether. I may content myself with believing that you will not have succeeded in being interesting, but I shall, of course, not attempt to demonstrate it, and you will be as indifferent to me as I am to you. I needn't remind you that there are all sorts of tastes: who can know it better? Some people, for excellent reasons, don't like to read about carpenters; others, for reasons even better, don't like to read about courtesans. Many object to Americans. Others (I believe they are mainly editors and publishers) won't look at Italians. Some readers don't like

---

[1] *Mumu.*

quiet subjects; others don't like bustling ones. Some enjoy a complete illusion, others the consciousness of large concessions. They choose their novels accordingly, and if they don't care about your idea they won't, *a fortiori*, care about your treatment."

So that it comes back very quickly, as I have said, to the liking: in spite of M. Zola, who reasons less powerfully than he represents, and who will not reconcile himself to this absoluteness of taste, thinking that there are certain things that people ought to like, and that they can be made to like. I am quite at a loss to imagine anything (at any rate in this matter of fiction) that people *ought* to like or to dislike. Selection will be sure to take care of itself, for it has a constant motive behind it. That motive is simply experience. As people feel life, so they will feel the art that is most closely related to it. This closeness of relation is what we should never forget in talking of the effort of the novel. Many people speak of it as a factitious, artificial form, a product of ingenuity, the business of which is to alter and arrange the things that surround us, to translate them into conventional, traditional moulds. This, however, is a view of the matter which carries us but a very short way, condemns the art to an eternal repetition of a few familiar *clichés*, cuts short its development, and leads us straight up to a dead wall. Catching the very note and trick, the strange irregular rhythm of life, that is the attempt whose strenuous force keeps Fiction upon her feet. In proportion as in what she offers us we see life *without* rearrangement do we feel that we are touching the truth; in proportion as we see it *with* rearrangement do we feel that we are being put off with a substitute, a compromise and convention. It is not uncommon to hear an extraordinary assurance of remark in regard to this matter of rearranging, which is often spoken of as if it were the last word of art. Mr. Besant seems to me in danger of falling into the great error with his rather unguarded talk about "selection." Art is essentially selection, but it is a selection whose main care is to be typical, to be inclusive. For many people art means rose-colored windowpanes, and selection means picking a bouquet for Mrs. Grundy. They will tell you glibly that artistic considerations have nothing to do with the disagreeable, with the ugly; they will rattle off shallow commonplaces about the province of art and the limits of art till you are moved to some wonder in return as to the province and the limits of ignorance. It appears to me that no one can ever have made a seriously artistic attempt without becoming conscious of an immense increase—a kind of revelation—of freedom. One perceives in that case—by the light of a heavenly ray—that the province of art is all life, all feeling, all observation, all vision. As Mr. Besant so justly intimates, it is all experience. That is a sufficient answer to those who maintain that it must not touch the sad things of life, who stick into its divine unconscious bosom little prohibitory inscriptions on the end of sticks, such as we see in public gardens—"It is forbidden to walk on the grass; it is forbidden to touch the flowers; it is not allowed to introduce dogs or to remain after dark; it is requested to keep to the right." The young aspirant in the line of fiction whom we continue to imagine will do nothing without taste, for in that case his freedom would be of little use to him; but the first advantage of his taste will be to reveal to him the absurdity of the little sticks and tickets. If he have taste, I must add, of course he will have ingenuity, and my disrespectful reference to that quality just now was not meant to imply that it is useless in fiction. But it is only a secondary aid; the first is a capacity for receiving straight impressions.

Mr. Besant has some remarks on the question of "the story" which I shall not attempt to criticize, though they seem to me to contain a singular ambiguity, because I do not think I understand them. I cannot see what is meant by talking as if there were a part of a novel which is the story and part of it which for mystical reasons is not—unless indeed the distinction be made in a sense in which it is difficult to suppose that any one should attempt to convey anything. "The story," if it represents anything, represents the subject, the idea, the *donnée* of the novel; and there is surely no "school"—Mr. Besant speaks of a school—which urges that a novel should be all treatment and no subject. There must assuredly be something to treat; every school is intimately conscious of that. This sense of the story being the idea, the starting-point, of the novel, is the only one that I see in which it can be spoken of as something different from its organic whole; and since in proportion as the work is successful the idea permeates and penetrates it, informs and animates it, so that every word and every punctuation-point contribute directly to the expression, in that proportion do we lose our sense of the story being a blade which may be drawn more or less out of its sheath. The story and the novel, the idea and the form, are the needle and thread, and I never heard of a guild of tailors who recommended the use of the thread without the needle, or the needle without the thread. Mr. Besant is not the only critic who may be observed to have spoken as if there were certain things in life which constitute stories, and certain others which do not. I find the same odd implication in an entertaining article in the *Pall Mall Gazette*, devoted, as it happens, to Mr. Besant's lecture. "The story is the thing!" says this graceful writer, as if with a tone of opposition to some other idea. I should think it was, as every painter who, as the time for "sending in" his picture looms in the distance, finds himself still in quest of a subject—as every belated artist not fixed about his theme will heartily agree. There are some subjects which speak to us and others which do not, but he would be a clever man who should undertake to give a rule—an *index expurgatorius*—by which the story and the no-story should be known apart. It is impossible (to me at least) to imagine any such rule which shall not be altogether arbitrary. The writer in the *Pall Mall* opposes the delightful (as I suppose) novel of *Margot la Balafrée* to certain tales in which "Bostonian nymphs" appear to have "rejected English dukes for psychological reasons." [1] I am not acquainted with the romance just designated, and can scarcely forgive the *Pall Mall* critic for not mentioning the name of the author, but the title appears to refer to a lady who may have received a scar in some heroic adventure.[2] I am inconsolable at not being acquainted with this episode, but am utterly at a loss to see why it is a story when the rejection (or acceptance) of a duke is not, and why a reason, psychological or other, is not a subject when a cicatrix is. They are all particles of the multitudinous life with which the novel deals, and surely no dogma which pretends to make it lawful to touch the one and unlawful to touch the other will stand for a moment on its feet. It is the special picture that must stand or fall, according as it seem to possess truth or to lack it. Mr. Besant does not, to my sense, light up the subject by intimating that a story must, under penalty of not being a story, consist of "adventures." Why of adventures more than of green spectacles? He mentions a category of impossible things, and among them he

---

[1 Probably a reference to James's short novel An *International Episode* (1879).—*Ed.*]
[2 *Balafrée* means "scarred on the face."—*Ed.*]

places "fiction without adventure." Why without adventure, more
than without matrimony, or celibacy, or parturition, or cholera, or
hydropathy, or Jansenism? This seems to me to bring the novel
back to the hapless little rôle of being an artificial, ingenious thing
—bring it down from its large, free character of an immense and
exquisite correspondence with life. And what *is* adventure, when it
comes to that, and by what sign is the listening pupil to recognize
it? It is an adventure—an immense one—for me to write this
little article; and for a Bostonian nymph to reject an English duke
is an adventure only less stirring, I should say, than for an English
duke to be rejected by a Bostonian nymph. I see dramas within
dramas in that, and innumerable points of view. A psychological
reason is, to my imagination, an object adorably pictorial; to catch
the tint of its complexion—I feel as if that idea might inspire one
to Titianesque efforts. There are few things more exciting to me,
in short, than a psychological reason, and yet, I protest, the novel
seems to me the most magnificent form of art. I have just been
reading, at the same time, the delightful story of *Treasure Island*,
by Mr. Robert Louis Stevenson and, in a manner less consecutive,
the last tale from M. Edmond de Goncourt, which is entitled
Chérie. One of these works treats of murders, mysteries, islands of
dreadful renown, hairbreadth escapes, miraculous coincidences and
buried doubloons. The other treats of a little French girl who
lived in a fine house in Paris, and died of wounded sensibility
because no one would marry her. I call *Treasure Island* delightful,
because it appears to me to have succeeded wonderfully in what
it attempts; and I venture to bestow no epithet upon *Chérie*,
which strikes me as having failed deplorably in what it attempts
—that is in tracing the development of the moral consciousness of
a child. But one of these productions strikes me as exactly as
much of a novel as the other, and as having a "story" quite as
much. The moral consciousness of a child is as much a part of
life as the islands of the Spanish Main, and the one sort of geography seems to me to have those "surprises" of which Mr. Besant
speaks quite as much as the other. For myself (since it comes back
in the last resort, as I say, to the preference of the individual), the
picture of the child's experience has the advantage that I can at
successive steps (an immense luxury, near to the "sensual pleasure"
of which Mr. Besant's critic in the *Pall Mall* speaks) say Yes or
No, as it may be, to what the artist puts before me. I have been

a child in fact, but I have been on a quest for a buried treasure only in supposition, and it is a simple accident that with M. de Goncourt I should have for the most part to say No. With George Eliot, when she painted that country with a far other intelligence, I always said Yes.

The most interesting part of Mr. Besant's lecture is unfortunately the briefest passage—his very cursory allusion to the "conscious moral purpose" of the novel. Here again it is not very clear whether he be recording a fact or laying down a principle; it is a great pity that in the latter case he should not have developed his idea. This branch of the subject is of immense importance, and Mr. Besant's few words point to considerations of the widest reach, not to be lightly disposed of. He will have treated the art of fiction but superficially who is not prepared to go every inch of the way that these considerations will carry him. It is for this reason that at the beginning of these remarks I was careful to notify the reader that my reflections on so large a theme have no pretension to be exhaustive. Like Mr. Besant, I have left the question of the morality of the novel till the last, and at the last I find I have used up my space. It is a question surrounded with difficulties, as witness the very first that meets us, in the form of a definite question, on the threshold. Vagueness, in such a discussion, is fatal, and what is the meaning of your morality and your conscious moral purpose? Will you not define your terms and explain how (a novel being a picture) a picture can be either moral or immoral? You wish to paint a moral picture or carve a moral statue: will you not tell us how you would set about it? We are discussing the Art of Fiction; questions of art are questions (in the widest sense) of execution; questions of morality are quite another affair, and will you not let us see how it is that you find it so easy to mix them up? These things are so clear to Mr. Besant that he has deduced from them a law which he sees embodied in English Fiction, and which is "a truly admirable thing and a great cause for congratulation." It is a great cause for congratulation indeed when such thorny problems become as smooth as silk. I may add that in so far as Mr. Besant perceives that in point of fact English Fiction has addressed itself preponderantly to these delicate questions he will appear to many people to have made a vain discovery. They will have been positively struck, on the contrary, with the moral timidity of the usual English novelist;

with his (or with her) aversion to face the difficulties with which
on every side the treatment of reality bristles. He is apt to be
extremely shy (whereas the picture that Mr. Besant draws is a
picture of boldness), and the sign of his work, for the most part,
is a cautious silence on certain subjects. In the English novel (by
which of course I mean the American as well), more than in any
other, there is a traditional difference between that which people
know and that which they agree to admit that they know, that
which they see and that which they speak of, that which they feel
to be a part of life and that which they allow to enter into literature. There is the great difference, in short, between what they talk
of in conversation and what they talk of in print. The essence of
moral energy is to survey the whole field, and I should directly reverse Mr. Besant's remark and say not that the English novel has a
purpose, but that it has a diffidence. To what degree a purpose in
a work of art is a source of corruption I shall not attempt to
inquire; the one that seems to me least dangerous is the purpose
of making a perfect work. As for our novel, I may say lastly on
this score that as we find it in England today it strikes me as
addressed in a large degree to "young people," and that this in
itself constitutes a presumption that it will be rather shy. There
are certain things which it is generally agreed not to discuss, not
even to mention, before young people. That is very well, but the
absence of discussion is not a symptom of the moral passion. The
purpose of the English novel—"a truly admirable thing, and a
great cause for congratulation"—strikes me therefore as rather
negative.

There is one point at which the moral sense and the artistic
sense lie very near together; that is in the light of the very obvious
truth that the deepest quality of a work of art will always be the
quality of the mind of the producer. In proportion as that intelligence is fine will the novel, the picture, the statue partake of
the substance of beauty and truth. To be constituted of such elements is, to my vision, to have purpose enough. No good novel
will ever proceed from a superficial mind; that seems to me an
axiom which, for the artist in fiction, will cover all needful moral
ground: If the youthful aspirant take it to heart it will illuminate
for him many of the mysteries of "purpose." There are many
other useful things that might be said to him, but I have come to
the end of my article, and can only touch them as I pass. The

critic in the *Pall Mall Gazette*, whom I have already quoted, draws attention to the danger, in speaking of the art of fiction, of generalizing. The danger that he has in mind is rather, I imagine, that of particularizing, for there are some comprehensive remarks which, in addition to those embodied in Mr. Besant's suggestive lecture, might without fear of misleading him be addressed to the ingenuous student. I should remind him first of the magnificence of the form that is open to him, which offers to sight so few restrictions and such innumerable opportunities. The other arts, in comparison, appear confined and hampered; the various conditions under which they are exercised are so rigid and definite. But the only condition that I can think of attaching to the composition of the novel is, as I have already said, that it be sincere. This freedom is a splendid privilege, and the first lesson of the young novelist is to learn to be worthy of it.

. . .

"Enjoy it as it deserves [I should say to him]; take possession of it, explore it to its utmost extent, publish it, rejoice in it. All life belongs to you, and do not listen either to those who would shut you up into corners of it and tell you that it is only here and there that art inhabits, or to those who would persuade you that this heavenly messenger wings her way outside of life altogether, breathing a superfine air, and turning away her head from the truth of things. There is no impression of life, no manner of seeing it and feeling it, to which the plan of the novelist may not offer a place; you have only to remember that talents so dissimilar as those of Alexandre Dumas and Jane Austen, Charles Dickens and Gustave Flaubert have worked in this field with equal glory. Do not think too much about optimism and pessimism; try and catch the color of life itself. In France today we see a prodigious effort (that of Émile Zola, to whose solid and serious work no explorer of the capacity of the novel can allude without respect), we see an extraordinary effort vitiated by a spirit of pessimism on a narrow basis. M. Zola is magnificent, but he strikes an English reader as ignorant; he has an air of working in the dark; if he had as much light as energy, his results would be of the highest value. As for the aberrations of a shallow optimism, the ground (of English fiction especially) is strewn with their brittle particles as with broken glass. If you must indulge in conclusions, let them have the taste of a wide knowledge. Remember that your first duty is to be as complete as possible—to make as perfect a work. Be generous and delicate and pursue the prize."

NOTES AND COMMENTS

James agreed with Besant that fiction should be taken seriously and should be true to life; what he opposed was too narrow a concept of "reality." Do you think that once he broadens the definition of reality, his theory of artistic freedom, with its opposition to formulas and rules, follows necessarily? James contended that form and content cannot be considered separately if reality is to be captured by a writer. Why? Do you agree?

James and Freud (in the essay that follows) both discuss the raw material of artistic creation, but their approach and emphasis are different because one is a novelist and the other a scientist. Must the concerns of each inevitably be opposed?

James is interested in understanding character and in reproducing, if not reality, "the air of reality," "the illusion of life." Does this contradict De Quincey's requirement that a serious writer must move his readers? Compare De Quincey's and James's views on the moral function of literature.

James's conception of reality makes the value of a novel depend more on the accuracy of the author's psychological insight than on the events of the story. Does the type of literature he praises ask more of a reader and, accordingly, reward him more? Do most books on current best-seller lists make such demands of a reader, or are they the kind of "happy-ending fiction" which James opposes in this essay?

SIGMUND FREUD

1856-1939

Freud found it fruitful to apply psychoanalytic techniques to the analysis of works of art because he believed that the roots of creativeness lie in the artist's unconscious. Creativity, he felt, is a complex process, demanding deeper explanation than that afforded by the theory that human behavior in any area is a completely conscious matter. By this approach to artistic creation Freud profoundly influenced modern literature and pointed to new directions in criticism. Among his works on the creative process are *Delusions and Dreams in Jensen's "Gradiva," Leonardo Da Vinci,* and *The Moses of Michelangelo.* In the following essay, published in 1908, he seeks to explain the creative powers of imaginative writers.

Creative Writers and Day-Dreaming

WE LAYMEN have always been intensely curious to know—like the Cardinal who put a similar question to Ariosto[1]—from what sources that strange being, the creative writer, draws his material, and how he manages to make such an impression on us with it and to arouse in us emotions of which, perhaps, we had not even thought ourselves capable. Our interest is only heightened the more by the fact that, if we ask him, the writer himself gives us

Reprinted from *Complete Psychological Works,* Vol. 9, by Sigmund Freud. Translated and edited by James Strachey. By permission of The Hogarth Press Ltd., London.
[1] Cardinal Ippolito d'Este was Ariosto's first patron, to whom he dedicated the *Orlando Furioso.* The poet's only reward was the question: "Where did you find so many stories, Lodovico?" [The footnotes for this essay were supplied by the translator.]

no explanation, or none that is satisfactory; and it is not at all weakened by our knowledge that not even the clearest insight into the determinants of his choice of material and into the nature of the art of creating imaginative form will ever help to make creative writers of *us*.

If we could at least discover in ourselves or in people like ourselves an activity which was in some way akin to creative writing! An examination of it would then give us a hope of obtaining the beginnings of an explanation of the creative work of writers. And, indeed, there is some prospect of this being possible. After all, creative writers themselves like to lessen the distance between their kind and the common run of humanity; they so often assure us that every man is a poet at heart and that the last poet will not perish till the last man does.

Should we not look for the first traces of imaginative activity as early as in childhood? The child's best-loved and most intense occupation is with his play or games. Might we not say that every child at play behaves like a creative writer, in that he creates a world of his own, or rather, rearranges the things of his world in a new way which pleases him? It would be wrong to think he does not take that world seriously; on the contrary, he takes his play very seriously and he expends large amounts of emotion on it. The opposite of play is not what is serious but what is real. In spite of all the emotion with which he cathects his world of play, the child distinguishes it quite well from reality; and he likes to link his imagined objects and situations to the tangible and visible things on the real world. This linking is all that differentiates the child's "play" from "phantasying."

The creative writer does the same as the child at play. He creates a world of phantasy which he takes very seriously—that is, which he invests with large amounts of emotion—while separating it sharply from reality. Language has preserved this relationship between children's play and poetic creation. It gives [in German] the name of *"Spiel"* ["play"] to those forms of imaginative writing which require to be linked to tangible objects and which are capable of representation. It speaks of a *"Lustspiel"* or *"Trauerspiel"* ["comedy" or "tragedy": literally, "pleasure play" or "mourning play"] and describes those who carry out the representation as *"Schauspieler"* ["players": literally "show-players"]. The unreality of the writer's imaginative world, however, has very important consequences for the technique of his art; for many things which, if they were real, could give no enjoyment, can do so in the play of phantasy, and many excitements which, in themselves, are actually distressing, can become a source of pleasure for the hearers and spectators at the performance of a writer's work.

There is another consideration for the sake of which we will dwell a moment longer on this contrast between reality and play. When the child has grown up and has ceased to play, and after he has been labouring for decades to envisage the realities of life with proper seriousness, he may one day find himself in a mental situation which once more undoes the contrast between play and reality. As an adult he can look back on the intense seriousness with which he once carried on his games in childhood; and, by equating his ostensibly serious occupations of to-day with his childhood games, he can throw off the too heavy burden imposed on him by life and win the high yield of pleasure afforded by *humour*.

As people grow up, then, they cease to play, and they seem to give up the yield of pleasure which they gained from playing. But whoever understands the human mind knows that hardly anything is harder for a man than to give up a pleasure which he has once experienced. Actually, we can never give anything up; we only exchange one thing for another. What appears to be a renunciation is really the formation of a substitute or surrogate. In the same way, the growing child, when he stops playing, gives up nothing but the link with real objects; instead of *playing*, he now *phantasies*. He builds castles in the air and creates what are called *daydreams*. I believe that most people construct phantasies at times in their lives. This is a fact which has long been overlooked and whose importance has therefore not been sufficiently appreciated.

People's phantasies are less easy to observe than the play of children. The child, it is true, plays by himself or forms a closed psychical system with other children for the purposes of a game; but even though he may not play his game in front of the grownups, he does not, on the other hand, conceal it from them. The adult, on the contrary, is ashamed of his phantasies and hides them from other people. He cherishes his phantasies as his most intimate possessions, and as a rule he would rather confess his misdeeds than tell anyone his phantasies. It may come about that for that reason he believes he is the only person who invents such phantasies and has no idea that creations of this kind are widespread among other people. This difference in the behaviour of a person who plays and a person who phantasies is accounted for by the motives of these two activities, which are nevertheless adjuncts to each other.

A child's play is determined by wishes: in point of fact by a single wish—one that helps in his upbringing—the wish to be big and grown up. He is always playing at being "grown up," and in his games he imitates what he knows about the lives of his elders. He has no reason to conceal this wish. With the adult, the case is different. On the one hand, he knows that he is expected not to go on playing or phantasying any longer, but to act in the real world; on the other hand, some of the wishes which give rise to his phantasies are of a kind which it is essential to conceal. Thus he is ashamed of his phantasies as being childish and as being unpermissible.

But, you will ask, if people make such a mystery of their phantasying, how is it that we know such a lot about it? Well, there is a class of human beings upon whom, not a god, indeed, but a stern goddess—Necessity—has allotted the task of telling what they suffer and what things give them happiness.[1] These are the victims of nervous illness, who are obliged to tell their phantasies, among other things, to the doctor by whom they expect to be cured by mental treatment. This is our best source of knowledge, and we have since found good reason to suppose that our patients tell us nothing that we might not also hear from healthy people.

Let us now make ourselves acquainted with a few of the characteristics of phantasying. We may lay it down that a happy person never phantasies, only an unsatisfied one. The motive forces of phantasies are unsatisfied wishes, and every single phantasy is the fulfilment of a wish, a correlation of unsatisfying reality. These motivating wishes vary according to the sex, character and

---

[1] This is an allusion to some well-known lines spoken by the poet-hero in the final scene of Goethe's *Torquato Tasso*:

Und wenn der Mensch in seiner Qual verstummt,
Gab mir ein Gott, zu sagen, wie ich leide.

"And when mankind is dumb in its torment, a god granted me to tell how I suffer."

circumstances of the person who is having the phantasy; but they fall naturally into two main groups. They are either ambitious wishes, which serve to elevate the subject's personality; or they are erotic ones. In young women the erotic wishes predominate almost exclusively, for their ambition is as a rule absorbed by erotic trends. In young men egoistic and ambitious wishes come to the fore clearly enough alongside of erotic ones. But we will not lay stress on the opposition between the two trends; we would rather emphasize the fact that they are often united. Just as, in many altar-pieces, the portrait of the donor is to be seen in a corner of the picture, so, in the majority of ambitious phantasies, we can discover in some corner or other the lady for whom the creator of the phantasy performs all his heroic deeds and at whose feet all his triumphs are laid. Here, as you see, there are strong enough motives for concealment; the well-brought-up young woman is only allowed a minimum of erotic desire, and the young man has to learn to suppress the excess of self-regard which he brings with him from the spoilt days of his childhood, so that he may find his place in a society which is full of other individuals making equally strong demands.

We must not suppose that the products of this imaginative activity—the various phantasies, castles in the air and day-dreams —are stereotyped or unalterable. On the contrary, they fit themselves in to the subject's shifting impressions of life, change with every change in his situation, and receive from every fresh active impression what might be called a "date-mark." The relation of a phantasy to time is in general very important. We may say that it hovers, as it were, between three times—the three moments of time which our ideation involves. Mental work is linked to some current impression, some provoking occasion in the present which has been able to arouse one of the subject's major wishes. From there it harks back to a memory of an earlier experience (usually an infantile one) in which this wish was fulfilled; and it now creates a situation relating to the future which represents a fulfilment of the wish. What it thus creates is a day-dream or phantasy, which carries about it traces of its origin from the occasion which provoked it and from the memory. Thus past, present and future are strung together, as it were, on the thread of the wish that runs through them.

A very ordinary example may serve to make what I have said

clear. Let us take the case of a poor orphan boy to whom you have given the address of some employer where he may perhaps find a job. On his way there he may indulge in a day-dream appropriate to the situation from which it arises. The content of his phantasy will perhaps be something like this. He is given a job, finds favour with his new employer, makes himself indispensable in the business, is taken into his employer's family, marries the charming young daughter of the house, and then himself becomes a director of the business, first as his employer's partner and then as his successor. In this phantasy, the dreamer has regained what he possessed in his happy childhood—the protecting house, the loving parents and the first objects of his affectionate feelings. You will see from this example the way in which the wish makes use of an occasion in the present to construct, on the pattern of the past, a picture of the future.

There is a great deal more that could be said about phantasies; but I will only allude as briefly as possible to certain points. If phantasies become over-luxuriant and over-powerful, the conditions are laid for an onset of neurosis or psychosis. Phantasies, moreover, are the immediate mental precursors of the distressing symptoms complained of by our patients. Here a broad by-path branches off into pathology.

I cannot pass over the relation of phantasies to dreams. Our dreams at night are nothing else than phantasies like these, as we can demonstrate from the interpretation of dreams. Language, in its unrivalled wisdom, long ago decided the question of the essential nature of dreams by giving the name of "day-dreams" to the airy creations of phantasy. If the meaning of our dreams usually remains obscure to us in spite of this pointer, it is because of the circumstance that at night there also arise in us wishes of which we are ashamed; these we must conceal from ourselves, and they have consequently been repressed, pushed into the unconscious. Repressed wishes of this sort and their derivatives are only allowed to come to expression in a very distorted form. When scientific work had succeeded in elucidating this factor of *dream-distortion*, it was no longer difficult to recognize that night-dreams are wish-fulfilments in just the same way as day-dreams—the phantasies which we all know so well.

So much for phantasies. And now for the creative writer. May we really attempt to compare the imaginative writer with the "dreamer in broad daylight," and his creations with day-dreams? Here we must begin by making an initial distinction. We must separate writers who, like the ancient authors of epics and trage- dies, take over their material ready-made, from writers who seem to originate their own material. We will keep to the latter kind, and, for the purposes of our comparison, we will choose not the writers most highly esteemed by the critics, but the less pretentious authors of novels, romances and short stories, who nevertheless have the widest and most eager circle of readers of both sexes. One feature above all cannot fail to strike us about the creations of these story-writers: each of them has a hero who is the centre of interest, for whom the writer tries to win our sympathy by every possible means and whom he seems to place under the protection of a special Providence. If, at the end of one chapter of my story, I leave the hero unconscious and bleeding from severe wounds, I am sure to find him at the beginning of the next being carefully nursed and on the way to recovery; and if the first volume closes with the ship he is in going down in a storm at sea, I am certain, at the opening of the second volume, to read of his miraculous rescue—a rescue without which the story could not proceed. The feeling of security with which I follow the hero through his peril- ous adventures is the same as the feeling with which a hero in real life throws himself into the water to save a drowning man or ex- poses himself to the enemy's fire in order to storm a battery. It is the true heroic feeling, which one of our best writers has expressed in an inimitable phrase: "Nothing can happen to *me!*" [1] It seems to me, however, that through this revealing characteristic or in- vulnerability we can immediately recognize His Majesty the Ego, the hero alike of every day-dream and of every story.

Other typical features of these egocentric stories point to the same kinship. The fact that all the women in the novel invariably fall in love with the hero can hardly be looked on as a portrayal of reality, but it is easily understood as a necessary constituent of a day-dream. The same is true of the fact that the other characters in the story are sharply divided into good and bad, in defiance of the variety of human characters that are to be observed in real life. The "good" ones are the helpers, while the "bad" ones are the

---

[1] *"Es kann mir nix g'schehen!"* This phrase from Anzengruber, the Viennese dramatist, was a favourite one of Freud's.

enemies and rivals, of the ego which has become the hero of the story.

We are perfectly aware that very many imaginative writings are far removed from the model of the naïve day-dream; and yet I cannot suppress the suspicion that even the most extreme deviations from that model could be linked with it through an uninterrupted series of transitional cases. It has struck me that in many of what are known as "psychological" novels only one person—once again the hero—is described from within. The author sits inside his mind, as it were, and looks at the other characters from outside. The psychological novel in general no doubt owes its special nature to the inclination of the modern writer to split up his ego, by self-observation, into many part-egos, and, in consequence, to personify the conflicting currents of his own mental life in several heroes. Certain novels, which might be described as "eccentric," seem to stand in quite special contrast to the type of the day-dream. In these, the person who is introduced as the hero plays only a very small active part; he sees the actions and sufferings of other people pass before him like a spectator. Many of Zola's later works belong to this category. But I must point out that the psychological analysis of individuals who are not creative writers, and who diverge in some respects from the so-called norm, has shown us analogous variations of the day-dream, in which the ego contents itself with the role of spectator.

If our comparison of the imaginative writer with the day-dreamer, and of poetical creation with the day-dream, is to be of any value, it must, above all, show itself in some way or other fruitful. Let us, for instance, try to apply to these authors' works the thesis we laid down earlier concerning the relation between phantasy and the three periods of time and the wish which runs through them; and, with its help, let us try to study the connections that exist between the life of the writer and his works. No one has known, as a rule, what expectations to frame in approaching this problem; and often the connection has been thought of in much too simple terms. In the light of the insight we have gained from phantasies, we ought to expect the following state of affairs. A strong experience in the present awakens in the creative writer a memory of an earlier experience (usually belonging to his childhood) from which there now proceeds a wish which finds its ful-

filment in the creative work. The work itself exhibits elements of
the recent provoking occasion as well as of the old memory.

Do not be alarmed at the complexity of this formula. I suspect
that in fact it will prove to be too exiguous a pattern. Nevertheless,
it may contain a first approach to the true state of affairs; and,
from some experiments I have made, I am inclined to think that
this way of looking at creative writings may turn out not unfruitful.
You will not forget that the stress it lays on childhood memories
in the writer's life—a stress which may perhaps seem puzzling—
is ultimately derived from the assumption that a piece of creative
writing, like a day-dream, is a continuation of, and a substitute for,
what was once the play of childhood.

We must not neglect, however, to go back to the kind of
imaginative works which we have to recognize, not as original
creations, but as the refashioning of ready-made and familiar material. Even here, the writer keeps a certain amount of independence, which can express itself in the choice of material and in
changes in it which are often quite extensive. In so far as the material is already at hand, however, it is derived from the popular
treasure-house of myths, legends and fairy tales. The study of con-
structions of folk-psychology such as these is far from being complete, but it is extremely probable that myths, for instance, are
distorted vestiges of the wishful phantasies of whole nations, the
secular dreams of youthful humanity.

You will say that, although I have put the creative writer first
in the title of my paper, I have told you far less about him than
about phantasies. I am aware of that, and I must try to excuse it
by pointing to the present state of our knowledge. All I have been
able to do is to throw out some encouragements and suggestions
which, starting from a study of phantasies, lead on to the problem
of the writer's choice of his literary material. As for the other
problem—by what means the creative writer achieves the emotional effects in us that are aroused by his creations—we have as
yet not touched on it at all. But I should like at least to point out
to you the path that leads from our discussion of phantasies to the
problems of poetical effects.

You will remember how I have said that the day-dreamer carefully conceals his phantasies from other people because he feels he
has reasons for being ashamed of them. I should now add that
even if he were to communicate them to us he could give us no

pleasure by his disclosures. Such phantasies, when we learn them, repel us or at least leave us cold. But when a creative writer presents his plays to us or tells us what we are inclined to take to be his personal day-dreams, we experience a great pleasure, and one which probably arises from the confluence of many sources. How the writer accomplishes this is his innermost secret; the essential *ars poetica* lies in the technique of overcoming the feeling of repulsion in us which is undoubtedly connected with the barriers that rise between each single ego and the others. We can guess two of the methods used by this technique. The writer softens the character of his egoistic day-dreams by altering and disguising it, and he bribes us by the purely formal—that is, aesthetic—yield of pleasure which he offers us in the presentation of his phantasies. We give the name of an *incentive bonus,* or a *fore-pleasure,* to a yield of pleasure such as this, which is offered to us so as to make possible the release of still greater pleasure arising from deeper psychical sources. In my opinion, all the aesthetic pleasure which a creative writer affords us has the character of a fore-pleasure of this kind, and our actual enjoyment of an imaginative work proceeds from a liberation of tensions in our minds. It may even be that not a little of this effect is due to the writer's enabling us thenceforward to enjoy our own day-dreams without self-reproach or shame. This brings us to the threshold of new, interesting and complicated enquiries; but also, at least for the moment, to the end of our discussion.

NOTES AND COMMENTS

It is important to recognize that in this essay Freud does not try to explain what creativity is or why a particular writer possesses it. He points out only that a writer applies his creative talent to the same raw materials we are all familiar with in childhood play and adult day-dreaming. He does suggest, however, that talent is what enables an artist to please us with a communication that might otherwise be unpalatable. De Quincey means the same thing, perhaps, when he claims that literature moves us. Would Freud agree with De Quincey that literature has a moral purpose?

Freud cites examples of "popular literature" to prove his point. Why would Henry James find his references to this type of literature distasteful? Freud also describes the communication between artist and reader. Does the relationship between the modern poet and the average citizen, as described by Ciardi, make this kind of communication impossible?

Freud comes very close to explaining why great works of art continue to live in ages and places remote from those in which they were created: to the extent that the artist deals with common human experiences he is striking chords which any person can respond to, despite differences of time, place, and circumstance. This is what is meant by "universality" in a work of art.

HENRI BERGSON

1859-1941

Henri Bergson, the immensely influential French philosopher, was an apostle of intuition and vitalism. To the rationalism of scientific thinkers of his day Bergson opposed the idea that we know really important things not through reason but through intuition, the meeting ground of reason, imagination, and emotion. In *Creative Evolution* he developed the notion of *élan vital*, his term for that quality which differentiates the living from the non-living: the living possesses a "vital impulse" (*élan vital*), precious in itself and unalterably opposed to the mechanical.

In *Laughter* Bergson discusses the comic spirit in terms of this central philosophic thesis. Laughter is a corrective for rigidity, a means of protecting the *élan vital* from whatever may reduce it to automatism.

FROM *Laughter*

WHAT DOES laughter mean? What is the basal element in the laughable? What common ground can we find between the grimace of a merry-andrew, a play upon words, an equivocal situation in a burlesque and a scene of high comedy? What method of distillation will yield us invariably the same essence from which so many different products borrow either their obtrusive odour or their delicate perfume? The greatest of thinkers, from Aristotle downwards, have tackled this little problem, which has a knack of baffling every effort, of slipping away and escaping only to bob up again, a pert challenge flung at philosophic speculation.

Our excuse for attacking the problem in our turn must lie in the fact that we shall not aim at imprisoning the comic spirit within a definition. We regard it, above all, as a living thing. However trivial it may be, we shall treat it with the respect due to life. We shall confine ourselves to watching it grow and expand. Passing by imperceptible gradations from one form to another, it will be seen to achieve the strangest metamorphoses. We shall disdain nothing we have seen. Maybe we may gain from this prolonged contact, for the matter of that, something more flexible than an abstract definition,—a practical, intimate acquaintance, such as springs from a long companionship. And maybe we may also find that, unintentionally, we have made an acquaintance that is useful. For the comic spirit has a logic of its own, even in its wildest eccentricities. It has a method in its madness. It dreams, I admit, but it conjures up in its dreams visions that are at once accepted and understood by the whole of a social group. Can it then fail to throw light for us on the way that human imagination works, and more particularly social, collective, and popular imagination? Begotten of real life and akin to art, should it not also have something of its own to tell us about art and life?

At the outset we shall put forward three observations which we look upon as fundamental. They have less bearing on the actually comic than on the field within which it must be sought.

1. The first point to which attention should be called is that the comic does not exist outside the pale of what is strictly *human*. A landscape may be beautiful, charming and sublime, or insignificant and ugly; it will never be laughable. You may laugh at an animal, but only because you have detected in it some human attitude or expression. You may laugh at a hat, but what you are making fun of, in this case, is not the piece of felt or straw, but the shape that men have given it,—the human caprice whose mould it has assumed. It is strange that so important a fact, and such a simple one too, has not attracted to a greater degree the attention of philosophers. Several have defined man as "an animal which laughs." They might equally well have defined him as an animal which is laughed at; for if any other animal, or some lifeless object, produces the same effect, it is always because of some resemblance to man, of the stamp he gives it or the use he puts it to.

Here I would point out, as a symptom equally worthy of notice, the *absence of feeling* which usually accompanies laughter. It seems as though the comic could not produce its disturbing effect unless it fell, so to say, on the surface of a soul that is thoroughly calm and unruffled. Indifference is its natural environment, for laughter has no greater foe than emotion. I do not mean that we could not laugh at a person who inspires us with pity, for instance, or even with affection, but in such a case we must, for the moment, put our affection out of court and impose silence upon our pity. In a society composed of pure intelligences there would probably be no more tears, though perhaps there would still be laughter; whereas highly emotional souls, in tune and unison with life, in whom every event would be sentimentally prolonged and re-echoed, would neither know nor understand laughter. Try, for a moment, to become interested in everything that is being said and done; act, in imagination, with those who act, and feel with those who feel; in a word, give your sympathy its widest expansion: as though at the touch of a fairy wand you will see the flimsiest of objects assume importance, and a gloomy hue spread over everything. Now step aside, look upon life as a disinterested spectator: many a drama will turn into a comedy. It is enough for us to stop our ears to the sound of music in a room, where dancing is going on, for the dancers at once to appear ridiculous. How many human actions would stand a similar test? Should we not see many of them suddenly pass from grave to gay, on isolating them from the accompanying music of sentiment? To produce the whole of its effect, then, the comic demands something like a momentary anesthesia of the heart. Its appeal is to intelligence, pure and simple.

This intelligence, however, must always remain in touch with other intelligences. And here is the third fact to which attention should be drawn. You would hardly appreciate the comic if you felt yourself isolated from others. Laughter appears to stand in need of an echo. Listen to it carefully: it is not an articulate, clear, well-defined sound; it is something which would fain be prolonged by reverberating from one to another, something beginning with a crash, to continue in successive rumblings, like thunder in a mountain. Still, this reverberation cannot go on for ever. It can travel within as wide a circle as you please: the circle remains, none the less, a closed one. Our laughter is always the laughter of a group. It may, perchance, have happened to you, when seated in a railway carriage or at *table d'hôte*, to hear travellers relating to one another stories which must have been comic to them, for they laughed heartily. Had you been one of their company, you would have laughed like them, but, as you were not, you had no desire whatever to do so. A man who was once asked why he did not weep at a sermon when everybody else was shedding tears replied: "I don't belong to the parish!" What that man thought of tears would be still more true of laughter. However spontaneous it seems, laughter always implies a kind of secret freemasonry, or even complicity, with other laughers, real or imaginary. How often has it been said that the fuller the theatre, the more uncontrolled the laughter of the audience! On the other hand, how often has the remark been made that many comic effects are incapable of translation from one language to another, because they refer to the customs and ideas of a particular social group! It is through not understanding the importance of this double fact that the comic has been looked upon as a mere curiosity in which the mind finds amusement, and laughter itself as a strange, isolated phenomenon, without any bearing on the rest of human activity. Hence those definitions which tend to make the comic into an abstract relation between ideas: "an intellectual contrast," "a patent absurdity," etc., definitions which, even were they really suitable to every form of the comic, would not in the least explain why the comic makes us laugh. How, indeed, should it come about that this particular logical relation, as soon as it is perceived, contracts, expands and shakes our limbs, whilst all other relations leave the body unaffected? It is not from this point of view that we shall approach the problem. To understand laughter, we must put it back into its natural environment, which is society, and above all must we determine the utility of its function, which is a social one. Such, let us say at once, will be the leading idea of all our investigations. Laughter must answer to certain requirements of life in common. It must have a *social* signification.

Let us clearly mark the point towards which our three preliminary observations are converging. The comic will come into being, it appears, whenever a group of men concentrate their attention on one of their number, imposing silence on their emotions and calling into play nothing but their intelligence. What, now, is the particular point on which their attention will have to be concentrated, and what will here be the function of intelligence? To reply to these questions will be at once to come to closer grips with the problem. But here a few examples have become indispensable.

2. A man, running along the street, stumbles and falls; the passers-by burst out laughing. They would not laugh at him, I imagine, could they suppose that the whim had suddenly seized him to sit down on the ground. They laugh because his sitting down is involuntary. Consequently, it is not his sudden change of attitude that raises a laugh, but rather the involuntary element in this change,—his clumsiness, in fact. Perhaps there was a stone on the road. He should have altered his pace or avoided the obstacle. Instead of that, through lack of elasticity, through absentmindedness and a kind of physical obstinacy, *as a result, in fact, of rigidity or of momentum*, the muscles continued to perform the same movement when the circumstances of the case called for something else. That is the reason of the man's fall, and also of the people's laughter.

Now, take the case of a person who attends to the petty occupations of his everyday life with mathematical precision. The objects around him, however, have all been tampered with by a mischievous wag, the result being that when he dips his pen into the inkstand he draws it out all covered with mud, when he fancies he is sitting down on a solid chair he finds himself sprawling on the floor, in a word his actions are all topsy-turvy or mere beating the air, while in every case the effect is invariably one of momentum. Habit has given the impulse: what was wanted was to check the movement or deflect it. He did nothing of the sort, but continued like a machine in the same straight line. The victim, then, of a practical joke is in a position similar to that of a runner who falls,—he is comic for the same reason. The laughable element in both cases consists of a certain *mechanical inelasticity*, just where one would expect to find the wideawake adaptability and the living pliableness of a human being. The only difference in the two cases is that the former happened of itself, whilst the latter was obtained artificially. In the first instance, the passer-by does nothing but look on, but in the second the mischievous wag intervenes.

All the same, in both cases the result has been brought about by an external circumstance. The comic is therefore accidental: it remains, so to speak, in superficial contact with the person. How is it to penetrate within? The necessary conditions will be fulfilled when mechanical rigidity no longer requires for its manifestation a stumbling-block which either the hazard of circumstance or human knavery has set in its way, but extracts by natural processes, from its own store, an inexhaustible series of opportunities for externally revealing its presence. Suppose, then, we imagine a mind always thinking of what it has just done and never of what it is doing, like a song which lags behind its accompaniment. Let us try to picture to ourselves a certain inborn lack of elasticity of both senses and intelligence, which brings it to pass that we continue to see what is no longer visible, to hear what is no longer audible, to say what is no longer to the point: in short, to adapt ourselves to a past and therefore imaginary situation, when we ought to be shaping our conduct in accordance with the reality which is present. This time the comic will take up its abode in the person himself; it is the person who will supply it with everything—matter and form, cause and opportunity. Is it then surprising that the absent-minded individual—for this is the character we have just been describing—has usually fired the imagination of comic authors? When La Bruyère came across this particular type, he realised, on analysing it, that he had got hold of a recipe for the wholesale manufacture of comic effects. As a matter of fact he overdid it, and gave us far too lengthy and detailed a description of *Ménalque*, coming back to his subject, dwelling and expatiating on it beyond all bounds.[1] The very facility of the subject fascinated him. Absentmindedness, indeed, is not perhaps the actual fountain-head of the comic, but surely it is contiguous to a certain stream of facts and fancies which flows straight from the fountain-head. It is situated, so to say, on one of the great natural watersheds of laughter.

Now, the effect of absentmindedness may gather strength in its turn. There is a general law, the first example of which we have just encountered, and which we will formulate in the following terms: when a certain comic effect has its origin in a certain cause, the more natural we regard the cause to be, the more comic shall we find the effect. Even now we laugh at absentmindedness when presented to us as a simple fact. Still more laughable will be the absentmindedness we have seen springing up and growing before our very eyes, with whose origin we are acquainted and whose life-history we can reconstruct. To choose a definite example: suppose a man has taken to reading nothing but romances of love and

---

[1 Jean de La Bruyère (1645-1696), in his *Characters*, an incisive commentary on the society of his time, presented a series of portraits of people—often real people thinly disguised—who exemplified various traits of character he discussed. Ménalque was one of these characters.—*Ed.*]

chivalry. Attracted and fascinated by his heroes, his thoughts and intentions gradually turn more and more towards them, till one fine day we find him walking among us like a somnambulist. His actions are distractions. But then his distractions can be traced back to a definite, positive cause. They are no longer cases of *absence* of mind, pure and simple; they find their explanation in the *presence* of the individual in quite definite, though imaginary, surroundings. Doubtless a fall is always a fall, but it is one thing to tumble into a well because you were looking anywhere but in front of you, it is quite another thing to fall into it because you were intent upon a star. It was certainly a star at which Don Quixote was gazing. How profound is the comic element in the over-romantic, Utopian bent of mind! And yet, if you reintroduce the idea of absentmindedness, which acts as a go-between you will see this profound comic element uniting with the most superficial type. Yes, indeed, these whimsical wild enthusiasts, these madmen who are yet so strangely reasonable, excite us to laughter by playing on the same chords within ourselves, by setting in motion the same inner mechanism, as does the victim of a practical joke or the passer-by who slips down in the street. They, too, are runners who fall and simple souls who are being hoaxed—runners after the ideal who stumble over realities, child-like dreamers for whom life delights to lie in wait. But, above all, they are past-masters in absentmindedness, with this superiority over their fellows that their absentmindedness is systematic and organised around one central idea, and that their mishaps are also quite coherent, thanks to the inexorable logic which reality applies to the correction of dreams, so that they kindle in those around them, by a series of cumulative effects, a hilarity capable of unlimited expansion.

Now, let us go a little further. Might not certain vices have the same relation to character that the rigidity of a fixed idea has to intellect? Whether as a moral kink or a crooked twist given to the will, vice has often the appearance of a curvature of the soul. Doubtless there are vices into which the soul plunges deeply with all its pregnant potency, which it rejuvenates and drags along with it into a moving circle of reincarnations. Those are tragic vices. But the vice capable of making us comic is, on the contrary, that which is brought from without, like a ready-made frame into which we are to step. It lends us its own rigidity instead of borrowing from us our flexibility. We do not render it more complicated; on the contrary, it simplifies us. Here . . . lies the essential difference between comedy and drama. A drama, even when portraying passions or vices that bear a name, so completely incorporates them in the person that their names are forgotten, their general characteristics effaced, and we no longer think of them at all, but rather of the person in whom they are assimilated; hence, the title of a drama can seldom be anything else than a proper noun. On the other hand, many comedies have a common noun as their title: *l'Avare, le Joueur*,[1] etc. Were you asked to think of a play capable of being called *le Jaloux*, for instance, you would find that *Sganarelle* or *George Dandin*[2] would occur to your mind, but not *Othello: le Jaloux* could only be the title of a comedy. The reason is that, however intimately vice, when comic, is associated with persons, it none the less retains its simple, independent existence, it remains the central character, present though invisible, to which the characters in flesh and blood on the stage are attached. At times it delights in dragging them down with its own weight and making them share in its tumbles. More frequently, however, it plays on them as on an instrument or pulls the strings as though they were puppets. Look closely: you will find that the art of the comic poet consists in making us so well acquainted with the particular vice, in introducing us, the spectators, to such a degree of intimacy with it, that in the end we get hold of some of the strings of the marionette with which he is playing, and actually work them ourselves; this it is that explains part of the pleasure we feel. Here, too, it is really a kind of automatism that makes us laugh—an automatism, as we have already remarked, closely akin to mere absentmindedness. To realise this more fully, it need only be noted that a comic character is generally comic in proportion to his ignorance of himself. The comic person is unconscious. As though wearing the ring of Gyges with reverse effect, he becomes invisible to himself while remaining visible to all the world. A character in a tragedy will make no change in his conduct because he will know how it is judged by us; he may continue therein even though fully conscious of what he is and feeling keenly the horror he inspires in us. But a defect that is ridiculous, as soon as it feels itself to be so, endeavours to modify itself or at least to appear as though it did.

[1] *L'Avare* (*The Miser*), by Molière, and *Le Joueur* (*The Gambler*), by Jean-François Regnard: both seventeenth-century French comedies.—Ed.]
[2] Comedies by Molière.—Ed.]

Were Harpagon[1] to see us laugh at his miserliness, I do not say that he would get rid of it, but he would either show it less or show it differently. Indeed, it is in this sense only that laughter "corrects men's manners." It makes us at once endeavour to appear what we ought to be, what some day we shall perhaps end in being.

It is unnecessary to carry this analysis any further. From the runner who falls to the simpleton who is hoaxed, from a state of being hoaxed to one of absentmindedness, from absentmindedness to wild enthusiasm, from wild enthusiasm to various distortions of character and will, we have followed the line of progress along which the comic becomes more and more deeply imbedded in the person, yet without ceasing, in its subtler manifestations, to recall to us some trace of what we noticed in its grosser forms, an effect of automatism and of inelasticity. Now we can obtain a first glimpse—a distant one, it is true, and still hazy and confused—of the laughable side of human nature and of the ordinary function of laughter.

What life and society require of each of us is a constantly alert attention that discerns the outlines of the present situation, together with a certain elasticity of mind and body to enable us to adapt ourselves in consequence. *Tension* and *elasticity* are two forces, mutually complementary, which life brings into play. If these two forces are lacking in the body to any considerable extent, we have sickness and infirmity and accidents of every kind. If they are lacking in the mind, we find every degree of mental deficiency, every variety of insanity. Finally, if they are lacking in the character, we have cases of the gravest inadaptability to social life, which are the sources of misery and at times the causes of crime. Once these elements of inferiority that affect the serious side of existence are removed—and they tend to eliminate themselves in what has been called the struggle for life—the person can live, and that in common with other persons. But society asks for something more; it is not satisfied with simply living, it insists on living well. What it now has to dread is that each one of us, content with paying attention to what affects the essentials of life, will, so far as the rest is concerned, give way to the easy automatism of acquired habits. Another thing it must fear is that the members of whom it is made up, instead of aiming after an increasingly delicate ad-

---

[1 The principal character of Molière's *L'Avare.—Ed.*]

justment of wills which will fit more and more perfectly into one another, will confine themselves to respecting simply the fundamental conditions of this adjustment: a cut-and-dried agreement among the persons will not satisfy it, it insists on a constant striving after reciprocal adaptation. Society will therefore be suspicious of all *inelasticity* of character, of mind and even of body, because it is the possible sign of a slumbering activity as well as of an activity with separatist tendencies, that inclines to swerve from the common centre round which society gravitates: in short, because it is the sign of an eccentricity. And yet, society cannot intervene at this stage by material repression, since it is not affected in a material fashion. It is confronted with something that makes it uneasy, but only as a symptom—scarcely a threat, at the very most a gesture. A gesture, therefore, will be its reply. Laughter must be something of this kind, a sort of *social gesture*. By the fear which it inspires, it restrains eccentricity, keeps constantly awake and in mutual contact certain activities of a secondary order which might retire into their shell and go to sleep, and in short, softens down whatever the surface of the social body may retain of mechanical inelasticity. Laughter, then, does not belong to the province of esthetics alone, since unconsciously (and even immorally in many particular instances) it pursues a utilitarian air of general improvement. And yet there is something esthetic about it, since the comic comes into being just when society and the individual, freed from the worry of self-preservation, begin to regard themselves as works of art. In a word, if a circle be drawn round those actions and dispositions—implied in individual or social life—to which their natural consequences bring their own penalties, there remains outside this sphere of emotion and struggle—and within a neutral zone in which man simply exposes himself to man's curiosity—a certain rigidity of body, mind and character that society would still like to get rid of in order to obtain from its members the greatest possible degree of elasticity and sociability. This rigidity is the comic, and laughter is its corrective.

NOTES AND COMMENTS

Bergson's analysis of the core of the comic rests on three assumptions: Only the human is laughable. Laughter demands a "momentary anesthesia of the heart." Laughter has social significance.

Most readers would probably agree with the first of these premises. The second, however, is not so obviously valid. Laughter is related to intelligence rather than to emotion, but does this mean, as Bergson says it does, that we cannot simultaneously feel for and laugh at the same object? (Consider, for example, your reaction to a comedian like Chaplin, or to a fictional character like Huckleberry Finn.)

Bergson's third premise—the social function of comedy—is related to his central point: that the comic stems from and acts as a corrective for rigidity in what should be alive and flexible. The inflexibility that shows itself as absent-mindedness, according to Bergson, is a classic source of the comic; and there are, of course, a multitude of other stock figures and stock situations. Try testing Bergson's thesis by applying it to the characters and situations exploited, in one way or another, by well-known comedians before the public today.

BERNARD GREBANIER

1903-

Among the writings of Bernard Grebanier, Professor of English Literature at Brooklyn College, are two lively books on Shakespearean plays: *The Heart of Hamlet* and *The Truth About Shylock*. Both challenge what Grebanier feels are mistaken notions that critics, actors, and the general public have come to hold about *Hamlet* and *The Merchant of Venice*. The following essay, taken from *The Heart of Hamlet*, is a general discussion of the nature of tragedy.

Melpomene: the Nature of Tragedy

A DISTASTE FOR all tragedy is sufficiently common among the vulgar. "Life is depressing enough," runs the platitude; "why go to the theater to be reminded of the fact? Give us Abbott and Costello or the Marx Brothers." Yet people of some sensitivity, while not necessarily eschewing low comedy, do find gratification in tragedy. They do not go to it to be depressed—that would be an idiotic exercise for anyone!—but because they find themselves, at the end of a good tragedy, emerging from the theater in a mood of chastened exaltation, a mood which makes life seem not less sad but more understandable and easier to bear—a mood which would be very difficult to define, had not Aristotle already so perfectly defined it.

Now, it is not implied that one who is enthralled by *Oedipus Tyrannus* could not delight in the antics of the Brothers Marx.

Reprinted from *The Heart of Hamlet* by Bernard Grebanier, by permission of Thomas Y. Crowell Company.

The demands of the human spirit are—luckily for the arts!—extensive. No one who willingly suffers with Lear will therefore the less enjoy roaring at Falstaff's ribaldry another day. There is nothing anomalous in a man's being elevated by *Parsifal* on Good Friday and anticipating eagerly a performance of *The Bartered Bride* a week later.[1] It is precisely because the tragic summons into play the most exalted capacities of the human spirit that it has been traditionally approached in a holy-day disposition.

We rightfully expect, the point is, from each of the multitudinous experiences available to us, the reward uniquely pertaining to it. The pleasures of a cool swim on a hot day defy analogy with the pleasures of a tennis match; those of champagne with those of a planked steak. We do not seek from painting what we receive from music. We no more expect to procure from Leonardo what we receive from Rubens than we expect to procure from the *Mass in B Minor* what we receive from *The Marriage of Figaro*.

If as a result of its peculiar resources no one of the arts can deliver the same meanings and comforts as another, and if because of the inevitable circumscriptions imposed by subject and technique no two works in the same art (or by the same artist) can convey identical meanings, it is none the less true that the comic spirit and the tragic spirit have each its own qualifications, and these cut across the limits of the various arts. Plainly, there were affinities of purpose in the creation of *Much Ado About Nothing*, the Overture to *The Barber of Seville*, the *Would-Be Gentleman*, certain paintings of Hogarth and Breughel and Teniers, *Vanity Fair*, some of Beethoven's *Scherzi*, and *The Importance of Being*

---

[1] Thus (*Patience*):

> "DUKE. Tell me, Major, are you fond of toffee?
> MAJOR. Very!
> COLONEL. We are all fond of toffee.
> ALL (the Dragoons). We are!
> DUKE. Yes, and toffee in moderation is a capital thing. But to *live* on toffee—toffee for breakfast, toffee for dinner, toffee for tea—to have it supposed that you care for nothing *but* toffee, and that you would consider yourself insulted if anything but toffee were offered to you—how would you like that?
> COLONEL. I can quite believe that under those circumstances, even toffee would become monotonous."
>
> [W. S. Gilbert, *Patience*, I]

For "toffee," read tragedy, melodrama, satire, comedy (high or low) or farce.

Earnest. The affinities are perhaps even stronger in *King Lear*, Beethoven's *Eroica*, *Paradise Lost*, the paintings on the ceiling of the Sistine Chapel, Miss Cather's *A Lost Lady*, and the *Saint Matthew Passion*.

That is, we anticipate from the tragic, whatever the art or particular work, a characteristic response. If we miss this response, we have been cheated of our due. Dreiser could call his novel *An American Tragedy*, Mr. Miller could present *Death of a Salesman* as a new kind of tragedy, Mr. Inge's *Come Back, Little Sheba* may have been hailed as a stirring tragedy—but moving though they may be, sincere as they unquestionably are, saddening or depressing as they have been found, tragedies they are not. For they do not fulfill the high function of tragedy, which, as Aristotle understood, is to provide for us "through pity and fear" the "proper purgation of these emotions."

It is to be hoped that no one will deem it stranger that Aristotle, because he lived twenty-three hundred years ago, could have precisely stated for all times[1] the purpose of tragedy than that Archimedes should not much later have discovered, as the world acknowledges he did discover, the fundamentals of hydromechanics on the famous occasion when he took a bath. Indeed, there is nothing at all odd in the fact that an "ancient" Greek should have understood the function of tragedy, when we remember how vital a part of civic life the witnessing of tragedy was to an Athenian.

Aristotle lived in an era peculiarly favorable, even for a man of his extraordinary sagacity, for the statement of eternal principles concerning tragedy. He was not in the position of that notorious German savant who wrote a disquisition on the elephant.[2] He did

---

[1] One must defend oneself against the contemporary tendency to consider everything written before 1950 outdated. One is no longer astonished to find a pair of critics say of a masterful story and its author that he "died in 1928 but this story . . . is as vital as when it was written" [J. Greene and E. Abell, *Stories of Sudden Truth* (New York, 1953), p. 80]. This in 1953! Accelerate this tempo a little and a man may expect his literary reputation "may outlive his life half a year."

[2] Though it can hardly be possible, there may be some fortunate who has not heard one of the many versions of this celebrated tale. If so, it seems only fair to deprive him herewith of that felicity: A number of eminent representatives of various cultures were asked to write a treatise on the elephant. The Englishman bade his man pack his traps, went off to Africa, lived with the elephant and hunted him; after six months he returned to England and wrote a book entitled *Elephant-Hunting in Africa*. The Frenchman went to

not have to evolve the principles of tragedy or decide out of hand what they ought to be. He lived in the age immediately following the enormous dramatic productivity that had begun with Aeschylus and continued with Sophocles, Euripides, and their contemporaries, who had been providing the Athenian citizens with their yearly experience of spiritual purgation. All he had to do, therefore, was to ask himself: what are the basic attributes of tragedy as exhibited in the works of these masters? What, despite the wide differences of their approaches to tragedy, had they all understood tragedy to be? Aristotle had only, thus, to deduce from many masterworks (the vast majority of which have been lost to us) just what is the *sine qua non* of tragedy—and that he managed to perfection.

To begin with, Aristotle implies quite plainly what constituted the role of tragedy in the life of the Athenian citizen. Tragedy had had a long and important history as a rite connected with the worship of the god Dionysus; by the time of the Golden Age in Athens, when the plays of Aeschylus and Sophocles were presented in the Theater of Dionysus, and tragedy, as Aristotle says, had found at last its "natural form," its function was both religious and medicinal. It would be fair to say that the ceremony of attending the tragedies in Athens during the festival of Dionysus was the religious equivalent of the Hebraic-Christian practice of fasting on the Day of Atonement or during Lent. The citizenry of Athens came to the theater on those days to achieve *katharsis*, purgation. The Athenian way of achieving spiritual cleansing was, of course, basically opposed to the Hebraic-Christian. The latter involves self-condemnation, the acknowledgment of personal sin, the beating of the evil back into the breast; the Greek, letting the sin flow out of one's system, the getting rid of the evil by affording it a channel through which to depart. (It is difficult to refrain from the conviction that psychiatrists might have starved from lack of patients in those days!)

Doubtless in more primitive times this purgation was achieved through the unlimited license then endorsed during the Dionysian

the *Bibliothèque Nationale*, where he spent two industrious years, after which he published a two-volume work, *bien documentée*, entitled *L'Éléphant et Ses Amours*. The Jew, naturally, wrote a treatise on *The Elephant and Zionism*. The German simply went home, asked his *frau* to make him a huge pot of black coffee, sat at the dining-room table, and there, the story concludes, *out of his inner consciousness* he evolved an elephant.

revels. But by the time of Aeschylus such merely animal methods were no longer adequate, and tragedy provided the perfect vehicle for the rite of *katharsis*. Then the Athenian went to the theater to participate in the tragic deed of some noble hero or heroine (tragedy rises above even the difference of sex); as he watched and hearkened he *became* Oedipus or Clytemnestra or Creon or Electra or Eteocles—he suffered with each, he experienced heroic passions, he fell spiritually as each hero or heroine fell—yet he remained safe in body and secure from guilt in soul. He became blind vicariously with Oedipus, but still had his own eyes; he helped direct Orestes' sword with Electra but himself rested innocent of the worst of all crimes, a mother's murder.[1]

And such must always be the function of tragedy. We all accumulate poisons from the inescapable frustrations of daily living; our disasters are wont (and for this we might offer thanks) to be only petty and mean; we are not allotted the scope for expending

---

[1] If the modern skeptic finds it difficult to accept the possibility of a whole population's being as aesthetic-minded as we here imply, let him recall the incomparable architecture, the hundreds of great tragedies and sculptures produced under the patronage of these people. Let him remember that it was Aeschylus, the sublimest poet among the tragedians, and Sophocles, the sublimest dramatist, to whom this populace with its applause most often awarded the coveted prize. There is no way of accounting for it, but despite our own empirical knowledge of the shabbiness of popular taste, we cannot deny that in that age the Athenians were an astonishing people. (Though still among the most charming people in the world, one can no longer say the same for their taste. Paying lip-reverence to their classical culture, they are now much more interested in their dull Byzantine past. As for their apprehension of beauty—! One will find the Acropolis fairly clear of Greeks on most days; they are busy trotting visitors off to see and admire an atrocity decorating the grave of a maiden buried in their Cemetery Number One, the work of a modern sculptor, depicting the lady lying near death on her couch, the folds of the sheet being so realistic that they seem actually to have been used a week! Around this horror crowds are always to be seen gaping in astounded delight.) The story of Sophocles' trial could have been true nowhere else and in no other era. The ninety-year-old dramatist was sued by his son, in an attempt to break Sophocles' will in favor of his illegitimate son's family, on a charge of his being mentally incompetent. In answer, the great old man simply read in court a passage from the masterpiece on which he was then engaged, *Oedipus at Colonus*, the tribute to Colonus, his native town. The court was so much moved by the magnificence of the poetry that the case was dismissed at once, and Sophocles carried home in honor to his dwelling. Where else could this have happened but in the Athens of his day?

Public taste, of course, has not at all times been at low ebb. It is well to remember that with the Elizabethan butcher, baker, and candlestick-maker, Shakespeare was the most popular playwright of the day.

ourselves on noble issues; we do not experience grand catastrophes, and thus venoms overflow within us and quench the inner light. We come, then, to tragedy for purgation from our spiritual ills. By participating in a noble tragedy such as our life does not afford, but Hamlet or Lear or Oedipus do enact, we come away chastened and cleansed, better prepared to take up the burdens of the day.

To speak in this manner is to speak of the social import of literature with validity. In truth, it is only when the arts fulfill their aesthetic obligations that they *can* be socially useful. We once knew a cellist, member of a string quartet, who professed despair, as was fashionable in the late 'thirties, over his inability to coordinate his "social conscience" with his music. How, for instance, was he to make a *Razoumovsky Quartet* contributory to social progress? When we were beginning to tire of these impasses of his and of his masochistic cries of *mea culpa*, we were struck with the perfect solution for his dilemma—though he considered it merely flippant. "If you really want to help the progress of humanity," we offered, "why don't you learn to play the cello better than you do?"

There has been much nonsense written in the twentieth century by critics who have given their economic, sociological, psychoanalytical—and most absurd of all—"Marxist" interpretations of the arts. What they have had to say may or may not be a contribution to economics, sociology, psychoanalysis, or history— but it is worse than irrelevant to the arts, worse even than merely vulgar. Worse, for it has been responsible for innumerable acts of mayhem against the arts and artists alike. Aesthetically-minded people are more, not less, sensitive to calls upon their conscience from the sufferings of humanity. It is easy to distract them from the creative fields in which they labor, with the reproof: "Is this a time to be concerned with such irrelevance as beauty?" That is a question which might just as appropriately have been asked of Dante, Watteau, or Brahms. For in what era have not suffering, carnage, and deprivation been abroad? Luckily for the world, such men have usually understood that there is sustenance man is always in need of, quite as much as of bread—sustenance they could endow us with only by cultivating unapologetically their best gifts. They have known that the riches they pour out for us must be for more than one era. It is not that one denies the possible value of making posters, marching songs, or bitter plays which will move men to picket for the thirty-hour week and higher wages. We all approve of decreased taxes, adequate defense, better sanitation, and municipal housing—and for such ends comedy and satire can agitate. Tragedy cannot. It does something more important. When high-minded creators, pushed to the wall by this class of critics, do less nobly than they could in order to propagandize against a social ill, let them consider whether the temporary disease they would cure is more pressing than that unceasing accumulation of spiritual frustrations that every man and every woman harbors within, and for which tragedy and the tragic spirit are the best anodynes. Even when we conquer the moon, as it seems we must, these frustrations will continue to require easement—in all probability, more than ever.

As for the various sociological interpretations of tragedies extant, how can such commentary illuminate or facilitate by a jot the experience for which tragedy is created? Of what avail is it to relate *Othello* to Shakespeare's economic status, personal marital experiences, social class, subconscious involvements? The purposes for which *Othello* exists are in no way affected by such knowledge; for, to begin with, and to end with, *Othello* fulfills the purposes of tragedy. It can therefore, for every man and every woman, purify the spirit, give insight into life, and bestow courage for the tensions of living. For these are the function of tragedy, and surely no nobler service is performed by any other kind of human activity. If this be error and upon us proved, we never writ nor no man ever suffered.

And these things it can do only by operating, as Aristotle observes, through the agency of the individual audience's emotions of pity and fear. Pity is self-explanatory. But what is this "fear," this *phobos?* The word used to be translated as "terror"; but nowadays "terror" is too much associated with sliding panels and disappearing staircases to be serviceable. This fear, which might perhaps be better rendered into modern English as "awe," is double: awe at man's insignificance in the face of the vast complexity, over which he can exercise no control, of God, Nature, and society—a complexity in the face of which he seems so puny and helpless; and awe, too, at the seed of divinity in man which, despite his very insignificance, prompts him to stand up against adversity, and will not allow him to bend his neck accommodatingly to the axe suspended over him.

A hero who is the victim of the forces operating upon him, who can be crushed by adversity, and who bows before the axe threatening him, may inspire but never fear. If Hamlet, however noble, were only the victim of the evil circumstances enmeshing him, and were discomfited by them to the extent that he could neither cope with nor combat them (this is perhaps the most popular of all misconceptions of his character), he would be no tragic hero, for he could inspire no awe, and hence would belong not in the glorious company of Oedipus, Lear, and Othello, but in that of Dickens' Little Nell. Mr. Butcher, although making an exception of Hamlet because he accepts the popular view of that hero's make-up, well says of the character of the tragic hero that it must have "in it some vital and spontaneous force which can make and mold circumstances. . . . It is of the battling, energetic type," and he agrees that "most" of Shakespeare's heroes are of this kind: "strong and dominant natures, they are of a militant quality of mind." [1]

Pity is not enough for the tragic sentiment—that is the error too many aspirants to tragic writing have not been at pains to circumvent. Pathos, which is easier to evoke than awe, does not by itself provide the tragic *katharsis*; unaccompanied by fear, it tends to depress, not cleanse. It is, moreover, but a step from mere pity for the victim to indignation against his oppressor; and when indignation intrudes powerfully the tragic sentiment is murdered. To be much inflamed against a villain, or society, or things in general—to be greatly indignant—is to be deprived of the curative effects upon the spirit of tragedy's purgation. There are occasions when we ought to be inflamed, no doubt—but they can never be the occasions when we can also be cleansed within. To say, as one must, that *An American Tragedy* and *Death of a Salesman* fall short of their pretensions is to question neither the power of their indictment nor their possible social usefulness; they simply do not rise to the dignity and unique function of tragedy. (Their authors' hopes that somehow these works might manage to encompass both indictment and tragedy have proved vain. The finished creation, like one's children, has a distressing way of being what it is, one's intentions notwithstanding!) The difficult task of combining tragedy and indictment depends for its success on a very delicate

---

[1] S. H. Butcher, *Aristotle's Theory of Poetry and Fine Art* (New York, 1951), pp. 351-2.

balance between these normally opposing elements. Ibsen, who rarely attempted pure tragedy, contrived this balance admirably in *Ghosts*. From this example alone it is possible to deduce that the secret lies in going no further than implication when one indicts in tragedy. In *Ghosts* our prime concern is neither with venereal disease nor the tyranny of the moral values of the past, but with the fall of Mrs. Alving, whose attempts to stand up against those specters are blasted by her own defects of character.

There is, let it be repeated, room for all kinds of expression, and a dramatist may prefer to write a play in the spirit of burning indignation or mockery or gentle raillery, but such a play is bent upon providing something more and a good deal less than the tragic *katharsis*. Ibsen and Chekhov have few peers among world dramatists, and there is no more reason why Ibsen should not have chosen to write *The Wild Duck* in a vein of ironic indictment or why Chekhov should not have chosen to write *The Cherry Orchard* in the comic spirit, than that Shakespeare, because he had written *Hamlet*, need have resisted penning the indignant arraignment of moral hypocrisy of *Measure for Measure*. This is not to charge these plays with artistic inadequacy; *The Wild Duck* is Ibsen at his greatest, *The Cherry Orchard* is beyond need of anyone's praise, and *Measure for Measure* for its poetry alone must ever be priceless. It is merely to remind one that none of them has been conceived in the vein of tragedy. Indeed, *Measure for Measure* and *The Wild Duck* are far more bitter than tragedy must ever attempt to be.

The merely pathetic, then, is not enough—not enough, that is, to solace the human spirit. Indeed, the pursuit of the merely pathetic is likely to skirt dangerously near the boundaries of the sentimental (i.e., false sentiment) and often falls over into it. The borderlines were not always clear, for instance, to so great an artist as Dickens. *Bleak House* is a great tragic novel if only because it contains Lady Dedlock; *The Old Curiosity Shop*, on the other hand, is vitiated into sentimentality because it contains Little Nell. It is related of Wilde that when someone asked him whether he had not been profoundly affected by the demise of Little Nell, he answered that a man must have a heart of stone who could read those pages without dying of laughter. Thus, mere pathos may have so little dignity as to defeat its own ends. Pity without fear cannot make for tragedy.

Now, as we have implied, the pity and fear required of us, the audience, are expressed chiefly during the course of our self-identification with the hero of a tragedy. As we attend the tragedy, *we* must be Lear, Electra, or Hamlet, so that at the conclusion we may feel that us the play

> with new acquist
> Of true experience from this great event
> With peace and consolation hath dismissed,
> And calm of mind, all passion spent.[1]
> [*Samson Agonistes*, 1755—end]

This hero, as Aristotle knew, must have certain qualifications, or else this self-identification on the part of the audience cannot take place. He cannot be a completely "virtuous man brought from prosperity to adversity," for that would only excite indignation— or, as Aristotle puts it, "it merely shocks us." Nor can he be a "bad man passing from adversity to prosperity," for that "possesses no single tragic quality"—we should be indignant here too, though for quite different reasons. Nor can he be an utter villain whose downfall we witness, for at that we should rejoice. The kind of hero with whom alone we can identify ourselves is one extreme in neither virtue nor vice, a man essentially good, whose misfortunes are brought about "by some error or frailty"—*hamartia*, as the Greek has it, the famous "tragic flaw" of literary parlance. "The single Greek word *hamartia*," as Mr. Lane Cooper reminds us, "lays emphasis upon the want of insight within the man, but is elastic enough to mean also the outward fault resulting from it."[2]

That is to say, the hero of a tragedy must be to a considerable extent the author of his own doom; he must fall because of some

---

[1] These famous lines, perfectly expressing the audience's ideal reaction to the fall of a tragic hero (in this play, Samson), were dictated by one of the earliest of the moderns to understand truly the meaning of Aristotle's words. Indeed, Milton, in the Foreword to *Samson Agonistes*, strongly emphasizes the curative, the medicinal function of tragedy when he says of tragedy that it "hath been ever held the gravest, moralest, and most profitable of all other poems (i.e., forms of literary composition); therefore said by Aristotle to be of power by raising pity and fear, or terror, to purge the mind of those and such-like passions, that is to temper and reduce them to just measure with a kind of delight, stirred up by reading or seeing those passions well imitated. Nor is Nature wanting in her own effects to make good his assertion: for so in physic things of melancholic hue and quality are used against melancholy, sour against sour, salt to remove salt humors."

[2] L. Cooper, *Aristotle on the Art of Poetry* (Ithaca, 1947), p. 40.

basic moral weakness. (Aristotle's word for "character" is *ethos*; as he sees it, character in tragedy means "moral constitution.") The hero of a tragedy, in other words, never falls only because of circumstances, Fate, or Destiny, but chiefly through some species of personal ethical blindness. No one can possibly identify himself with a man or woman who suffers catastrophe only through some accident. By definition an accident is a happening that cannot be anticipated, and must therefore necessarily be left out of account. An accident is an occurrence that can be explained by no ordinary human logic, in which we are accustomed to move from cause to effect. When a man suffers accident the cause is outside his control and we cannot put ourselves in his place. For these reasons, in a world of ever-recurring accidents we are all compelled to live as though they did not occur; if we were not, in dread of the unpredictable we should never dare to step out of our houses—indeed, should never dare move from a chair, which, moreover, would have to be discreetly placed well out of the possible descent of a chandelier.

There is no misconception more prevalent than the vulgar one which credits the classic Greek tragedies with exhibiting the remorseless operation of Fate. Many careless textbooks have perpetuated this untruth, and book reviewers are forever describing some modern work showing the agency of blind Destiny as being in that respect "like a Greek tragedy." Poor Oedipus is always being subpoenaed as an analogy for the hero of such a book. In point of fact, no tragic hero is more completely the author of his own doom than Oedipus; he builds his own funeral pyre log by log, impelled as he is by his *hamartia*, his tragic flaw—overweeningness, heedlessness, wilfulness.

Consider his actions, as they are revealed to us in the play. Raised by the king and queen of Corinth as their son, he was disturbed at a feast by a drunkard's slighting insinuations about his origins. Oedipus begged the King and Queen to reveal the facts of his birth, but their answers were so evasive that he journeyed to the oracle to learn the truth. But, characteristically, the oracle answered a question he had not asked, and it spoke of his murdering his father and committing incest with his mother. Horrified at these words, in order to escape such a fate Oedipus vowed never to return to Corinth. Although virtuous, Oedipus was however also an exceedingly heedless man. Since he had consulted the oracle only because he was unsure of his parentage, he could, if completely rational, also have taken care, to avoid the terrible future prophesied, never to kill any man old enough to be his father and never to mate with any woman clearly older than himself. Yet before long, refusing to clear the road of Laius' carriage, he slew his father in a fit of wrath; and soon thereafter he recklessly allowed himself to be wedded to the widowed Jocasta, his mother. It is beside the point that he did not know either to be his actual parents. He had been given sufficient warning for him to have avoided both deeds.[1] Read in any other light than through these facts, which are a part of Sophocles' play, Oedipus Tyrannus will never mean what its author intended or its original audiences understood. Oedipus a victim of Fate would not be a tragic Oedipus, only a pathetic one.[2]

Since accidents do occur they are naturally represented in tragedy. They could hardly fail to be. For, in a manner of speaking, everything that happens to an individual, everything that occurs without his first having willed it, is an "accident," whether it be the unheralded appearance of a human being at one's threshold or the lateness of the morning train. But such accidents, whatever their consequences—and we are aware that the tardiness of a train may be but the first of a series of destructive events—in tragedy must be represented (if they contribute to the catastrophe) as cooperating with the hero's tragic flaw. For instance, the lateness of

---

[1] There is nowhere a more brilliant study of this play than in Professor H. D. F. Kitto's Greek Tragedy (2d edition, revised, London, 1950), pp. 135-41. He says, "Sophocles is not trying to make us feel that an inexorable destiny or a malignant god is guiding the events."

[2] The same sort of admonition must be made about Romeo and Juliet, a play almost universally misunderstood. The fault here is somewhat Shakespeare's. He was still near the beginning of his career, was writing his first good tragedy, and unsure of himself (as the verse's alternation between lyrical sublimity and fumbling fatuousness demonstrates). In this play he toyed with the idea of setting a prologue before each act, but apparently gave up after writing only two—which he would have done wisely to remove; they are of no consequence to the tragedy. Unhappily the first prologue speaks of Romeo and Juliet as "a pair of star-crossed lovers," and the phrase has been taken up by criticism without regard to the transactions of the plot. It is a far better play than the words imply. If the love of Romeo and Juliet were crossed only by their evil stars, they would be merely victims of circumstances, not tragic figures, as they are. They would be two well-meaning weaklings with whom we cannot possibly identify ourselves. As it is, the work clearly exhibits them falling as a result of the tragic flaw they both share—heedlessness.

a train may contribute to tragic catastrophe if we feel it is our hero's characteristic fault that, knowing the undependability of the company's services, he made no provision for the contingency of lateness. Or, the sudden appearance of another human being at the threshold may contribute to our hero's fall if we feel that some aspect of their relationship is owing to a defect in our hero's character. In short, in a tragedy it is the hero's personal shortcoming which starts the rocks tumbling down the cliff; and accidents of time and place may convert the inconsequential falling of a few rocks into a destructive avalanche. Tragedy ever reminds us that each man lives in a world over which his control begins abruptly to cease in the area contiguous to the exterior side of his own skin. It *is* disastrously unlucky that Desdemona loses the handkerchief precisely when she does lose it: her handkerchief lost on any other day might have caused no trouble at all; on that particular day Othello because of his tragic flaw has already allowed his mind to be poisoned against her. But, on the other hand, were Othello other than he is and she other than she is, no catastrophe need have ensued because of that loss. It *is* disastrously unlucky for Macbeth (and for Duncan too!) as well as for Lady Macbeth that the King comes to stay at their castle on that of all nights: on any other occasion Macbeth might not have been steeled for the bloody deed; on that night he was prepared to murder. On the other hand, people do accept the hospitality of those whom they have benefited, arise without a gash the next morning, hale and hearty, and leave their hosts in no danger of the electric chair. In tragedy, the hero's tragic flaw sows a wind that reaps the whirlwind.

The classic tragic flaw, the *hamartia* exhibited by the heroes and heroines of Greek tragedy, is some species of rashness, or as Mr. Butcher tentatively states it, an "error of judgment arising from a hasty or careless view of the special case; an error which in some degree is morally culpable, as it might have been avoided." For us "overweeningness" or "heedlessness" is the most satisfactory designation in our language for the rashness found in the classic tragic hero.[1] Tragedy reminds us, because of the fatal overweening-

---

[1] Mr. Butcher would probably not be quite satisfied with either word. He knows that Sophocles' *Oedipus Tyrannus* was in Aristotle's judgment the ideal tragedy, and therefore feels that any description of *hamartia* must be one to account for the hero of that play—a view in which we heartily concur. But, incredibly enough, this great scholar actually can say of Oedipus: "His

ness of the hero, of the necessity of remaining modest before the gods. We must never for a minute forget, no matter how favorable appearances may be to us, that we can hardly manage ourselves, much less the rest of the world. The tragic hero is a man whom we admire, often love, but who at a crucial moment—even as you and I—forgets discretion, has the illusion that he can manipulate a course of events just because he chooses to view them a certain way. Oedipus is brave, fearless, and generous, but he is utterly reckless about his own conduct; because he *intends* to avoid the crimes predicted by the oracle, he feels foolishly safe and takes insufficient precautions to prevent their commission. The oracle is no more responsible for the crimes he commits than the three witches are for Macbeth's murdering Duncan. Oracle and witches are simply the voice of the vast complex of affairs, full of pitfalls for all of us, the voice that warns us to moderate our wilfulness and live with intelligence. Catastrophic for us if we feel so superior to the world's chances that we disregard the warning or prefer to interpret it as a signal to plunge ahead wherever our will would lead us! Indeed, as the truth narrows inch by inch closer to Oedipus, we see him questioning himself less than ever; rather, that characteristic overweeningness of his makes him turn against Creon, who only wishes him well, and against sightless Tiresias, whose only guilt is that he sees the truth to which Oedipus (though in possession of his eyes) blinds himself. For all his qualities, Oedipus is a stubborn man who cannot be prevented from destroying his own peace. Such a man is Lear, who out of similar stubbornness turns against Cordelia and Kent, who love him most, just because they speak truth too bluntly to be palatable to his bad temper. Such an overweening man is Othello; pure of soul, if ever man was, lofty in principle, courageous, wholly unselfish and unassuming, he yet permits himself to forget all he has reason

---

character was not the determining factor in his fortunes. He, if any man, was in a genuine sense the victim of circumstances." Hence, Professor Butcher decides that the meaning of *hamartia* cannot be, after all, limited to "either a defect of character or a single passionate or inconsiderate act," and must include the possibility of an error for which the hero is not responsible. Thus the door is opened to mere accident as the cause of the tragic catastrophe, and hence to the banishing of all possible self-identification with the hero. The conception of *Oedipus Tyrannus* earlier discussed in this chapter brings the play into uniformity with the rest of Greek tragic drama, as it unquestionably must have been for Aristotle, who admired it above all other tragedies.

to know his wife to be ("My life upon her faith!"),[1] and, having lost his judgment, allows his overwrought emotions to lead him to disaster. This overweeningness destroys Romeo and Juliet; we are not disposed to hold it against them when first love precipitates them into recklessness, as we cannot hold it against Lear, Othello, and Oedipus that they are overweening, for these are beings who evoke our affection, not our censure; but we are forced to recognize, if we understand Shakespeare's play correctly, that had Romeo and Juliet taken a few pains to conciliate their families, who were all too ready to make peace, their love might have ended happily.

It is interesting to observe that we can identify ourselves only with men and women who have such flaws, and not at all with a flawless character. It is not only because we know privately how imperfect we are. It is rather because a flawless man, if he suffers catastrophe, having no error that can bring about his doom, can fall only through forces external to himself, i.e., by accident or Fate. As graphic illustration we may consult the difference in our feelings about the deaths of Paris and Romeo in the same play. Romeo is far from perfect. Before he meets Juliet, he is obviously insincere, a mooncalf in love with love, affected—is saved from being a bore, indeed, only because his faults are so common to youth. Paris, on the other hand, is an entirely attractive character, and remains so throughout the play. A lesser artist, since our sympathies are to be with Romeo, would have made a rival lover something of a villain. But Shakespeare has strengthened the pathos by making us feel that, barring the fact that she does not love him, Juliet might do much worse than marry Paris. His love for her is beyond question; he is respectful to Capulet; he is forbearing at Friar Lawrence's cell when Juliet is almost rude to him, and answers her curtness with gentlest affection; he is overwhelmed with grief at the news of her supposed death; and the depth of his affections is to be gauged by his quietly going to pay his obsequies with perfumed water, flowers, and devotion when she has been entombed, and vowing to continue these services to her memory nightly thereafter. He is killed only because he wishes to protect the sanctity of the dead from what he conceives to be the vengeance of a Montague. He is innocent of a single unpleasant trait or deed. He knows of no marriage between the lovers, is even

---

[1] *Othello*, I, iii, 296.

unaware they have met. He is a person entirely sinned against, a fact untrue of Romeo. And yet we cannot identify ourselves with Paris because, entirely admirable though he is, he is only a victim of circumstance. While with Romeo, who is less ideal than Paris, we can identify ourselves because he is the author of his own doom, because he possesses a tragic flaw. This paradox is quite characteristic of true tragedy.

There are other qualifications for the tragic hero besides this *hamartia*. Though most of the subjects of Greek tragedy were taken from the treasuries of mythology, Aristotle wisely observes that tragedy need not confine itself to traditional stories. But, because of the plays he knew, he suggested that the tragic hero should be one "highly renowned and prosperous." This dictum was perverted during the English Restoration to mean only high social rank, and in that distorted garb fathered many a dull so-called Heroic Tragedy in which the hero owned no distinction beyond his being a prince and nourishing a propensity toward pompous oratory—a man unable to arouse any sympathy. A man of social eminence with the soul of a mouse cannot be tragic. No one is a candidate for tragedy just because his name appears in the *Almanac de Gotha* or the *Social Register*—a fact no one there listed will deplore. The heroes "highly renowned and prosperous" of Greek lore were, of course, men and women of position, but they were renowned even more for their personal accomplishments and qualities. We must, therefore, in consequence of literary experience since then, modify Aristotle's suggestion to include men and women, whatever their rank in society, who are *above the average in personal qualities*. Thomas Hardy's Jude, though of humblest origin, is a true tragic hero by power of his unconquerable thirst for learning and a larger life, the unyielding search for which raises him above his fellows. Social position is not a basic requirement for a tragic hero; what is essential is an internal quality which sets him apart from the herd—which makes him, in short, not bend his head to the axe, as the average man will do. The same spiritual superiority of his heroes in Conrad's novels rates these stories among the noblest tragic works in fiction, perhaps the best in English in the last three-quarters of a century—those simple, sometimes even rough, souls who when adverse fortune corners them prefer to go down to disaster rather than part with a few rags of personal honor, all they have to cover themselves with in their dolorous pass. The death of these men is a loss to the world; the world is poorer for their falling from its ranks. So, while Jude and Lord Jim are tragic characters, Dreiser's Clyde Griffiths and Mr. Miller's Salesman are not, because, though we pity them, their fall involves no loss to humanity, no awe. With the tragic hero something more than himself goes down to defeat.

For this reason we may add that a hero with inner qualities above the average is likely to be a more impressive one if he comes from an important place in society. Such a man involves the destinies of more lives than his own. A tragic hero of rank carries along with him to ruin more than can a man from humbler walks of life. The death of Abraham Lincoln, for example, was a greater tragic fact (for North and South) than the death of any Union or Confederate soldier. Milton had in Samson the perfect symbol for the tragic hero, who when he brings the edifice down upon his own head also causes general ruin. A hero of lofty place is also more tragic because he falls from a greater height; a fall from ten stories is bound to be more catastrophic than one from a doorstep. The fall of an eagle weighs more with us than the fall of a sparrow. As the Gentleman says of Lear:

> A sight most pitiful in the meanest wretch,
> Past speaking of in a king! [1]

Shakespeare's tragic heroes all satisfy both requirements. They are all men and women superior to the average; and Lear is a king, Macbeth becomes one, Cleopatra is a queen, Hamlet is a prince, Coriolanus and Othello are the very props of the state, Brutus is the cause of civil war, and Romeo and Juliet are the offspring of Verona's two leading families. These two attributes will also be found in the tragic figures who stand close to the central character in importance: Cassius is second only by personal choice to Brutus, Desdemona is the daughter of a leading senator, Lady Macbeth becomes a queen, Cordelia is first a princess and then a queen, and Antony (of *Antony and Cleopatra*) is one of the twin pillars sustaining the world.

Now, since self-identification on the part of the audience with the hero is the root of the cathartic experience in tragedy, how, it may be asked, is one to identify oneself with a man who, unlike

---

[1] *King Lear*, IV, vi, 208-9.

ourselves, is above the average? The naturalists[1] since Zola have indeed maintained that it is with the average man that audiences can more readily identify. Isn't he more like ourselves than General Othello, Prince Hamlet, or King Lear? Isn't his very mediocrity closer to our own experience? Zola, Dreiser, James T. Farrell, Arthur Miller (we exempt the hero of his fine tragedy, A View from the Bridge), William Inge, and their peers have valiantly labored to keep their heroes within the dimensions of averageness and mediocrity. Not only their heroes but their heroes' experiences are run-of-the-mill, within the petty scope of our own everyday experiences. On the face of it, logic would seem to indicate that you and I can more easily be the Salesman or Clyde Griffiths than Prince Hamlet or King Lear. But this is not actually the case, for at least two reasons, one psychological, the other aesthetic.

For a very human cause, no individual can identify himself with an average man as hero. What normal human being ever thinks of himself as average? We may know that the trivialities of our own lives will not bear objective representation; modesty, for instance, bids us remember that the occasion on which we missed a step and sprained an ankle could be a dramatic one only to ourselves. But just the same we are all aware of stately potentialities for tragedy, all kinds of noble capacities which the world ignores in us but to which, given the opportunity, we would rise. What unattractive woman but sees in the mirror somewhere in her face a hint of beauty? What cringing coward but knows that when the right moment strikes he will seize occasion? We are all endowed with "one grace, one wonder at the least," which saves us from undifferentiating submergence in the sea of the general. To ourselves none of us is mediocre. And hence, those convincingly average people created by the naturalists we view with an almost impersonal kind of sympathy. Those men and women are pathetic, perhaps—but they cannot be ourselves because they lack our dimensions, our potentialities. As for the sub-average creations of Mr. Steinbeck and Mr. Erskine Caldwell, there is, of course, no possibility of our identification with them, and they loom most

---

[1] We employ the term despite the objections of some current practitioners of naturalism to being designated otherwise than as realists. They consider "naturalism" an insult. But some word is surely called for to distinguish the method of a Flaubert from that of a Zola, that of a Willa Cather from that of a Dreiser.

real when they figure comically, as they do, for instance, in *Tobacco Road*.

Another reason why we cannot identify ourselves with the hero of the naturalists proceeds from aesthetic considerations. As we have observed, a completed creation, just because it has its own entity, takes on a life of its own, always something in excess of its author's intentions. The distinction between realism and naturalism is that the realist *selects* his materials from everyday reality while the naturalist, traditionally concerned with the representation of average people, studiously presents quasi-scientifically the sense of *all* the facts of everyday reality. Thus the naturalist achieves his reality by surrounding his characters with a thousand little details of everyday experience. We see from which side of the bed our hero rises, so to speak, observe the tone of the water after he has made his ablutions, note the brand of toothpaste he uses, and so on—these facts being important for our comprehension of his life. This is that spirit of scientific documentation which Zola called for and which his followers have strictly adhered to. Yet, strangely enough, our familiarity with the persons of these stories, as the work makes its leisurely way to its conclusion, grows more and more remote, and the figures become less and less realizable. Only the details take on vividness, not the people connected with them. That is why the *Iliad* is a greater book than *For Whom the Bell Tolls*, despite its paraphernalia of gods, goddesses, and antique warfare. Priam pleading for his son's remains voices the grief of all stricken men in time of loss, and Hector taking leave of his wife speaks with the tongue of all men saying farewell. In Mr. Hemingway's novel there is no single occurrence of such moving universality; the events of his story belong to our day, his gods are our gods, and his warfare our warfare, but from his characters we stand, however well-wishing, aloof; they end by being little more than names to us.

It is the persons with whom we identify ourselves; we can identify ourselves with any happenings only if we can identify ourselves with the person to whom they occur. It matters not whether there are ghosts or witches in the world; what does matter is how Hamlet and Macbeth behave (that is, how *we* behave) in encountering them. It is beside the point to ask whether any girl is likely to procure the perfect husband by his correct choice among three caskets; what is to the point is that Shakespeare makes that experience entirely real because Portia and Bassanio are real. Now, the reader of the naturalistic novel, while the details are accumulating *en masse*, is by degrees being further and further cut off from self-identification. *An American Tragedy* is utterly successful in depicting a thoroughly average young man, raised in an average environment in a particular part of the West, going to work in a particular Midwestern city and having characteristic experiences of average boys in such an employment, getting into the difficulties in which average boys entangle themselves, escaping to an average community in a particular part of New York State, and there falling into a pattern leading to disaster. I accept the picture[1] but it means little to me personally because the accent has been placed upon his environment, and I have lived in totally different environments. None of the experiences of Clyde's youth and adolescence were mine; I knew no such parents, no such teachers, had no fellow bellhops, never associated with factory girls, never nursed as a glamorous ideal canoeing on the lake with small-town "aristocracy" or playing bridge with them. That is, I do not associate myself with the man of whom I must remember that he gets up on the left side of the bed and uses toothpaste X, when I myself get up on the right side of the bed and use tooth-powder Y. The very precision of the details excludes me.

Now, realism as practised by Jane Austen, Balzac, Tolstoi, Flaubert, Dickens (at his best), Thackeray, Meredith, Hardy, Henry James, Miss Cather, and Mr. Faulkner (among others) avoids this dehumanizing process. The very act of selection, though the material is taken from everyday experience, by omitting these particularizing details tends to elevate the characters above the

---

[1] But I reject its indictment of American justice. Dreiser is outraged that, though Clyde did not murder Roberta but only (wanting her dead) *allowed* her to drown when he could have saved her, his hero should have capital punishment visited upon him. A monumental second volume is devoted to retracing the events of the story as a powerful arraignment of the law. But it makes little difference that Clyde is technically innocent; he surely is as morally culpable of a death he could easily have prevented as if his hand had pushed Roberta under the waters. His excuse, the excuse of mediocrity, that he just did not save her but certainly did not actually kill her, alienates us from sympathy, and we cannot share Dreiser's indignation at the miscarriage of justice. The real failure of this novel is demonstrated by the fact that Roberta, in despite of the author, manages to be something of a tragic figure because of the quality of her love for Clyde. Her rising to tragedy disqualifies him as a tragic figure. If we identify with her, we must take sides against him.

realm of the average, makes them lifelike but larger than life—as
they ought to be—places them with the universal rather than the
commonplace; and, as Aristotle observes, it is the business of the
literary creator to "express the universal." Without respect to
tragedy, it will be seen that the characters created by Ibsen and
Chekhov, both realists, are not deluged by minuteness of detail;
their figures are universal. Emma Bovary emerges not as a commonplace woman but as a woman whose tragic failing is common
to all women; Flaubert's severe selectivity in recording her life has
made her universal; as a result we recognize in Emma's disaster
that any woman who allows the characteristically feminine dis-
satisfaction with the attainable to have free rein will plunge herself and all connected with her into misery. Much the same may
be said of Anna Karenina and Miss Cather's Lost Lady, both
creations of superb realists. With these women all men and women
can identify themselves, for they are not typed but universal. The
great persons of literary creation are both entirely themselves and
at the same time so deeply rooted in our common humanity that
they are we too.

From our vantage point the old quarrel between romanticism
and realism has no meaning. "The Poet is not an Historian," says
Aristotle. It is the business of the historian to record what has
actually happened, the particular event; it is that of the man of
letters to deal with what "in a given situation might well happen
—a sequence of events that is possible," [1] i.e., possible in the sense
of being credible. Romanticism and realism are therefore merely
matters of preference dictated by the creator's own temperament
—which, in truth, may itself so vary that the same author may
produce at different times pieces of realism and romanticism, as
was the case with Flaubert, Ibsen, Hauptmann, Hamsun, and
Strindberg. For the purposes of literature it matters not whether a
writer's plot is the fiction of his imagination or the product of his
experience and observation of everyday living—provided that he
knows men and women as they are—of the past or of the present,
set in the country or set in the town. Both romanticism and
realism have justified themselves by their creations; by their fruits
we know them to merit equal praise. Shakespeare's plays and Flaubert's *Madame Bovary* would be enough to make argument su-

---

[1] Cooper, *op. cit.*, p. 31.

perfluous, and readers of judgment turn to both schools with equal enthusiasm. For the *reality* of the plot has nothing to do with whether its locale be in an impossible Forest of Arden or an actually existing Lyons or London, its time an imagined sixteenth century or an observed twentieth. "A sequence of events which, though actually impossible, looks reasonable should be preferred by the poet to what, though really possible, seems incredible," says Aristotle.[1] Daily, events occur which would be impossible to make credible in the telling, yet the genius of a Shakespeare can make the advent of Hamlet's father's ghost an experience of fear-inspiring reality. We will accept any story as real, no matter how related or unrelated to our own experience, if it offers the characters the opportunity to behave in universal human fashion, for with that we can always identify ourselves. We all have occasion to encounter ghosts, though they come not from beyond the grave, who appear before us to lay upon us their own stern behests.

And thus the great persons of literature are not only lifelike; they take on more reality than life itself. We come to know Shakespeare's Beatrice, Hamlet, Othello, Desdemona, Iago, Isabella, Cordelia, Kent, and Coriolanus better than we know our own brothers and sisters. For we know these exciting beings completely, could predict how they would behave in a given situation. We can be sure, for instance, that if Beatrice had been Othello's wife no tragedy could have ensued; she would have ridiculed him into rationality with a barrage of well-aimed sarcasms until he spoke his suspicions, which she would have summarily routed with merriment; before she was through with him, he would have been on his knees begging forgiveness. Isabella, on the other hand, would have turned on him in blazing moral indignation and shamed him into sense; Cleopatra would have ensnared him with her enchantingly perverse moods until he drowned his thoughts in passionate embraces. We can be sure, too, that Hamlet in Othello's place would have been quicker to suspect Iago than Desdemona; that Kent, with his blunt loyalty to those he loves, would have pierced through the villain's lies. We know that Desdemona, for all her exquisite delicacy, would have answered Lear not in Cordelia's style, which threw the aging monarch so completely off balance that he lost all perspective, but in the manner she answered

---

[1] Cooper, *op. cit.*, p. 80.

Brabantio, which answer, despite the folly of the question, saved
her father's face before the assembled court. Benedick would
never have looked at Ophelia twice, though Claudio would have
adored her; Hamlet, with Portia at his side, would have solved
his problems without catastrophe to her or himself. We know
these people completely; our brothers and sisters, whom we ought
to know better than them, have a way—alas!—of behaving quite
unpredictably. The flesh-and-blood reality of the great creations
of the literary masters is, indeed, one of the chief solaces in life
for us. So long as we share with them our common humanity, none
of us can ever be alone.

    None of the world's writers can offer that solace to the extent
that Shakespeare does; no other writer exercises our sense of one-
ness with our fellow human beings in as lively a way as he. It is
for this reason that all the scholarly knowledge in the world will
not bring the student within sight of Shakespeare if he come unaccompanied by his common humanity. The call upon that common humanity is not, as in Milton, opulently orchestrated with
thrilling literary reference; one returns from Milton rewarded in
direct proportion to one's previous saturation in the sea of the
world's great books. Literary reference plays an almost negligible
role (though no knowledge is negligible when reading him) in the
apprehension of Shakespeare; in him the appeal is always based
upon experiences common to human relationships.[1] The simplest
of Italian barbers who can honestly find *Hamlet* a play *molto sim-
patico* basks more surely in the warmth of Shakespeare's sun than
the most ponderous of scholars who cherishes no passion for literature beyond one for sources, dates, editions, and commas. Naturally, all that kind of knowledge can lead one all the closer to
Shakespeare—provided one also brings along his heart. It was the
great Bradley himself who, with his vast erudition, could speak
with admiration of "that native strength and justice of perception,
and that habit of reading with an eager mind, which make many

---

    [1] It is here that the professional scholars are always erring. Their enthusi-
asms over the "findings" of their researches impel them constantly to blind
themselves to meanings in Shakespeare which are obvious enough in the light
of ordinary human relationships, in favor of bloodless interpretations which
bring the poet closer to his contemporaries and sources but further away from
what is eternally true in human nature.

an unscholarly lover of Shakespeare a far better critic than many a Shakespeare scholar." [1]

Having cleared some ground, as we now approach Shakespeare's work we must make it plain that we are not interested in appraising either him or *Hamlet*. A man must be a fool to stand in front of Pike's Peak and say, "I like you," or stick out his tongue and say, "I don't like you." Pike's Peak will be there long after this little man is forgotten, and so will Shakespeare and his *Hamlet*. We can choose only either to be blind or to see. And it is not the people who love the arts most who are forever appraising them; rather they are too busy experiencing the arts to have much patience with talk about them. They are too busy listening to Beethoven to participate in the recurrent epistolary warfare in the *Times* arguing the greater merits of the *Third*, *Fifth*, *Seventh*, or *Ninth Symphony*; they probably feel as they listen to each that *it* is the greatest, or rather that each symphony, having a complete and perfect life of its own, is as great as it need be. (And they probably feel, too, that nothing disqualifies the *Sixth* or the *Eighth* either.) This weighing of comparative greatness among things superlatively great is the most absurd of follies. Criticism and discussion are defensible only to the extent that they can enrich the experience of the work of art. Such alone is the apologia for whatever bypaths of criticism we feel obliged to trace in this work. . . .

Though there is little likelihood that Shakespeare could have known Aristotle's *Poetics*, we find him in all the principles we have drawn therefrom thoroughly Aristotelian. When we consider how utterly different were the history, technique, and theatrical requirements of the Athenian drama, we are all the more struck with the timeless truth of Aristotle's deductions, so that in these funda-

---

[1] These words, prefatory to one of the few monumental volumes of Shakespearean commentary [A. C. Bradley, *Shakespearean Tragedy*, London, 1929], never palatable to a certain type of "scholar," are probably with relief thrown with the book into the discard by such as pronounce Bradley's brilliant volume "superseded" by later "findings." He is far too perceptive ever to be superseded; and when he is wrong he never loses one's respect. His delicate appreciation of Shakespeare's tragic power and his own scope will both survive centuries of new scholarly discoveries about dates, editions, and sources. We find ourselves in total disagreement with his view of *Hamlet*—though nothing better has ever been written upon *Lear* than his lectures—and we love him even for his errors, for he writes like a poet himself, and with the vivacity born of love for his subject.

mentals Shakespeare's tragedies illustrate them as completely as do Sophocles'.[1] If Aristotle could have known Shakespeare's tragedies, he might have gone further than Ben Jonson, and said to him:

> I will not lodge thee by
> Euripides, bid Aeschylus to lie
> A little farther off, to make thee room:
> Thou art a monument without a tomb.[2]

But can we single out any tendency, can we phrase any philosophy implied in Shakespeare's tragedies when they are considered as a whole, as surely as we can for great world dramatists like Aeschylus, Sophocles, Euripides, Molière, Ibsen, and Chekhov?

Two qualities are obviously to be found in his plays—comedies, histories, and tragedies alike—and these are: an infinite compassion for human beings and an incomparable understanding of the operations of the human soul. He has made us comprehend the involved processes which motivate so bloodchilling a scoundrel as Iago[3] no less than the almost saintly forbearance of a Helena.

---

[1] From this generalization we exclude Shakespeare's very early and inept *Titus Andronicus*. Some scholars deny his authorship of a work so repellent in plot as this. But the master's hand is to be discerned (though unsteady) in its often by-no-means contemptible verse. (Shakespeare's verse, like Shakespeare's understanding, was far less Elizabethan than Shakespearean.) There should be nothing shocking that the world's greatest poet-dramatist should have written one of the world's worst plays before he was mature enough to write so many of the world's best. Most of Milton's earliest verse is dismal, as he himself was well aware when, at twenty-four, he deplored his lack of "inward ripeness" ["On His Having Arrived at the Age of Twenty-Three," 7]. Yet *Paradise Lost* is nonpareil in narrative poetry. These instances, which could be multiplied (e.g., Shelley, Whitman, Beethoven, Wagner), are a proof of how much self-discipline and growth are involved in the highest expressions of genius.

[2] Ben Jonson's "To the Memory of My Beloved Master William Shakespeare," 19-22:

> I will not lodge thee by
> *Chaucer, or Spenser, or bid Beaumont lie*
> *A little farther off, to make thee room:*
> *Thou art a monument without a tomb.*

[3] Among his villains there are only two whose wickedness is not explained —Goneril and Regan, more like harpies than normal flesh and blood. It is of no avail to say of them flippantly that they are incomprehensible because they are women. Shakespeare knew what he was creating, and he needed these two horrors to complete his gallery of portraits. Anyone who has lived with any thought in the twentieth century must acknowledge that here and there we meet with a creature, like a Hitler or a Stalin and the demons who clustered

Dostoievski has often been mentioned as more nearly Shakespeare's peer than any other writer in this compassion and this comprehension, and surely the great Russian has few equals in these respects. But an important difference exists between the two. Dostoievski's compassion, vast as it is, has a moral unbalance at its root: he is so anxious to understand evil that before he is through with it he has banished it as a kind of human delusion; he washes it away in tears—is, in short, at basis a sentimentalist. Shakespeare, even when weakest, in his early plays, is not once guilty of sentimentality; no writer is more completely free of that taint. (It would never have occurred to him, for example, to select a prostitute as the saintliest of his women.) Ever careful to account for evil, in so far as it can be accounted for, and eager to understand it, he never confuses good and evil. Evil is never depicted by him as only good intentions gone astray. We may have every understanding of the wickedness of Iago or Edmund, may even a little pity them, but we have never any doubt that they are a menace nor do we cease wishing to see their wickedness thwarted. The sanity of distinguishing both between what is good and what is evil, and between the cause of evil and the evil itself, is fundamental in Shakespeare's view of the world. And it is fundamental to a healthy functioning of the body politic; without it all must be chaos.[1] We must learn to understand what we can of the causes of evil; we must exercise ourselves to help abolish these causes, in so far as they can be abolished, but the evil itself must be punished if we are to survive. We may understand that the gangster-killer may be somewhat a product of the slums (choosing thus to overlook the bright ornaments of society who grew up in the same districts), but we do not therefore hand him a machine-gun and

about them in mutual sympathy, whom no psychological theory can explain, incarnations of evil as they seem to be. To the indignant devotee of professional psychology one merely observes that whatever could be said about the factors which "condition" a Hitler could be said about countless others who in no way resembled him: men born the same year, in the same kind of house and street in the same city, to parents of comparable temperaments and income, brought up during the same crucial years, subject to the same disillusionments and deprivations. Many of these others became not Hitlers but his victims.

[1] The anthropologists have copiously demonstrated to us that what is an evil in one culture may be a good in another. But they have also thereby proved—a conclusion some of them evade—that every society *has* a good and an evil, that ethical distinctions are *sine qua non* to the existence of the race.

say, "Go ahead, my boy, we understand your impulse to murder!" We must be busy clearing slums but we must also safely remove the killer.

This unmatched compassion and this limitless understanding are not peculiar, however, to the tragedies. What then do we find in the tragedies? Those plays are corrupted by the schools into little moral sermons. *Macbeth*, a favorite victim, is everywhere perverted into a lecture on the dangers of ambition. Ambition is, of course, not necessarily wicked. It is evil only when it spurs men, as it does spur Macbeth, to work evil; but it also provokes some men to noble acts from which thousands reap benefits. Macbeth's *hamartia*, although universally so described, could not then be ambition; no one could take exception if his ambition led him to hope for elevation by the exercise of his military talents, in the fashion which saw his appointment to Cawdor. His tragic flaw is an overweeningness, a recklessness of consequences and the prices he must pay for his acts, even though he knows what these will be like—a heedlessness which moves him to give free rein to his ambition through murderous acts, through means he should firmly reject. Shakespeare's profound wisdom disinclined him from propounding such abstract saws as that "honesty is the best policy," or "ambition is wicked." Honesty, generally, is good. But if a doctor announced to a woman that her husband had six months to live, knowing that his words would kill her, the goodness of his honesty would be open to question. Shakespeare, quite to the contrary, everywhere demonstrates that he feels with his Friar Lawrence:

> For nought so vile that on the earth doth live
> But to the earth some special good doth give,
> Nor aught so good, but, strained from that fair use,
> Revolts from true birth, stumbling on abuse:
> Virtue itself turns vice, being misapplied,
> And vice sometime's by action dignified.
> [*Romeo and Juliet*, II, iii, 17-22]

No one better knew than Shakespeare the bottomless truth of the dictum, "By their fruits ye shall know them." He does not imply that love, for instance, is either good or bad. It is good in so far as it transforms Romeo and Juliet overnight from a callow youth and an insipid girl into two adults of passion and glowing imagination;

but it is bad in so far as it makes them reckless. One might as well *accuse* them of love as Macbeth of ambition. Love is good in that it causes Cleopatra and Antony to rise majestically above their egotisms and opportunisms; but it is bad in that it makes them heedless on the road they travel together. One cannot make any moral generalizations about love, honesty, patriotism, and so on —only about the particular acts which they motivate.

Nor can we pretend that Shakespeare's tragedies exhibit the triumph of the virtuous. He knew that there is no neat distribution of rewards and punishment in this world, as was the case with Archibald the All-Right's Gentle Jane, who "was good as gold,"

> And when she grew up she was given in marriage
> To a first-class earl who keeps his carriage!

and his Teasing Tom who "was a very bad boy,"

> The consequence was he was lost totally,
> And married a girl in the *corps de bally!*
> [W. S. Gilbert, *Patience*, II]

Shakespeare knew that such is but wishful thinking about life. Rather do we witness, as we must in life, the prolonged success of the Iagos, Edmunds, Gonerils and Regans, Siciniuses and Junius Brutuses; and, what is more anguishing, the heartbreaking sufferings of the Hamlets, Othellos, Lears, and Cordelias. Indeed, Shakespeare's tragic figures suffer all out of proportion to their faults, as they would in life. For merely possessing a bad temper and stubbornness did ever man suffer more than Lear?

The neoclassical period of English literature, committed by its narrow interpretation of ethical values to the doctrine of "poetic justice," was mightily disturbed by Shakespeare's failure to reward the good. It approved, rather, the morality of Richardson in *Pamela, or Virtue Rewarded*, in which Lord B., after vainly chasing Pamela over six volumes in an attempt to seduce her, in the end rewards her endurance by marrying her. The neoclassicists were, therefore, pleased when Tate revised *King Lear* to restore Lear to his throne at the conclusion and marry Cordelia, spared death, to the deserving Kent. This travesty of Shakespeare's tragedy won the approval even of Samuel Johnson; and this was the version the public saw on the boards for something like a century and a quarter. But Shakespeare would have no traffic with these facile dispensations of justice. He had deliberately, in writing *Lear*, altered the original ending, which found the king once more in possession of his kingdom, to make it a true tragedy. He knew that we are never granted in life a gold star for every act of good conduct or sacrifice, nor are the wicked always rapidly checked in their careers. Sometimes in his tragedies a man of noble deeds (Brutus, Hamlet, Othello), sometimes a man of wicked deeds (Macbeth) goes down to ruin.

But, nevertheless, there is a meaning in the conclusions of his tragedies. If the man fighting on the side of goodness does go down to ruin at the catastrophe of a tragedy, so do those who act in behalf of wickedness. Hamlet is dead, but so are Claudius, Gertrude, Polonius, and Laertes. Othello and Desdemona die, but Iago is to suffer death by torture. Lear and Cordelia perish, but so do Cornwall, Regan, Goneril, and Edmund. And when the smoke clears after the general disaster, who remain in command of the ruined field to build life anew? Almost always exclusively the forces for goodness.[1] Hamlet is dead, but the well-balanced Horatio and the courageous Fortinbras carry on; Othello dies but a wiser Cassio continues; Lear is dead but Kent and a sager Albany and Edgar survive; in *Macbeth* the forces for right are plainly triumphant; in *Romeo and Juliet* the rival families outdo each other in offering peace and atonement at the end. The world is thus left in the capable hands of the good, and all that has been evil has perished in the fall of the hero.

In other words, Shakespeare seems to be saying that although the good man may go down to defeat, goodness itself cannot. This is the peculiarly Shakespearean version of *katharsis*. Shakespeare's tragic endings remind us that overweeningness may hurl the noblest to the dust, but he bids us also not despair about the world, only to look into ourselves. For goodness, he knows, in the long run, though the struggle be protracted and arduous and may seem momentarily to fall to the evil, cannot be extinguished. He seems to imply what Milton later expressly states:

> Virtue may be assailed, but never hurt,
> Surprised by unjust force, but not enthralled,
> Yea even that which mischief meant most harm,

---

[1] The exceptions are the "Roman" plays, where Shakespeare, limited by well-known history, seems to have chosen a tragic ending consonant with the type history-play.

> Shall in the happy trial prove most glory.
> But evil on itself shall back recoil,
> And mix no more with goodness, when at last
> Gathered like scum, and settled to itself
> It shall be in eternal restless change
> Self-fed and self-consumed: if this fail
> The pillared firmament is rottenness,
> And earth's base built on stubble.
>
> [*Comus*, 588-598]

Evil, as so many poets have insisted, can in the event only prove temporary, for it carries the seeds of its own dissolution within itself.

What then? If life has meaning, Shakespeare seems to say, it is in the living of life itself, in participating, as we must, in the struggle

> Where evil wars in that design immense
> With good, the gear of God's beneficence.

NOTES AND COMMENTS

Grebanier feels that recent critics with sociological, economic, and other "irrelevant" viewpoints have failed to illuminate the true meaning of tragedy. Consequently, he says, the modern reader would do well to return to Aristotle's idea that the function of tragedy is to arouse "pity and fear" in the spectator. Why, according to Grebanier, is Aristotle's view preferable to the socially conscious ideas of tragedy embodied in the works of Arthur Miller or Émile Zola? Why are external circumstances unsatisfying in arousing tragic emotions? Reconsider, in the light of Grebanier's essay, those modern movies and plays which, in your opinion, are tragedies.

Compare the attitudes of James and De Quincey toward the morality of a work of art with Grebanier's interpretation of Shakespeare's morality. Grebanier disagrees with neoclassic interpetations of Shakespeare. Do you find his criticisms justified by Johnson's "Preface to Shakespeare," or is he perhaps in closer harmony with Johnson than he realizes?

SAMUEL JOHNSON

1709-1784

Samuel Johnson, the last of the neoclassicists, both summed up and transcended the literary era which justified its canons of taste by appeal to the classics of ancient Greece and Rome. His encyclopedic knowledge, the judiciousness of his pronouncements, and, most of all, his prodigious achievement made him the literary dictator of late eighteenth-century England. Recognized first as a poet, he later wrote *Rasselas*, a "philosophical romance," one of the precursors of the modern novel. His essays in *The Rambler* and *The Idler*—periodicals he produced almost without assistance—influenced the manners, morals, and taste of the rising middle class. His dictionary—again compiled virtually single-handed—was the first in English of sufficient authority to establish standards of usage for more than a century. And all this says nothing of his greatest work, *The Lives of the Poets*, a high-water mark of English criticism.

The preface to Johnson's edition of Shakespeare, published in 1765, is one of the masterpieces of the neoclassic tradition. But Johnson, here as elsewhere, is more than a neoclassicist. Because of his intense personal engagement with the literature he wrote about, he was able to go beyond the accepted critical principles of his age when they proved too narrow to permit a just appraisal of the works he loved. The "Preface to Shakespeare," in its balance and forcefulness, has influenced almost every succeeding Shakespearean critic.

FROM *Preface to* *The Plays of William Shakespeare, 1765*

THAT PRAISES are without reason lavished on the dead, and that the honors due only to excellence are paid to antiquity, is a complaint likely to be always continued by those who, being able to add nothing to truth, hope for eminence from the heresies of paradox; or those who, being forced by disappointment upon consolatory expedients, are willing to hope from posterity what the present age refuses and flatter themselves that the regard which is yet denied by envy will be at last bestowed by time.

Antiquity, like every other quality that attracts the notice of mankind, has undoubtedly votaries that reverence it, not from reason, but from prejudice. Some seem to admire indiscriminately whatever has been long preserved, without considering that time has sometimes cooperated with chance; all perhaps are more willing to honor past than present excellence; and the mind contemplates genius through the shades of age, as the eye surveys the sun through artificial opacity. The great contention of criticism is to find the faults of the moderns and the beauties of the ancients. While an author is yet living, we estimate his powers by his worst performance; and when he is dead, we rate them by his best.

To works, however, of which the excellence is not absolute and definite, but gradual and comparative; to works not raised upon principles demonstrative and scientific, but appealing wholly to observation and experience, no other test can be applied than length of duration and continuance of esteem. What mankind have long possessed they have often examined and compared; and if they persist to value the possession, it is because frequent comparisons have confirmed opinion in its favor. As among the works of nature no man can properly call a river deep or a mountain high, without the knowledge of many mountains and many rivers; so, in the productions of genius, nothing can be styled excellent till it has been compared with other works of the same kind. Demonstration immediately displays its power and has nothing to hope or fear from the flux of years; but works tentative and experimental must be estimated by their proportion to the general and collective ability of man, as it is discovered in a long succession of endeavors. Of the first building that was raised, it might be with certainty determined that it was round or square, but whether it was spacious or lofty must have been referred to time. The Pythagorean scale of numbers was at once discovered to be perfect; but the poems of Homer we yet know not to transcend the common limits of human intelligence but by remarking that nation after nation, and century after century, has been able to do little more than transpose his incidents, new-name his characters, and paraphrase his sentiments.

The reverence due to writings that have long subsisted arises, therefore, not from any credulous confidence in the superior wisdom of past ages or gloomy persuasion of the degeneracy of mankind, but is the consequence of acknowledged and indubitable positions, that what has been longest known has been most considered, and what is most considered is best understood.

The poet of whose works I have undertaken the revision may now begin to assume the dignity of an ancient and claim the privilege of established fame and prescriptive veneration. He has long outlived his century, the term commonly fixed as the test of literary merit. Whatever advantages he might once derive from personal allusions, local customs, or temporary opinions have for many years been lost; and every topic of merriment or motive of sorrow which the modes of artificial life afforded him now only obscure the scenes which they once illuminated. The effects of favor and competition are at an end; the tradition of his friendships and his enmities have perished; his works support no opinion with arguments nor supply any faction with invectives; they can neither indulge vanity nor gratify malignity; but are read without any other reason than the desire of pleasure and are therefore praised only as pleasure is obtained; yet, thus unassisted by interest or passion, they have passed through variations of taste and changes of manners, and, as they devolved from one generation to another, have received new honors at every transmission.

But because human judgment, though it be gradually gaining upon certainty, never becomes infallible; and approbation, though long continued, may yet be only the approbation of prejudice or fashion; it is proper to inquire by what peculiarities of excellence Shakespeare has gained and kept the favor of his countrymen.

Nothing can please many, and please long, but just representations of general nature. Particular manners can be known to few, and therefore few only can judge how nearly they are copied. The irregular combinations of fanciful invention may delight awhile by that novelty of which the common satiety of life sends us all in quest; but the pleasures of sudden wonder are soon exhausted, and the mind can only repose on the stability of truth.

Shakespeare is, above all writers, at least above all modern writers, the poet of nature, the poet that holds up to his readers a faithful mirror of manners and of life. His characters are not modified by the customs of particular places, unpracticed by the rest of the world; by the peculiarities of studies or professions which can operate but upon small numbers; or by the accidents of transient fashions or temporary opinions: they are the genuine progeny of common humanity, such as the world will always supply, and observation will always find. His persons act and speak by the influence of those general passions and principles by which all minds are agitated and the whole system of life is continued in motion. In the writings of other poets a character is too often an individual; in those of Shakespeare it is commonly a species.

It is from this wide extension of design that so much instruction is derived. It is this which fills the plays of Shakespeare with practical axioms and domestic wisdom. It was said of Euripides that every verse was a precept; and it may be said of Shakespeare that from his works may be collected a system of civil and economical prudence. Yet his real power is not shown in the splendor of particular passages, but by the progress of his fable and the tenor of his dialogue; and he that tries to recommend him by select quotations will succeed like the pedant in Hierocles, who, when he offered his house to sale, carried a brick in his pocket as a specimen.

It will not easily be imagined how much Shakespeare excels in accommodating his sentiments to real life but by comparing him with other authors. It was observed of the ancient schools of declamation that the more diligently they were frequented, the more was the student disqualified for the world, because he found nothing there which he should ever meet in any other place. The same remark may be applied to every stage but that of Shakespeare. The theater, when it is under any other direction, is peopled by such characters as were never seen, conversing in a language which was never heard, upon topics which will never arise in the commerce of mankind. But the dialogue of this author is often so evidently determined by the incident which produces it, and is pursued with so much ease and simplicity, that it seems scarcely to claim the merit of fiction, but to have been gleaned by diligent selection out of common conversation and common occurrences.

Upon every other stage the universal agent is love, by whose power all good and evil is distributed and every action quickened or retarded. To bring a lover, a lady, and a rival into the fable; to entangle them in contradictory obligations, perplex them with oppositions of interest, and harass them with violence of desires inconsistent with each other; to make them meet in rapture and part in agony, to fill their mouths with hyperbolical joy and outrageous sorrow, to distress them as nothing human ever was distressed, to deliver them as nothing human ever was delivered, is the business of a modern dramatist. For this, probability is violated, life is misrepresented, and language is depraved. But love is only one of many passions; and as it has no great influence upon the sum of life, it has little operation in the dramas of a poet who caught his ideas from the living world and exhibited only what he saw before him. He knew that any other passion, as it was regular or exorbitant, was a cause of happiness or calamity.

Characters thus ample and general were not easily discriminated and preserved, yet perhaps no poet ever kept his personages more distinct from each other. I will not say with Pope that every speech may be assigned to the proper speaker, because many speeches there are which have nothing characteristical; but, perhaps, though some may be equally adapted to every person, it will be difficult to find any that can be properly transferred from the present possessor to another claimant. The choice is right, when there is reason for choice.

Other dramatists can only gain attention by hyperbolical or aggravated characters, by fabulous and unexampled excellence or depravity, as the writers of barbarous romances invigorated the reader by a giant and a dwarf; and he that should form his expectations of human affairs from the play, or from the tale, would be equally deceived. Shakespeare has no heroes; his scenes are occupied only by men, who act and speak as the reader thinks that he should himself have spoken or acted on the same occasion. Even where the agency is supernatural, the dialogue is level with life. Other writers disguise the most natural passions and most frequent incidents; so that he who contemplates them in the book will not know them in the world. Shakespeare approximates the remote and familiarizes the wonderful; the event which he represents will not happen, but, if it were possible, its effects would probably be such as he has assigned; and it may be said that he has not only shown human nature as it acts in real exigences, but as it would be found in trials to which it cannot be exposed.

This, therefore, is the praise of Shakespeare, that his drama is the mirror of life; that he who has mazed his imagination in following the phantoms which other writers raise up before him, may here be cured of his delirious ecstasies by reading human sentiments in human language, by scenes from which a hermit may estimate the transactions of the world and a confessor predict the progress of the passions.

His adherence to general nature has exposed him to the censure of critics who form their judgments upon narrower principles. Dennis and Rymer think his Romans not sufficiently Roman;[1] and Voltaire censures his kings as not completely royal. Dennis is offended that Menenius, a senator of Rome, should play the buffoon; and Voltaire perhaps thinks decency violated when the Danish usurper is represented as a drunkard. But Shakespeare always makes nature predominate over accident; and, if he preserves the essential character, is not very careful of distinctions superinduced and adventitious. His story requires Romans or kings, but he thinks only on men. He knew that Rome, like every other city, had men of all dispositions; and wanting a buffoon, he went into the senate house for that which the senate house would certainly have afforded him. He was inclined to show an usurper and a murderer not only odious, but despicable; he therefore added drunkenness to his other qualities, knowing that kings love wine like other men, and that wine exerts its natural power upon kings. These are the petty cavils of petty minds; a poet overlooks the casual distinction of country and condition, as a painter, satisfied with the figure, neglects the drapery.

The censure which he has incurred by mixing comic and tragic scenes, as it extends to all his works, deserves more consideration. Let the fact be first stated and then examined.

Shakespeare's plays are not in the rigorous and critical sense

---

[1 Dennis and Rymer, earlier eighteenth-century critics, were much concerned with "decorum." This neoclassic idea insisted that the dramatist observe a code of proprieties which made realistic representation virtually impossible and condemned much of Shakespeare as hopelessly vulgar. Though English tragedies composed under its aegis are notorious for their static dullness, Racine and Corneille succeeded in using the conventions "decorum" demanded to produce the greatest French dramas.—Ed.]

either tragedies or comedies, but compositions of a distinct kind; exhibiting the real state of sublunary nature, which partakes of good and evil, joy and sorrow, mingled with endless variety of proportion and innumerable modes of combination; and express- ing the course of the world, in which the loss of one is the gain of another; in which, at the same time, the reveller is hasting to his wine, and the mourner burying his friend; in which the malig- nity of one is sometimes defeated by the frolic of another; and many mischiefs and many benefits are done and hindered without design.

Out of this chaos of mingled purposes and casualties the ancient poets, according to the laws which custom had prescribed, selected some the crimes of men, and some their absurdities; some the momentous vicissitudes of life, and some the lighter occur- rences; some the terrors of distress, and some the gaieties of prosperity. Thus rose the two modes of imitation, known by the names of *tragedy* and *comedy*, compositions intended to promote different ends by contrary means, and considered as so little allied that I do not recollect among the Greeks or Romans a single writer who attempted both.

Shakespeare has united the powers of exciting laughter and sorrow not only in one mind but in one composition. Almost all his plays are divided between serious and ludicrous characters, and, in the successive evolutions of the design, sometimes produce seriousness and sorrow, and sometimes levity and laughter.

That this is a practice contrary to the rules of criticism will be readily allowed; but there is always an appeal open from criti- cism to nature. The end of writing is to instruct; the end of poetry is to instruct by pleasing. That the mingled drama may convey all the instruction of tragedy or comedy cannot be denied, because it includes both in its alternations of exhibition and approaches nearer than either to the appearance of life, by showing how great machinations and slender designs may promote or obviate one another, and the high and the low co-operate in the general sys- tem by unavoidable concatenation.

It is objected that by this change of scenes the passions are interrupted in their progression, and that the principal event, being not advanced by a due gradation of preparatory incidents, wants at last the power to move, which constitutes the perfection of dramatic poetry. This reasoning is so specious that it is received as true even by those who in daily experience feel it to be false. The interchanges of mingled scenes seldom fail to produce the intended vicissitudes of passion. Fiction cannot move so much but that the attention may be easily transferred; and though it must be allowed that pleasing melancholy be sometimes interrupted by unwelcome levity, yet let it be considered likewise that melancholy is often not pleasing, and that the disturbance of one man may be the relief of another; that different auditors have different habitudes; and that, upon the whole, all pleasure consists in variety.

The players, who in their edition divided our author's works into comedies, histories, and tragedies, seem not to have distinguished the three kinds by any very exact or definite ideas.

An action which ended happily to the principal persons, however serious or distressful through its intermediate incidents, in their opinion constituted a comedy. This idea of a comedy continued long amongst us; and plays were written which, by changing the catastrophe, were tragedies today and comedies tomorrow.

Tragedy was not in those times a poem of more general dignity of elevation than comedy; it required only a calamitous conclusion, with which the common criticism of the age was satisfied, whatever lighter pleasure it afforded in its progress.

History was a series of actions, with no other than chronological succession, independent on each other, and without any tendency to introduce or regulate the conclusion. It is not always very nicely distinguished from tragedy. There is not much nearer approach to unity of action in the tragedy of *Antony and Cleopatra* than in the history of *Richard the Second*. But a history might be continued through many plays; as it had no plan, it had no limits.

Through all these denominations of the drama, Shakespeare's mode of composition is the same: an interchange of seriousness and merriment, by which the mind is softened at one time and exhilarated at another. But whatever be his purpose, whether to gladden or depress, or to conduct the story, without vehemence or emotion, through tracts of easy and familiar dialogue, he never fails to attain his purpose; as he commands us, we laugh or mourn, or sit silent with quiet expectation, in tranquillity without indifference.

When Shakespeare's plan is understood, most of the criticisms of Rymer and Voltaire vanish away. The play of *Hamlet* is opened, without impropriety, by two sentinels; Iago bellows at Brabantio's window without injury to the scheme of the play, though in terms which a modern audience would not easily endure; the character of Polonius is seasonable and useful; and the gravediggers themselves may be heard with applause.

Shakespeare engaged in dramatic poetry with the world open before him; the rules of the ancients were yet known to few; the public judgment was unformed; he had no example of such fame as might force him upon imitation, nor critics of such authority as might restrain his extravagance; he therefore indulged his natural disposition; and his disposition, as Rymer has remarked, led him to comedy. In tragedy he often writes, with great appearance of toil and study, what is written at last with little felicity; but, in his comic scenes, he seems to produce, without labor, what no labor can improve. In tragedy he is always struggling after some occasion to be comic; but in comedy he seems to repose, or to luxuriate, as in a mode of thinking congenial to his nature. In his tragic scenes there is always something wanting, but his comedy often surpasses expectation or desire. His comedy pleases by the thoughts and the language, and his tragedy for the greater part by incident and action. His tragedy seems to be skill, his comedy to be instinct.

The force of his comic scenes has suffered little diminution, from the changes made by a century and a half, in manners or in words. As his personages act upon principles arising from genuine passion, very little modified by particular forms, their pleasures and vexations are communicable to all times and to all places; they are natural, and therefore durable. The adventitious peculiarities of personal habits are only superficial dyes, bright and pleasing for a little while, yet soon fading to a dim tinct, without any remains of former lustre; but the discriminations of true passion are the colors of nature; they pervade the whole mass and can only perish with the body that exhibits them. The accidental compositions of heterogeneous modes are dissolved by the chance which combined them; but the uniform simplicity of primitive qualities neither admits increase nor suffers decay. The sand heaped by one flood is scattered by another, but the rock always continues in its place. The stream of time, which is continually washing the dissoluble fabrics of other poets, passes without injury by the adamant of Shakespeare.

If there be, what I believe there is, in every nation a style which never becomes obsolete, a certain mode of phraseology so consonant and congenial to the analogy and principles of its respective language as to remain settled and unaltered; this style is probably to be sought in the common intercourse of life, among those who speak only to be understood, without ambition of elegance. The polite are always catching modish innovations, and the learned depart from established forms of speech in hope of finding or making better; those who wish for distinction forsake the vulgar, when the vulgar is right; but there is a conversation above grossness and below refinement, where propriety resides, and where this poet seems to have gathered his comic dialogue. He is therefore more agreeable to the ears of the present age than any other author equally remote and among his other excellencies deserves to be studied as one of the original masters of our language.

These observations are to be considered not as unexceptionably constant, but as containing general and predominant truth. Shakespeare's familiar dialogue is affirmed to be smooth and clear, yet not wholly without ruggedness or difficulty; as a country may be eminently fruitful, though it has spots unfit for cultivation; his characters are praised as natural, though their sentiments are sometimes forced and their actions improbable; as the earth upon the whole is spherical, though its surface is varied with protuberances and cavities.

Shakespeare with his excellencies has likewise faults, and faults sufficient to obscure and overwhelm any other merit. I shall show them in the proportion in which they appear to me, without envious malignity or superstitious veneration. No question can be more innocently discussed than a dead poet's pretensions to renown; and little regard is due to that bigotry which sets candor higher than truth.

His first defect is that to which may be imputed most of the evil in books or in men. He sacrifices virtue to convenience and is so much more careful to please than to instruct that he seems to write without any moral purpose. From his writings indeed a system of social duty may be selected, for he that thinks reasonably must think morally; but his precepts and axioms drop casually from him; he makes no just distribution of good or evil, nor is always careful to show in the virtuous a disapprobation of the wicked; he carries his persons indifferently through right and wrong and at the close dismisses them without further care and leaves their examples to operate by chance. This fault the barbarity of his age cannot extenuate; for it is always a writer's duty to make the world better, and justice is a virtue independent on time or place.

The plots are often so loosely formed that a very slight consideration may improve them, and so carelessly pursued that he seems not always fully to comprehend his own design. He omits opportunities of instructing or delighting which the train of his story seems to force upon him, and apparently rejects those exhibitions which would be more affecting, for the sake of those which are more easy.

It may be observed that in many of his plays the latter part is evidently neglected. When he found himself near the end of his work, and in view of his reward, he shortened the labor to snatch the profit. He therefore remits his efforts where he should most vigorously exert them, and his catastrophe is improbably produced or imperfectly represented.

He had no regard to distinction of time or place, but gives to one age or nation, without scruple, the customs, institutions, and opinions of another, at the expense not only of likelihood but of possibility. These faults Pope has endeavored, with more zeal than judgment, to transfer to his imagined interpolators. We need not wonder to find Hector quoting Aristotle,[1] when we see the loves of Theseus and Hippolyta combined with the Gothic mythology of fairies.[2] Shakespeare, indeed, was not the only violator of chronology, for in the same age Sidney, who wanted not the advantages of learning, has, in his *Arcadia*, confounded the pastoral with the feudal times, the days of innocence, quiet, and security, with those of turbulence, violence, and adventure.

In his comic scenes he is seldom very successful when he engages his characters in reciprocations of smartness and contests of sarcasm; their jests are commonly gross, and their pleasantry licentious; neither his gentlemen nor his ladies have much delicacy nor are sufficiently distinguished from his clowns by any appearance of refined manners. Whether he represented the real conversation of his time is not easy to determine. The reign of Elizabeth is commonly supposed to have been a time of stateliness, formality, and reserve; yet perhaps the relaxations of that severity were not

---

[1] *Troilus and Cressida*, II. ii. 166-167.
[2] *A Midsummer Night's Dream*, throughout.

very elegant. There must, however, have been always some modes of gaiety preferable to others, and a writer ought to choose the best.

In tragedy his performance seems constantly to be worse as his labor is more. The effusions of passion which exigence forces out are for the most part striking and energetic; but whenever he solicits his invention, or strains his faculties, the offspring of his throes is tumor, meanness, tediousness, and obscurity.

In narration he affects a disproportionate pomp of diction and a wearisome train of circumlocution and tells the incident imperfectly in many words which might have been more plainly delivered in few. Narration in dramatic poetry is naturally tedious, as it is unanimated and inactive and obstructs the progress of the action; it should therefore always be rapid and enlivened by frequent interruption. Shakespeare found it an incumbrance and, instead of lightening it by brevity, endeavored to recommend it by dignity and splendor.

His declamations or set speeches arc commonly cold and weak, for his power was the power of nature; when he endeavored, like other tragic writers, to catch opportunities of amplification, and, instead of inquiring what the occasion demanded, to show how much his stores of knowledge could supply, he seldom escapes without the pity or resentment of his reader.

It is incident to him to be now and then entangled with an unwieldy sentiment, which he cannot well express and will not reject; he struggles with it awhile, and, if it continues stubborn, comprises it in words such as occur and leaves it to be disentangled and evolved by those who have more leisure to bestow upon it.

Not that always where the language is intricate the thought is subtle, or the image always great where the line is bulky; the equality of words to things is very often neglected, and trivial sentiments and vulgar ideas disappoint the attention to which they are recommended by sonorous epithets and swelling figures.

But the admirers of this great poet have most reason to complain when he approaches nearest to his highest excellence and seems fully resolved to sink them in dejection and mollify them with tender emotions by the fall of greatness, the danger of innocence, or the crosses of love.[1] What he does best, he soon

[1 Johnson intends "sink them in dejection" as praise. His criticism is that Shakespeare limits his most powerful passages by introducing elements which distract the reader from the emotions he has so effectively produced.—Ed.]

ceases to do. He is not long soft and pathetic without some idle conceit or contemptible equivocation. He no sooner begins to move than he counteracts himself; and terror and pity, as they are rising in the mind, are checked and blasted by sudden frigidity.

A quibble is to Shakespeare what luminous vapors are to the traveler; he follows it at all adventures; it is sure to lead him out of his way and sure to engulf him in the mire. It has some malignant power over his mind, and its fascinations are irresistible. Whatever be the dignity or profundity of his disquisition, whether he be enlarging knowledge or exalting affection, whether he be *amusing* attention with incidents or enchaining it in suspense, let but a quibble spring up before him, and he leaves his work unfinished. A quibble is the golden apple for which he will always turn aside from his career or stoop from his elevation. A quibble, poor and barren as it is, gave him such delight that he was content to purchase it by the sacrifice of reason, propriety, and truth. A quibble was to him the fatal Cleopatra for which he lost the world and was content to lose it.

It will be thought strange that in enumerating the defects of this writer I have not yet mentioned his neglect of the unities,[1] his violation of those laws which have been instituted and established by the joint authority of poets and critics.

For his other deviations from the art of writing, I resign him to critical justice, without making any other demand in his favor than that which must be indulged to all human excellence: that his virtues be rated with his failings. But from the censure which this irregularity may bring upon him, I shall, with due reverence to that learning which I must oppose, adventure to try how I can defend him.

His histories, being neither tragedies nor comedies, are not subject to any of their laws; nothing more is necessary to all the praise which they expect than that the changes of action be so prepared as to be understood, that the incidents be various and affecting, and the characters consistent, natural, and distinct. No other unity is intended, and therefore none is to be sought.

[1 The neoclassic theory of the "unities" required that a correct dramatist give his play not only unity of plot but also unity of time and place. That is, he was to use only one set and to limit his action to 24 hours. Aristotle was cited as the authority for the rule. It is, however, based upon a misreading of both the letter and the spirit of the *Poetics.—Ed.*]

In his other works he has well enough preserved the unity of action. He has not, indeed, an intrigue regularly perplexed and regularly unraveled; he does not endeavor to hide his design only to discover it, for this is seldom the order of real events, and Shakespeare is the poet of nature; but his plan has commonly, what Aristotle requires, a beginning, a middle, and an end; one event is concatenated with another, and the conclusion follows by easy consequence. There are perhaps some incidents that might be spared, as in other poets there is much talk that only fills up time upon the stage; but the general system makes gradual advances, and the end of the play is the end of expectation.

To the unities of time and place he has shown no regard; and perhaps a nearer view of the principles on which they stand will diminish their value and withdraw from them the veneration which, from the time of Corneille, they have very generally received, by discovering that they have given more trouble to the poet than pleasure to the auditor.

The necessity of observing the unities of time and place arises from the supposed necessity of making the drama credible. The critics hold it impossible that an action of months or years can be possibly believed to pass in three hours; or that the spectator can suppose himself to sit in the theater while ambassadors go and return between distant kings, while armies are levied and towns besieged, while an exile wanders and returns, or till he whom they saw courting his mistress shall lament the untimely fall of his son. The mind revolts from evident falsehood, and fiction loses its force when it departs from the resemblance of reality.

From the narrow limitation of time necessarily arises the contraction of place. The spectator, who knows that he saw the first act at Alexandria, cannot suppose that he sees the next at Rome, at a distance to which not the dragons of Medea could, in so short a time, have transported him; he knows with certainty that he has not changed his place; and he knows that place cannot change itself; that what was a house cannot become a plain; that what was Thebes can never be Persepolis.

Such is the triumphant language with which a critic exults over the misery of an irregular poet and exults commonly without resistance or reply. It is time, therefore, to tell him by the authority of Shakespeare, that he assumes, as an unquestionable principle, a position which, while his breath is forming it into words, his understanding pronounces to be false. It is false, that any representation is mistaken for reality; that any dramatic fable in its materiality was ever credible, or, for a single moment, was ever credited.

The objection arising from the impossibility of passing the first hour at Alexandria and the next at Rome, supposes that when the play opens the spectator really imagines himself at Alexandria and believes that his walk to the theater has been a voyage to Egypt, and that he lives in the days of Antony and Cleopatra. Surely he that imagines this may imagine more. He that can take the stage at one time for the palace of the Ptolemies may take it in half an hour for the promontory of Actium. Delusion, if delusion be admitted, has no certain limitation; if the spectator can be once persuaded that his old acquaintances are Alexander and Caesar, that a room illuminated with candles is the plain of Pharsalia or the bank of Granicus, he is in a state of elevation above the reach of reason or of truth, and from the heights of empyrean poetry may despise the circumscriptions of terrestrial nature. There is no reason why a mind thus wandering in ecstasy should count the clock, or why an hour should not be a century in that calenture of the brains that can make the stage a field.

The truth is that the spectators are always in their senses and know, from the first act to the last that the stage is only a stage, and that the players are only players. They come to hear a certain number of lines recited with just gesture and elegant modulation. The lines relate to some action, and an action must be in some place; but the different actions that complete a story may be in places very remote from each other; and where is the absurdity of allowing that space to represent first Athens and then Sicily which was always known to be neither Sicily nor Athens, but a modern theater.

By supposition, as place is introduced, time may be extended; the time required by the fable elapses for the most part between the acts; for, of so much of the action as is represented, the real and poetical duration is the same. If in the first act preparations for war against Mithridates are represented to be made in Rome, the event of the war may, without absurdity, be represented in the catastrophe as happening in Pontus; we know that there is neither war nor preparation for war; we know that we are neither in Rome nor Pontus; that neither Mithridates nor Lucullus are before us. The drama exhibits successive imitations of successive actions; and why may not the second imitation represent an action that happened years after the first, if it be so connected with it that nothing but time can be supposed to intervene? Time is, of all modes of existence, most obsequious to the imagination; a lapse of years is as easily conceived as a passage of hours. In contemplation we easily contract the time of real actions and therefore willingly permit it to be contracted when we only see their imitation.

It will be asked how the drama moves if it is not credited. It is credited with all the credit due to a drama. It is credited, whenever it moves, as a just picture of a real original; as representing to the auditor what he would himself feel if he were to do or suffer what is there feigned to be suffered or to be done. The reflection that strikes the heart is not that the evils before us are real evils, but that they are evils to which we ourselves may be exposed. If there be any fallacy, it is not that we fancy the players, but that we fancy ourselves unhappy for a moment; but we rather lament the possibility than suppose the presence of misery, as a mother weeps over her babe when she remembers that death may take it from her. The delight of tragedy proceeds from our consciousness of fiction; if we thought murders and treasons real, they would please no more.

Imitations produce pain or pleasure, not because they are mistaken for realities, but because they bring realities to mind. When the imagination is recreated by a painted landscape, the trees are not supposed capable to give us shade, or the fountains coolness; but we consider how we should be pleased with such fountains playing beside us and such woods waving over us. We are agitated in reading the history of *Henry the Fifth*, yet no man takes his book for the field of Agincourt. A dramatic exhibition is a book recited with concomitants that increase or diminish its effect. Familiar comedy is often more powerful in the theater than on the page; imperial tragedy is always less. The humor of Petruchio may be heightened by grimace; but what voice or what gesture can hope to add dignity or force to the soliloquy of Cato? [1]

A play read affects the mind like a play acted. It is therefore evident that the action is not supposed to be real; and it follows that between the acts a longer or shorter time may be allowed to pass, and that no more account of space or duration is to be taken

[1] Addison, *Cato*, V. i.

by the auditor of a drama than by the reader of a narrative, before whom may pass in an hour the life of a hero or the revolutions of an empire.

Whether Shakespeare knew the unities and rejected them by design, or deviated from them by happy ignorance, it is, I think, impossible to decide and useless to inquire. We may reasonably suppose that, when he rose to notice, he did not want the counsels and admonitions of scholars and critics, and that he at last deliberately persisted in a practice, which he might have begun by chance. As nothing is essential to the fable but unity of action, and as the unities of time and place arise evidently from false assumptions, and, by circumscribing the extent of the drama, lessen its variety, I cannot think it much to be lamented that they were not known by him, or not observed; nor, if such another poet could arise, should I very vehemently reproach him that his first act passed at Venice and his next in Cyprus.[1] Such violations of rules merely positive become the comprehensive genius of Shakespeare, and such censures are suitable to the minute and slender criticism of Voltaire:

> Non usque adeo permiscuit imis
> Longus summa dies ut non, si voce Metelli
> Serventur leges, malint a Caesare tolli.[2]

Yet when I speak thus slightly of dramatic rules, I cannot but recollect how much wit and learning may be produced against me; before such authorities I am afraid to stand, not that I think the present question one of those that are to be decided by mere authority, but because it is to be suspected that these precepts have not been so easily received but for better reasons than I have yet been able to find. The result of my inquiries, in which it would be ludicrous to boast of impartiality, is that the unities of time and place are not essential to a just drama; that, though they may sometimes conduce to pleasure, they are always to be sacrificed to the nobler beauties of variety and instruction; and that a play written with nice observation of critical rules is to be contemplated as an elaborate curiosity, as the product of superfluous and ostenta-

---

[1] *Othello*, Acts I and II.

[2] Lucan, *Pharsalia*, III. 138-140: "The passage of time has not wrought such confusion that the laws, rather than be saved by Metullus, would not prefer to be saved by Caesar."

tious art, by which is shown, rather what is possible, than what is necessary.

He that, without diminution of any other excellence, shall preserve all the unities unbroken deserves the like applause with the architect who shall display all the orders of architecture in a citadel without any deduction from its strength; but the principal beauty of a citadel is to exclude the enemy, and the greatest graces of a play are to copy nature and instruct life.

NOTES AND COMMENTS

In spite of his independence of mind, Johnson was a child of his age. His insistence that moralizing or teaching is a necessary function of poetry and his conviction that Shakespeare was a greater writer of comedies than of tragedies may puzzle the modern reader, but such opinions were commonly held in his day. Similarly, Johnson's praise of Shakespeare for presenting characters who are species rather than individuals is rather startling. But in the light of his discussion of Claudius in *Hamlet* and the foolish senator in *Julius Caesar*, do you think the strangeness lies more in his terminology than in his ideas?

In the nineteenth century Romantic critics condemned Johnson for his style, which they found pompous and artificial. If one insists that the best style is the most nearly colloquial, Johnson surely is at fault, but just as surely, he achieves by his carefully balanced sentences and rounded periods an effect not possible to a less formal manner.

There is balance also in Johnson's method of argumentation. The opening sections, for instance, are a debate upon the validity of equating what is good with what is old. Note Johnson's balanced resolution of the question in the fourth paragraph, the point at which his style, his rhetoric, and his judgment meet. Does a similar technique govern the development of the rest of the selection?

Johnson was not the first to attack the unities and the notion of verisimilitude to which their supporters appealed. His stature and the forcefulness of his argument against this rather sterile idea that the stage must conform literally to the conditions of off-stage reality did, however, end the discussion in his own time. But the issue is a perennial one. For a more recent critic's animadversions against a theory which literalizes the stage, see Walter Kerr's *How Not to Write a Play*. For a discussion of the dangers of an over-literal approach in another art form, look again at Henry James's "The Art of Fiction."

ALDOUS HUXLEY

1894-

Aldous Huxley comes of a family associated with science for almost a century: his grandfather was Thomas Henry Huxley, whose writings on evolution earned him the nickname "Darwin's Bulldog"; his brother is the biologist Julian Huxley (see page 391). But Aldous Huxley's career recalls rather that of another of his famous relatives, his great-uncle Matthew Arnold, the pre-eminent Victorian spokesman for the humanist tradition. A novelist and essayist, Huxley began by writing satires—*Antic Hay, Brave New World, Point Counter Point, Eyeless in Gaza*, among others—which reflected caustically on the twentieth century's limiting preoccupation with the material. In his later works, like *Time Must Have a Stop*, he has considered the view of life metaphysics and religion can provide.

This essay, which appeared in 1925 in *Along the Road*, represents the earlier Huxley and his mordant view of contemporary civilization.

Popular Music

THERE IS a certain jovial, bouncing, hoppety little tune with which any one who has spent even a few weeks in Germany, or has been tended in childhood by a German nurse, must be very familiar. Its name is "Ach, du lieber Augustin." It is a merry little affair in three-four time; in rhythm and melody so simple, that the village idiot could sing it after a first hearing; in sentiment so inno-

Reprinted from *Along the Road* by Aldous Huxley. Copyright renewed 1953 by Aldous Huxley. By permission of Harper and Brothers and Chatto and Windus Ltd., London.

cent that the heart of the most susceptible maiden would not
quicken by a beat a minute at the sound of it. Rum ti-tiddle, Um
tum tum, Um tum tum, Um tum tum: Rum ti-tiddle, Um tum
tum, Um tum tum, TUM. By the very frankness of its cheerful
imbecility the thing disarms all criticism.

Now for a piece of history. "Ach, du lieber Augustin" was
composed in 1770, and it was the first waltz. The first waltz! I
must ask the reader to hum the tune to himself, then to think of
any modern waltz with which he may be familiar. He will find in
the difference between the tunes a subject richly suggestive of interesting meditations.

The difference between "Ach, du lieber Augustin" and any
waltz tune composed at any date from the middle of the nineteenth century onwards, is the difference between one piece of
music almost completely empty of emotional content and another,
densely saturated with amorous sentiment, languor and voluptuous-
ness. The susceptible maiden who, when she hears "Ach, du lieber
Augustin," feels no emotions beyond a general sense of high spirits
and cheerfulness, is fairly made to palpitate by the luscious strains
of the modern waltz. Her soul is carried swooning along, over
waves of syrup; she seems to breathe an atmosphere heavy with
ambergris and musk. From the jolly little thing it was at its birth,
the waltz has grown into the voluptuous, heart-stirring affair with
which we are now familiar.

And what has happened to the waltz has happened to all
popular music. It was once innocent but is now provocative; once
pellucid, now richly clotted; once elegant, now deliberately barbarous. Compare the music of *The Beggar's Opera* with the music
of a contemporary revue. They differ as life in the garden of Eden
differed from life in the artistic quarter of Gomorrah. The one is
prelapsarian in its airy sweetness, the other is rich, luscious and
loud with conscious savagery.

The evolution of popular music has run parallel on a lower
plane, with the evolution of serious music. The writers of popular
tunes are not musicians enough to be able to invent new forms of
expression. All they do is to adapt the discoveries of original
geniuses to the vulgar taste. Ultimately and indirectly, Beethoven
is responsible for all the languishing waltz tunes, all the savage
jazzings, for all that is maudlin and violent in our popular music.
He is responsible because it was he who first devised really effective

musical methods for the direct expression of emotion. Beethoven's emotions happened to be noble; moreover, he was too intellectual a musician to neglect the formal, architectural side of music. But unhappily he made it possible for composers of inferior mind and character to express in music their less exalted passions and vulgarer emotions. He made possible the weakest sentimentalities of Schumann, the baroque grandiosities of Wagner, the hysterics of Scriabine; he made possible the waltzes of all the Strausses, from the *Blue Danube* to the waltz from *Salome*. And he made possible, at a still further remove, such masterpieces of popular art as "You made me love you" and "That coal black mammy of mine."

For the introduction of a certain vibrant sexual quality into music, Beethoven is perhaps less directly responsible than the nineteenth-century Italians. I used often to wonder why it was that Mozart's operas were less popular than those of Verdi, Leoncavallo and Puccini. You couldn't ask for more, or more infectiously "catchy" tunes than are to be found in *Figaro* or *Don Giovanni*. The music though "classical," is not obscure, nor forbiddingly complex. On the contrary it is clear, simple with that seemingly easy simplicity which only consummate genius can achieve and thoroughly engaging. And yet for every time *Don Giovanni* is played, *La Bohème* is played a hundred. *Tosca* is at least fifty times as popular as *Figaro*. And if you look through a catalogue of gramophone records you will find that, while you can buy *Rigoletto* complete in thirty discs, there are not more than three records of *The Magic Flute*. This seems at first sight extremely puzzling. But the reason is not really far to seek. Since Mozart's day composers have learned the art of making music throatily and palpitatingly sexual. The arias of Mozart have a beautiful clear purity which renders them utterly insipid compared with the sobbing, catch-in-the-throaty melodies of the nineteenth-century Italians. The public, having accustomed itself to this stronger and more turbid brewage, finds no flavor in the crystal songs of Mozart.

No essay on modern popular music would be complete without some grateful reference to Rossini, who was, as far as I know, the first composer to show what charms there are in vulgar melody. Melodies before Rossini's day were often exceedingly commonplace and cheap; but almost never do they possess that almost indefinable quality of low vulgarity which adorns some of the most successful of Rossini's airs, and which we recognize as being some-how a modern, contemporary quality. The methods which Rossini employed for the achievement of his melodic vulgarity are not easy to analyze. His great secret, I fancy, was the very short and easily memorable phrase frequently repeated in different parts of the scale. But it is easiest to define by example. Think of Moses' first aria in *Moses in Egypt*. That is an essentially vulgar melody; and it is quite unlike the popular melodies of an earlier date. Its affinities are with the modern popular tune. It is to his invention of vulgar tunes that Rossini owed his enormous contemporary success. Vulgar people before his day had to be content with Mozart's delicate airs. Rossini came and revealed to them a more congenial music. That the world fell down and gratefully worshiped him is not surprising. If he has long ceased to be popular, that is because his successors, profiting by his lessons, have achieved in his own vulgar line triumphs of which he could not have dreamed.

Barbarism has entered popular music from two sources—from the music of barbarous people, like the Negroes, and from serious music which has drawn upon barbarism for its inspiration. The technique of being barbarous effectively has come, of course, from serious music. In the elaboration of this technique no musicians have done more than the Russians. If Rimsky-Korsakoff had never lived, modern dance music would not be the thing it is.

Whether, having grown inured to such violent and purely physiological stimuli as the clashing and drumming, the rhythmic throbbing and wailing glissandos of modern jazz music can supply, the world will ever revert to something less crudely direct, is a matter about which one cannot prophesy. Even serious musicians seem to find it hard to dispense with barbarism. In spite of the monotony and the appalling lack of subtlety which characterize the process, they persist in banging away in the old Russian manner, as though there were nothing more interesting or exciting to be thought of. When, as a boy, I first heard Russian music, I was carried off my feet by its wild melodies, its persistent, its relentlessly throbbing rhythms. But my excitement grew less and less with every hearing. Today no music seems to me more tedious. The only music a civilized man can take unfailing pleasure in is civilized music. If you were compelled to listen every day of your life to a single piece of music, would you choose Stravinsky's "Oiseau de Feu" or Beethoven's "Grosse Fuge"? Obviously, you would choose the fugue, if only for its intricacy and because there is more in it to occupy the mind than in the Russian's too simple rhythms. Composers seem to forget that we are, in spite of everything and though appearances may be against us, tolerably civilized. They overwhelm us not merely with Russian and negroid noises, but with Celtic caterwaulings on the black notes, with dismal Spanish wailings, punctuated by the rattle of the castanets and the clashing harmonies of the guitar. When serious composers have gone back to civilized music—and already some of them are turning from barbarism—we shall probably hear a corresponding change for the more refined in popular music. But until serious musicians lead the way, it will be absurd to expect the vulgarizers to change their style.

NOTES AND COMMENTS

Huxley, writing about music as a man of letters, can permit himself in the interests of liveliness and emphasis the sort of generalizations a musician would avoid. But the generalizations need testing. How much do you think modern popular music owes to the serious music composed "from the middle of the nineteenth century onwards"? One thinks immediately, of course, of "pop" songs based on melodies borrowed from Chopin, Tchaikovsky, and others. But is there a connection between Stravinsky's "The Rite of Spring" and jazz—or even rock 'n' roll?

Perhaps Huxley in places pushes his point a little too far. In his discussion of barbarism, does he fail to distinguish between the vulgar and the primitive? Can truly primitive music—certain folk music, for example, or African work songs and ritual music—be vulgar at all? Does some popular music (Gershwin's, perhaps) express emotion both directly and tastefully?

The question of emotion in music is complex. Bach and Mozart never expressed emotion as Wagner did in the "Liebestod" from *Tristan und Isolde,* but would they have been writing music if they had not expressed emotion at all?

CLEMENT GREENBERG

1909-

Clement Greenberg, an artist himself, has written extensively on modern art and its place in twentieth-century culture for such magazines as *The Nation*, *Partisan Review*, and *Horizon*. He has also published book-length studies of Joan Miró and Henri Matisse. This essay reveals his concern not only for abstract art but for art itself.

The Case for Abstract Art

MANY PEOPLE SAY that the kind of art our age produces is one of the major symptoms of what's wrong with the age. The disintegration and, finally, the disappearance of recognizable images in painting and sculpture, like the obscurity in advanced literature, are supposed to reflect a disintegration of values in society itself. Some people go further and say that abstract, nonrepresentational art is pathological art, crazy art, and that those who practice it and those who admire and buy it are either sick or silly. The kindest critics are those who say it's all a joke, a hoax, and a fad, and that modernist art in general, or abstract art in particular, will soon pass. This sort of thing is heard or read pretty constantly, but in some years more often than others.

There seems to be a certain rhythm in the advance in popularity of modernist art, and a certain rhythm in the counter-attacks which try to stem it. More or less the same works or arguments are used in all the polemics, but the targets usually change. Once it

Reprinted from *Adventures of the Mind*, copyright 1958, 1959 by the Curtis Publishing Company. By permission of the author.

was the impressionists who were a scandal, next it was Van Gogh and Cézanne, then it was Matisse, then it was cubism and Picasso, after that Mondrian, and now it is Jackson Pollock. The fact that Pollock was an American shows, in a backhanded way, how important American art has lately become.

Some of the same people who attack modernist art in general, or abstract art in particular, happen also to complain that our age has lost those habits of disinterested contemplation, and that capacity for enjoying things as ends in themselves and for their own sake, which former ages are supposed to have cultivated. This idea has been advanced often enough to convert it into a cliché. I hate to give assent to a cliché, for it is almost always an over-simplification, but I have to make an exception in this case. While I strongly doubt that disinterested contemplation was as unalloyed or as popular in ages past as is supposed, I do tend to agree that we could do with more of it in this time, and especially in this country.

I think a poor life is lived by any one who doesn't regularly take time out to stand and gaze, or sit and listen, or touch, or smell, or brood, without any further end in mind, simply for the satisfaction gotten from that which is gazed at, listened to, touched, smelled or brooded upon. We all know, however, that the climate of Western life, and particularly of American life, is not conducive to this kind of thing; we are all too busy making a living. This is another cliché, of course. And still a third cliché says that we should learn from Oriental society how to give more of ourselves to the life of the spirit, to contemplation and meditation, and to the appreciation of what is satisfying or beautiful in its own sole right. This last is not only a cliché, but a fallacy, since most Orientals are even more preoccupied than we are with making a living. I hope that I myself am not making a gross and reductive simplification when I say that so much of Oriental contemplative and aesthetic discipline strikes me as a technique for keeping one's eyes averted from ugliness and misery.

Every civilization and every tradition of culture seem to possess capacities for self-cure and self-correction that go into operation automatically, unbidden. If the given tradition goes too far in one direction it will usually try to right itself by going equally far in the opposite one. There is no question but that our Western civilization, especially in its American variant, devotes more mental energy than any other to the production of material things and services; and that, more than any other, it puts stress on interested, purposeful activity in general. This is reflected in our art, which, as has been frequently observed, puts such great emphasis on movement and development and resolution, on beginnings, middles, and endings—that is, on dynamics. Compare Western music with any other kind, or look at Western literature, for that matter, with its relatively great concern with plot and over-all structure and its relatively small concern with tropes and figures and ornamental elaborations; think of how slow-moving Chinese and Japanese poetry is by comparison with ours, and how much it delights in static situations; and how uncertain the narrational logic of non-Western fiction tends to be. Think of how encrusted and convoluted Arabic poetry is by contrast even with our most euphuistic lyrical verse. And as for non-Western music, does it not almost always, and literally, strike us as more monotonous than ours?

Well, how does Western art compensate for, correct, or at least qualify its emphasis on the dynamic—an emphasis that may or may not be excessive? And how does Western life itself compensate for, correct, or at least qualify its obsession with material production and purposeful activity? I shall not here attempt to answer the latter question. But in the realm of art an answer is beginning to emerge of its own accord, and the shape of part of that answer is abstract art.

Abstract decoration is almost universal, and Chinese and Japanese calligraphy is quasi-abstract—abstract to the extent that a few occidentals can read the characters of Chinese or Japanese writing. But only in the West, and only in the last fifty years, have such things as abstract pictures and free-standing pieces of abstract sculpture appeared. What makes the big difference between these and abstract decorations is that they are, exactly, pictures and free-standing sculpture—solo works of art meant to be looked at for their own sake and with full attention, and not as the adjuncts, incidental aspects, or settings of things other than themselves. These abstract pictures and pieces of sculpture challenge our capacity for disinterested contemplation in a way that is more concentrated and, I dare say, more conscious than anything else I know of in art. Music is an essentially abstract art, but even at its most rarefied and abstract, and whether it's Bach's or the middle-period Schoenberg's music, it does not offer this challenge in quite the same way or degree. Music tends from a beginning through a middle toward an ending. We wait to see how it "comes out"— which is what we also do with literature. Of course, the *total* experience of literature and music is completely disinterested, but it becomes that only at a further remove. While undergoing the experience we are caught up and expectant as well as detached— disinterested and at the same time interested in a way resembling that in which we are interested in how things turn out in real life. I exaggerate to make my point—aesthetic experience *has* to be disinterested, and when it is genuine it always is, even when bad works of art are involved—but the distinctions I've made and those I've still to make are valid nevertheless.

With representational painting it is something like what it is with literature. This has been said before, many times before, but usually in order to criticize representational painting in what I think is a wrongheaded when not downright silly way. What I mean when I say, in this context, that representational painting is like literature, is that it tends to involve us in the interested as well as the disinterested by presenting us with the images of things that are inconceivable outside time and action. This goes even for landscapes and flower pieces and still lifes. It is not simply that we sometimes tend to confuse the attractiveness of the things represented in a picture with the quality of the picture itself. And it is not only that attractiveness as such has nothing to do with the abiding success of a work of art. What is more fundamental is that the meaning—as distinct from the attractiveness—of what is represented becomes truly inseparable from the representation itself. That Rembrandt confined impasto—thick paint, that is— to his highlights, and that in his later portraits especially these coincide with the ridges of the noses of his subjects is important to the artistic effect of these portraits. And that the effectiveness of the impasto, as impasto—as an abstract element of technique— coincides with its effectiveness as a means of showing just how a nose looks under a certain kind of light is also genuinely important. And that the lifelike delineation of the nose contributes to the evocation of the personality of the individual to whom the nose belongs is likewise important. And the manner and degree of insight into that individual's personality which Rembrandt exhibits in his portrait is important too. None of these factors can be, or ought to be, separated from the legitimate effect of the portrait as a picture pure and simple.

But once we have to do with personalities and lifelikeness we have to do with things from which we cannot keep as secure a distance for the sake of disinterestedness as we can, say, from abstract decoration. As it happens, the whole tendency of our Western painting, up until the later stages of impressionism, was to make distance and detachment on the part of the spectator as insecure as possible. It laid more of a stress than any other tradition on creating a sculpture-like, or photographic, illusion of the third dimension, on thrusting images at the eye with a lifelikeness that brought them as close as possible to their originals. Because of their sculptural vividness, Western paintings tend to be far less quiet, far more agitated and active—in short, far more explicitly dynamic—than most non-Western paintings do. And they involve the spectator to a much greater extent in the practical and actual aspects of the things they depict and represent.

We begin to wonder what we think of the people shown in Rembrandt's portraits, *as* people; whether or not we would like to walk through the terrain shown in a Corot landscape; about the life stories of the burghers we see in a Steen painting; we react in a less than disinterested way to the attractiveness of the models, real or ideal, of the personages in a Renaissance painting. And once we begin to do this we begin to participate in the work of art in a so-to-speak practical way. In itself this participation may not be improper, but it does become so when it begins to shut out all other factors. This it has done and does, all too often. Even though the connoisseurs have usually been able in the long run to prefer the picture of a dwarf by Velasquez to that of a pretty girl by Howard Chandler Christy, the enjoyment of pictorial and sculptural art in our society has tended, on every other level than that of professional connoisseurship, to be excessively "literary," and to center too much on merely technical feats of copying.

But, as I've said, every tradition of culture tends to try to correct one extreme by going to its opposite. And when our Western tradition of painting came up at last with reservations about its forthright naturalism, these quickly took the form of an equally forthright antinaturalism. These reservations started with late impressionism, and have now culminated in abstract art. I don't at all wish to be understood as saying that it all happened because some artist or artists decided it was time to curb the excesses of realistic painting, and that the main historical significance of abstract art lies in its function as an antidote to these. Nor do I wish to be understood as assuming that realistic or naturalistic art inherently needs, or ever needed, such a thing as an antidote. The motivations, conscious and unconscious, of the first modernist artists, and of present modernists as well, were and are quite different. Impressionism itself started as an effort to push naturalism further than ever before. And all through the history of art—not only in recent times—consequences have escaped intentions.

It is on a different, and more impersonal and far more general level of meaning and history that our culture has generated abstract art as an antidote. On that level this seemingly new kind of art has emerged as an epitome of almost everything that disinterested contemplation requires, and as both a challenge and a reproof to a society that exaggerates, not the necessity, but the intrinsic value of purposeful and interested activity. Abstract art comes, on this level, as a relief, an arch-example of something that does not have to mean, or be useful for, anything other than itself. And it seems fitting, too, that abstract art should at present flourish most in this country. If American society is indeed given over as no other society has been to purposeful activity and material production, then it is right that it should be reminded, in extreme terms, of the essential nature of disinterested activity.

Abstract art does this in very literal and also in very imaginative ways. First, it does not exhibit the illusion or semblance of things we are already familiar with in real life; it gives us no imaginary space through which to walk with the mind's eye; no imaginary objects to desire or not desire; no imaginary people to like or dislike. We are left alone with shapes and colors. These may or may not remind us of real things; but if they do, they usually do so incidentally or accidentally—on our own responsibility as it were; and the genuine enjoyment of an abstract picture does not ordinarily depend on such resemblances.

Second, pictorial art in its highest definition is static; it tries to overcome movement in space or time. This is not to say that the eye does not wander over a painted surface, and thus travel in both space and time. When a picture presents us with an illusion of real space, there is all the more inducement for the eye to do such wandering. But ideally the whole of a picture should be taken in at a glance; its unity should be immediately evident, and the supreme quality of a picture, the highest measure of its power to move and control the visual imagination, should reside in its unity. And this is something to be grasped only in an indivisible instant of time. No expectancy is involved in the true and pertinent experience of a painting; a picture, I repeat, does not "come out" the way a story, or a poem, or a piece of music does. It's all there at once, like a sudden revelation. This "at-onceness" an abstract picture usually drives home to us with greater singleness and clarity than a representational painting does. And to apprehend this "at-onceness" demands a freedom of mind and untrammeledness of eye that constitute "at-onceness" in their own right. Those who have grown capable of experiencing this know what I mean. You are summoned and gathered into one point in the continuum of duration. The picture does this to you, willy-nilly, regardless of whatever else is on your mind; a mere glance at it creates the attitude required for its appreciation, like a stimulus that elicits an automatic response. You become all attention, which means that you become, for the moment, selfless and in a sense entirely identified with the object of your attention.

The "at-onceness" which a picture or a piece of sculpture enforces on you is not, however, single or isolated. It can be repeated in a succession of instants, in each one remaining an "at-onceness," an instant all by itself. For the cultivated eye, the picture repeats its instantaneous unity like a mouth repeating a single word.

This pinpointing of the attention, this complete liberation and concentration of it, offers what is largely a new experience to most people in our sort of society. And it is, I think, a hunger for this particular kind of experience that helps account for the growing popularity of abstract art in this country: for the way it is taking over in the art schools, the galleries, and the museums. The fact that fad and fashion are also involved does not invalidate what I say. I know that abstract art of the latest variety—that originating with painters like Pollock and Georges Mathieu—has gotten associated with progressive jazz and its cultists; but what of it? That Wagner's music became associated with German ultranationalism, and that Wagner was Hitler's favorite composer, still doesn't detract from its sheer quality as music. That the present vogue for folk music started, back in the 1930's, among the Communists doesn't make our liking for it any the less genuine, or take anything away from folk music itself. Nor does the fact that so much gibberish gets talked and written about abstract art compromise it, just as the gibberish in which art criticism in general abounds, and abounds increasingly, doesn't compromise art in general.

One point, however, I want to make glaringly clear. Abstract art is not a special kind of art; no hard-and-fast line separates it from representational art; it is only the latest phase in the development of Western art as a whole, and almost every "technical" device of abstract painting is already to be found in the realistic painting that preceded it. Nor is it a superior kind of art. I still know of nothing in abstract painting, aside perhaps from some of the near-abstract cubist works that Picasso, Braque and Léger executed between 1910 and 1914, which matches the highest achievements of the old masters. Abstract painting may be a purer, more quintessential form of pictorial art than the representational kind, but this does not of itself confer quality upon an abstract picture. The ratio of bad abstract painting to good is actually much greater than the ratio of bad to good representational painting. Nonetheless, the very best painting, the major painting, of our age is almost exclusively abstract. Only on the middle and lower levels of quality, on the levels below the first-rate—which is, of course, where most of the art that gets produced places itself—only there is the better painting preponderantly representational.

On the plane of culture in general, the special, unique value of abstract art, I repeat, lies in the high degree of detached contemplativeness that its appreciation requires. Contemplativeness is demanded in greater or lesser degree for the appreciation of every kind of art, but abstract art tends to present this requirement in quintessential form, at its purest, least diluted, most immediate. If abstract art—as does happen nowadays—should chance to be the first kind of pictorial art we learn to appreciate, the chances are that when we go to other kinds of pictorial art—to the old masters, say, and I hope we all do go to the old masters eventually—we shall find ourselves all the better able to enjoy them. That is, we shall be able to experience them with less intrusion of irrelevancies, therefore more fully and more intensely.

The old masters stand or fall, their pictures succeed or fail, on the same ultimate basis as do those of Mondrian or any other abstract artist. The abstract formal unity of a picture by Titian is more important to its quality than what that picture images. To return to what I said about Rembrandt's portraits, the whatness of what is imaged is not unimportant—far from it—and cannot be separated, really, from the formal qualities that result from the way it is imaged. But it is a fact, in my experience, that representational paintings are essentially and most fully appreciated when the identities of what they represent are only secondarily present to our consciousness. Baudelaire said he could grasp the quality of a painting by Delacroix when he was still too far away from it to make out the images it contained, when it was still only a blur of colors. I think it was really on this kind of evidence that critics and connoisseurs, though they were almost always unaware of it, discriminated between the good and the bad in the past. Put to it, they more or less unconsciously dismissed from their minds the connotations of Rubens' nudes when assessing and experiencing the final worth of his art. They may have remained aware of the pinkness as a *nude* pinkness, but it was a pinkness and a nudity devoid of most of their usual associations.

Abstract paintings do not confront us with such problems. Or at least the frequenting of abstract art can train us to relegate them automatically to their proper place; and in doing this we refine our eyes for the appreciation of non-abstract art. That has been my own experience. That it is still relatively rare can be explained perhaps by the fact that most people continue to come to painting through academic art—the kind of art they see in ads and in magazines—and when and if they discover abstract art it comes as such an overwhelming experience that they tend to forget everything produced before. This is to be deplored, but it does not negate the value, actual or potential, of abstract art as an introduction to the fine arts in general, and as an introduction, too, to habits of disinterested contemplation. In this respect, the value of abstract art will, I hope, prove far greater in the future than it has yet. Not only can it confirm instead of subverting tradition; it can teach us, by example, how valuable so much in life can be made without being invested with ulterior meanings. How many people I know who have hung abstract pictures on their walls and found themselves gazing at them endlessly, and then exclaiming, "I don't know what there is in that painting, but I can't take my eyes off it." This kind of bewilderment is salutary. It does us good not to be able to explain, either to ourselves or to others, what we enjoy or love; it expands our capacity for experience.

NOTES AND COMMENTS

Unlike most defenders of abstract art, Greenberg does not attempt to demonstrate that abstract art is *better* than representational art but that the two ultimately are based upon the same principles and have the same end: the creation of a "formal unity" that exists solely in order to be contemplated. Do you feel this is a valid assessment of the function of art? Is Greenberg's conviction that abstract art can teach the viewer to "see" representational art better in accord with his central argument?

Greenberg maintains that to enjoy a picture as a picture one needs to be detached. Our tendency to "participate" in representational art is, therefore, really a distraction, a temptation that pulls us away from true contemplation. If there is no museum within easy reach, study some prints of works by Titian, Rembrandt or Da Vinci to see what you can discover about your own way of enjoying traditional art. Test your reaction to abstract art by looking at some works of Jackson Pollock or Kandinsky. You may find certain pictures—such as El Greco's "View of Toledo" or Van Gogh's "The Cypresses"—that suggest a fusion of the two styles since they are as abstract as they are representational. Do such pictures bear out Greenberg's central point that abstract art differs not in kind but only in degree from representational art?

Greenberg, like many other commentators on contemporary civilization, thinks that western culture is too much preoccupied with "purposeful activity." Do you think this criticism is justified by prevailing attitudes toward art in this country—even among people who think they know and appreciate the arts?

KNOWLEDGE
AND LEARNING

❧ Because all men agree that nothing so much distinguishes the human race from the rest of creation as its ability to learn, it is almost impossible to discuss education only intellectually. The subject is so central to man's conception of himself that those who write about it most reasonably tend also to write about it with most intensity. Consider, for instance, the depth of Cardinal Newman's commitment to the ideal of the liberally educated man or the contempt with which Bertrand Russell denounces institutions which, in propagandizing instead of teaching, debase education and betray the students who trust them. It is almost impossible to be unaware of the emotion which informs C. S. Lewis's vision of man swallowed up by the Nature he thinks he controls. C. P. Snow sees, perhaps, something of the same vision, but the danger for him lies in a very different kind of ignorance.

Thus, though all four of these essayists discuss the human duty to educate the young from varying, even conflicting points of view, they all care equally about the duty itself. And possibly Thurber, in his way, cares just as much.

JOHN HENRY CARDINAL NEWMAN

1801-1890

John Henry Cardinal Newman became in 1851 the first rector of the Catholic University of Ireland, an institution founded to give Irish Catholics the education they needed if Ireland was ever to emerge from the stagnation and poverty centuries of foreign domination and penal laws had produced. The venture was an abysmal failure. After seven years, during which his duties included fund-raising and teaching elementary courses, Newman returned to London. The Irish were suspicious of even so sympathetic an Englishman as he. The practical problems the university encountered were legion. But most serious of all, there was no agreement between Newman and the Irish clergy, the school's patrons, about what a university was supposed to be. The clergy wanted a seminary to inculcate moral virtue in the young, joined to a sort of trade school to give students the means to better themselves economically. Newman, nurtured in the liberal tradition of Oxford, believed that higher education has as its proper end not the salvation of the soul but the development of the mind. *The Idea of a University*, the series of discourses and commentaries in which he set forth his ideal and its justification, failed to persuade his colleagues. Since his day, however, the book has come to be recognized as a classic statement of the nature and purpose of a liberal education.

In much of the book Newman seeks to show what a liberal education is *not*, to clear away the preconceptions which lead people to think it should develop professional skill or moral virtue. Discourse VI, "Knowledge Viewed in Relation to Learning," argues that the goal of liberal education is not the amassing of factual knowledge or "learning," but rather the achievement of an "enlargement of mind," the philosophic discipline in virtue of which one can judge and order knowledge and experience.

Knowledge Viewed in Relation to Learning

1. IT WERE WELL if the English, like the Greek language, possessed some definite word to express, simply and generally, intellectual proficiency or perfection, such as "health," as used with reference to the animal frame, and "virtue," with reference to our moral nature. I am not able to find such a term; talent, ability, genius belong distinctly to the raw material, which is the subject matter, not to that excellence which is the result of exercise and training. When we turn, indeed, to the particular kinds of intellectual perfection, words are forthcoming for our purpose, as, for instance, judgment, taste, and skill; yet even these belong, for the most part, to powers or habits bearing upon practice or upon art, and not to any perfect condition of the intellect, considered in itself. Wisdom, again, is certainly a more comprehensive word than any other, but it has a direct relation to conduct, and to human life. Knowledge, indeed, and science express purely intellectual ideas, but still not a state or quality of the intellect; for knowledge, in its ordinary sense, is but one of its circumstances, denoting a possession or a habit; and science has been appropriated to the subject matter of the intellect, instead of belonging in English, as it ought to do, to the intellect itself. The consequence is that, on an occasion like this, many words are necessary in order, first, to bring out and convey what surely is no difficult idea in itself—that of the cultivation of the intellect as an end; next, in order to recommend what surely is no unreasonable object; and lastly, to describe and make the mind realize the particular perfection in which that object consists. Everyone knows practically what are the constituents of health or of virtue; and everyone recognizes health and virtue as ends to be pursued; it is otherwise with intellectual excellence, and this must be my excuse, if I seem to anyone to be bestowing a good deal of labour on a preliminary matter.

In default of a recognized term, I have called the perfection or virtue of the intellect by the name of philosophy, philosophical knowledge, enlargement of mind, or illumination, terms which are not uncommonly given to it by writers of this day: but, whatever name we bestow on it, it is, I believe, as a matter of history, the business of a university to make this intellectual culture its direct scope, or to employ itself in the education of the intellect—just as the work of a hospital lies in healing the sick or wounded, of a riding or fencing school, or of a gymnasium, in exercising the limbs, of an almshouse, in aiding and solacing the old, of an orphanage, in protecting innocence, of a penitentiary, in restoring the guilty. I say, a university, taken in its bare idea, and before we view it as an instrument of the Church, has this object and this mission; it contemplates neither moral impression nor mechanical production; it professes to exercise the mind neither in art nor in duty; its function is intellectual culture; here it may leave its scholars, and it has done its work when it has done as much as this. It educates the intellect to reason well in all matters, to reach out towards truth, and to grasp it.

*   *   *   *   *

3. I suppose the prima-facie view which the public at large would take of a university, considering it as a place of education, is nothing more or less than a place for acquiring a great deal of knowledge on a great many subjects. Memory is one of the first developed of the mental faculties; a boy's business when he goes to school is to learn, that is, to store up things in his memory. For some years his intellect is little more than an instrument for taking in facts, or a receptacle for storing them; he welcomes them as fast as they come to him; he lives on what is without; he has his eyes ever about him; he has a lively susceptibility of impressions; he imbibes information of every kind; and little does he make his own in a true sense of the word, living rather upon his neighbours all around him. He has opinions, religious, political, and literary, and, for a boy, is very positive in them and sure about them; but he gets them from his schoolfellows, or his masters, or his parents, as the case may be. Such as he is in his other relations, such also is he in his school exercises; his mind is observant, sharp, ready, retentive; he is almost passive in the acquisition of knowledge. I say this in no disparagement of the idea of a clever boy. Geography, chronology, history, language, natural history, he heaps up the matter of these studies as treasures for a future day. It is the seven years of plenty with him: he gathers in by handfuls, like the Egyptians, without counting; and though, as time goes on, there is exercise for his argumentative powers in the elements of mathematics, and for

his taste in the poets and orators, still, while at school, or at least, till quite the last years of his time, he acquires, and little more; and when he is leaving for the university, he is mainly the creature of foreign influences and circumstances, and made up of accidents, homogeneous or not, as the case may be. Moreover, the moral habits, which are a boy's praise, encourage and assist this result; that is, diligence, assiduity, regularity, despatch, persevering application; for these are the direct conditions of acquisition, and naturally lead to it. Acquirements, again, are emphatically producible, and at a moment; they are a something to show, both for master and scholar; an audience, even though ignorant themselves of the subjects of an examination, can comprehend when questions are answered and when they are not. Here again is a reason why mental culture is in the minds of men identified with the acquisition of knowledge.

The same notion possesses the public mind when it passes on from the thought of a school to that of a university: and with the best of reasons so far as this, that there is no true culture without acquirements, and that philosophy presupposes knowledge. It requires a great deal of reading, or a wide range of information, to warrant us in putting forth our opinions on any serious subject; and without such learning the most original mind may be able indeed to dazzle, to amuse, to refute, to perplex, but not to come to any useful result or any trustworthy conclusion. There are indeed persons who profess a different view of the matter, and even act upon it. Every now and then you will find a person of vigorous or fertile mind, who relies upon his own resources, despises all former authors, and gives the world, with the utmost fearlessness, his views upon religion, or history, or any other popular subject. And his works may sell for a while; he may get a name in his day; but this will be all. His readers are sure to find on the long run that his doctrines are mere theories, and not the expression of facts, that they are chaff instead of bread, and then his popularity drops as suddenly as it rose.

Knowledge then is the indispensable condition of expansion of mind, and the instrument of attaining to it; this cannot be denied, it is ever to be insisted on; I begin with it as a first principle; however, the very truth of it carries men too far, and confirms to them the notion that it is the whole of the matter. A narrow mind is thought to be that which contains little knowledge; and an enlarged mind, that which holds a great deal; and what seems to put the matter beyond dispute is the fact of the great number of studies which are pursued in a university, by its very profession. Lectures are given on every kind of subject; examinations are held; prizes awarded. There are moral, metaphysical, physical professors; professors of languages, of history, of mathematics, of experimental science. Lists of questions are published, wonderful for their range and depth, variety and difficulty; treatises are written, which carry upon their very face the evidence of extensive reading or multifarious information; what then is wanting for mental culture to a person of large reading and scientific attainments? what is grasp of mind but acquirement? where shall philosophical repose be found but in the consciousness and enjoyment of large intellectual possessions?

And yet this notion is, I conceive, a mistake, and my present business is to show that it is one, and that the end of a liberal education is not mere knowledge, or knowledge considered in its *matter;* and I shall best attain my object by actually setting down some cases, which will be generally granted to be instances of the process of enlightenment or enlargement of mind, and others which are not, and thus, by the comparison, you will be able to judge for yourselves, Gentlemen, whether knowledge, that is, acquirement, is after all the real principle of the enlargement, or whether that principle is not rather something beyond it.

4. For instance, let a person, whose experience has hitherto been confined to the more calm and unpretending scenery of these islands, whether here or in England, go for the first time into parts where physical nature puts on her wilder and more awful forms, whether at home or abroad, as into mountainous districts; or let one, who has ever lived in a quiet village, go for the first time to a great metropolis—then I suppose he will have a sensation which perhaps he never had before. He has a feeling not in addition or increase of former feelings, but of something different in its nature. He will perhaps be borne forward, and find for a time that he has lost his bearings. He has made a certain progress, and he has a consciousness of mental enlargement; he does not stand where he did, he has a new centre, and a range of thoughts to which he was before a stranger.

Again, the view of the heavens which the telescope opens upon us, if allowed to fill and possess the mind, may almost whirl it round and make it dizzy. It brings in a flood of ideas, and is rightly called an intellectual enlargement, whatever is meant by the term.

And so again, the sight of beasts of prey and other foreign animals, their strangeness, the originality (if I may use the term) of their forms and gestures and habits and their variety and independence of each other, throw us out of ourselves into another creation, and as if under another Creator, if I may so express the temptation which may come on the mind. We seem to have new faculties, or a new exercise for our faculties, by this addition to our knowledge; like a prisoner who, having been accustomed to wear manacles or fetters, suddenly finds his arms and legs free.

Hence physical science generally, in all its departments, as bringing before us the exuberant riches and resources, yet the orderly course, of the universe, elevates and excites the student, and at first, I may say, almost takes away his breath, while in time it exercises a tranquilizing influence upon him.

Again, the study of history is said to enlarge and enlighten the mind, and why? because, as I conceive, it gives it a power of judging of passing events, and of all events, and a conscious superiority over them, which before it did not possess.

And in like manner, what is called seeing the world, entering into active life, going into society, travelling, gaining acquaintance with the various classes of the community, coming into contact with the principles and modes of thought of various parties, interests, and races, their views, aims, habits and manners, their religious creeds and forms of worship—gaining experience how various yet how alike men are, how low minded, how bad, how opposed, yet how confident in their opinions; all this exerts a perceptible influence upon the mind, which it is impossible to mistake, be it good or be it bad, and is popularly called its enlargement.

And then again, the first time the mind comes across the arguments and speculations of unbelievers, and feels what a novel light they cast upon what he has hitherto accounted sacred; and still more, if it gives in to them and embraces them, and throws off as so much prejudice what it has hitherto held, and, as if waking from a dream, begins to realize to its imagination that there is now no such thing as law and the transgression of law, that sin is a phantom, and punishment a bugbear, that it is free to sin, free to enjoy the world and the flesh; and still further, when it does enjoy them, and reflects that it may think and hold just what it will, that "the world is all before it where to choose," and what system to build up as its own private persuasion; when this torrent of wilful thoughts rushes over and inundates it, who will deny that the fruit of the tree of knowledge, or what the mind takes for knowledge, has made it one of the gods, with a sense of expansion and elevation, an intoxication in reality, still, so far as the subjective state of the mind goes, an illumination? Hence the fanaticism of individuals or nations who suddenly cast off their Maker. Their eyes are opened; and, like the judgment-stricken king in the tragedy, they see two suns, and a magic universe, out of which they look back upon their former state of faith and innocence with a sort of contempt and indignation, as if they were then but fools, and the dupes of imposture.

On the other hand, religion has its own enlargement, and an enlargement, not of tumult, but of peace. It is often remarked of uneducated persons, who have hitherto thought little of the unseen world, that, on their turning to God, looking into themselves, regulating their hearts, reforming their conduct, and meditating on death and judgment, heaven and hell, they seem to become, in point of intellect, different beings from what they were. Before, they took things as they came, and thought no more of one thing than another. But now every event has a meaning; they have their own estimate of whatever happens to them; they are mindful of times and seasons, and compare the present with the past; and the world, no longer dull, monotonous, unprofitable, and hopeless, is a various and complicated drama, with parts and an object, and an awful moral.

5. Now from these instances, to which many more might be added, it is plain, first, that the communication of knowledge certainly is either a condition or the means of that sense of enlargement or enlightenment, of which at this day we hear so much in certain quarters: this cannot be denied; but next, it is equally plain that such communication is not the whole of the process. The enlargement consists, not merely in the passive reception into the mind of a number of ideas hitherto unknown to it, but in the mind's energetic and simultaneous action upon and towards and among those new ideas, which are rushing in upon it. It is the action of a formative power, reducing to order and meaning the matter of our acquirements; it is a making the objects of our knowl-

edge subjectively our own, or, to use a familiar word, it is a digestion of what we receive, into the substance of our previous state
of thought; and without this no enlargement is said to follow.
There is no enlargement unless there be a comparison of ideas one
with another, as they come before the mind, and a systematizing
of them. We feel our minds to be growing and expanding *then*,
when we not only learn, but refer what we learn to what we know
already. It is not the mere addition to our knowledge that is the
illumination; but the locomotion, the movement onwards, of that
mental centre, to which both what we know, and what we are
learning, the accumulating mass of our acquirements, gravitates.
And therefore a truly great intellect, and recognized to be such
by the common opinion of mankind, such as the intellect of
Aristotle, or of St. Thomas, or of Newton, or of Goethe (I purposely take instances within and without the Catholic pale, when
I would speak of the intellect as such) is one which takes a connected view of old and new, past and present, far and near, and
which has an insight into the influence of all these one on another;
without which there is no whole, and no centre. It possesses the
knowledge, not only of things, but also of their mutual and true
relations; knowledge, not merely considered as acquirement, but as
philosophy.

Accordingly, when this analytical, distributive, harmonizing
process is away, the mind experiences no enlargement, and is not
reckoned as enlightened or comprehensive, whatever it may add
to its knowledge. For instance, a great memory, as I have already
said, does not make a philosopher, any more than a dictionary can
be called a grammar. There are men who embrace in their minds a
vast multitude of ideas, but with little sensibility about their real
relations towards each other. These may be antiquarians, annalists,
naturalists; they may be learned in the law; they may be versed in
statistics; they are most useful in their own place; I should shrink
from speaking disrespectfully of them; still, there is nothing in
such attainments to guarantee the absence of narrowness of mind.
If they are nothing more than well-read men, or men of information, they have not what specially deserves the name of culture of
mind, or fulfils the type of liberal education.

In like manner, we sometimes fall in with persons who have
seen much of the world, and of the men who, in their day, have
played a conspicuous part in it, but who generalize nothing, and

have no observation, in the true sense of the word. They abound in information in detail, curious and entertaining, about men and things; and having lived under the influence of no very clear or settled principles, religious or political, they speak of every one and every thing, only as so many phenomena, which are complete in themselves, and lead to nothing, not discussing them, or teaching any truth, or instructing the hearer, but simply talking. No one would say that these persons, well informed as they are, had attained to any great culture of intellect or to philosophy.

The case is the same still more strikingly where the persons in question are beyond dispute men of inferior powers and deficient education. Perhaps they have been much in foreign countries, and they receive, in a passive, otiose, unfruitful way, the various facts which are forced upon them there. Seafaring men, for example, range from one end of the earth to the other; but the multiplicity of external objects which they have encountered forms no symmetrical and consistent picture upon their imagination; they see the tapestry of human life, as it were on the wrong side, and it tells no story. They sleep, and they rise up, and they find themselves, now in Europe, now in Asia; they see visions of great cities and wild regions; they are in the marts of commerce, or amid the islands of the South; they gaze on Pompey's Pillar, or on the Andes; and nothing which meets them carries them forward or backward, to any idea beyond itself. Nothing has a drift or relation; nothing has a history or a promise. Everything stands by itself, and comes and goes in its turn, like the shifting scenes of a show, which leave the spectator where he was. Perhaps you are near such a man on a particular occasion, and expect him to be shocked or perplexed at something which occurs; but one thing is much the same to him as another, or, if he is perplexed, it is as not knowing what to say, whether it is right to admire, or to ridicule, or to disapprove, while conscious that some expression of opinion is expected from him; for in fact he has no standard of judgment at all, and no landmarks to guide him to a conclusion. Such is mere acquisition, and, I repeat, no one would dream of calling it philosophy.

6. Instances, such as these, confirm, by the contrast, the conclusion I have already drawn from those which preceded them. That only is true enlargement of mind which is the power of viewing many things at once as one whole, of referring them

severally to their true place in the universal system, of understanding their respective values, and determining their mutual dependence. Thus is that form of universal knowledge, of which I have on a former occasion spoken, set up in the individual intellect, and constitutes its perfection. Possessed of this real illumination, the mind never views any part of the extended subject matter of knowledge without recollecting that it is but a part, or without the associations which spring from this recollection. It makes everything in some sort lead to everything else; it would communicate the image of the whole to every separate portion, till that whole becomes in imagination like a spirit, everywhere pervading and penetrating its component parts, and giving them one definite meaning. Just as our bodily organs, when mentioned, recall their function in the body, as the word "creation" suggests the Creator, and "subjects" a sovereign, so, in the mind of the philosopher, as we are abstractedly conceiving of him, the elements of the physical and moral world, sciences, arts, pursuits, ranks, offices, events, opinions, individualities, are all viewed as one, with correlative functions, and as gradually by successive combinations converging, one and all, to the true centre.

To have even a portion of this illuminative reason and true philosophy is the highest state to which nature can aspire, in the way of intellect; it puts the mind above the influences of chance and necessity, above anxiety, suspense, unsettlement, and superstition, which is the lot of the many. Men, whose minds are possessed with some one object, take exaggerated views of its importance, are feverish in the pursuit of it, make it the measure of things which are utterly foreign to it, and are startled and despond if it happens to fail them. They are ever in alarm or in transport. Those, on the other hand, who have no object or principle whatever to hold by, lose their way, every step they take. They are thrown out, and do not know what to think or say, at every fresh juncture; they have no view of persons, or occurrences, or facts, which c⸱ me suddenly upon them, and they hang upon the opinion of others, for want of internal resources. But the intellect, which has been disciplined to the perfection of its powers, which knows, and thinks while it knows, which has learned to leaven the dense mass of facts and events with the elastic force of reason, such an intellect cannot be partial, cannot be exclusive, cannot be impetuous, cannot be at a loss, cannot but be patient, collected, and majestically calm, because it discerns the end in every beginning, the origin in every end, the law in every interruption, the limit in each delay; because it ever knows where it stands, and how its path lies from one point to another. It is the τετράγωνος[1] of the Peripatetic, and has the "nil admirari"[2] of the Stoic:

> Felix qui potuit rerum cognoscere causas,
> Atque metus omnes, et inexorabile fatum
> Subjecit pedibus, strepitumque Acherontis avari.[3]

There are men who, when in difficulties, originate at the moment vast ideas or dazzling projects; who, under the influence of excitement, are able to cast a light, almost as if from inspiration, on a subject or course of action which comes before them; who have a sudden presence of mind equal to any emergency, rising with the occasion, and an undaunted magnanimous bearing, and an energy and keenness which is but made intense by opposition. This is genius, this is heroism; it is the exhibition of a natural gift, which no culture can teach, at which no institution can aim; here, on the contrary, we are concerned, not with mere nature, but with training and teaching. That perfection of the intellect, which is the result of education, and its *beau ideal*, to be imparted to individuals in their respective measures, is the clear, calm, accurate vision and comprehension of all things, as far as the finite mind can embrace them, each in its place, and with its own characteristics upon it. It is almost prophetic from its knowledge of history; it is almost heart-searching from its knowledge of human nature; it has almost supernatural charity from its freedom from littleness and prejudice; it has almost the repose of faith, because nothing can startle it; it has almost the beauty and harmony of heavenly contemplation, so intimate is it with the eternal order of things and the music of the spheres.

7. And now, if I may take for granted that the true and adequate end of intellectual training and of a university is not learning or acquirement, but rather is thought or reason exercised upon knowledge, or what may be called philosophy, I shall be in a

---

[1 *Tetragonos*, "four-cornered," an epithet used by the disciples of Aristotle, the Peripatetics, to symbolize the fully balanced mind.—*Ed.*]

[2 To be astonished at nothing.—*Ed.*]

[3 Virgil, *Georgics*, ll. 190-193: "Happy is he who could know the causes of things and put under his feet all fears and inexorable fate and the roar of greedy Acheron."—*Ed.*]

position to explain the various mistakes which at the present day
beset the subject of university education.

I say then, if we would improve the intellect, first of all we
must ascend; we cannot gain real knowledge on a level; we must
generalize, we must reduce to method, we must have a grasp of
principles, and group and shape our acquisitions by means of them.
It matters not whether our field of operation be wide or limited;
in every case, to command it, is to mount above it. Who has not
felt the irritation of mind and impatience created by a deep, rich
country, visited for the first time, with winding lanes, and high
hedges, and green steeps, and tangled woods, and everything smiling indeed, but in a maze? The same feeling comes upon us in a
strange city, when we have no map of its streets. Hence you hear
of practised travellers, when they first come into a place, mounting
some high hill or church tower, by way of reconnoitring its neighbourhood. In like manner, you must be above your knowledge,
not under it, or it will oppress you; and the more you have of it,
the greater will be the load. The learning of a Salmasius or a
Burman, unless you are its master, will be your tyrant. "Imperat
aut servit";[1] if you can wield it with a strong arm, it is a great
weapon; otherwise,

> Vis consili expers
> Mole ruit suâ.[2]

You will be overwhelmed, like Tarpeia, by the heavy wealth which
you have exacted from tributary generations.

Instances abound; there are authors who are as pointless as
they are inexhaustible in their literary resources. They measure
knowledge by bulk, as it lies in the rude block, without symmetry,
without design. How many commentators are there on the classics,
how many on Holy Scripture, from whom we rise up, wondering at
the learning which has passed before us, and wondering why it
passed! How many writers are there of ecclesiastical history, such
as Mosheim or Du Pin, who, breaking up their subject into
details, destroy its life, and defraud us of the whole by their anxiety about the parts! The sermons, again, of the English divines
in the seventeenth century, how often are they mere repertories of

---

[1] It rules or it serves.—*Ed.*]
[2] Brute force bereft of wisdom falls to ruin by its own weight (Horace,
Odes, III, iv, 65).—*Ed.*]

miscellaneous and officious learning! Of course Catholics also may read without thinking; and in their case, equally as with Protestants, it holds good, that such knowledge is unworthy of the name, knowledge which they have not thought through, and thought out. Such readers are only possessed by their knowledge, not possessed of it; nay, in matter of fact they are often even carried away by it, without any volition of their own. Recollect, the memory can tyrannize, as well as the imagination. Derangement, I believe, has been considered as a loss of control over the sequence of ideas. The mind, once set in motion, is henceforth deprived of the power of initiation, and becomes the victim of a train of associations, one thought suggesting another, in the way of cause and effect, as if by a mechanical process, or some physical necessity. No one who has had experience of men of studious habits but must recognize the existence of a parallel phenomenon in the case of those who have overstimulated the memory. In such persons reason acts almost as feebly and as impotently as in the madman; once fairly started on any subject whatever, they have no power of self-control; they passively endure the succession of impulses which are evolved out of the original exciting cause; they are passed on from one idea to another and go steadily forward, plodding along one line of thought in spite of the amplest concessions of the hearer, or wandering from it in endless digression in spite of his remonstrances. Now if, as is very certain, no one would envy the madman the glow and originality of his conceptions, why must we extol the cultivation of that intellect, which is the prey, not indeed of barren fancies but of barren facts, of random intrusions from without, though not of morbid imaginations from within? And in thus speaking, I am not denying that a strong and ready memory is in itself a real treasure; I am not disparaging a well-stored mind, though it be nothing besides, provided it be sober, any more than I would despise a bookseller's shop—it is of great value to others, even when not so to the owner. Nor am I banishing, far from it, the possessors of deep and multifarious learning from my ideal university; they adorn it in the eyes of men; I do but say that they constitute no type of the results at which it aims; that it is no great gain to the intellect to have enlarged the memory at the expense of faculties which are indisputably higher.

8. Nor indeed am I supposing that there is any great danger, at least in this day, of overeducation; the danger is on the other

side. I will tell you, Gentlemen, what has been the practical error
of the last twenty years—not to load the memory of the student
with a mass of undigested knowledge, but to force upon him so
much that he has rejected all. It has been the error of distracting
and enfeebling the mind by an unmeaning profusion of subjects;
of implying that a smattering in a dozen branches of study is not
shallowness, which it really is, but enlargement, which it is not; of
considering an acquaintance with the learned names of things and
persons, and the possession of clever duodecimos, and attendance
on eloquent lecturers, and membership with scientific institutions,
and the sight of the experiments of a platform and the specimens
of a museum, that all this was not dissipation of mind, but progress. All things now are to be learned at once, not first one thing,
then another, not one well, but many badly. Learning is to be
without exertion, without attention, without toil; without grounding, without advance, without finishing. There is to be nothing
individual in it; and this, forsooth, is the wonder of the age. What
the steam engine does with matter, the printing press is to do with
mind; it is to act mechanically, and the population is to be passively, almost unconsciously enlightened by the mere multiplication and dissemination of volumes. Whether it be the schoolboy, or
the schoolgirl, or the youth at college, or the mechanic in the
town, or the politician in the senate, all have been the victims in
one way or other of this most preposterous and pernicious of delusions. Wise men have lifted up their voices in vain; and at length,
lest their own institutions should be outshone and should disappear in the folly of the hour; they have been obliged, as far as
they could with a good conscience, to humour a spirit which they
could not withstand, and make temporizing concessions at which
they could not but inwardly smile.

It must not be supposed that because I so speak, therefore
I have some sort of fear of the education of the people: on the
contrary, the more education they have, the better, so that it is
really education. Nor am I an enemy to the cheap publication of
scientific and literary works, which is now in vogue: on the
contrary, I consider it a great advantage, convenience, and gain;
that is, to those to whom education has given a capacity for using
them. Further, I consider such innocent recreations as science and
literature are able to furnish will be a very fit occupation of the
thoughts and the leisure of young persons, and may be made the

means of keeping them from bad employments and bad companions. Moreover, as to that superficial acquaintance with chemistry, and geology, and astronomy, and political economy, and modern history, and biography, and other branches of knowledge, which periodical literature and occasional lectures and scientific institutions diffuse through the community, I think it a graceful accomplishment, and a suitable, nay, in this day a necessary accomplishment, in the case of educated men. Nor, lastly, am I disparaging or discouraging the thorough acquisition of any one of these studies, or denying that, as far as it goes, such thorough acquisition is a real education of the mind. All I say is, call things by their right names, and do not confuse together ideas which are essentially different. A thorough knowledge of one science and a superficial acquaintance with many are not the same thing; a smattering of a hundred things or a memory for detail is not a philosophical or comprehensive view. Recreations are not education; accomplishments are not education. Do not say, the people must be educated, when, after all, you only mean amused, refreshed, soothed, put into good spirits and good humour, or kept from vicious excesses. I do not say that such amusements, such occupations of mind, are not a great gain; but they are not education. You may as well call drawing and fencing education, as a general knowledge of botany or conchology. Stuffing birds or playing stringed instruments is an elegant pastime, and a resource to the idle, but it is not education; it does not form or cultivate the intellect. Education is a high word; it is the preparation for knowledge, and it is the imparting of knowledge in proportion to that preparation. We require intellectual eyes to know withal, as bodily eyes for sight. We need both objects and organs intellectual; we cannot gain them without setting about it; we cannot gain them in our sleep, or by haphazard. The best telescope does not dispense with eyes; the printing press or the lecture room will assist us greatly, but we must be true to ourselves, we must be parties in the work. A university is, according to the usual designation, an alma mater, knowing her children one by one, not a foundry, or a mint, or a treadmill.

9. I protest to you, Gentlemen, that if I had to choose between a so-called university, which dispensed with residence and tutorial superintendence, and gave its degrees to any person who passed an examination in a wide range of subjects, and a university

which had no professors or examinations at all, but merely brought a number of young men together for three or four years, and then sent them away as the University of Oxford is said to have done some sixty years since, if I were asked which of these two methods was the better discipline of the intellect—mind, I do not say which is *morally* the better, for it is plain that compulsory study must be a good and idleness an intolerable mischief—but if I must determine which of the two courses was the more successful in training, moulding, enlarging the mind, which sent out men the more fitted for their secular duties, which produced better public men, men of the world, men whose names would descend to posterity, I have no hesitation in giving the preference to that university which did nothing over that which exacted of its members an acquaintance with every science under the sun. And, paradox as this may seem, still if results be the test of systems, the influence of the public schools and colleges of England, in the course of the last century, at least will bear out one side of the contrast as I have drawn it. What would come, on the other hand, of the ideal systems of education which have fascinated the imagination of this age, could they ever take effect, and whether they would not produce a generation frivolous, narrow-minded, and resourceless, intellectually considered, is a fair subject for debate; but so far is certain, that the universities and scholastic establishments, to which I refer, and which did little more than bring together first boys and then youths in large numbers, these institutions, with miserable deformities on the side of morals, with a hollow profession of Christianity, and a heathen code of ethics—I say, at least they can boast of a succession of heroes and statesmen, of literary men and philosophers, of men conspicuous for great natural virtues, for habits of business, for knowledge of life, for practical judgment, for cultivated tastes, for accomplishments, who have made England what it is—able to subdue the earth, able to domineer over Catholics.

How is this to be explained? I suppose as follows: When a multitude of young men, keen, open-hearted, sympathetic, and observant, as young men are, come together and freely mix with each other, they are sure to learn one from another, even if there be no one to teach them; the conversation of all is a series of lectures to each, and they gain for themselves new ideas and views, fresh matter of thought, and distinct principles for judging and acting, day by day. An infant has to learn the meaning of the information which its senses convey to it, and this seems to be its employment. It fancies all that the eye presents to it to be close to it, till it actually learns the contrary, and thus by practice does it ascertain the relations and uses of those first elements of knowledge which are necessary for its animal existence. A parallel teaching is necessary for our social being, and it is secured by a large school or a college; and this effect may be fairly called in its own department an enlargement of mind. It is seeing the world on a small field with little trouble; for the pupils or students come from very different places, and with widely different notions, and there is much to generalize, much to adjust, much to eliminate, there are interrelations to be defined, and conventional rules to be established, in the process, by which the whole assemblage is moulded together, and gains one tone and one character.

Let it be clearly understood, I repeat it, that I am not taking into account moral or religious considerations; I am but saying that that youthful community will constitute a whole, it will embody a specific idea, it will represent a doctrine, it will administer a code of conduct, and it will furnish principles of thought and action. It will give birth to a living teaching, which in course of time will take the shape of a self-perpetuating tradition, or a *genius loci*, as it is sometimes called; which haunts the home where it has been born, and which imbues and forms, more or less, and one by one, every individual who is successively brought under its shadow. Thus it is that, independent of direct instruction on the part of superiors, there is a sort of self-education in the academic institutions of Protestant England; a characteristic tone of thought, a recognized standard of judgment is found in them, which, as developed in the individual who is submitted to it, becomes a twofold source of strength to him, both from the distinct stamp it impresses on his mind, and from the bond of union which it creates between him and others—effects which are shared by the authorities of the place, for they themselves have been educated in it, and at all times are exposed to the influence of its ethical atmosphere. Here then is a real teaching, whatever be its standards and principles, true or false; and it at least tends towards cultivation of the intellect; it at least recognizes that knowledge is something more than a sort of passive reception of scraps and details; it is a something, and it does a something, which never will issue

from the most strenuous efforts of a set of teachers, with no mutual
sympathies and no intercommunion, of a set of examiners with
no opinions which they dare profess, and with no common
principles, who are teaching or questioning a set of youths who do
not know them, and do not know each other, on a large number
of subjects, different in kind, and connected by no wide philosophy, three times a week, or three times a year, or once in three
years, in chill lecture rooms or on a pompous anniversary.

10. Nay, self-education in any shape, in the most restricted
sense, is preferable to a system of teaching which, professing so
much, really does so little for the mind. Shut your college gates
against the votary of knowledge, throw him back upon the search-
ings and the efforts of his own mind; he will gain by being spared
an entrance into your Babel. Few indeed there are who can dispense with the stimulus and support of instructors, or will do anything at all if left to themselves. And fewer still (though such
great minds are to be found), who will not, from such unassisted
attempts, contract a self-reliance and a self-esteem, which are not
only moral evils, but serious hindrances to the attainment of truth.
And next to none, perhaps, or none, who will not be reminded
from time to time of the disadvantage under which they lie, by
their imperfect grounding, by the breaks, deficiencies, and irregularities of their knowledge, by the eccentricity of opinion and the
confusion of principle which they exhibit. They will be too often
ignorant of what everyone knows and takes for granted, of that
multitude of small truths which fall upon the mind like dust,
impalpable and ever accumulating; they may be unable to converse, they may argue perversely, they may pride themselves on
their worst paradoxes or their grossest truisms, they may be full of
their own mode of viewing things, unwilling to be put out of their
way, slow to enter into the minds of others; but, with these and
whatever other liabilities upon their heads, they are likely to have
more thought, more mind, more philosophy, more true enlargement, than those earnest but ill-used persons who are forced to
load their minds with a score of subjects against an examination,
who have too much on their hands to indulge themselves in thinking or investigation, who devour premise and conclusion together
with indiscriminate greediness, who hold whole sciences on faith,
and commit demonstrations to memory, and who too often, as
might be expected, when their period of education is passed, throw

up all they have learned in disgust, having gained nothing really by their anxious labours, except perhaps the habit of application.

Yet such is the better specimen of the fruit of that ambitious system which has of late years been making way among us: for its result on ordinary minds, and on the common run of students, is less satisfactory still; they leave their place of education simply dissipated and relaxed by the multiplicity of subjects, which they have never really mastered, and so shallow as not even to know their shallowness. How much better, I say, is it for the active and thoughtful intellect, where such is to be found, to eschew the college and the university altogether than to submit to a drudgery so ignoble, a mockery so contumelious! How much more profitable for the independent mind, after the mere rudiments of education, to range through a library at random, taking down books as they meet him, and pursuing the trains of thought which his mother wit suggests! How much healthier to wander into the fields, and there with the exiled Prince to find "tongues in the trees, books in the running brooks!" How much more genuine an education is that of the poor boy in the poem[1]—a poem, whether in conception or in execution, one of the most touching in our language—who, not in the wide world, but ranging day by day around his widowed mother's home, "a dexterous gleaner" in a narrow field, and with only such slender outfit

> as the village school and books a few
> Supplied,

contrived from the beach, and the quay, and the fisher's boat, and the inn's fireside, and the tradesman's shop, and the shepherd's walk, and the smuggler's hut, and the mossy moor, and the screaming gulls, and the restless waves, to fashion for himself a philosophy and a poetry of his own!

NOTES AND COMMENTS

In this Discourse Newman intends simultaneously to enlighten and persuade a not necessarily sympathetic audience. To accomplish

---

[1] Crabbe's "Tales of the Hall." This poem, let me say, I read on its first publication, above thirty years ago, with extreme delight, and have never lost my love of it; and on taking it up lately, found I was even more touched by it than heretofore. A work which can please in youth and age, seems to fulfil (in logical language) the *accidental definition* of a classic. [A further course of twenty years has past, and I bear the same witness in favour of this poem.]

his end, he defines, distinguishes, presents examples and analogies, even employs shock tactics. Trace the development of the Discourse to see what means he uses to prepare his audience for the rather startling opinion he expounds in section 9.

Newman is acknowledged to be one of the greatest masters of English prose. To study closely the way in which his balanced, periodic sentences achieve sonority and power, imitate one of his carefully built paragraphs, for example the first one in section 3, which discusses the typical learning processes of schoolboys.

Imagine how Newman might comment on the contemporary American educational scene. What would he think of majors and minors and "distribution" requirements (so many courses in the humanities, so many in the social and physical sciences)? Would he find that American schools and colleges put too much emphasis on the acquisition of facts? How would he react to educational television? Would he approve of bull sessions and kaffee-klatsches?

JAMES THURBER

1894-1961

James Thurber's chronicles and cartoons of the unexpected, bewildering, or lugubrious problems that can beset the ordinary man have
enduring appeal for American readers. His essays and stories are collected in such books as *My World—and Welcome to It*, *The Beast in
Me and Other Animals*, and *Fables for Our Time*. And no writer or
artist ever devoted so much consideration to the traumata of dogs
(*Thurber's Dogs*).

"University Days" is taken from *My Life and Hard Times*, an
account of Thurber's youth in Columbus, Ohio. His view of university
life is much more personal than Newman's and far less ideal.

University Days

I PASSED ALL the other courses that I took at my University,
but I could never pass botany. This was because all botany students
had to spend several hours a week in a laboratory looking through
a microscope at plant cells, and I could never see through a microscope. I never once saw a cell through a microscope. This used
to enrage my instructor. He would wander around the laboratory
pleased with the progress all the students were making in drawing
the involved and, so I am told, interesting structure of flower
cells, until he came to me. I would just be standing there. "I can't
see anything," I would say. He would begin patiently enough,
explaining how anybody can see through a microscope, but he

James Thurber

would always end up in a fury, claiming that I could *too* see through a microscope but just pretended that I couldn't. "It takes away from the beauty of flowers anyway," I used to tell him. "We are not concerned with beauty in this course," he would say. "We are concerned solely with what I may call the *mechanics* of flars." "Well," I'd say, "I can't see anything." "Try it just once again," he'd say, and I would put my eye to the microscope and see nothing at all, except now and again a nebulous milky substance—a phenomenon of maladjustment. You were supposed to see a vivid, restless clockwork of sharply defined plant cells. "I see what looks like a lot of milk," I would tell him. This, he claimed, was the result of my not having adjusted the microscope properly, so he would readjust it for me, or rather, for himself. And I would look again and see milk.

I finally took a deferred pass, as they called it, and waited a year and tried again. (You had to pass one of the biological sciences or you couldn't graduate.) The professor had come back from vacation brown as a berry, bright-eyed, and eager to explain cell-structure again to his classes. "Well," he said to me, cheerily, when we met in the first laboratory hour of the semester, "we're going to see cells this time, aren't we?" "Yes, sir," I said. Students to right of me and to left of me and in front of me were seeing cells; what's more, they were quietly drawing pictures of them in their notebooks. Of course, I didn't see anything.

"We'll try it," the professor said to me, grimly, "with every adjustment of the microscope known to man. As God is my witness, I'll arrange this glass so that you see cells through it or I'll give up teaching. In twenty-two years of botany, I—" He cut off abruptly for he was beginning to quiver all over, like Lionel Barrymore, and he genuinely wished to hold onto his temper; his scenes with me had taken a great deal out of him.

So we tried it with every adjustment of the microscope known to man. With only one of them did I see anything but blackness or the familiar lacteal opacity, and that time I saw, to my pleasure and amazement, a variegated constellation of flecks, specks, and dots. These I hastily drew. The instructor, noting my activity, came back from an adjoining desk, a smile on his lips and his eyebrows high in hope. He looked at my cell drawing. "What's that?" he demanded, with a hint of a squeal in his voice. "That's what I saw," I said. "You didn't, you didn't, you *did*n't!" he screamed, losing control of his temper instantly, and he bent over and squinted into the microscope. His head snapped up. "That's your eye!" he shouted. "You've fixed the lens so that it reflects! You've drawn your eye!"

Another course that I didn't like, but somehow managed to pass, was economics. I went to that class straight from the botany class, which didn't help me any in understanding either subject. I used to get them mixed up. But not as mixed up as another student in my economics class who came there direct from a physics laboratory. He was a tackle on the football team, named Bolenciecwcz. At that time Ohio State University had one of the best football teams in the country, and Bolenciecwcz was one of its outstanding stars. In order to be eligible to play it was necessary for him to keep up in his studies, a very difficult matter, for while he was not dumber than an ox he was not any smarter. Most of his professors were lenient and helped him along. None gave him more hints, in answering questions, or asked him simpler ones than the economics professor, a thin, timid man named Bassum. One day when we were on the subject of transportation and distribution, it came Bolenciecwcz's turn to answer a question. "Name one means of transportation," the professor said to him. No light came into the big tackle's eyes. "Just any means of transportation," said the professor. Bolenciecwcz sat staring at him. "That is," pursued the professor, "any medium, agency, or method of going from one place to another." Bolenciecwcz had the look of a man who is being led into a trap. "You may choose among steam, horse-drawn, or electrically propelled vehicles," said the instructor. "I might suggest the one which we commonly take in making long journeys across land." There was a profound silence in which everybody stirred uneasily, including Bolenciecwcz and Mr. Bassum. Mr. Bassum abruptly broke this silence in an amazing manner. "Choo-choo-choo," he said, in a low voice, and turned instantly scarlet. He glanced appealingly around the room. All of us, of course, shared Mr. Bassum's desire that Bolenciecwcz should stay abreast of the class in economics, for the Illinois game, one of the hardest and most important of the season, was only a week off. "Toot, toot, too-toooooooot!" some student with a deep voice moaned, and we all looked encouragingly at Bolenciecwcz. Somebody else gave a fine imitation of a locomotive letting off steam. Mr. Bassum himself rounded off the little show. "Ding, dong,

ding, dong," he said, hopefully. Bolenciecwcz was staring at the
floor now, trying to think, his great brow furrowed, his huge hands
rubbing together, his face red.

"How did you come to college this year, Mr. Bolenciecwcz?"
asked the professor. "*Chuf*fa chuffa, *chuf*fa chuffa."

"M'father sent me," said the football player.

"What on?'" asked Bassum.

"I git an 'lowance," said the tackle, in a low, husky voice,
obviously embarrassed.

"No, no," said Bassum. "Name a means of transportation.
What did you *ride* here on?"

"Train," said Bolenciecwcz.

"Quite right," said the professor. "Now, Mr. Nugent, will
you tell us——"

If I went through anguish in botany and economics—for different reasons—gymnasium work was even worse. I don't even like
to think about it. They wouldn't let you play games or join in the
exercises with your glasses on and I couldn't see with mine off. I
bumped into professors, horizontal bars, agricultural students, and
swinging iron rings. Not being able to see, I could take it but I
couldn't dish it out. Also, in order to pass gymnasium (and you
had to pass it to graduate) you had to learn to swim if you didn't
know how. I didn't like the swimming pool, I didn't like swimming, and I didn't like the swimming instructor, and after all these
years I still don't. I never swam but I passed my gym work anyway, by having another student give my gymnasium number (978)
and swim across the pool in my place. He was a quiet, amiable
blonde youth, number 473, and he would have seen through a
microscope for me if we could have got away with it, but we
couldn't get away with it. Another thing I didn't like about gymnasium work was that they made you strip the day you registered.
It is impossible for me to be happy when I am stripped and being
asked a lot of questions. Still, I did better than a lanky agricultural
student who was cross-examined just before I was. They asked
each student what college he was in—that is, whether Arts, Engineering, Commerce, or Agriculture. "What college are you in?"
the instructor snapped at the youth in front of me. "Ohio State
University," he said promptly.

It wasn't that agricultural student but it was another a whole
lot like him who decided to take up journalism, possibly on the

ground that when farming went to hell he could fall back on
newspaper work. He didn't realize, of course, that that would be
very much like falling back full-length on a kit of carpenter's tools.
Haskins didn't seem cut out for journalism, being too embarrassed
to talk to anybody and unable to use a typewriter, but the editor
of the college paper assigned him to the cow barns, the sheep
house, the horse pavilion, and the animal husbandry department
generally. This was a genuinely big "beat," for it took up five times
as much ground and got ten times as great a legislative appropria-
tion as the College of Liberal Arts. The agricultural student knew
animals, but nevertheless his stories were dull and colorlessly written. He took all afternoon on each of them, on account of having
to hunt for each letter on the typewriter. Once in a while he had
to ask somebody to help him hunt. "C" and "L," in particular,
were hard letters for him to find. His editor finally got pretty
much annoyed at the farmer-journalist because his pieces were so
uninteresting. "See here, Haskins," he snapped at him one day,
"Why is it we never have anything hot from you on the horse
pavilion? Here we have two hundred head of horses on this campus—more than any other university in the Western Conference
except Purdue—and yet you never get any real low down on them.
Now shoot over to the horse barns and dig up something lively."
Haskins shambled out and came back in about an hour; he said
he had something. "Well, start it off snappily," said the editor.
"Something people will read." Haskins set to work and in a couple
of hours brought a sheet of typewritten paper to the desk; it was a
two-hundred-word story about some disease that had broken out
among the horses. Its opening sentence was simple but arresting.
It read: "Who has noticed the sores on the tops of the horses in
the animal husbandry building?"

Ohio State was a land grant university and therefore two
years of military drill was compulsory. We drilled with old Spring-
field rifles and studied the tactics of the Civil War even though
the World War was going on at the time. At 11 o'clock each morning thousands of freshmen and sophomores used to deploy over
the campus, moodily creeping up on the old chemistry building.
It was good training for the kind of warfare that was waged at
Shiloh but it had no connection with what was going on in
Europe. Some people used to think there was German money
behind it, but they didn't dare say so or they would have been

thrown in jail as German spies. It was a period of muddy thought and marked, I believe, the decline of higher education in the Middle West.

As a soldier I was never any good at all. Most of the cadets were glumly indifferent soldiers, but I was no good at all. Once General Littlefield, who was commandant of the cadet corps, popped up in front of me during regimental drill and snapped, "You are the main trouble with this university!" I think he meant that my type was the main trouble with the university but he may have meant me individually. I was mediocre at drill, certainly—that is, until my senior year. By that time I had drilled longer than anybody else in the Western Conference, having failed at military at the end of each preceding year so that I had to do it all over again. I was the only senior still in uniform. The uniform which, when new, had made me look like an interurban railway conductor, now that it had become faded and too tight made me look like Bert Williams in his bellboy act. This had a definitely bad effect on my morale. Even so, I had become by sheer practise little short of wonderful at squad manoeuvres.

One day General Littlefield picked our company out of the whole regiment and tried to get it mixed up by putting it through one movement after another as fast as we could execute them: squads right, squads left, squads on right into line, squads right about, squads left front into line, etc. In about three minutes one hundred and nine men were marching in one direction and I was marching away from them at an angle of forty degrees, all alone. "Company, halt!" shouted General Littlefield, "That man is the only man who has it right!" I was made a corporal for my achievement.

The next day General Littlefield summoned me to his office. He was swatting flies when I went in. I was silent and he was silent too, for a long time. I don't think he remembered me or why he had sent for me, but he didn't want to admit it. He swatted some more flies, keeping his eyes on them narrowly before he let go with the swatter. "Button up your coat!" he snapped. Looking back on it now I can see that he meant me although he was looking at a fly, but I just stood there. Another fly came to rest on a paper in front of the general and began rubbing its hind legs together. The general lifted the swatter cautiously. I moved restlessly and the fly flew away. "You startled him!" barked General Littlefield, looking at me severely. I said I was sorry. "That won't help the situation!" snapped the general, with cold military logic. I didn't see what I could do except offer to chase some more flies toward his desk, but I didn't say anything. He stared out the window at the faraway figures of co-eds crossing the campus toward the library. Finally, he told me I could go. So I went. He either didn't know which cadet I was or else he forgot what he wanted to see me about. It may have been that he wished to apologize for having called me the main trouble with the university; or maybe he had decided to compliment me on my brilliant drilling of the day before and then at the last minute decided not to. I don't know. I don't think about it much any more.

NOTES AND COMMENTS

Granted that Thurber's humor is based on a kind of understated exaggeration—e.g., "for while he was not dumber than an ox he was not any smarter"—he nonetheless puts his finger on some of the major obstacles to wisdom to be encountered on an American campus. For instance, how much "enlargement of the mind" is one likely to acquire by exchanging ideas with Bolenciecwcz or Haskins? And in what way do gym or the ROTC open up to the student "a range of thoughts to which he was before a stranger"?

BERTRAND RUSSELL

1872-

Bertrand Russell's first great achievements were in the realm of logic and mathematics: *Principia Mathematica*, on which he collaborated with Alfred North Whitehead, is a classic in its field. He is most widely known, however, for his writings on philosophic and social questions and for books like *The ABC of Relativity* (from which a selection appears on page 381), which seek to open to the layman the new worlds of scientific discovery. But in all his works Russell is ever the humanist and stylist; he was awarded the Nobel Prize for literature in 1950.

The present essay, with its insistence that education must lead students to accept the future with excitement and hope, suggests in its austere lucidity why Russell has devoted so much of his career to teaching non-specialists about the radically new in mathematics and physics.

Education

NO POLITICAL THEORY is adequate unless it is applicable to children as well as to men and women. Theorists are mostly childless, or, if they have children, they are carefully screened from the disturbances which would be caused by youthful turmoil. Some of them have written books on education, but without, as a rule, having any actual children present to their minds while they wrote. Those educational theorists who have had a knowledge of children, such as the inventors of Kindergarten and the Montessori system,

Reprinted from *Principles of Social Reconstruction* by Bertrand Russell. By permission of George Allen & Unwin Ltd., London.

have not always had enough realization of the ultimate goal of education to be able to deal successfully with advanced instruction. I have not the knowledge either of children or of education which would enable me to supply whatever defects there may be in the writings of others. But some questions, concerning education as a political institution, are involved in any hope of social reconstruction, and are not usually considered by writers on educational theory. It is these questions that I wish to discuss.

The power of education in forming character and opinion is very great and very generally recognized. The genuine beliefs, though not usually the professed precepts, of parents and teachers are almost unconsciously acquired by most children; and even if they depart from these beliefs in later life, something of them remains deeply implanted, ready to emerge in a time of stress or crisis. Education is, as a rule, the strongest force on the side of what exists and against fundamental change: threatened institutions, while they are still powerful, possess themselves of the educational machine, and instil a respect for their own excellence into the malleable minds of the young. Reformers retort by trying to oust their opponents from their position of vantage. The children themselves are not considered by either party; they are merely so much material, to be recruited into one army or the other. If the children themselves were considered, education would not aim at making them belong to this party or that, but at enabling them to choose intelligently between the parties; it would aim at making them able to think, not at making them think what their teachers think. Education as a political weapon could not exist if we respected the rights of children. If we respected the rights of children, we should educate them so as to give them the knowledge and the mental habits required for forming independent opinions; but education as a political institution endeavors to form habits and to circumscribe knowledge in such a way as to make one set of opinions inevitable.

The two principles of *justice* and *liberty*, which cover a very great deal of the social reconstruction required, are not by themselves sufficient where education is concerned. Justice, in the literal sense of equal rights, is obviously not wholly possible as regards children. And as for liberty, it is, to begin with, essentially negative: it condemns all avoidable interference with freedom, without giving a positive principle of construction. But education is essentially constructive, and requires some positive conception of what constitutes a good life. And although liberty is to be respected in education as much as is compatible with instruction, and although a very great deal more liberty than is customary can be allowed without loss to instruction, yet it is clear that some departure from complete liberty is unavoidable if children are to be taught anything, except in the case of unusually intelligent children who are kept isolated from more normal companions. This is one reason for the great responsibility which rests upon teachers: the children must, necessarily, be more or less at the mercy of their elders, and cannot make themselves the guardians of their own interests. Authority in education is to some extent unavoidable, and those who educate have to find a way of exercising authority in accordance with the *spirit* of liberty.

Where authority is unavoidable, what is needed is *reverence*. A man who is to educate really well, and is to make the young grow and develop into their full stature, must be filled through and through with the spirit of reverence. It is reverence towards others that is lacking in those who advocate machine-made cast-iron systems: militarism, capitalism, Fabian scientific organization, and all the other prisons into which reformers and reactionaries try to force the human spirit. In education, with its codes of rules emanating from a Government office, its large classes and fixed curriculum and overworked teachers, its determination to produce a dead level of glib mediocrity, the lack of reverence for the child is all but universal. Reverence requires imagination and vital warmth; it requires most imagination in respect of those who have least actual achievement or power. The child is weak and superficially foolish, the teacher is strong, and in an every-day sense wiser than the child. The teacher without reverence, or the bureaucrat without reverence, easily despises the child for these outward inferiorities. He thinks it is his duty to "mold" the child: in imagination he is the potter with the clay. And so he gives to the child some unnatural shape, which hardens with age, producing strains and spiritual dissatisfactions, out of which grow cruelty and envy, and the belief that others must be compelled to undergo the same distortions.

The man who has reverence will not think it his duty to "mold" the young. He feels in all that lives, but especially in human beings, and most of all in children, something sacred, indefinable, unlimited, something individual and strangely precious, the growing principle of life, an embodied fragment of the dumb striving of the world. In the presence of a child he feels an unaccountable humility—a humility not easily defensible on any rational ground, and yet somehow nearer to wisdom than the easy self-confidence of many parents and teachers. The outward helplessness of the child and the appeal of dependence make him conscious of the responsibility of a trust. His imagination shows him what the child may become, for good or evil, how its impulses may be developed or thwarted, how its hopes must be dimmed and the life in it grow less living, how its trust will be bruised and its quick desires replaced by brooding will. All this gives him a longing to help the child in its own battle; he would equip and strengthen it, not for some outside end proposed by the State or by any other impersonal authority, but for the ends which the child's own spirit is obscurely seeking. The man who feels this can wield the authority of an educator without infringing the principle of liberty.

It is not in a spirit of reverence that education is conducted by States and Churches and the great institutions that are subservient to them. What is considered in education is hardly ever the boy or girl, the young man or young woman, but almost always, in some form, the maintenance of the existing order. When the individual is considered, it is almost exclusively with a view to worldly success—making money or achieving a good position. To be ordinary, and to acquire the art of getting on, is the ideal which is set before the youthful mind, except by a few rare teachers who have enough energy of belief to break through the system within which they are expected to work. Almost all education has a political motive: it aims at strengthening some group, national or religious or even social, in the competition with other groups. It is this motive, in the main, which determines the subjects taught, the knowledge offered and the knowledge withheld, and also decides what mental habits the pupils are expected to acquire. Hardly anything is done to foster the inward growth of mind and spirit; in fact, those who have had most education are very often atrophied in their mental and spiritual life, devoid of impulse, and possessing only certain mechanical aptitudes which take the place of living thought.

Some of the things which education achieves at present must continue to be achieved by education in any civilized country. All children must continue to be taught how to read and write, and some must continue to acquire the knowledge needed for such professions as medicine or law or engineering. The higher education required for the sciences and the arts is necessary for those to whom it is suited. Except in history and religion and kindred matters, the actual instruction is only inadequate, not positively harmful. The instruction might be given in a more liberal spirit, with more attempt to show its ultimate uses; and of course much of it is traditional and dead. But in the main it is necessary, and would have to form a part of any educational system.

It is in history and religion and other controversial subjects that the actual instruction is positively harmful. These subjects touch the interests by which schools are maintained; and the interests maintain the schools in order that certain views on these subjects may be instilled. History, in every country, is so taught as to magnify that country: children learn to believe that their own country has always been in the right and almost always victorious, that it has produced almost all the great men, and that it is in all respects superior to all other countries. Since these beliefs are flattering, they are easily absorbed, and hardly ever dislodged from instinct by later knowledge.

The false ideals as to the history of the world which are taught in the various countries are of a kind which encourages strife and serves to keep alive a bigoted nationalism. If good relations between States were desired, one of the first steps ought to be to submit all teaching of history to an international commission, which should produce neutral textbooks free from the patriotic bias which is now demanded everywhere.

Exactly the same thing applies to religion. Elementary schools are practically always in the hands either of some religious body or of a State which has a certain attitude towards religion.

The result: . . . free inquiry is checked, and on the most important matter in the world the child is met with dogma or with stony silence.

It is not only in elementary education that these evils exist. In more advanced education they take subtler forms, and there is more attempt to conceal them, but they are still present. Eton and Oxford set a certain stamp upon a man's mind, just as a Jesuit College does. It can hardly be said that Eton and Oxford have a *conscious* purpose, but they have a purpose which is none the less strong and effective for not being formulated. In almost all who have been through them they produce a worship of "good form," which is as destructive to life and thought as the medieval Church. "Good form" is quite compatible with superficial open-mindedness, a readiness to hear all sides, and a certain urbanity towards opponents. But it is not compatible with fundamental open-mindedness, or with any inward readiness to give weight to the other side. Its essence is the assumption that what is most important is a certain kind of behavior, a behavior which minimizes friction between equals and delicately impresses inferiors with a conviction of their own crudity. As a political weapon for preserving the privileges of the rich in a snobbish democracy it is unsurpassable. As a means of producing an agreeable social *milieu* for those who have money with no strong beliefs or unusual desires it has some merit. In every other respect it is abominable.

The evils of "good form" arise from two sources: its perfect assurance of its own rightness, and its belief that correct manners are more to be desired than intellect, or artistic creation, or vital energy, or any of the other sources of progress in the world. Perfect assurance, by itself, is enough to destroy all mental progress in those who have it. And when it is combined with contempt for the angularities and awkwardnesses that are almost invariably associated with great mental power, it becomes a source of destruction to all who come in contact with it. "Good form" is itself dead and incapable of growth; and by its attitude to those who are without it it spreads its own death to many who might otherwise have life. The harm which it has done to well-to-do Englishmen, and to men whose abilities have led the well-to-do to notice them, is incalculable.

The prevention of free inquiry is unavoidable so long as the purpose of education is to produce belief rather than thought, to compel the young to hold positive opinions on doubtful matters rather than to let them see the doubtfulness and be encouraged to independence of mind. Education ought to foster the wish for truth, not the conviction that some particular creed is the truth. But it is creeds that hold men together in fighting organizations: Churches, States, political parties. It is intensity of belief in a creed that produces efficiency in fighting: victory comes to those who feel the strongest certainty about matters on which doubt is the only rational attitude. To produce this intensity of belief and this efficiency in fighting, the child's nature is warped, and its free outlook is cramped, by cultivating inhibitions as a check to the growth of new ideas. In those whose minds are not very active the result is the omnipotence of prejudice; while the few whose thought cannot be wholly killed become cynical, intellectually hopeless, destructively critical, able to make all that is living seem foolish, unable themselves to supply the creative impulses which they destroy in others.

The success in fighting which is achieved by suppressing freedom of thought is brief and very worthless. In the long run mental vigor is as essential to success as it is to a good life. The conception of education as a form of drill, a means of producing unanimity through slavishness, is very common, and is defended chiefly on the ground that it leads to victory. Those who enjoy parallels from ancient history will point to the victory of Sparta over Athens to enforce their moral. But it is Athens that has had power over men's thoughts and imaginations, not Sparta: any one of us, if we could be born again into some past epoch, would rather be born an Athenian than a Spartan. And in the modern world so much intellect is required in practical affairs that even the external victory is more likely to be won by intelligence than by docility. Education in credulity leads by quick stages to mental decay; it is only by keeping alive the spirit of free inquiry that the indispensable minimum of progress can be achieved.

Certain mental habits are commonly instilled by those who are engaged in educating: obedience and discipline, ruthlessness in the struggle for worldly success, contempt towards opposing groups, and an unquestioning credulity, a passive acceptance of the teacher's wisdom. All these habits are against life. Instead of obedience and discipline, we ought to aim at preserving independence and impulse. Instead of ruthlessness, education should try to develop justice in thought. Instead of contempt, it ought to instil reverence, and the attempt at understanding; towards the opinions of others it ought to produce, not necessarily acquiescence, but only such opposition as is combined with imaginative apprehension and a clear realization of the grounds for opposition. Instead of credulity, the object should be to stimulate constructive doubt, the love of mental adventure, the sense of worlds to conquer by enterprise and boldness in thought. Contentment with the *status quo*, and subordination of the individual pupil to political aims, owing to the indifference to the things of the mind, are the immediate causes of these evils; but beneath these causes there is one more fundamental, the fact that education is treated as a means of acquiring power over the pupil, not as a means of nourishing his own growth. It is in this that lack of reverence shows itself; and it is only by more reverence that a fundamental reform can be effected.

Obedience and discipline are supposed to be indispensable if order is to be kept in a class, and if any instruction is to be given. To some extent this is true; but the extent is much less than it is thought to be by those who regard obedience and discipline as in themselves desirable. Obedience, the yielding of one's will to outside direction, is the counterpart of authority. Both may be necessary in certain cases. Refractory children, lunatics, and criminals may require authority, and may need to be forced to obey. But in so far as this is necessary it is a misfortune: what is to be desired is the free choice of ends with which it is not necessary to interfere. . . .

If we took education seriously, and thought it as important to keep alive the minds of children as to secure victory in war, we should conduct education quite differently: we should make sure of achieving the end, even if the expense were a hundredfold greater than it is.

Discipline, as it exists in schools, is very largely an evil. There is a kind of discipline which is necessary to almost all achievement, and which perhaps is not sufficiently valued by those who react against the purely external discipline of traditional methods. The desirable kind of discipline is the kind that comes from within, which consists in the power of pursuing a distant object steadily, foregoing and suffering many things on the way. This involves the subordination of impulse to will, the power of a directing action by large creative desires even at moments when they are not vividly alive. Without this, no serious ambition, good or bad, can be realized, no consistent purpose can dominate. This kind of discipline is very necessary, but can only result from strong desires for ends not immediately attainable, and can only be produced by education if education fosters such desires, which it seldom does at present. Such discipline springs from one's own will, not from outside authority. It is not this kind which is sought in most schools, and it is not this kind which seems to me an evil.

Ruthlessness in the economic struggle will almost unavoidably be taught in schools so long as the economic structure of society remains unchanged. This must be particularly the case in middle-class schools, which depend for their numbers upon the good opinion of parents, and secure the good opinion of parents by advertising the successes of pupils. This is one of many ways in which the competitive organization of the State is harmful. Spontaneous and disinterested desire for knowledge is not at all uncommon in the young, and might be easily aroused in many in whom it remains latent. But it is remorselessly checked by teachers who think only of examinations, diplomas, and degrees.

Passive acceptance of the teacher's wisdom is easy to most boys and girls. It involves no effort of independent thought, and seems rational because the teacher knows more than his pupils; it is moreover the way to win the favor of the teacher unless he is a very exceptional man. Yet the habit of passive acceptance is a disastrous one in later life. It causes men to seek a leader and to accept as a leader whoever is established in that position. It makes the power of Churches, Governments, party caucuses, and all the other organizations by which plain men are misled into supporting old systems which are harmful to the nation and to themselves. It is possible that there would not be much independence of thought even if education did everything to promote it; but there would certainly be more than there is at present. If the object were to make pupils think, rather than to make them accept certain conclusions, education would be conducted quite differently: there would be less rapidity of instruction and more discussion, more occasions when pupils were encouraged to express themselves, more attempt to make education concern itself with matters in which the pupils felt some interest.

Above all, there would be an endeavor to rouse and stimulate the love of mental adventure. . . .

It will be said that the joy of mental adventure must be rare, that there are few who can appreciate it, and that ordinary education can take no account of so aristocratic a good. I do not believe this. The joy of mental adventure is far commoner in the young than in grown men and women. Among children it is very common, and grows naturally out of the period of make-believe and fancy. It is rare in later life because everything is done to kill it during education. Men fear thought as they fear nothing else on earth—more than ruin, more even than death. Thought is subversive and revolutionary, destructive and terrible; thought is merciless to privilege, established institutions, and comfortable habits; thought is anarchic and lawless, indifferent to authority, careless of the well-tried wisdom of the ages. Thought looks into the pit of hell and is not afraid. It sees man, a feeble speck, surrounded by unfathomable depths of silence; yet it bears itself proudly, as unmoved as if it were lord of the universe. Thought is great and swift and free, the light of the world, and the chief glory of man.

But if thought is to become the possession of many, not the privilege of the few, we must have done with fear. It is fear that holds men back—fear lest their cherished beliefs should prove delusions, fear lest the institutions by which they live should prove harmful, fear lest they themselves should prove less worthy of respect than they have supposed themselves to be. "Should the working man think freely about property? Then what will become of us, the rich? Should young men and young women think freely about sex? Then what will become of morality? Should soldiers think freely about war? Then what will become of military discipline? Away with thought! Back into the shades of prejudice, lest property, morals, and war should be endangered! Better men should be stupid, slothful, and oppressive than that their thoughts should be free. For if their thought were free they might not think as we do. And at all costs this disaster must be averted." So the opponents of thought argue in the unconscious depths of their souls. And so they act in their churches, their schools, and their universities.

No institution inspired by fear can further life. Hope, not fear, is the creative principle in human affairs. All that has made man great has sprung from the attempt to secure what is good, not from the struggle to avert what was thought evil. It is because modern education is so seldom inspired by a great hope that it so seldom achieves a great result. The wish to preserve the past rather than the hope of creating the future dominates the minds of those who control the teaching of the young. Education should not aim at a passive awareness of dead facts, but at an activity directed towards the world that our efforts are to create. It should be inspired, not by a regretful hankering after the extinct beauties of Greece and the Renaissance, but by a shining vision of the society that is to be, of the triumphs that thought will achieve in the time to come, and of the ever-widening horizon of man's survey over the universe. Those who are taught in this spirit will be filled with life and hope and joy, able to bear their part in bringing to mankind a future less somber than the past, with faith in the glory that human effort can create.

NOTES AND COMMENTS

In this essay Russell is thinking primarily of English institutions and English education, but he believes his argument is universally applicable. Is the overemphasis on "status" and "adjustment" of which we Americans are often accused partly due to the kind of betrayal of education Russell condemns? It would be unfair to say that American schools, on the whole, inculcate the sort of snobbery that he describes. But do our schools foster the peculiarly American reverse snobbery of *mistrusting* "good form"?

Russell denies Cardinal Newman's thesis (in *The Idea of a University*) that the church and liberal education can benefit each other. But Russell and Newman may have some convictions in common. For example, are Russell's "joy of mental adventure" and Newman's "philosophic habit of mind" complementary?

If one agrees with Russell that the institutions which control education—the church, the state, a dominant social class—are concerned not with the child but with their own self-perpetuation, a question remains: Where are we to find the fund of reverence and humility, to say nothing of learning, that can open young minds to knowledge?

C. S. LEWIS

1898-

The scholarly reputation of C. S. Lewis, who holds the Chair of Medieval and Renaissance English Literature at Cambridge University, rests firmly on such works as *The Allegory of Love*, perhaps the best single study of that curious medieval invention, the courtly love tradition. He is also an apologist for Christianity, especially for what he sees as its essential humanism—a view he presents in treatises like *Miracles* or *The Problem of Pain*, and in such other works as *The Screwtape Letters*, a set of exhortations to a young "guardian devil" from a more experienced fiend. He has also embodied his convictions in a series of metaphysical science-fiction novels, *Out of the Silent Planet*, *Perelandra*, and *That Hideous Strength*.

In *The Abolition of Man* Lewis argues his belief in the necessity of *Tao*. He uses this Chinese word, meaning "the way," to signify a doctrine that moral absolutes exist in the universe as surely as scientific laws and that these absolutes determine good and evil in human action just as gravity determines that apples fall down instead of up. As the term he chooses suggests, Lewis believes that such a doctrine is a part of the tradition of any civilization which has achieved a "wisdom" —not only of Judeo-Christian civilization, but of the Oriental cultures as well. This selection from the book is concerned with what Lewis thinks a denial of *Tao* may lead to in the realm of education.

FROM *The Abolition of Man*

It came burning hot into my mind, whatever he said and however he flattered, when he got me home to his house, he would sell me for a slave.

BUNYAN

"MAN'S CONQUEST of Nature" is an expression often used to describe the progress of applied science. "Man has Nature whacked" said someone to a friend of mine not long ago. In their context the words had a certain tragic beauty, for the speaker was dying of tuberculosis. "No matter," he said, "I know I'm one of the casualties. Of course there are casualties on the winning as well as on the losing side. But that doesn't alter the fact that it is winning." I have chosen this story as my point of departure in order to make it clear that I do not wish to disparage all that is really beneficial in the process described as "Man's conquest," much less all the real devotion and self-sacrifice that has gone to make it possible. But having done so I must proceed to analyse this conception a little more closely. In what sense is Man the possessor of increasing power over Nature?

Let us consider three typical examples: the aeroplane, the wireless, and the contraceptive. In a civilized community, in peacetime, anyone who can pay for them may use these things. But it cannot strictly be said that when he does so he is exercising his own proper or individual power over Nature. If I pay you to carry me, I am not therefore myself a strong man. Any or all of the three things I have mentioned can be withheld from some men by other men—by those who sell, or those who allow the sale, or those who own the sources of production, or those who make the goods. What we call Man's power is, in reality, a power possessed by some men which they may, or may not, allow other men to profit by. Again, as regards the powers manifested in the aeroplane or the wireless, Man is as much the patient or subject as the possessor, since he is the target both for bombs and for propaganda. And as regards

Reprinted from *The Abolition of Man* by C. S. Lewis. Copyright 1944 by The Macmillan Company. By permission of The Macmillan Company and Geoffrey Bles Ltd., London.

contraceptives, there is a paradoxical, negative sense in which all possible future generations are the patients or subjects of a power wielded by those already alive. By contraception simply, they are denied existence; by contraception used as a means of selective breeding, they are, without their concurring voice, made to be what one generation, for its own reasons, may choose to prefer. From this point of view, what we call Man's power over Nature turns out to be a power exercised by some men over other men with Nature as its instrument.

It is, of course, a commonplace to complain that men have hitherto used badly, and against their fellows, the powers that science has given them. But that is not the point I am trying to make. I am not speaking of particular corruptions and abuses which an increase of moral virtue would cure: I am considering what the thing called "Man's power over Nature" must always and essentially be. No doubt, the picture could be modified by public ownership of raw materials and factories and public control of scientific research. But unless we have a world state this will still mean the power of one nation over others. And even within the world state or the nation it will mean (in principle) the power of majorities over minorities, and (in the concrete) of a government over the people. And all long-term exercises of power, especially in breeding, must mean the power of earlier generations over later ones.

The latter point is not always sufficiently emphasized, because those who write on social matters have not yet learned to imitate the physicists by always including Time among the dimensions. In order to understand fully what Man's power over Nature, and therefore the power of some men over other men, really means, we must picture the race extended in time from the date of its emergence to that of its extinction. Each generation exercises power over its successors: and each, in so far as it modifies the environment bequeathed to it and rebels against tradition, resists and limits the power of its predecessors. This modifies the picture which is sometimes painted of a progressive emancipation from tradition and a progressive control of natural processes resulting in a continual increase of human power. In reality, of course, if any one age really attains, by eugenics and scientific education, the power to make its descendants what it pleases, all men who live after it are the patients of that power. They are weaker, not stronger: for though we may have put wonderful machines in their hands we have pre-ordained how they are to use them. And if, as is almost certain, the age which had thus attained maximum power over posterity were also the age most emancipated from tradition, it would be engaged in reducing the power of its predecessors almost as drastically as that of its successors. And we must also remember that, quite apart from this, the later a generation comes—the nearer it lives to that date at which the species becomes extinct—the less power it will have in the forward direction, because its subjects will be so few. There is therefore no question of a power vested in the race as a whole steadily growing as long as the race survives. The last men, far from being the heirs of power, will be of all men most subject to the dead hand of the great planners and conditioners and will themselves exercise least power upon the future. The real picture is that of one dominant age—let us suppose the hundredth century A.D.—which resists all previous ages most successfully and dominates all subsequent ages most irresistibly, and thus is the real master of the human species. But even within this master generation (itself an infinitesimal minority of the species) the power will be exercised by a minority smaller still. Man's conquest of Nature, if the dreams of some scientific planners are realized, means the rule of a few hundreds of men over billions upon billions of men. There neither is nor can be any simple increase of power on Man's side. Each new power won by man is a power over man as well. Each advance leaves him weaker as well as stronger. In every victory, besides being the general who triumphs, he is also the prisoner who follows the triumphal car.

I am not yet considering whether the total result of such ambivalent victories is a good thing or a bad. I am only making clear what Man's conquest of Nature really means and especially that final stage in the conquest, which, perhaps, is not far off. The final stage is come when Man by eugenics, by pre-natal conditioning, and by an education and propaganda based on a perfect applied psychology, has obtained full control over himself. *Human* nature will be the last part of Nature to surrender to Man. The battle will then be won. We shall have "taken the thread of life out of the hand of Clotho" and be henceforth free to make our species whatever we wish it to be. The battle will indeed be won. But who, precisely, will have won it?

For the power of Man to make himself what he pleases means, as we have seen, the power of some men to make other men what they please. In all ages, no doubt, nurture and instruction have, in some sense, attempted to exercise this power. But the situation to which we must look forward will be novel in two respects. In the first place, the power will be enormously increased. Hitherto the plans of educationalists have achieved very little of what they attempted and indeed, when we read them—how Plato would have every infant "a bastard nursed in a bureau," and Elyot[1] would have the boy see no men before the age of seven and, after that, no women,[2] and how Locke wants children to have leaky shoes and no turn for poetry[3]—we may well thank the beneficent obstinacy of real mothers, real nurses, and (above all) real children for preserving the human race in such sanity as it still possesses. But the man-moulders of the new age will be armed with the powers of an omnicompetent state and an irresistible scientific technique: we shall get at last a race of conditioners who really can cut out all posterity in what shape they please. The second difference is even more important. In the older systems both the kind of man the teachers wished to produce and their motives for producing him were prescribed by the Tao—a norm to which the teachers themselves were subject and from which they claimed no liberty to depart. They did not cut men to some pattern they had chosen. They handed on what they had received: they initiated the young neophyte into the mystery of humanity which over-arched him and them alike. It was but old birds teaching young birds to fly. This will be changed. Values are now mere natural phenomena. Judgements of value are to be produced in the pupil as part of the conditioning. Whatever Tao there is will

---

[1 Sir Thomas Elyot (c. 1490-1546), scholar and diplomat, author of The Boke Named the Governour.—Ed.]

[2] The Boke Named the Governour, I, iv: "Al men except physitions only shulde be excluded and kepte out of the norisery." I, vi: "After that a childe is come to seuen yeres of age . . . the most sure counsaille is to withdrawe him from all company of women."

[3] Some Thoughts concerning Education, ¶ 7: "I will also advise his Feet to be wash'd every Day in cold Water, and to have his Shoes so thin that they might leak and let in Water, whenever he comes near it." ¶ 174: "If he have a poetick vein, 'tis to me the strangest thing in the World that the Father should desire or suffer it to be cherished or improved. Methinks the Parents should labour to have it stifled and suppressed as much as may be." Yet Locke is one of our most sensible writers on education.

be the product, not the motive, of education. The conditioners
have been emancipated from all that. It is one more part of
Nature which they have conquered. The ultimate springs of
human action are no longer, for them, something given. They
have surrendered—like electricity: it is the function of the Conditioners to control, not to obey them. They know how to *produce*
conscience and decide what kind of conscience they will produce.
They themselves are outside, above. For we are assuming the last
stage of Man's struggle with Nature. The final victory has been
won. Human nature has been conquered—and, of course, has
conquered, in whatever sense those words may now bear.

The Conditioners, then, are to choose what kind of artificial
Tao they will, for their own good reasons, produce in the Human
race. They are the motivators, the creators of motives. But how
are they going to be motivated themselves? For a time, perhaps,
by survivals, within their own minds, of the old "natural" *Tao*.
Thus at first they may look upon themselves as servants and
guardians of humanity and conceive that they have a "duty" to do
it "good." But it is only by confusion that they can remain in this
state. They recognize the concept of duty as the result of certain
processes which they can now control. Their victory has consisted
precisely in emerging from the state in which they were acted
upon by those processes to the state in which they use them as
tools. One of the things they now have to decide is whether they
will, or will not, so condition the rest of us that we can go on
having the old idea of duty and the old reactions to it. How can
duty help them to decide that? Duty itself is up for trial: it cannot
also be the judge. And "good" fares no better. They know quite
well how to produce a dozen different conceptions of good in us.
The question is which, if any, they should produce. No conception
of good can help them to decide. It is absurd to fix on one of the
things they are comparing and make it the standard of comparison.

To some it will appear that I am inventing a factitious difficulty for my Conditioners. Other, more simple-minded, critics
may ask "Why should you suppose they will be such bad men?"
But I am not supposing them to be bad men. They are, rather, not
men (in the old sense) at all. They are, if you like, men who have
sacrificed their own share in traditional humanity in order to
devote themselves to the task of deciding what "Humanity" shall
henceforth mean. "Good" and "bad," applied to them, are words

without content: for it is from them that the content of these words is henceforward to be derived. Nor is their difficulty factitious. We might suppose that it was possible to say "After all, most of us want more or less the same things—food and drink and sexual intercourse, amusement, art, science, and the longest possible life for individuals and for the species. Let them simply say, This is what we happen to like, and go on to condition men in the way most likely to produce it. Where's the trouble?" But this will not answer. In the first place, it is false that we all really like the same things. But even if we did, what motive is to impel the Conditioners to scorn delights and live laborious days in order that we, and posterity, may have what we like? Their duty? But that is only the *Tao*, which they may decide to impose on us, but which cannot be valid for them. If they accept it, then they are no longer the makers of conscience but still its subjects, and their final conquest over Nature has not really happened. The preservation of the species? But why should the species be preserved? One of the questions before them is whether this feeling for posterity (they know well how it is produced) shall be continued or not. However far they go back, or down, they can find no ground to stand on. Every motive they try to act on becomes at once a *petitio*. It is not that they are bad men. They are not men at all. Stepping outside the *Tao*, they have stepped into the void. Nor are their subjects necessarily unhappy men. They are not men at all: they are artefacts. Man's final conquest has proved to be the abolition of Man.

Yet the Conditioners will act. When I said just now that all motives fail them, I should have said all motives except one. All motives that claim any validity other than that of their felt emotional weight at a given moment have failed them. Everything except the *sic volo, sic jubeo*[1] has been explained away. But what never claimed objectivity cannot be destroyed by subjectivism. The impulse to scratch when I itch or to pull to pieces when I am inquisitive is immune from the solvent which is fatal to my justice, or honour, or care for posterity. When all that says "it is good" has been debunked, what says "I want" remains. It cannot be exploded or "seen through" because it never had any pretensions. The Conditioners, therefore, must come to be motivated simply by

_____

[1 What I want, I command.—*Ed*.]

their own pleasure. I am not here speaking of the corrupting influence of power nor expressing the fear that under it our Conditioners will degenerate. The very words *corrupt* and *degenerate* imply a doctrine of value and are therefore meaningless in this context. My point is that those who stand outside all judgements of value cannot have any ground for preferring one of their own impulses to another except the emotional strength of that impulse. We may legitimately hope that among the impulses which arise in minds thus emptied of all "rational" or "spiritual" motives, some will be benevolent. I am very doubtful myself whether the benevolent impulses, stripped of that preference and encouragement which the *Tao* teaches us to give them and left to their merely natural strength and frequency as psychological events, will have much influence. I am very doubtful whether history shows us one example of a man who, having stepped outside traditional morality and attained power, has used that power benevolently. I am inclined to think that the Conditioners will hate the conditioned. Though regarding as an illusion the artificial conscience which they produce in us their subjects, they will yet perceive that it creates in us an illusion of meaning for our lives which compares favourably with the futility of their own: and they will envy us as eunuchs envy men. But I do not insist on this, for it is mere conjecture. What is not conjecture is that our hope even of a "conditioned" happiness rests on what is ordinarily called "chance"—the chance that benevolent impulses may on the whole predominate in our Conditioners. For without the judgement "Benevolence is good"—that is, without re-entering the *Tao*—they can have no ground for promoting or stabilizing their benevolent impulses rather than any others. By the logic of their position they must just take their impulses as they come, from chance. And Chance here means Nature. It is from heredity, digestion, the weather, and the association of ideas, that the motives of the Conditioners will spring. Their extreme rationalism, by "seeing through" all "rational" motives, leaves them creatures of wholly irrational behaviour. If you will not obey the *Tao*, or else commit suicide, obedience to impulse (and therefore, in the long run, to mere "nature") is the only course left open.

At the moment, then, of Man's victory over Nature, we find the whole human race subjected to some individual men, and those individuals subjected to that in themselves which is purely "natural"—to their irrational impulses. Nature, untrammelled by values, rules the Conditioners and, through them, all humanity. Man's conquest of Nature turns out, in the moment of its consummation, to be Nature's conquest of Man. Every victory we seemed to win has led us, step by step, to this conclusion. All Nature's apparent reverses have been but tactical withdrawals. We thought we were beating her back when she was luring us on. What looked to us like hands held up in surrender was really the opening of arms to enfold us for ever. If the fully planned and conditioned world (with its *Tao* a mere product of the planning) comes into existence, Nature will be troubled no more by the restive species that rose in revolt against her so many millions of years ago, will be vexed no longer by its chatter of truth and mercy and beauty and happiness. *Ferum victorem cepit:*[1] and if the eugenics are efficient enough there will be no second revolt, but all sunk beneath the Conditioners, and the Conditioners beneath her, till the moon falls or the sun grows cold.

NOTES AND COMMENTS

If Bertrand Russell detests the propaganda which too often substitutes for education, Lewis gazes with horror at its utmost extension: a world divided into Conditioners and their victims. Though Russell says nothing about *Tao*, what would his attitude be toward a concept which gives such importance to tradition? Would Russell and Lewis be more in agreement in their evaluation of reformers in education? (Note what Russell says about "theorists," and Lewis about "educationalists.")

Lewis's thought is so closely reasoned that to judge the validity of his argument one must trace carefully the logic by which he proceeds from Man's conquest of Nature to Nature's conquest of Man. Does the meaning he assigns to *Tao* suggest a flaw in his reasoning?

The piece depends for its effect not only on logic but also on prose rhythms and on the chilling phrases in which Lewis expresses his dread of man's ultimate destruction. Note, for instance, the last sentence of the essay.

---

[1] "(Captive Greece) conquered her wild conqueror." A phrase from the *Epistles* of Horace, referring to the influence of the arts and culture of Greece upon the conquering Romans.—Ed.]

C. P. SNOW

1905-

C. P. Snow lives in two worlds. He is the author of a cycle of novels, *Strangers and Brothers* (including *The Masters, The Conscience of the Rich,* and *The Affair*), which is generally recognized as a major achievement of twentieth-century English fiction. He is, as well, a physicist whose "working existence" has been spent among scientists; during World War II, for instance, he was director for the British government of recruitment for scientific research.

Because of his double competence Snow can discuss the modern age's most vexing intellectual problem, the dichotomy between science and the humanities, with an authority denied most of the others who have considered it. The following essay is an abstract of *The Two Cultures and the Scientific Revolution*, originally written to be delivered at Cambridge University as the 1959 Rede Lecture.

The Conflict of Cultures

BY TRAINING I am a scientist; by vocation I am a writer. For thirty years I have had to be in touch with scientists as part of a working existence. During the same thirty years I was trying to shape the books I wanted to write, which in due course took me among writers. It was through living among these groups and through moving regularly from one to the other and back again that I became occupied with the problem of what I call the "two cultures." For constantly I felt I was moving among two groups— comparable in intelligence, not grossly different in social origin, earning about the same incomes—who had almost ceased to communicate at all, who in intellectual, moral and psychological climate had so little in common that they might have inhabited different worlds.

As a result of this cultural dichotomy, I believe the intellectual life of the whole of Western society is increasingly being split into two polar groups. When I say the intellectual life I mean to include also a large part of our practical life, because I should be the last person to suggest the two can at the deepest level be distinguished. At one pole we have the literary intellectuals who, incidentally, while no one was looking, took to referring to themselves as "intellectuals" as though there were no others.

Literary intellectuals are at one pole—at the other, scientists; and, as the most representative, the physical scientists. Between the two lies a gulf of mutual incomprehension. The two groups have, moreover, a curious, distorted image of each other. Their attitudes are so different that even on the level of emotion they find little common ground.

Nonscientists tend to think of scientists as brash and boastful. Nonscientists have a rooted impression that the scientists are shallowly optimistic, unaware of man's condition. On the other hand, the scientists believe that the literary intellectuals are totally lacking in foresight, peculiarly unconcerned with their brother men, in a deep sense anti-intellectual, anxious to restrict both art and thought to the existential moment. Some of this subterranean backchat is not entirely baseless—though it is all destructive. Much of it rests on misinterpretations which are dangerous. I would now like to deal with two of the most profound of these misinterpretations.

First, concerning the nonscientists' impression that scientists are blankly optimistic. This accusation depends upon a confusion between the individual experience and the social experience, between the individual condition of man and his social condition. Most of the scientists I have known well have felt—just as deeply as the nonscientists I have known well—that the individual condition of each of us is tragic. Each of us is alone. Sometimes we escape from solitariness through love or affection or perhaps creative moments; but those triumphs of life are pools of light we make for ourselves, while the edge of the road is black. Each of us dies alone.

Some scientists I have known have had faith in revealed religion. Perhaps with them the sense of the tragic condition is not so strong. I don't know. With most people of deep feeling, however high-spirited and happy they are—sometimes most with those who are happiest and most high-spirited—this tragic awareness seems to be in the fibers, part of the weight of life. That is as true of the scientists I have known as of anyone.

But nearly all scientists—and this is where the color of hope comes in—would see no reason why, just because the individual condition is tragic, so must the social condition be. Most of our fellow human beings, for instance, are underfed and die before their time. In the crudest terms, that is the social condition.

There is a moral trap which comes through the insight into man's loneliness; it tempts one to sit back, complacent in one's unique tragedy, and let the others go without a meal. As a group the scientists fall into that trap less than others. They are inclined to be impatient to see if something can be done and inclined to think that it can be done, until it's proved otherwise. That is their real optimism, and it's an optimism that the rest of us badly need.

In reverse this same spirit, tough and good and determined to fight it out at the side of their brother men, has made scientists regard the other culture's social attitudes as contemptible. That viewpoint is too facile; some of those attitudes are contemptible, but they are a temporary phase and not representative.

I remember being cross-examined by a scientist of distinction. "Why do most writers take on social opinions which would have been thought distinctly uncivilized and *démodé* at the time of the Plantagenets? Weren't they not only politically silly but politically wicked?"

The honest answer was that there was, in fact, a connection, which literary persons were culpably slow to see, between some kinds of early twentieth-century art and the most imbecile expressions of antisocial feeling. But though many of those antisocial writers dominated literary sensibility for a generation, that is no longer so, or at least to nothing like the same extent. Literature changes more slowly than science. It hasn't the same automatic corrective, and so its misguided periods are longer. But it is ill-considered of scientists to judge writers on the evidence of the period 1914-50.

Those are two of the misunderstandings between the two cultures. But is this arbitrary division defensible? Are these in reality two cultures? I believe the scientific culture is really a culture, not only in an intellectual but also in an anthropological sense.

The scientists' culture is intensive, rigorous and constantly in action. Their culture contains a great deal of argument, usually more rigorous and almost always at a higher conceptual level, than literary arguments—and even though the scientists cheerfully use words in senses which literary intellectuals don't recognize, the senses are exact ones. For example, "subjective," in contemporary technological jargon, means "divided according to subjects"; "objective" means "directed toward an object."

Remember, scientists are very intelligent men. Their culture is in many ways an exacting and admirable one. It doesn't contain much art, with the exception—an important exception—of music. It involves verbal exchange; insistent argument; long-playing records; color photography; the ear; to some extent the eye.

Of books, though, there is very little; of novels, history, poetry, plays, almost nothing. It isn't that scientists are not interested in the psychological or moral or social life. In the social life they certainly are interested, more than most of us. In the moral, they are by and large the soundest group of intellectuals we have; there is a moral component right in the grain of science itself, and almost all scientists form their own judgments of the moral life. It isn't that they lack the interests. It is more that the whole literature of the traditional culture doesn't seem to them to be relevant to those interests. They are, of course, dead wrong.

But what about the other side? The nonscientific culture is impoverished, too—perhaps more seriously, because it is vainer about it. The literary intellectuals still like to pretend that the traditional culture is the whole of culture, as though the natural order—the sciences—didn't exist; as though the exploration of the natural order were of no interest either in its own value or its consequences; as though the scientific edifice of the physical world were not, in its intellectual depth, complexity and articulation, the most beautiful and wonderful collective work of the mind of man. Yet most nonscientists have no conception of that edifice at all.

As with the tone-deaf, they don't know what they miss. They give a pitying chuckle at the news of scientists who have never read a major work of English literature. They dismiss them as ignorant specialists. Yet their own ignorance and their own specialization is just as startling. A good many times I have been present at gatherings of people who, by the standards of the traditional culture, are thought highly educated and who have with considerable gusto been expressing their incredulity at the illiteracy of scientists. Once or twice I have been provoked and have asked the company how many of them could describe the Second Law of Thermodynamics. The response was cold; it was also negative. Yet I was asking something which is about the scientific equivalent of "Have you read a work of Shakespeare's?"

I now believe that if I had asked an even simpler question —such as, "What do you mean by mass, or acceleration?", which is the scientific equivalent of saying, "Can you read?"—not more than one in ten of the highly educated would have felt that I was speaking the same language. So the great edifice of modern physics goes up, and the majority of the cleverest people in the Western world have about as much insight into it as their neolithic ancestors would have had.

The reasons for the existence of the two cultures are many, deep and complex. I want to isolate one which is not so much a reason as a correlative, something which winds in and out of any of these discussions. It can be said simply, and it is this: If we ignore the scientific culture, then the rest of Western intellectuals have never tried, wanted or been able to understand the industrial revolution, much less to accept it.

All over the West the first wave of the industrial revolution crept on without anyone's noticing what was happening. It was destined to become in our own time by far the biggest transformation in society since the discovery of agriculture. In fact, those two revolutions, the agricultural and the industrial-scientific, are the only qualitative changes in social living that men have ever known. But the traditional culture didn't notice; or when it did notice, didn't like what it saw.

Almost none of the talent, almost none of the imaginative energy of the nineteenth century went back into the revolution which was producing the wealth. The traditional culture became more abstracted from it as society became more wealthy, trained its young men for administration, for the purpose of perpetuating the traditional culture itself, but never in any circumstances to equip them to understand the revolution or take part in it. Farsighted men were beginning to see, before the middle of the nineteenth century, that in order to go on producing wealth, society needed to train some of its bright minds in science, particularly in applied science. Few listened. The traditional culture didn't listen at all; and the pure scientists, such as there were, didn't listen very eagerly.

Thus the academics had nothing to do with the industrial revolution. So far as there was any thinking in nineteenth-century industry, it was left to cranks and clever workmen. The industrial revolution received very little educated talent. It had to make do with the guidance handy men could give it—sometimes, of course, handy men like Henry Ford, with a dash of genius.

Of course, one truth is straightforward—industrialization is the only hope of the poor. I use the word "hope" in a crude and prosaic sense. It is all very well for us, sitting pretty, to think that material standards of living don't matter. In fact, to deny this attitude is now to be accused of "materialism." It is all very well for one, as a personal choice, to reject industrialization. Do a modern Walden, if you like and, if you go without much food, see most of your children die in infancy; despise the comforts of literacy; accept twenty years off your own life—then I respect you for the strength of your aesthetic revulsion. But I don't respect you in the slightest if, even passively, you try to impose the same choice on others who are not free to choose.

The industrial revolution looked very different according to whether one saw it from above or below. To people who saw it from below there was no question that the industrial revolution was less bad than what had gone before. The only question was how to make it better.

In a more sophisticated sense that is still the question. In the advanced countries we have realized in a rough-and-ready way what the old industrial revolution brought with it—a great increase of population, because applied science went hand in hand with medical science and medical care; enough to eat, for a similar reason; everyone able to read and write, because an industrial society can't work without a broad base of literacy. Health, food, education—nothing but the industrial revolution could have spread them right down to the very poor.

Those are primary gains. There are losses, too, of course; one of which is that organizing a society for industry makes it easy to organize it for all-out war. But the gains remain. They are the matrix of our social hope. And yet, do we understand how they have happened? Have we begun to comprehend even the old industrial revolution, much less the new scientific revolution in which we stand? There never was anything more necessary to comprehend.

By the industrial revolution I mean the gradual use of machines, the employment of men and women in factories, the change from a population of agricultural laborers to a population largely engaged in making things in factories and distributing them when they were made.

Out of the industrial revolution grew another change, closely related to the first, but far more deeply scientific. This change comes from the application of real science to industry. I believe the industrial changes involving electronics, atomic energy and automation are in cardinal respects different in kind from any we have experienced before and will change the world much more. It is this transformation that, in my view, is entitled to the name of "scientific revolution." This is the material basis of our lives, or more exactly, the social plasma of which we are a part. And we know almost nothing about it.

Why aren't we coping with the scientific revolution? How are we going to meet our future, both our cultural and practical future? I believe both phases of the question lead to the same conclusion. If one begins by thinking only of the intellectual life or only of the social life, one comes to a point where it becomes manifest that our education has failed us.

I don't pretend that any country has got its education perfect. In some ways the Russians and Americans are both more actively dissatisfied with their educational establishment than the English —at least they are taking more drastic steps to change it. That may be because they are more sensitive to the world they are living in. I have no doubt that, though neither of them has got the answer right, they are a good deal nearer than we in England. We do some things much better than either of them. In educational tactics we are often more gifted than the Russians or the Americans. In educational strategy, in contrast, we are only playing at it.

The differences between the three systems are revelatory. The English teach a far smaller proportion of their children up to the

age of eighteen, and take a far smaller proportion even of those
they do teach up to the level of a university degree. The old pattern of training a small elite has never been broken, though it
has been slightly bent. Within that pattern the English have kept
their national passion for specialization, and we work our clever
young up to the age of twenty-one far harder than the Americans,
though no harder than the Russians. At eighteen English science
specialists know more science than their contemporaries anywhere,
though they know less of anything else.

The American strategy is different in kind. They take everyone, the entire population up to eighteen, in high schools and
educate them very loosely and generally. Their problem is to inject
some rigor—in particular, some fundamental mathematics and
science—into this loose education. A very large proportion of the
eighteen-year-olds then go to college; and this college education is,
like the school education, much more diffuse and less professional
than its English counterpart. At the end of four years the American young men and women are usually not so well-trained pro-
fessionally as their English equivalents—though I think it is fair
comment to say that a higher proportion of the best of them, having been run on a looser rein, retain their creative zest. Real severity
enters with the Ph.D. At that level the Americans suddenly begin
to work their students much harder than the English do.

The Russian high-school education is much less specialized
than the English, much more arduous than the American. It is so
arduous that for the nonacademic it seems to have proved too
tough, and they are trying other methods for students from fifteen
to seventeen. The general method has been to put everyone
through a kind of continental *lycée* course, with a sizable component, more than 40 per cent, of science and mathematics.
Everyone has to do all subjects. At the university this general
education ceases abruptly; and for the last three years of the five-
year course the specialization is more intensive than that found in
either England or America.

With some qualifications, I believe, the Russians have judged
the situation sensibly. They have a deeper insight into the scientific
revolution than the English or the Americans. The gap between
the cultures doesn't seem to be anything like so wide as it is in
the West.

The Russians have judged what kind and number of educated

men and women a country needs to come out on top in the scientific revolution. I am going to over-simplify, but their estimate, and I believe it's pretty nearly right, is this: First of all, as many alpha-plus scientists as the country can produce. No country has many of them. Provided the schools and universities are there, it doesn't matter much what you teach these individuals. They will look after themselves.

Second, a much larger stratum of alpha professionals—these are the people who are going to do the supporting research, the high-class design and development. Third, another stratum educated to a college-degree level. Some of these will do the secondary technical jobs, but some will take major responsibility, particularly in the human jobs. The proper use of such men depends upon a different distribution of ability from the one that now holds. As the scientific revolution goes on, the call for these men will be something we haven't imagined—though the Russians have. They will be required in thousands upon thousands and they will need all the human development that a university education can give them. It is here, perhaps, most of all that our insight has been fogged.

Fourth and last, politicians and administrators—an entire community—who know enough science to have a sense of what the scientists are talking about.

That, or something like that, is the specification for the scientific revolution. I want now to go on to an issue which will, in the world view, count more. That issue is that the people in the industrialized countries are getting richer, and those in the nonindustrialized countries are at best standing still; so the gap between the industrialized countries and the rest is widening daily. On the world scale this is the gap between the rich and the poor.

Among the rich are the United States, the white Commonwealth countries, Great Britain, most of Europe and the U.S.S.R. China is betwixt and between, not yet over the industrial hump, but probably getting there. The poor are all the rest. In the rich countries people are living longer, eating better, working less. In a poor country like India the expectation of life is less than half what it is in England. In all nonindustrialized countries people are still working as laboriously as they have always had to work, from neolithic times until our own. Life for the overwhelming majority

of mankind has always been nasty, brutish and short. It is so in
the poor countries still.

This disparity between the rich and the poor has been noticed.
It has been noticed most acutely by the poor. And because they
have noticed it, it won't last long. Whatever else—in the world we
know—survives to the year 2000, that won't. Once the trick of
getting rich is known, as it now is, the world can't survive half rich
and half poor.

The West has got to help in this transformation. The trouble
is that the West with its divided cultures finds it hard to grasp
just how big and, above all, just how fast the transformation must
be.

The comforting assurances, given from top to bottom, that in
100 or 200 years things may be slightly better for have-nots only
madden. Pronouncements such as one still hears from old hands
on Asia or on Africa—"Why, it will take those people five hundred
years to get up to our standard!"—are both suicidal and techno-
logically illiterate.

The fact is, the social enrichment of a poor country has already been proved possible. Someone said when the first atomic
bomb went off that the only important secret is now let out—the
thing works. After that, any determined country could make the
bomb, given a few years. In the same way, the only secret of the
Russian and Chinese industrialization is that they've brought it off.
That is what Asians and Africans have noticed. It took the Russians about forty years, starting with something of an industrial
base—czarist industry wasn't negligible—but interrupted by a civil
war and then the greatest war of all. The Chinese started with
much less of an industrial base but haven't been interrupted, and
it looks as though it would not take them much more than half
the time.

The Russian and Chinese transformations are being made
with inordinate effort and with great suffering. Much of the suffering was unnecessary; the horror is hard to look at straight, standing
in the same decades. Yet these examples have proved that common men can show astonishing fortitude in chasing tomorrow.

The transformations have also proved something which only
the scientific culture can take in its stride. It is simply that tech-

nology is rather easy. Or more exactly, technology is the branch of human experience that people can learn with predictable results. For a long time the West misjudged this very badly. Somehow we've made ourselves believe that the whole of technology was a more or less incommunicable art. It's true enough that we start with a certain advantage, not so much because of tradition, I think, as because our children play with mechanical toys. They are picking up pieces of applied science before they can read. That is an advantage we haven't made the most of.

The curious thing is that none of that seems to matter much. For the task of totally industrializing a major country, as in China today, it takes only will to train enough scientists and engineers and technicians. Will, and quite a small number of years. There is no evidence that any country or race is better than any other in scientific teachability; there is a good deal of evidence that all are much alike. Tradition and technical background seem to count for surprisingly little.

There is no getting away from it; it is technically possible to carry out the scientific revolution in India, Africa, Southeast Asia, Latin America and the Middle East within fifty years. There is no excuse for Western man not to know this, and not to know that this is the one way out through the three menaces which stand in our way—H-bomb war, over-population and the gap between the rich and the poor. This is one of the situations where the worst crime is innocence.

Since the gap between the rich countries and the poor can be removed, it will be. If we are shortsighted, inept, incapable either of good will or enlightened self-interest, then it may be removed to the accompaniment of war and starvation—but removed it will be. The questions are how and by whom.

To those questions one can only give partial answers; but that may be enough to set us thinking. The scientific revolution on a world scale needs capital first and foremost—capital in all forms, including capital machinery. The poor countries, until they have got beyond a certain point on the industrial curve, cannot accumulate that capital. That is why the gap between rich and poor is widening. The capital must come from outside.

There are only two possible sources. One is the West, which means mainly the United States, the other is the U.S.S.R. Even the United States hasn't infinite resources of such capital. If the

West or Russia tried to do it alone, it would mean an effort greater than either had to make industrially in the last war. If they both took part it wouldn't mean that order of sacrifice—though in my view it's optimistic to think, as some wise men do, that it would mean no sacrifice at all. The scale of the operation requires that it would have to be a national one. Private industry, even the biggest private industry, can't touch it, and in no sense is it a fair business risk.

The second requirement, and as important as capital, is men. That is, trained scientists and engineers adaptable enough to devote themselves to a foreign country's industrialization for at least ten years out of their lives. Here, unless and until the Americans and the English educate themselves both sensibly and imaginatively, the Russians have a clear edge. This is where their educational policy has already paid big dividends. They have such men to spare if they are needed. The English haven't, and the Americans aren't much better off. Imagine, for example, that the United States and British governments had agreed to help the Indians to carry out a major industrialization, similar in scale to the Chinese. Imagine that the capital could be found. It would then require something like 10,000 to 20,000 engineers from the United States and England to help get the thing going. At present we couldn't find them.

That is the size of the problem—an immense capital outlay, an immense investment in men, both scientists and linguists, most of whom the West does not yet possess—with rewards negligible in the short term, apart from doing the job, and in the long term most uncertain.

People will ask me, "This is all very fine and large. But you are supposed to be a realistic man. Can you possibly believe that men will behave as you say they ought to? Can you imagine a political technique in parliamentary societies like the United States or England by which any such plan could become real?"

This is fair comment. I can only reply that I don't know. I confess, and I should be less than honest if I didn't, that I can't see the political technique through which the good human capabilities of the West can get into action. The best one can do, and it is a poor best, is to nag away. That is perhaps too easy a palliative for one's own disquiet. For though I don't know how we can do what we need to do, or whether we shall do anything at all, I do know this—if we don't do it, the Communist countries will in time.

If that is how it turns out we shall have failed, both practically and morally. At best, the West will have become an enclave in a different world. Are we resigning ourselves to that? History is merciless to failure. In any case, if that happens we shall not be writing the history.

Meanwhile, there are steps to be taken which aren't outside the powers of reflective people. Education isn't the total solution to this problem, but without education the West can't even begin to cope. All the arrows point the same way. Closing the gap between our cultures is a necessity in the most abstract intellectual sense, as well as in the most practical. When those two senses have grown apart, then no society is going to be able to think with wisdom. For the sake of the intellectual life, for the sake of the Western society living precariously as rich among the poor, for the sake of the poor who needn't be poor if there is intelligence in the world, it is obligatory for the English and the Americans and the whole West to look at our education with fresh eyes. This is one of the cases where the English and the Americans have the most to learn from each other. We have each a good deal to learn from the Russians, if we are not too proud. Incidentally, the Russians have a good deal to learn from us too.

Isn't it time we began? The danger is that we have been brought up to think as though we had all the time in the world. We have very little time. So little that I dare not guess at it.

NOTES AND COMMENTS

When Snow speaks of the "gulf of mutual incomprehension" between the scientist and the literary intellectual, he is not referring simply to a problem of language. To see how wide he thinks the gulf is, investigate what he means by culture "in an anthropological sense." And to determine whether Snow is justified in seeing this dichotomy, you might ask an English instructor if he knows the Second Law of Thermodynamics, or a science teacher is he can define iambic pentameter. Ask either of them if he knows the date of the fall of Constantinople.

Snow's essay, with its serious discussion of the most urgent contemporary issues, provides an excellent focal point for comparing the views of the writers in this section. Contrast, for example, Snow's preoccupation with the practical needs of society and Newman's concern with what makes an educated man. Snow asks the West to build an educational system to perpetuate a civilization, and praises the Russians for their effective use of education for essentially political ends. Consider how Russell might react to Snow's position.

To Snow, technological progress is a boon; to C. S. Lewis it is mankind's potential destroyer. But is there a relationship between Lewis's *Tao* and the "moral component" Snow finds "right in the grain of science itself"? And can Snow's "specification for the scientific revolution" be seen as an attempt not to condition men but to prevent the conquest of Man by Nature?

PERSPECTIVES

✑§ The ultimate wisdom to almost any man is that which shows
him an ordered universe, a cosmos in which he has a place. The
essays in this section are concerned with the search for such a
wisdom. John Donne, who lived in the seventeenth century, is a
spokesman for Christian humanism, a tradition which organized
all knowledge of the material world and of man in the light of
Judeo-Christian teaching. Though neither Donne nor the men in
preceding centuries were born to wisdom—they had to acquire it
through their own questioning and their own understanding—they
nonetheless lived within a tradition that provided a starting point
for speculation and was for most men its end as well. But Donne's
generation is perhaps the last for which this tradition was fully
alive. Swift, in the eighteenth century, voiced his fear for its passing; to Stevenson, in the nineteenth, it was no more than a memory. And no new perspective which could attract the allegiance of
a majority of men has taken its place.

The rest of the essays are devoted to the diverse perspectives
the twentieth century offers. H. L. Mencken, who praises the
beauty of Christianity and condemns its doctrine, wants a view
of life that will permit men to live in dignity without religion;
Julian Huxley sees man's dignity and status established through

biological evolution, and Bertrand Russell explains the change in perspective relativity demands. There are, on the other hand, those who are convinced that neither science nor any other purely human means is sufficient for the achievement of a cosmic vision. Martin D'Arcy, who shares this point of view, speculates that a synthesis of twentieth-century science and traditional religious dogma might provide a new perspective for an ordered universe within which man could be at home.

JOHN DONNE

1573-1631

The young John Donne, an Elizabethan man-about-town who wrote brilliant, sometimes cynical love poetry, hoped to rise in the Court of Elizabeth I by means of his talent and learning. But he ended his chances for worldly success when he eloped with his patron's niece. As he expressed it shortly after their marriage: "John Donne, Anne Donne, Undone."

But Donne's later life belied his gloomy prophecy. Though he never became the important courtier he had hoped to be, he rose, after taking orders in the Anglican Church, to be Dean of St. Paul's and, through his sermons, his meditations, and his poetry, one of the foremost spokesmen of 17th-century Anglicanism. He is a spokesman, furthermore, who appeals particularly to twentieth-century readers because he, too, lived in a time of intellectual and spiritual turmoil. Christian humanism was still a living tradition providing a coherent view of man and his place in the universe. But if men like Donne, whose lives forced them to be aware of the social, religious and political upheavals of the age, were to accept the tradition at all, they had to come to it by way of very personal wrestling with very private doubts. Thus, though Donne's doctrine is wholly traditional, his expression of it rings with the power and intensity only conviction attained with difficulty can give.

The "Devotions for Emergent Occasions" marked the stages of a serious illness Donne suffered in 1623. Number XVII, written as he listened from what he and others felt might be his deathbed to the tolling of funeral bells, is the most famous of his prose writings.

Devotion XVII

Nunc lento sonitu dicunt,	Now, this Bell tolling softly
Morieris.	for another, saies to me,
	Thou must die.

PERCHANCE HE for whom this bell tolls may be so ill, as that he knows not it tolls for him; and perchance I may think myself so much better than I am, as that they who are about me, and see my state, may have caused it to toll for me, and I know not that. The church is catholic, universal, so are all her actions; all that she does belongs to all. When she baptizes a child, that action concerns me; for that child is thereby connected to that head which is my head too, and ingrafted into that body whereof I am a member. And when she buries a man, that action concerns me: all mankind is of one author, and is one volume; when one man dies, one chapter is not torn out of the book, but translated into a better language; and every chapter must be so translated; God employs several translators; some pieces are translated by age, some by sickness, some by war, some by justice; but God's hand is in every translation, and his hand shall bind up all our scattered leaves again for that library where every book shall lie open to one another. As therefore the bell that rings to a sermon calls not upon the preacher only, but upon the congregation to come, so this bell calls us all; but how much more me, who am brought so near the door by this sickness. There was a contention as far as a suit (in which both piety and dignity, religion and estimation, were mingled), which of the religious orders should ring to prayers first in the morning; and it was determined, that they should ring first that rose earliest. If we understand aright the dignity of this bell that tolls for our evening prayer, we would be glad to make it ours by rising early, in that application, that it might be ours as well as his, whose indeed it is. The bell doth toll for him that thinks it doth; and though it intermit again, yet from that minute that that occasion wrought upon him, he is united to God. Who casts not up his eye to the sun when it rises? but who takes off his eye from a comet when that breaks out? Who bends not his ear to any bell which upon any occasion rings? but who can remove it from that bell which is passing a piece of himself out of this world? No man is an island, entire of itself; every man is a piece of the continent, a part of the main. If a clod be washed away by the sea, Europe is the less, as well as if a promontory were, as well as if a manor of thy friend's or of thine own were: any man's death diminishes me, because I am involved in mankind, and therefore never send to know for whom the bell tolls; it tolls for thee. Neither can we call this a begging of misery, or a borrowing of misery, as though we were not miserable enough of ourselves, but must fetch in more from the next house, in taking upon us the misery of our neighbors. Truly it were an excusable covetousness if we did, for affliction is a treasure, and scarce any man hath enough of it. No man hath affliction enough that is not matured and ripened by it, and made fit for God by that affliction. If a man carry treasure in bullion, or in a wedge of gold, and have none coined into current money, his treasure will not defray him as he travels. Tribulation is a treasure in the nature of it, but it is not current money in the use of it, except we get nearer and nearer our home, Heaven, by it. Another man may be sick too, and sick to death, and this affliction may lie in his bowels, as gold in a mine, and be of no use to him; but this bell, that tells me of his affliction, digs out and applies that gold to me: if by this consideration of another's danger I take mine own into contemplation, and so secure myself, by making my recourse to my God, who is our only security.

NOTES AND COMMENTS

Donne was first and foremost a poet, and his is necessarily a poetic prose. Trace the tolling of the bell through the Devotion to see how it unifies the content, symbolizes the ideas, and acts as the refrain of the meditation upon man in relation to God, to other men, to pain, and to death.

The most famous phrases in the Devotion—"No man is an island" and "Never send to know for whom the bell tolls: it tolls for thee"—express Donne's conviction that the human race is one. Where does he find the source of such unity? Is he concerned, as most contemporary readers would be, with the humanitarian aspects of the principle? Why, for instance, does he wish to take upon himself the affliction and misery of his neighbor? Is he expressing the kind of one-world, anti-national view that Rebecca West finds so dangerous? Do any of the other commentators on politics and society in this book—Macdonald, Shaw, Burke, Ortega y Gasset—seem to be writing from a point of view similar to Donne's?

Consider more closely Donne's attitude toward suffering. Why can he accept it? Would it be possible even for those who do not share his perspective to agree with him that a man can be "matured and ripened" by affliction?

JONATHAN SWIFT

1667-1745

Jonathan Swift, the greatest English satirist, wrote the following essay to oppose an attempt to repeal the Test Act of 1673. This Act was supposed to safeguard the position of the Established Church by requiring civil or political officeholders to receive the sacrament of the Lord's Supper according to the practice of the Church of England. It is hard now to see the Act as other than unjust, but Swift, though himself a clergyman of the Anglican Church of Ireland, was not concerned only with the prerogatives of the church he served. He felt the waning force of the great tradition of Christian humanism; since he believed that the Established Church was one of the few institutions that could defend what was for him the cornerstone of civilization, he dreaded any measure that would whittle away its power and influence.

The irony of the essay, however, cuts two ways: it is directed not just against the dissenters or freethinkers who wanted to repeal the Test Act but also, and more important, against "nominal" Christians whose failure to pay more than lip service to the religion they professed could allow it to be destroyed by default.

An Argument to Prove that the
Abolishing of Christianity in England

May, as Things Now Stand, Be Attended with Some Incon-
veniences, and Perhaps Not Produce Those Many Good
Effects Proposed Thereby.

Written in the Year 1708.

I AM VERY sensible what a weakness and presumption it is to
reason against the general humour and disposition of the world.
I remember it was with great justice, and a due regard to the freedom both of the public and the press, forbidden upon severe penalties to write, or discourse, or lay wagers against the Union,[1] even
before it was confirmed by parliament, because that was looked
upon as a design to oppose the current of the people, which, besides the folly of it, is a manifest breach of the fundamental law
that makes this majority of opinion the voice of God. In like manner, and for the very same reasons, it may perhaps be neither safe
nor prudent to argue against the abolishing of Christianity at a
juncture when all parties appear so unanimously determined upon
the point, as we cannot but allow from their actions, their discourses, and their writings. However, I know not how, whether
from the affectation of singularity or the perverseness of human
nature, but so it unhappily falls out that I cannot be entirely of
this opinion. Nay, although I were sure an order were issued out
for my immediate prosecution by the Attorney-General, I should
still confess that in the present posture of our affairs at home or
abroad, I do not yet see the absolute necessity of extirpating the
Christian religion from among us.

This perhaps may appear too great a paradox even for our
wise and paradoxical age to endure; therefore I shall handle it

---

[1 The Act of Union, 1707, joined England and Scotland in one kingdom.
There was much opposition to the Act from many quarters. Swift feared that
the position of the Church of England might be weakened by such close ties
with a nation dominated by Presbyterianism.—Ed.]

with all tenderness, and with the utmost deference to that great
and profound majority which is of another sentiment.

And yet the curious may please to observe, how much the
genius of a nation is liable to alter in half an age. I have heard it
affirmed for certain by some very old people, that the contrary
opinion was even in their memories as much in vogue as the other
is now; and, that a project for the abolishing of Christianity would
then have appeared as singular, and been thought as absurd, as it
would be at this time to write or discourse in its defence.

Therefore I freely own that all appearance are against me. The
system of the Gospel, after the fate of other systems, is generally
antiquated and exploded; and the mass or body of the common
people, among whom it seems to have had its latest credit, are
now grown as much ashamed of it as their betters; opinion like
fashions always descending from those of quality to the middle
sort, and thence to the vulgar, where at length they are dropped
and vanish.

But here I would not be mistaken, and must therefore be so
bold as to borrow a distinction from the writers on the other side
when they make a difference between nominal and real Trinitari-
ans. I hope no reader imagines me so weak to stand up in the defence of real Christianity, such as used in primitive times (if we
may believe the authors of those ages) to have an influence upon
men's belief and actions: to offer at the restoring of that would
indeed be a wild project; it would be to dig up foundations; to
destroy at one blow all the wit and half the learning of the kingdom; to break the entire frame and constitution of things; to ruin
trade, extinguish arts and sciences with the professors of them;
in short, to turn our courts, exchanges, and shops into deserts; and
would be full as absurd as the proposal of Horace, where he ad-
vises the Romans all in a body to leave their city and seek a new
seat in some remote part of the world by way of cure for the corruption of their manners.

Therefore I think this caution was in itself altogether unnecessary, (which I have inserted only to prevent all possibility of
cavilling) since every candid reader will easily understand my discourse to be intended only in defence of nominal Christianity; the
other having been for some time wholly laid aside by general consent, as utterly inconsistent with our present schemes of wealth
and power.

But why we should therefore cast off the name and title of Christians, although the general opinion and resolution be so violent for it, I confess I cannot (with submission) apprehend the consequence necessary. However, since the undertakers propose such wonderful advantages to the nation by this project, and advance many plausible objections against the system of Christianity, I shall briefly consider the strength of both, fairly allow them their greatest weight, and offer such answers as I think most reasonable. After which I will beg leave to show what inconvenience may possibly happen by such an innovation in the present posture of our affairs.

First, one great advantage proposed by the abolishing of Christianity is, that it would very much enlarge and establish liberty of conscience, that great bulwark of our nation, and of the *Protestant* Religion, which is still too much limited by *priestcraft* notwithstanding all the good intentions of the legislature, as we have lately found by a severe instance. For it is confidently reported that two young gentlemen of great hopes, bright wit, and profound judgment, who upon a thorough examination of causes and effects, and by the mere force of natural abilities, without the least tincture of learning, having made a discovery that there was no God, and generously communicating their thoughts for the good of the public, were some time ago, by an unparalleled severity, and upon I know not what *obsolete* law, broke *only* for blasphemy. And as it hath been wisely observed, if persecution once begins, no man alive knows how far it may reach, or where it will end.

In answer to all which, with deference to wiser judgments, I think this rather shows the necessity of a *nominal* religion among us. Great wits love to be free with the highest objects; and if they cannot be allowed a *God* to revile or renounce, they will *speak evil of dignities*, abuse the government, and reflect upon the ministry; which I am sure few will deny to be of much more pernicious consequence, according to the saying of Tiberius, *Deorum offensa diis curæ*.[1] As to the particular fact related, I think it is not fair to argue from one instance, perhaps another cannot be produced; yet (to the comfort of all those who may be apprehensive of persecution) blasphemy we know is freely spoke a million of times in every coffeehouse and tavern, or wherever else *good company* meet.

[1 "Insults to the gods are the concern of the gods."—*Ed*.]

It must be allowed indeed, that to break an English free-born officer only for blasphemy, was, to speak the gentlest of such an action, a very high strain of absolute power. Little can be said in
excuse for the general; perhaps he was afraid it might give offence
to the allies, among whom, for aught I know, it may be the custom
of the country to believe a God. But if he argued, as some have
done, upon a mistaken principle, that an officer who is guilty of
speaking blasphemy, may some time or other proceed so far as to
raise a mutiny, the consequence is by no means to be admitted;
for surely the commander of an English army is likely to be but
ill obeyed whose soldiers fear and reverence him as little as they do
a deity.

It is further objected against the Gospel System, that it obliges
men to the belief of things too difficult for freethinkers, and such
who have shaken off the prejudices that usually cling to a confined
education. To which I answer, that men should be cautious how
they raise objections which reflect upon the wisdom of the nation.
Is not every body freely allowed to believe whatever he pleases,
and to publish his belief to the world whenever he thinks fit, especially if it serve to strengthen the party which is in the right?
Would any indifferent foreigner, who should read the trumpery
lately written by Asgill, Tindal, Toland, Coward,[1] and forty more,
imagine the Gospel to be our rule of faith, and confirmed by parliaments? Does any man either believe, or say he believes, or desire
to have it thought that he says he believes one syllable of the
matter? And is any man worse received upon that score, or does
he find his want of *nominal* faith a disadvantage to him in the pursuit of any civil or military employment? What if there be an old
dormant statute or two against him? Are they not now obsolete,
to a degree, that Empson and Dudley[2] themselves if they were now
alive, would find it impossible to put them in execution?

It is likewise urged that there are, by computation, in this kingdom above ten thousand parsons, whose revenues added to those
of my lords the bishops would suffice to maintain at least two
hundred young gentlemen of wit and pleasure, and freethinking,
enemies to priestcraft, narrow principles, pedantry, and prejudices;
who might be an ornament to the Court and Town: and then,

[1 Well-known freethinkers of the day. See below, pages 359 and 360.—
Ed.]

[2 Agents of Henry VIII with a genius for reviving obsolete statutes in
the service of the King's greed.—*Ed.*]

again, so great a number of able (bodied) divines might be a recruit to our fleet and armies. This indeed appears to be a consideration of some weight: but then, on the other side, several things deserve to be considered likewise: as, first, whether it may not be thought necessary that in certain tracts of country, like what we call parishes, there should be *one* man at least of abilities to read and write. Then it seems a wrong computation that the revenues of the Church throughout this island would be large enough to maintain two hundred young gentlemen, or even half that number, after the present refined way of living; that is, to allow each of them such a rent, as in the modern form of speech, would make them *easy*. But still there is in this project a greater mischief behind; and we ought to beware of the woman's folly who killed the hen that every morning laid her a golden egg. For, pray what would become of the race of men in the next age, if we had nothing to trust to besides the scrofulous, consumptive productions, furnished by our men of wit and pleasure, when having squandered away their vigour, health and estates, they are forced by some disagreeable marriage to piece up their broken fortunes, and entail rottenness and politeness on their posterity? Now, here are ten thousand persons reduced by the wise regulations of Henry the Eighth,[1] to the necessity of a low diet, and moderate exercise, who are the only great restorers of our breed, without which the nation would in an age or two become but one great hospital.

Another advantage proposed by the abolishing of Christianity is the clean gain of one day in seven, which is now entirely lost, and consequently the kingdom one seventh less considerable in trade, business, and pleasure; beside the loss to the public of so many stately structures now in the hands of the Clergy, which might be converted into theatres, exchanges, market-houses, common dormitories, and other public edifices.

I hope I shall be forgiven a hard word, if I call this a perfect cavil. I readily own there has been an old custom time out of mind for people to assemble in the churches every Sunday, and that

---

[1 This refers to Henry's despoiling of clerical holdings at the time of the break with Rome. Though Swift, as an Anglican clergyman, approved of Henry's forays against Roman Catholicism, he felt, as did many other Church of England clerics, that such property should have been given to the Anglican Establishment instead of being either taken into Henry's treasury or given to laymen.—*Ed.*]

shops are still frequently shut, in order as it is conceived, to preserve the memory of that ancient practice, but how this can prove
a hindrance to business or pleasure is hard to imagine. What if the
men of pleasure are forced one day in the week to game at home
instead of the chocolate-house? Are not the taverns and coffee-
houses open? Can there be a more convenient season for taking a
dose of physic? Are fewer claps got upon Sundays than other days?
Is not that the chief day for traders to sum up the accounts of the
week, and for lawyers to prepare their briefs? But I would fain
know how it can be pretended that the churches are misapplied?
Where are more appointments and rendezvouzes of gallantry?
Where more care to appear in the foremost box with greater advantage of dress? Where more meetings for business? Where more
bargains driven of all sorts? And where so many conveniences or
enticements to sleep?

There is one advantage greater than any of the foregoing,
proposed by the abolishing of Christianity: that it will utterly extinguish parties among us, by removing those factious distinctions
of High and Low Church, of Whig and Tory, Presbyterian and
Church of England, which are now so many grievous clogs upon
public proceedings, and dispose men to prefer the gratifying themselves, or depressing their adversaries, before the most important
interest of the state.

I confess, if it were certain that so great an advantage would
redound to the nation by this expedient, I would submit and be
silent: but will any man say, that if the words *whoring, drinking,
cheating, lying, stealing,* were by act of parliament ejected out of
the English tongue and dictionaries, we should all awake next
morning chaste and temperate, honest and just, and lovers of
truth. Is this a fair consequence? Or, if the physicians would forbid
us to pronounce the words *pox, gout, rheumatism* and *stone,*
would that expedient serve like so many talismans to destroy the
diseases themselves? Are party and faction rooted in men's hearts
no deeper than phrases borrowed from religion, or founded upon
no firmer principles? And is our language so poor that we cannot
find other terms to express them? Are *envy, pride, avarice* and *ambition* such ill nomenclators, that they cannot furnish appellations
for their owners? Will not *heydukes* and *mamalukes, mandarins*
and *potshaws,* or any other words formed at pleasure, serve to distinguish those who are in the ministry from others who *would be*

in it *if they could?* What, for instance, is easier than to vary the form of speech, and instead of the word church, make it a question in politics, whether the Monument be in danger? Because religion was nearest at hand to furnish a few convenient phrases, is our invention so barren, we can find no other? Suppose, for argument sake, that the Tories favoured Margarita, the Whigs Mrs. Tofts, and the Trimmers Valentini,[1] would not *Margaritians, Toftians* and *Valentinians* be very tolerable marks of distinction? The *Prasini* and *Veneti*, two most virulent factions in Italy, began (if I remember right) by a distinction of colours in ribbons, which we might do with as good a grace about the dignity of the blue and the green, and would serve as properly to divide the Court, the Parliament, and the Kingdom between them, as any terms of art whatsoever borrowed from religion. Therefore, I think, there is little force in this objection against Christianity, or prospect of so great an advantage as is proposed in the abolishing of it.

It is again objected, as a very absurd ridiculous custom, that a set of men should be suffered, much less employed and hired, to bawl one day in seven against the lawfulness of those methods most in use towards the pursuit of greatness, riches and pleasure, which are the constant practice of all men alive on the other six. But this objection is, I think, a little unworthy so refined an age as ours. Let us argue this matter calmly. I appeal to the breast of any polite freethinker, whether in the pursuit of gratifying a predominant passion, he hath not always felt a wonderful incitement by reflecting it was a thing forbidden; and therefore we see, in order to cultivate this taste, the wisdom of the nation hath taken special care that the ladies should be furnished with prohibited silks, and the men with prohibited wine: and indeed it were to be wished that some other prohibitions were promoted, in order to improve the pleasures of the town which for want of such expedients begin already, as I am told, to flag and grow languid, giving way daily to cruel inroads from the spleen.[2]

It is likewise proposed as a great advantage to the public, that

---

[1 Italian singers then in vogue. Since the last of these was a male soprano, Swift properly assigns him to the Trimmers, who refused to be committed to either side but preferred to stay safely in the middle.—*Ed.*]

[2 The fashionable malady in the eighteenth century—even Queen Anne suffered from it. It covered a number of symptoms, especially boredom and melancholy.—*Ed.*]

if we once discard the system of the Gospel, all religion will of course be banished for ever; and consequently, along with it, those grievous prejudices of education, which under the names of virtue, conscience, honour, justice, and the like, are so apt to disturb the peace of human minds, and the notions whereof are so hard to be eradicated by right reason or freethinking, sometimes during the whole course of our lives.

Here, first, I observe how difficult it is to get rid of a phrase which the world is once grown fond of, although the occasion that first produced it be entirely taken away. For several years past if a man had but an ill-favoured nose, the deep-thinkers of the age would some way or other contrive to impute the cause to the prejudice of his education. From this fountain are said to be derived all our foolish notions of justice, piety, love of our country, all our opinions of God, or a future state, Heaven, Hell, and the like: and there might formerly perhaps have been some pretence for this charge. But so effectual care has been since taken to remove those prejudices, by an entire change in the methods of education, that (with honour I mention it to our polite innovators) the young gentlemen who are now on the scene seem to have not the least tincture left of those infusions, or string of those weeds; and, by consequence, the reason for abolishing nominal Christianity upon that pretext is wholly ceased.

For the rest, it may perhaps admit a controversy, whether the banishing all notions of religion whatsoever, would be convenient for the vulgar. Not that I am in the least of opinion with those who hold religion to have been the invention of politicians to keep the lower part of the world in awe by the fear of invisible powers; unless mankind were then very different from what it is now: for I look upon the mass or body of our people here in England to be as freethinkers, that is to say as staunch unbelievers, as any of the highest rank. But I conceive some scattered notions about a superior power to be of singular use for the common people, as furnishing excellent materials to keep children quiet when they grow peevish, and providing topics of amusement in a tedious winter-night.

Lastly, it is proposed as a singular advantage, that the abolishing of Christianity will very much contribute to the uniting of Protestants, by enlarging the terms of communion so as to take in all sorts of dissenters, who are now shut out of the pale upon account of a few ceremonies which all sides confess to be things indifferent: that this alone will effectually answer the great ends of a scheme for comprehension, by opening a large noble gate at which all bodies may enter; whereas the chaffering with dissenters, and dodging about this or the other ceremony, is but like opening a few wickets, and leaving them at jar, by which no more than one can get in at a time, and that not without stooping, and sideling, and squeezing his body.

To all this I answer, that there is one darling inclination of mankind, which usually affects to be a retainer to religion, although she be neither its parent, its godmother, or its friend; I mean the spirit of opposition that lived long before Christianity, and can easily subsist without it. Let us, for instance, examine wherein the opposition of sectaries among us consists, we shall find Christianity to have no share in it at all. Does the Gospel any where prescribe a starched, squeezed countenance, a stiff, formal gait, a singularity of manners and habit, or any affected modes of speech different from the reasonable part of mankind? [1] Yet, if Christianity did not lend its name to stand in the gap, and to employ or divert these humours, they must of necessity be spent in contraventions to the laws of the land, and disturbance of the public peace. There is a portion of enthusiasm[2] assigned to every nation which, if it hath not proper objects to work on, will burst out and set all into a flame. If the quiet of a state can be bought by only flinging men a few ceremonies to devour, it is a purchase no wise man would refuse. Let the mastiffs amuse themselves about a sheep's skin stuffed with hay, provided it will keep them from worrying the flock. The institution of convents abroad seems in one point a strain of great wisdom, there being few irregularities in human passions, that may not have recourse to vent themselves in some of those orders, which are so many retreats for the speculative, the melancholy, the proud, the silent, the politic and the morose, to spend themselves, and evaporate the noxious particles; for each of whom we in this island are forced to provide a several

---

[1 Swift is referring to the Dissenters (as Puritans were called in his day), who dressed austerely and used biblical words and phrases, as well as "thee" and "thou," instead of those more commonly in use.—*Ed.*]

[2 Used pejoratively in eighteenth-century England to sum up the passions which got in the way of rational behavior, urging a man to go counter to the common sense of the people.—*Ed.*]

sect of religion to keep them quiet. And whenever Christianity shall be abolished, the legislature must find some other expedient to employ and entertain them. For what imports it how large a gate you open, if there will be always left a number who place a pride and a merit in refusing to enter?

Having thus considered the most important objections against Christianity, and the chief advantages proposed by the abolishing thereof, I shall now with equal deference and submission to wiser judgments as before, proceed to mention a few inconveniences that may happen, if the Gospel should be repealed; which perhaps the projectors may not have sufficiently considered.

And first, I am very sensible how much the gentlemen of wit and pleasure are apt to murmur, and be shocked at the sight of so many daggled-tail parsons, who happen to fall in their way, and offend their eyes: but at the same time, these wise reformers do not consider what an advantage and felicity it is for great wits to be always provided with objects of scorn and contempt, in order to exercise and improve their talents, and divert their spleen from falling on each other or on themselves; especially when all this may be done without the least imaginable *danger to their persons*.

And to urge another argument of a parallel nature: if Christianity were once abolished, how could the freethinkers, the strong reasoners, and the men of profound learning, be able to find another subject so calculated in all points whereon to display their abilities? What wonderful productions of wit should we be deprived of, from those whose genius by continual practice hath been wholly turned upon raillery and invectives against religion, and would therefore never be able to shine or distinguish themselves upon any other subject. We are daily complaining of the great decline of wit among us, and would we take away the greatest, perhaps the only topic we have left? Who would ever have suspected Asgill [1] for a wit, or Toland for a philosopher, if the inexhaustible stock of Christianity had not been at hand to provide them with materials? What other subject, through all art or nature, could have produced Tindal for a profound author, or furnished him with readers? It is the wise choice of the subject that alone adorns and distinguishes the writer. For, had an hundred such pens as

---

[1 John Asgill, who believed that men could achieve eternal life without passing through death. For Toland and Tindal, see below.—*Ed.*]

these been employed on the side of religion, they would have immediately sunk into silence and oblivion.

Nor do I think it wholly groundless, or my fears altogether imaginary, that the abolishing of Christianity may perhaps bring the Church in danger, or at least put the senate to the trouble of another securing vote. I desire I may not be mistaken; I am far from presuming to affirm or think that the Church is in danger at present, or as things now stand; but we know not how soon it may be so when the Christian religion is repealed. As plausible as this project seems, there may a dangerous design lurk under it. Nothing can be more notorious, than that the Atheists, Deists, Socinians, Anti-trinitarians, and other subdivisions of freethinkers, are persons of little zeal for the present ecclesiastical establishment: Their declared opinion is for repealing the Sacramental Test; they are very indifferent with regard to ceremonies; nor do they hold the *jus divinum*[1] of Episcopacy. Therefore this may be intended as one politic step towards altering the constitution of the Church established, and setting up Presbytery in the stead, which I leave to be further considered by those at the helm.

In the last place, I think nothing can be more plain, than that by this expedient, we shall run into the evil we chiefly pretend to avoid; and that the abolishment of the Christian religion will be the readiest course we can take to introduce popery. And I am the more inclined to this opinion, because we know it has been the constant practice of the Jesuits to send over emissaries, with instructions to personate themselves members of the several prevailing sects among us. So it is recorded, that they have at sundry times appeared in the guise of Presbyterians, Anabaptists, Independents and Quakers, according as any of these were most in credit; so since the fashion hath been taken up of exploding religion, the popish missionaries have not been wanting to mix with the freethinkers; among whom, Toland, the great oracle of the Anti-Christians is an Irish priest, the son of an Irish priest;[2] and the most learned and ingenious author of a book called *The Rights of the Christian Church*,[3] was in a proper juncture reconciled to

---

[1 Divine right.—*Ed.*]
[2 Born a Roman Catholic, though he became a Protestant at the age of 16.—*Ed.*]
[3 Matthew Tindal, who professed Catholicism temporarily during the reign of James II.—*Ed.*]

the Romish faith, whose true son, as appears by an hundred passages in his treatise, he still continues. Perhaps I could add some others to the number; but the fact is beyond dispute, and the reasoning they proceed by is right: for, supposing Christianity to be extinguished, the people will never be at ease till they find out some other method of worship; which will as infallibly produce superstition, as this will end in popery.

And therefore, if notwithstanding all I have said, it shall still be thought necessary to have a bill brought in for repealing Christianity, I would humbly offer an amendment; that instead of the word *Christianity*, may be put *Religion* in general; which I conceive will much better answer all the good ends proposed by the projectors of it. For, as long as we leave in being a God and his providence, with all the necessary consequences which curious and inquisitive men will be apt to draw from such premises, we do not strike at the root of the evil although we should ever so effectually annihilate the present scheme of the Gospel. For, of what use is freedom of thought, if it will not produce freedom of action, which is the sole end, how remote soever in appearance, of all objections against Christianity? And therefore, the freethinkers consider it as a sort of edifice, wherein all the parts have such a mutual dependence on each other, that if you happen to pull out one single nail, the whole fabric must fall to the ground. This was happily expressed by him who had heard of a text brought for proof of the Trinity, which in an ancient manuscript was differently read; he thereupon immediately took the hint, and by a sudden deduction of a long *sorites*, most logically concluded; Why, if it be as you say, I may safely whore and drink on, and defy the parson. From which, and many the like instances easy to be produced, I think nothing can be more manifest, than that the quarrel is not against any particular points of hard digestion in the Christian system, but against religion in general; which, by laying restraints on human nature, is supposed the great enemy to the freedom of thought and action.

Upon the whole, if it shall still be thought for the benefit of Church and State, that Christianity be abolished, I conceive however, it may be more convenient to defer the execution to a time of peace, and not venture in this conjuncture to disoblige our allies, who, as it falls out, are all Christians, and many of them, by the prejudices of their education, so bigoted as to place a sort of pride in the appellation. If upon being rejected by them, we are to trust to an alliance with the Turk, we shall find ourselves much deceived: for, as he is too remote, and generally engaged in war with the Persian emperor, so his people would be more scandalized at our infidelity than our Christian neighbours. Because the Turks are not only strict observers of religious worship, but what is worse, believe a God; which is more than is required of us even while we preserve the name of Christians.

To conclude: whatever some may think of the great advantages to trade by this favourite scheme, I do very much apprehend that in six months' time after the act is passed for the extirpation of the Gospel, the Bank and East-India Stock may fall at least one *percent*. And since that is fifty times more than ever the wisdom of our age thought fit to venture for the *preservation* of Christianity, there is no reason we should be at so great a loss, merely for the sake of *destroying* it.

NOTES AND COMMENTS

Swift's irony is based on a curious use of logic: he argues against a premise he sees as false by seeming to accept it and then carrying it to its absurd—sometimes terrifying—conclusions. One such premise is that there is no point in defending real Christianity, which is already quite dead; Swift's argument is in behalf of "nominal Christianity," which, as he says, still has a certain strength and usefulness. But since "nominal Christianity" is more hollow than hallowed, Swift can satirize attitudes toward religion that exist throughout English society —in the government, in the realm of wit and learning, among the military, in the Church itself and the various sects, in polite circles, in the merchant class, among the common people.

Swift is concerned with another, more fundamental premise when he speaks of the "uses" of Christianity. What is the attitude toward truth and other things of the spirit that makes a defense of Christianity on such a utilitarian basis possible? Is it in any way related to Swift's devastating conclusion that we might as well retain nominal Christianity since "the Bank and East-India Stock may fall at least one *percent*" if it is abolished? Does it tie in also with the early part of the essay in which Swift speaks of the disasters that may follow upon the re-introduction of real Christianity?

Throughout most of this essay Swift is ironic: the simple-minded, objective good will of his tone is belied by the straight-faced absurdities of his words. Is there, however, any point in the essay when he speaks directly, when a careful reader should be prepared to take his words at face value? If so, does his shift in tone weaken the essay, or does one of the premises he develops give him scope enough to present his viewpoint openly as well as ironically?

ROBERT LOUIS STEVENSON

1850-1894

Robert Louis Stevenson is best remembered for his adventure novels (*Kidnapped, The Master of Ballantrae,* and *Treasure Island*) and for *A Child's Garden of Verses,* but he also wrote stories and essays on an immense range of subjects. The present essay, with its praise of "unconcern and brazen boldness in the face of death," has special poignance in view of the fact that Stevenson from his early childhood suffered precarious health, and his writings were indeed the achievements of one to whom prudence would have suggested that he ought not "embark upon any work much more considerable than a half-penny post card."

The essay is interesting also as a reflection of late nineteenth-century thought. One hears much about "Victorian optimism," an optimism based on faith in science and the conviction that evolutionary progress is inevitable. That not everyone shared this outlook can be seen in Stevenson's praise of men who live with gaiety and courage in a world whose surface beauty overlies a reality of danger, disorder, and uncertainty.

Æs Triplex[1]

THE CHANGES wrought by death are in themselves so sharp and final, and so terrible and melancholy in their consequences, that the thing stands alone in man's experience, and has no parallel upon earth. It outdoes all other accidents because it is the

[1 *Æs triplex,* triple brass. From one of Horace's *Odes:* "Oak and triple brass bound the heart of him who first entrusted his frail craft to the wild sea."—*Ed.*]

last of them. Sometimes it leaps suddenly upon its victims, like a Thug; sometimes it lays a regular siege and creeps upon their citadel during a score of years. And when the business is done, there is sore havoc made in other people's lives, and a pin knocked out by which many subsidiary friendships hung together. There are empty chairs, solitary walks, and single beds at night. Again, in taking away our friends, death does not take them away utterly, but leaves behind a mocking, tragical, and soon intolerable residue, which must be hurriedly concealed. Hence a whole chapter of sights and customs striking to the mind, from the pyramids of Egypt to the gibbets and dule trees of mediaeval Europe. The poorest persons have a bit of pageant going towards the tomb; memorial stones are set up over the least memorable; and, in order to preserve some show of respect for what remains of our old loves and friendships, we must accompany it with much grimly ludicrous ceremonial, and the hired undertaker parades before the door. All this, and much more of the same sort, accompanied by the eloquence of poets, has gone a great way to put humanity in error; nay, in many philosophies the error has been embodied and laid down with every circumstance of logic; although in real life the bustle and swiftness, in leaving people little time to think, have not left them time enough to go dangerously wrong in practice.

As a matter of fact, although few things are spoken of with more fearful whisperings than this prospect of death, few have less influence on conduct under healthy circumstances. We have all heard of cities in South America built upon the side of fiery mountains, and how, even in this tremendous neighbourhood, the inhabitants are not a jot more impressed by the solemnity of mortal conditions than if they were delving gardens in the greenest corner of England. There are serenades and suppers and much gallantry among the myrtles overhead; and meanwhile the foundation shudders underfoot, the bowels of the mountain growl, and at any moment living ruin may leap sky-high into the moonlight, and tumble man and his merry-making in the dust. In the eyes of very young people, and very dull old ones, there is something indescribably reckless and desperate in such a picture. It seems not credible that respectable married people, with umbrellas, should find appetite for a bit of supper within quite a long distance of a fiery mountain; ordinary life begins to smell of high-handed debauch when it is carried on so close to a catastrophe; and even cheese and salad, it seems, could hardly be relished in such circumstances without something like a defiance of the Creator. It should be a place for nobody but hermits dwelling in prayer and maceration, or mere born-devils drowning care in a perpetual carouse.

And yet, when one comes to think upon it calmly, the situation of these South American citizens forms only a very pale figure for the state of ordinary mankind. This world itself, travelling blindly and swiftly in overcrowded space, among a million other worlds travelling blindly and swiftly in contrary directions, may very well come by a knock that would set it into explosion like a penny squib. And what, pathologically looked at, is the human body with all its organs, but a mere bagful of petards? The least of these is as dangerous to the whole economy as the ship's powder-magazine to the ship; and with every breath we breathe, and every meal we eat, we are putting one or more of them in peril. If we clung as devotedly as some philosophers pretend we do to the abstract idea of life, or were half as frightened as they make out we are, for the subversive accident that ends it all, the trumpets might sound by the hour and no one would follow them into battle—the blue-peter might fly at the truck,[1] but who would climb into a sea-going ship? Think (if these philosophers were right) with what a preparation of spirit we should affront the daily peril of the dinner-table: a deadlier spot than any battlefield in history, where the far greater proportion of our ancestors have miserably left their bones! What woman would ever be lured into marriage, so much more dangerous than the wildest sea? And what would it be to grow old? For, after a certain distance, every step we take in life we find the ice growing thinner below our feet, and all around us and behind us we see our contemporaries going through. By the time a man gets well into the seventies, his continued existence is a mere miracle; and when he lays his old bones in bed for the night, there is an overwhelming probability that he will never see the day. Do the old men mind it, as a matter of fact? Why, no. They were never merrier; they have their grog at night, and tell the raciest stories; they hear of the death of people about their own age, or even younger, not as if it was a grisly warn-

---

[1 The blue-peter is a blue flag with a white square in the center, hoisted as a signal that a ship is about to leave port. A truck is a small piece of wood fixed to the top of a mast and containing holes for signal ropes.—*Ed.*]

ing, but with a simple childlike pleasure at having outlived some
one else; and when a draught might puff them out like a guttering
candle, or a bit of a stumble shatter them like so much glass, their
old hearts keep sound and unaffrighted, and they go on, bubbling
with laughter, through years of man's age compared to which the
valley at Balaklava was as safe and peaceful as a village cricket-
green on Sunday. It may fairly be questioned (if we look to the
peril only) whether it was a much more daring feat for Curtius
to plunge into the gulf, than for any old gentleman of ninety to
doff his clothes and clamber into bed.

Indeed, it is a memorable subject for consideration, with what
unconcern and gaiety mankind pricks on along the Valley of the
Shadow of Death. The whole way is one wilderness of snares, and
the end of it, for those who fear the last pinch, is irrevocable
ruin. And yet we go spinning through it all, like a party for the
Derby. Perhaps the reader remembers one of the humorous devices
of the deified Caligula: how he encouraged a vast concourse of
holiday-makers on to his bridge over Baiae Bay; and when they
were in the height of their enjoyment, turned loose the Praetorian
guards among the company, and had them tossed into the sea.
This is no bad miniature of the dealings of nature with the transitory race of man. Only, what a chequered picnic we have of it, even
while it lasts! and into what great waters, not to be crossed by any
swimmer, God's pale Praetorian throws us over in the end!

We live the time that a match flickers; we pop the cork of a
ginger-beer bottle, and the earthquake swallows us on the instant.
Is it not odd, is it not incongruous, is it not, in the highest sense
of human speech, incredible, that we should think so highly of the
ginger-beer, and regard so little the devouring earthquake? The
love of Life and the fear of Death are two famous phrases that
grow harder to understand the more we think about them. It is a
well-known fact that an immense proportion of boat accidents
would never happen if people held the sheet in their hands instead
of making it fast; and yet, unless it be some martinet of a professional mariner or some landsman with shattered nerves, every one
of God's creatures makes it fast. A strange instance of man's unconcern and brazen boldness in the face of death!

We confound ourselves with metaphysical phrases, which we
import into daily talk with noble inappropriateness. We have no
idea of what death is, apart from its circumstances and some of

its consequences to others; and although we have some experience
of living, there is not a man on earth who has flown so high into
abstraction as to have any practical guess at the meaning of the
word *life*. All literature, from Job and Omar Khayam to Thomas
Carlyle or Walt Whitman, is but an attempt to look upon the
human state with such largeness of view as shall enable us to rise
from the consideration of living to the Definition of Life. And our
sages give us about the best satisfaction in their power when they
say that it is a vapour, or a show, or made out of the same stuff
with dreams. Philosophy, in its more rigid sense, has been at the
same work for ages; and after a myriad bald heads have wagged
over the problem, and piles of words have been heaped one upon
another into dry and cloudy volumes without end, philosophy has
the honour of laying before us, with modest pride, her contribution towards the subject: that life is a Permanent Possibility of
Sensation. Truly a fine result! A man may very well love beef, or
hunting, or a woman; but surely, surely, not a Permanent Possibility of Sensation! He may be afraid of a precipice, or a dentist,
or a large enemy with a club, or even an undertaker's man; but
not certainly of abstract death. We may trick with the word life
in its dozen senses until we are weary of tricking; we may argue in
terms of all the philosophies on earth, but one fact remains true
throughout—that we do not love life, in the sense that we are
greatly preoccupied about its conservation; that we do not, properly
speaking, love life at all, but living. Into the views of the least
careful there will enter some degree of providence; no man's eyes
are fixed entirely on the passing hour; but although we have some
anticipation of good health, good weather, wine, active employment, love, and self-approval, the sum of these anticipations does
not amount to anything like a general view of life's possibilities
and issues; nor are those who cherish them most vividly, at all the
most scrupulous of their personal safety. To be deeply interested
in the accidents of our existence, to enjoy keenly the mixed texture
of human experience, rather leads a man to disregard precautions,
and risk his neck against a straw. For surely the love of living is
stronger in an Alpine climber roping over a peril, or a hunter riding
merrily at a stiff fence, than in a creature who lives upon a diet and
walks a measured distance in the interest of his constitution.

There is a great deal of very vile nonsense talked upon both
sides of the matter: tearing divines reducing life to the dimensions

of a mere funeral procession, so short as to be hardly decent; and melancholy unbelievers yearning for the tomb as if it were a world too far away. Both sides must feel a little ashamed of their performances now and again when they draw in their chairs to dinner. Indeed, a good meal and a bottle of wine is an answer to most standard works upon the question. When a man's heart warms to his viands, he forgets a great deal of sophistry, and soars into a rosy zone of contemplation. Death may be knocking at the door, like the Commander's statue; we have something else in hand, thank God, and let him knock. Passing bells are ringing all the world over. All the world over, and every hour, some one is parting company with all his aches and ecstasies. For us also the trap is laid. But we are so fond of life that we have no leisure to entertain the terror of death. It is a honeymoon with us all through, and none of the longest. Small blame to us if we give our whole hearts to this glowing bride of ours, to the appetites, to honour, to the hungry curiosity of the mind, to the pleasure of the eyes in nature, and the pride of our own nimble bodies.

We all of us appreciate the sensations; but as for caring about the Permanence of the Possibility, a man's head is generally very bald, and his senses very dull, before he comes to that. Whether we regard life as a lane leading to a dead wall—a mere bag's end, as the French say—or whether we think of it as a vestibule or gymnasium, where we wait our turn and prepare our faculties for some more noble destiny; whether we thunder in a pulpit, or pule in little atheistic poetry-books, about its vanity and brevity; whether we look justly for years of health and vigour, or are about to mount into a bath-chair, as a step towards the hearse; in each and all of these views and situations there is but one conclusion possible: that a man should stop his ears against paralysing terror, and run the race that is set before him with a single mind. No one surely could have recoiled with more heartache and terror from the thought of death than our respected lexicographer;[1] and yet we know how little it affected his conduct, how wisely and boldly he walked, and in what a fresh and lively vein he spoke of life. Already an old man, he ventured on his Highland tour; and his heart, bound with triple brass, did not recoil before twenty-seven individual cups of tea. As courage and intelligence are the two

---

[1 Samuel Johnson.—Ed.]

qualities best worth a good man's cultivation, so it is the first part of intelligence to recognise our precarious estate in life, and the first part of courage to be not at all abashed before the fact. A frank and somewhat headlong carriage, not looking too anxiously before, not dallying in maudlin regret over the past, stamps the man who is well armoured for this world.

And not only well armoured for himself, but a good friend and a good citizen to boot. We do not go to cowards for tender dealing; there is nothing so cruel as panic; the man who has least fear for his own carcase, has most time to consider others. That eminent chemist who took his walks abroad in tin shoes, and subsisted wholly upon tepid milk, had all his work cut out for him in considerate dealings with his own digestion. So soon as prudence has begun to grow up in the brain, like a dismal fungus, it finds its first expression in a paralysis of generous acts. The victim begins to shrink spiritually; he develops a fancy for parlours with a regulated temperature, and takes his morality on the principle of tin shoes and tepid milk. The care of one important body or soul becomes so engrossing, that all the noises of the outer world begin to come thin and faint into the parlour with the regulated temperature; and the tin shoes go equably forward over blood and rain. To be overwise is to ossify; and the scruple-monger ends by standing stockstill. Now the man who has his heart on his sleeve, and a good whirling weathercock of a brain, who reckons his life as a thing to be dashingly used and cheerfully hazarded, makes a very different acquaintance of the world, keeps all his pulses going true and fast, and gathers impetus as he runs, until, if he be running towards anything better than wildfire, he may shoot up and become a constellation in the end. Lord look after his health, Lord have a care of his soul, says he; and he has at the key of the position, and swashes through incongruity and peril towards his aim. Death is on all sides of him with pointed batteries, as he is on all sides of all of us; unfortunate surprises gird him round; mim-mouthed friends and relations hold up their hands in quite a little elegiacal synod about his path: and what cares he for all this? Being a true lover of living, a fellow with something pushing and spontaneous in his inside, he must, like any other soldier, in any other stirring, deadly warfare, push on at his best pace until he touch the goal. "A peerage or Westminster Abbey!" cried Nelson in his bright, boyish, heroic manner. These are great incentives; not for any of these, but for the plain satisfaction of living, of being about their business in some sort or other, do the brave, serviceable men of every nation tread down the nettle danger, and pass flyingly over all the stumbling-blocks of prudence. Think of the heroism of Johnson, think of that superb indifference to mortal limitation that set him upon his dictionary, and carried him through triumphantly until the end! Who, if he were wisely considerate of things at large, would ever embark upon any work much more considerable than a halfpenny post card? Who would project a serial novel, after Thackeray and Dickens had each fallen in mid-course? Who would find heart enough to begin to live, if he dallied with the consideration of death?

And, after all, what sorry and pitiful quibbling all this is! To forego all the issues of living in a parlour with a regulated temperature—as if that were not to die a hundred times over, and for ten years at a stretch! As if it were not to die in one's own lifetime, and without even the sad immunities of death! As if it were not to die, and yet be the patient spectators of our own pitiable change! The Permanent Possibility is preserved, but the sensations carefully held at arm's length, as if one kept a photographic plate in a dark chamber. It is better to lose health like a spendthrift than to waste it like a miser. It is better to live and be done with it, than to die daily in the sickroom. By all means begin your folio; even if the doctor does not give you a year, even if he hesitates about a month, make one brave push and see what can be accomplished in a week. It is not only in finished undertakings that we ought to honour useful labour. A spirit goes out of the man who means execution, which outlives the most untimely ending. All who have meant good work with their whole hearts, have done good work, although they may die before they have the time to sign it. Every heart that has beat strong and cheerfully has left a hopeful impulse behind it in the world, and bettered the tradition of mankind. And even if death catch people, like an open pitfall, and in mid-career, laying out vast projects, and planning monstrous foundations, flushed with hope, and their mouths full of boastful language, they should be at once tripped up and silenced: is there not something brave and spirited in such a termination? and does not life go down with a better grace, foaming in full body over a precipice, than miserably straggling to an end in sandy deltas? When the Greeks made their fine saying that those whom the gods love die young, I cannot help believing they had this sort of death also in their eye. For surely, at whatever age it overtake the man, this is to die young. Death has not been suffered to take so much as an illusion from his heart. In the hot-fit of life, a-tiptoe on the highest point of being, he passes at a bound on to the other side. The noise of the mallet and chisel is scarcely quenched, the trumpets are hardly done blowing, when, trailing with him clouds of glory, this happy-starred, full-blooded spirit shoots into the spiritual land.

NOTES AND COMMENTS

Stevenson, like Donne, hears "passing bells" tolling, but whereas Donne makes them an occasion for recollection, Stevenson sees gallantry in ignoring them. One could explain the difference simply by saying that Donne is morbid and Stevenson a man who delights in life. But the unity the image of the tolling bell gives Donne's essay implies that for him death has its place in an ordered universe. On the other hand, note the images Stevenson uses not only for death, but for the general condition of human life. Death, for instance, is a Thug; life on the edge of a volcano is a "very pale figure for the state of ordinary mankind"; the earth travels "blindly and swiftly in overcrowded space." A further analysis of his metaphors suggests that Stevenson's concern is not really with death but with disorder. Do their differing attitudes toward death, then, stem less from the degree to which Stevenson and Donne accept life than from the different perspectives from which they view it?

Consider also Stevenson's comments on abstractions. Men, he says, love not *life* but *living*, for it is the process of living, not life in the abstract, that they know. Very little reflection would persuade most of us that he is right: life is dear to us not as an idea but because of the particular experiences it offers us. But though we love living, we *can* think about life. Stevenson has only contempt for philosophers who offer as a definition of life only the "Permanent Possibility of Sensation." Is his anti-intellectualism related to his conviction that one lives well only when he does *not* heed the "passing bell"?

H. L. MENCKEN

1880-1956

H. L. Mencken, journalist, essayist, editor of the *Smart Set* and the *American Mercury*, was America's outstanding "debunker" in the 1920's. He delighted in attacking popularly accepted notions with wit, skepticism, and irreverence. He irritated and outraged his readers to shock them into accepting unconventional points of view, although in the process his arguments against the weaknesses of democracy and the gaucheries of American culture sometimes suffered from exaggeration. "Believe in free speech to the last limits of the endurable," he once said, applying this distinctly American credo to others as well as to himself. He envisioned himself as the "American Voltaire, the enemy of all puritans, the heretic in the Sunday school, the one-man demolition crew of the genteel tradition, the unregenerate neighborhood brat who stretches a string in the alley to trip the bourgeoisie on its pious homeward journey." [1] The present essay is taken from *Treatise on the Gods.*

The Poetry of Christianity

CHRISTIANITY, as religions run in the world, is scarcely to be described as belonging to the first rank. It is full of vestiges of the barbaric cults that entered into it, and some of them are shocking to common sense, as to common decency. The old polytheism lingers on in the preposterous concept of the Trinity, defectively concealed by metaphysical swathings that are worse, if anything,

[1] Alistair Cooke in his introduction to *The Vintage Mencken.*

than the idea itself. The Atonement is a reminder of blood sacrifice and the Eucharist of the pharmacology of cannibals. Judaism, in its theology, is far simpler and more plausible. So is Parseeism. A Parsee is not doomed to Hell for neglecting a sacrament, like a Catholic or a Baptist, nor is the Hell ahead of him, supposing he lands there on other counts, the savage and incredible chamber of horrors that Christians fear. He believes vaguely that his soul will go marching on after death, but he doesn't believe that it will go marching on forever; soon or late, he is taught, the whole cosmos must come to an end and start all over again. Buddhism leans the same way; it rejects immortality as not only unimaginable, but also as unendurable. Confucianism evades the question as unanswerable. It teaches that the dead survive, but doesn't pretend to say how long. On the ethical side it is much more rational than Christianity, and very much more humane, for its chief prophets and law-givers have not been ignorant fanatics but highly civilized men, some of them philosophers comparable to Plato or Aristotle. Even Moslemism, in this department, is superior to Christianity, if only because its ethical system forms a connected and consistent whole. In Christianity the problem of evil, a serious difficulty in all religions that pretend to be logical, is enormously complicated by the plain conflict between the ethical teaching of the Old Testament and that of the New. Is God jealous or tolerant, vengeful or forgiving, a harsh and haughty monarch or a loving father? It is possible to answer these questions any way you choose, and to find revelation to support you. Christian theologians have been trying to dispose of them for nineteen centuries, but they still afflict every believer with any capacity, however slight, for anything reasonably describable as reflection.

But in one respect, at least, Christianity is vastly superior to every other religion in being today, and indeed, to all save one of the past: it is full of a lush and lovely poetry. The Bible is unquestionably the most beautiful book in the world. Allow everything you please for the barbaric history in the Old Testament and the silly Little Bethel theology in the New, and there remains a series of poems so overwhelmingly voluptuous and disarming that no other literature, old or new, can offer a match for it. Nearly all of it comes from the Jews, and their making of it constitutes one of the most astounding phenomena in human history. Save for a small minority of superior individuals, nearly unanimously agnostic, there is not much in their character, as the modern world knows them, to suggest a genius for exalted thinking. Even Ernest Renan, who was very friendly to them, once sneered at the *esprit sémitique* as *sans étendu, sans diversité,* and *sans philosophie.* As commonly encountered, they strike other peoples as predominantly unpleasant, and everywhere on earth they seem to be disliked. This dislike, despite their own belief to the contrary, has nothing to do with their religion: it is founded, rather, on their bad manners, their curious lack of tact. They have an extraordinary capacity for offending and alarming the *Goyim,* and not infrequently, from the earliest days down to our own time, it has engendered brutal wars upon them. Yet these same rude, unpopular and often unintelligent folk, from time almost immemorial, have been the chief dreamers of the Western world, and beyond all comparison its greatest poets. It was Jews who wrote the magnificent poems called the Psalms, the Song of Solomon, and the Books of Job and Ruth; it was Jews who set platitudes to deathless music in Proverbs; and it was Jews who gave us the Beatitudes, the Sermon on the Mount, the incomparable ballad of the Christ Child, and the twelfth chapter of Romans. I incline to believe that the scene recounted in John VIII, 3-11, is the most poignant drama ever written in the world, as the Song of Solomon is unquestionably the most moving love song, and the Twenty-third Psalm the greatest of hymns. All these transcendent riches Christianity inherits from a little tribe of sedentary Bedouins, so obscure and unimportant that secular history scarcely knows them. No heritage of modern man is richer and none has made a more brilliant mark upon human thought, not even the legacy of the Greeks.

All this, of course, may prove either one of two things: that the Jews, in their heyday, were actually superior to all the great peoples who disdained them, or that poetry is only an inferior art. My private inclination is to embrace the latter hypothesis, but I do not pause to argue the point. The main thing is that Christianity, alone among the modern world religions, has inherited an opulent aesthetic content, and is thus itself a work of art. Its external habiliments, of course, are not unique. There are Buddhist temples that are quite as glorious as the Gothic cathedrals, and in Shinto there is a dramatic liturgy that is at least as impressive as the Roman Mass. But no other religion is so beautiful in its very

substance—none other can show anything to match the great
strophes of flaming poetry which enter into every Christian gesture
of ceremonial and give an august inner dignity to Christian sacred
music. Nor does any other, not even the parent Judaism, rest upon
so noble a mythology. The story of Jesus, as it is told in the
Synoptic Gospels, and especially in Luke, is touching beyond
compare. It is, indeed, the most lovely story that the human
fancy has ever devised, and the fact that large parts of it cannot
be accepted as true surely does no violence to its effectiveness, for
it is of the very essence of poetry that it is not true: its aim is not
to record facts but to conjure up entrancing impossibilities. The
story of Jesus is the sempiternal Cinderella story, lifted to cosmic
dimensions. Beside it the best that you will find in the sacred
literature of Moslem and Brahman, Parsee and Buddhist, seems
flat, stale and unprofitable.

Moreover, it has the power, like all truly great myths, of
throwing off lesser ones, apparently in an endless stream. The
innumerable legends of the saints, many of them of great beauty,
are mainly no more than variations of one detail or another of
the fable of Jesus, and so are many of the stories that Christianity
has concocted out of what were, in the first place, pagan materials
—for example, that of Santa Claus. The human appeal of all this
poetry is so extraordinarily potent that it promises to survive the
decay of Christianity. Everyone has observed how Jews and infidels
succumb in Christendom to the spirit of Christmas. What is less
noted is the fact that among Christians themselves there is a growing tendency, when they throw off Christian theology, to salvage
Christian poetry. This is plainly visible in the organized lovey-
dovey that began with the Rotary movement and has since
proliferated so enormously in the United States, with tentacles
reaching out to not a few foreign lands. Robert S. and Helen M.
Lynd tell us, in *Middletown*, how, in the typical American community they describe, Rotary threatens to become a substitute for
Christianity, to the grave damage of churches and clergy. It is not,
of course, a theological system; it is simply a poetical system.
Starting out in 1905 on a you-tickle-me-and-I'll-tickle-you basis, it
quickly took on overtones of aspiration, and today its main purpose
seems to be to convince emulous but unimaginative men that it
offers a way to something resembling salvation on this earth—that
its puerile mumbo-jumbo can convert stock-brokers, insurance

agents and used-car dealers into passable imitatiuns of Francis Xavier. The grandiose imbecility called Christian Science is tarred with the same stick. It is certainly not a science, not even in the lame sense that spiritualism and psychotherapy are, and no Christian theologian save a hopeless dipsomaniac would venture to call it Christianity. It is simply a kind of poetry—an organized and unquestioning belief in the palpably not true.

The thirst for such poetry, in the long run, may displace the old fear of the brutal and implacable gods. Something of the sort, in fact, was once envisaged by H. G. Wells, who proposed abandoning the Christian Scriptures in favor of a new Bible made up of extracts from Shakespeare, Shelley, Thomas Jefferson, Abraham Lincoln and Karl Marx—all of them poets, though some of them didn't know it. Upton Sinclair, the American Gnostic, went a step further: he undertook to write a sort of New Testament of his own, with incidental help from such thinkers as Frances E. Willard, Henry George, Dr. Albert Abrams, and Sacco and Vanzetti. The late Hitler had a somewhat similar scheme, and the lamented New Dealers played with one in which the Holy Saints were to be displaced by Roosevelt II, Eleanor Roosevelt and a host of lesser semi-divinities, including, I suppose, the go-getting Roosevelt boys. Such efforts to substitute poetry for theology may be expected to multiply in the near future, for the world is plainly entering upon a new stage of myth-making. The two things, indeed, are much alike, for both are based on the doctrine that it is better to believe what is false than to suffer what is true. That was undoubtedly a sound philosophy in the days when the great religions were born and the great poems were written; it may even be sound enough, at least for all save a small minority of men, today. But it is hard to imagine it continuing sound forever. That modern man still needs such consolations is no more than proof that the emancipation of the human mind has just begun—that he is yet much nearer to the ape than he is to the cherubim. Once he attains to anything approaching a genuine mastery of his environment that will become as irrational to him as the old belief in ghosts, witches and demoniacal possession. Religion, in fact, is already a burden to him. It sends fears to haunt him—fears which stalk upon him out of the shadows of the Ages of Faith, the Apostolic Age, the Age of the Great Migrations, the Stone Age. Its time-binding afflicts him with moral ideas born of the needs of primitive

and long-forgotten peoples—ideas violently out of harmony with
the new conditions of life that his own immense curiosity and
ingenuity have set up. It is, in its very nature, a machine for scar-
ing; it must needs fail and break down as man gains more and more
knowledge, for knowledge is not only power; it is also courage.

It may be that, by thus moving away from religion man will
be losing something. Perhaps the theologians are right when they
argue that, whatever the falsity of their premises, they are at least
more or less sound in their conclusions: that religion, taking it by
and large, at least makes human beings happier. But that, after
all, begs the question, for it is only a romantic delusion that makes
happiness the one end of progress. It may be, for all we know, the
Übermensch[1] of the future will do without the boozy delusions of
well being that we now call by that name. His prophet, Friedrich
Nietzsche, has, in fact, hinted as much: his motto, says Nietzsche,
will be, "Be hard!" To sentimentalists breathing Christian air this
is revolting. They see in it only a counsel of brutality. But, as
William James long ago pointed out, there is a hardness of the
mind as well as a hardness of the fist, and we probably owe to it
every advance that we have made away from the brutes—even the
long, tortured advance toward kindness, charity, tolerance, tenderness, common decency. It has won for us, not only the concept of
the immutability of natural laws, but also the concept of the
mutability of all laws made by man. It has made us wary of our
feelings at the same time that it has given us confidence in our
growing store of fact. The truly civilized man, it seems to me, has
already got away from the old puerile demand for a "meaning in
life." It needs no esoteric significance to be interesting to him. His
satisfactions come, not out of a childish confidence that some
vague and gaseous god, hidden away in some impossible sky, made
him for a lofty purpose and will preserve him to fulfill it, but out
of a delight in the operations of the universe about him and of his
own mind. It delights him to exercise that mind, regardless of the
way it takes him, just as it delights the lower animals, including
those of his own species, to exercise their muscles. If he really
differs qualitatively from those lower animals, as all the theologians
agree, then that is the proof of it. It is not a soul that he has

[1] Superman.—*Ed.*]

acquired; it is a way of thinking, a way of looking at the universe, a way of facing the impenetrable dark that must engulf him in the end, as it engulfs the birds of the air and the protozoa in the sea ooze.

Thus he faces death the inexorable—not, perhaps, with complete serenity, but at least with dignity, calm, a gallant spirit. If he has not proved positively that religion is not true, then he has at least proved that it is not necessary. Men may live decently without it and they may die courageously without it. But not, of course, *all* men. The capacity for that proud imperturbability is still rare in the race—maybe as rare as the capacity for honor. For the rest there must be faith, as there must be morals. It is their fate to live absurdly, flogged by categorical imperatives of their own shallow imagining, and to die insanely, grasping for hands that are not there. Once, in my days as an active journalist, I attended one such poor fellow in his last moments. With the Seventh Commandment in mind, he had butchered his erring wife, and was now about to pay his debt to the Sixth. A devout Baptist, he was attended by a clergyman of his faith, and gave over his last hours to prayers to and praises of the Yahweh who had dealt with him so cruelly. When, finally the sheriff came to his cell and summoned him to the gallows he broke into a loud, confident recitation of the Twenty-third Psalm. Thus the last scene:

The march begins—first the sheriff, then the condemned with his arms bound, and then the clergyman.

THE CONDEMNED—(*Loudly*) The Lord is my shepherd; I shall not want. He maketh me to lie down in green pastures. (*They reach the foot of the gallows.*) He leadeth me beside the still waters. He restoreth my soul. (*They mount the steps.*) He leadeth me in the paths of righteousness for His name's sake. Yea, though I walk through the valley of the shadow of death (*The sheriff binds his legs*) I will fear no evil: for thou art with me; thy rod and thy staff they comfort me. (*The sheriff adjusts the noose.*) Thou preparest a table before me in the presence of mine enemies; thou anointest my head with oil; my cup runneth over. (*The sheriff signals to the hangman.*) Surely goodness and mercy shall follow me all the days of my life: and I will dwell in the house of——

The drop falls.

As an American I naturally spend most of my time laughing, but that time I did not laugh.

NOTES AND COMMENTS

What exactly does Mencken mean in this essay by "poetry"? Does the word as he uses it have more than one meaning? Also consider his use of "myth" and "legend." Do the three terms occasionally overlap?

The last part of the essay, dealing with the need for religion and man's possible development beyond it, seems better reasoned and more pertinent than the first part, which is full of Mencken's typical excesses —sweeping generalizations, dogmatic prejudices, disproportionate praise (of the "poetry") and intemperate contempt (of the religion and the people who produced it). Does the first part show Mencken himself as less emancipated than he realizes? Is it possible that by admiring the "poetry" he is really explaining the attraction he feels toward a religion his rationality rejects? Do you think that his attack on religion sounds dated—perhaps because it is no longer shocking or unique?

Remember, however, that it was just this kind of vigorous, free-wheeling, even outrageous writing which made Mencken's reputation in his heyday. Do you find that, in spite of the exaggerations and excesses, it still has a certain amount of appeal?

In connection with this essay and Julian Huxley's (page 391), you may be interested to read Shaw's Preface to *Back to Methuselah*. His views on science and religion are brilliantly set forth in that piece.

BERTRAND RUSSELL

1872-

The following selection consists of the first chapter and excerpts from the last chapter of *The ABC of Relativity*, written in 1925 and revised in 1958. In the first chapter Russell is not trying to explain what relativity is, how it was discovered, or how scientists use the theory; those subjects are discussed later in the book. Here he is concerned merely with explaining why Einstein's theories about relativity are considered so important in all twentieth-century thinking, and describing the sort of things relativity deals with.

The last chapter discusses the philosophical implications of relativity. It also states exceptionally well the modern physicist's view of the limitations as well as the importance of his subject. (For biographical information about Russell, see page 308.)

FROM *The ABC of Relativity*

EVERYBODY KNOWS that Einstein did something astonishing, but very few people know exactly what it was that he did. It is generally recognized that he revolutionized our conception of the physical world, but the new conceptions are wrapped up in mathematical technicalities. It is true that there are innumerable popular accounts of the theory of relativity, but they generally cease to be intelligible just at the point where they begin to say something important. The authors are hardly to blame for this. Many of the new ideas can be expressed in non-mathematical language, but they are none the less difficult on that account. What is demanded is a change in our imaginative picture of the world—a picture

Reprinted by permission of George Allen & Unwin Ltd., London.

which has been handed down from remote, perhaps pre-human, ancestors, and has been learned by each one of us in early childhood. A change in our imagination is always difficult, especially when we are no longer young. The same sort of change was demanded by Copernicus, when he taught that the earth is not stationary and the heavens do not revolve about it once a day. To us now there is no difficulty in this idea, because we learned it before our mental habits had become fixed. Einstein's ideas, similarly, will seem easier to generations which grow up with them; but for us a certain effort of imaginative reconstruction is unavoidable.

In exploring the surface of the earth, we make use of all our senses, more particularly of the senses of touch and sight. In measuring lengths, parts of the human body are employed in pre-scientific ages: a "foot," a "cubit," a "span" are defined in this way. For longer distances, we think of the time it takes to walk from one place to another. We gradually learn to judge distance roughly by the eye, but we rely upon touch for accuracy. Moreover it is touch that gives us our sense of "reality." Some things cannot be touched: rainbows, reflections in looking-glasses, and so on. These things puzzle children, whose metaphysical speculations are arrested by the information that what is in the looking-glass is not "real." Macbeth's dagger was unreal because it was not "sensible to feeling as to sight." Not only our geometry and physics, but our whole conception of what exists outside us, is based upon the sense of touch. We carry this even into our metaphors: a good speech is "solid," a bad speech is "gas," because we feel that a gas is not quite "real."

In studying the heavens, we are debarred from all senses except sight. We cannot touch the sun, or travel to it; we cannot walk round the moon, or apply a foot-rule to the Pleiades. Nevertheless, astronomers have unhesitatingly applied the geometry and physics which they found serviceable on the surface of the earth, and which they had based upon touch and travel. In doing so, they brought down trouble on their heads, which it was left for Einstein to clear up. It turned out that much of what we learned from the sense of touch was unscientific prejudice, which must be rejected if we are to have a true picture of the world.

An illustration may help us to understand how much is impossible to the astronomer as compared with the man who is

interested in things on the surface of the earth. Let us suppose
that a drug is administered to you which makes you temporarily
unconscious, and that when you wake you have lost your memory
but not your reasoning powers. Let us suppose further that while
you were unconscious you were carried into a balloon, which, when
you come to, is sailing with the wind on a dark night—the night
of the fifth of November if you are in England, or of the fourth of
July if you are in America. You can see fireworks which are being
sent off from the ground, from trains, and from aeroplanes travelling in all directions, but you cannot see the ground or the trains
or the aeroplanes because of the darkness. What sort of picture of
the world will you form? You will think that nothing is permanent:
there are only brief flashes of light, which, during their short
existence, travel through the void in the most various and bizarre
curves. You cannot touch these flashes of light, you can only see
them. Obviously your geometry and your physics and your metaphysics will be quite different from those of ordinary mortals. If
an ordinary mortal were with you in the balloon, you would find
his speech unintelligible. But if Einstein were with you, you would
understand him more easily than the ordinary mortal would,
because you would be free from a host of preconceptions which
prevent most people from understanding him.

The theory of relativity depends, to a considerable extent,
upon getting rid of notions which are useful in ordinary life but
not to our drugged balloonist. Circumstances on the surface of the
earth, for various more or less accidental reasons, suggest conceptions which turn out to be inaccurate, although they have come
to seem like necessities of thought. The most important of these
circumstances is that most objects on the earth's surface are fairly
persistent and nearly stationary from a terrestrial point of view.
If this were not the case, the idea of going on a journey would not
seem so definite as it does. If you want to travel from King's Cross
to Edinburgh, you know that you will find King's Cross where it
has always been, that the railway line will take the course that it
did when you last made the journey, and that Waverley Station
in Edinburgh will not have walked up to the Castle. You therefore
say and think that you have travelled to Edinburgh, not that
Edinburgh has travelled to you, though the latter statement would
be just as accurate. The success of this common-sense point of
view depends upon a number of things which are really of the

nature of luck Suppose all the houses in London were perpetually moving about, like a swarm of bees; suppose railways moved and changed their shapes like avalanches; and finally suppose that material objects were perpetually being formed and dissolved like clouds. There is nothing impossible in these suppositions. But obviously what we call a journey to Edinburgh would have no meaning in such a world. You would begin, no doubt, by asking the taxi-driver: "Where is King's Cross this morning?" At the station you would have to ask a similar question about Edinburgh, but the booking-office clerk would reply: "What part of Edinburgh do you mean, sir? Prince's Street has gone to Glasgow, the Castle has moved up into the Highlands, and Waverley Station is under water in the middle of the Firth of Forth." And on the journey the stations would not be staying quiet, but some would be travelling north, some south, some east or west, perhaps much faster than the train. Under these conditions you could not say where you were at any moment. Indeed the whole notion that one is always in some definite "place" is due to the fortunate immobility of most of the large objects on the earth's surface. The idea of "place" is only a rough practical approximation: there is nothing logically necessary about it, and it cannot be made precise.

If we were not much larger than an electron, we should not have this impression of stability, which is only due to the grossness of our senses. King's Cross, which to us looks solid, would be too vast to be conceived except by a few eccentric mathematicians. The bits of it that we could see would consist of little tiny points of matter, never coming into contact with each other, but perpetually whizzing round each other in an inconceivably rapid ballet-dance. The world of our experience would be quite as mad as the one in which the different parts of Edinburgh go for walks in different directions. If—to take the opposite extreme—you were as large as the sun and lived as long, with a corresponding slowness of perception, you would again find a higgledy-piggledy universe without permanence—stars and planets would come and go like morning mists, and nothing would remain in a fixed position relatively to anything else. The notion of comparative stability which forms part of our ordinary outlook is thus due to the fact that we are about the size we are, and live on a planet of which the surface is not very hot. If this were not the case, we should not find pre-relativity physics intellectually satisfying. Indeed we should never have invented such theories. We should have had to arrive at relativity physics at one bound, or remain ignorant of scientific laws. It is fortunate for us that we were not faced with this alternative, since it is almost inconceivable that one man could have done the work of Euclid, Galileo, Newton and Einstein. Yet without such an incredible genius physics could hardly have been discovered in a world where the universal flux was obvious to non-scientific observation.

In astronomy, although the sun, moon, and stars continue to exist year after year, yet in other respects the world we have to deal with is very different from that of everyday life. As already observed, we depend exclusively on sight: the heavenly bodies cannot be touched, heard, smelt or tasted. Everything in the heavens is moving relatively to everything else. The earth is going round the sun, the sun is moving, very much faster than an express train, towards a point in the constellation Hercules, the "fixed" stars are scurrying hither and thither like a lot of frightened hens. There are no well-marked places in the sky, like King's Cross and Edinburgh. When you travel from place to place on the earth, you say the train moves and not the stations, because the stations preserve their topographical relations to each other and the surrounding country. But in astronomy it is arbitrary which you call the train and which the station: the question is to be decided purely by convenience and as a matter of convention.

In this respect, it is interesting to contrast Einstein and Copernicus. Before Copernicus, people thought that the earth stood still and the heavens revolved about it once a day. Copernicus taught that "really" the earth rotates once a day, and the daily revolution of sun and stars is only "apparent." Galileo and Newton endorsed this view, and many things were thought to prove it—for example, the flattening of the earth at the poles, and the fact that bodies are heavier there than at the equator. But in the modern theory the question between Copernicus and his predecessors is merely one of convenience; all motion is relative, and there is no difference between the two statements: "the earth rotates once a day" and "the heavens revolve about the earth once a day." The two mean exactly the same thing, just as it means the same thing if I say that a certain length is six feet or two yards. Astronomy is easier if we take the sun as fixed than if we take the earth, just as accounts are easier in decimal coinage.

But to say more for Copernicus is to assume absolute motion, which is a fiction. All motion is relative, and it is a mere convention to take one body as at rest. All such conventions are equally legitimate, though not all are equally convenient.

There is another matter of great importance, in which astronomy differs from terrestrial physics because of its exclusive dependence upon sight. Both popular thought and old-fashioned physics used the notion of "force," which seemed intelligible because it was associated with familiar sensations. When we are walking, we have sensations connected with our muscles which we do not have when we are sitting still. In the days before mechanical traction, although people could travel by sitting in their carriages, they could see the horses exerting themselves, and evidently putting out "force" in the same way as human beings do. Everybody knew from experience what it is to push or pull, or to be pushed or pulled. These very familiar facts made "force" seem a natural basis for dynamics. But Newton's law of gravitation introduced a difficulty. The force between two billiard balls appeared intelligible because we know what it feels like to bump into another person; but the force between the earth and the sun, which are ninety-three million miles apart, was mysterious. Newton himself regarded this "action at a distance" as impossible, and believed that there was some hitherto undiscovered mechanism by which the sun's influence was transmitted to the planets. However, no such mechanism was discovered, and gravitation remained a puzzle. The fact is that the whole conception of "force" is a mistake. The sun does not exert any force on the planets; in Einstein's law of gravitation, the planet only pays attention to what it finds in its own neighbourhood. The way in which this works [can] be explained . . . for the present we are only concerned with the necessity of abandoning the notion of "force," which was due to misleading conceptions derived from the sense of touch.

As physics has advanced, it has appeared more and more that sight is less misleading than touch as a source of fundamental notions about matter. The apparent simplicity in the collision of billiard balls is quite illusory. As a matter of fact the two billiard balls never touch at all; what really happens is inconceivably complicated, but is more analogous to what happens when a comet penetrates the solar system and goes away again than to what common sense supposes to happen.

Most of what we have said hitherto was already recognized by physicists before Einstein invented the theory of relativity. "Force" was known to be merely a mathematical fiction, and it was generally held that motion is a merely relative phenomenon—that is to say, when two bodies are changing their relative position, we cannot say that one is moving while the other is at rest, since the occurrence is merely a change in their relation to each other. But a great labour was required in order to bring the actual procedure of physics into harmony with these new convictions. Newton believed in force and in absolute space and time; he embodied these beliefs in his technical methods, and his methods remained those of later physicists. Einstein invented a new technique, free from Newton's assumptions. But in order to do so he had to change fundamentally the old ideas of space and time, which had been unchallenged from time immemorial. This is what makes both the difficulty and the interest of his theory.

The philosophical consequences of relativity are neither so great nor so startling as is sometimes thought. It throws very little light on time-honoured controversies, such as that between realism and idealism. Some people think that it supports Kant's view that space and time are "subjective" and are "forms of intuition." I think such people have been misled by the way in which writers on relativity speak of "the observer." It is natural to suppose that the observer is a human being, or at least a mind; but he is just as likely to be a photographic plate or a clock. That is to say, the odd results as to the difference between one "point of view" and another are concerned with "point of view" in a sense applicable to physical instruments just as much as to people with perceptions. The "subjectivity" concerned in the theory of relativity is a *physical* subjectivity, which would exist equally if there were no such things as minds or senses in the world.

Moreover, it is a strictly limited subjectivity. The theory does not say that *everything* is relative; on the contrary, it gives a technique for distinguishing what is relative from what belongs to a physical occurrence in its own right. If we are going to say that the theory supports Kant about space and time, we shall have to say that it refutes him about space-time. In my view, neither statement is correct. I see no reason why, on such issues, philosophers should not all stick to the views they previously held. There were no conclusive arguments on either side before, and there are none now; to hold either view shows a dogmatic rather than a scientific temper.

Nevertheless, when the ideas involved in Einstein's work have become familiar, as they will do when they are taught in schools, certain changes in our habits of thought are likely to result, and to have great importance in the long run.

One thing which emerges is that physics tells us much less about the physical world than we thought it did. Almost all the "great principles" of traditional physics turn out to be like the "great law" that there are always three feet to a yard; others turn out to be downright false. . . .

It is a curious fact—of which relativity is not the only illustration—that, as reasoning improves, its claims to the power of proving facts grow less and less. Logic used to be thought to teach us how to draw inferences; now, it teaches us rather how not to draw inferences. Animals and children are terribly prone to inference: a horse is surprised beyond measure if you take an unusual turning. When men began to reason, they tried to justify the inferences that they had drawn unthinkingly in earlier days. A great deal of bad philosophy and bad science resulted from this propensity. "Great principles," such as the "uniformity of nature," the "law of universal causation," and so on, are attempts to bolster up our belief that what has often happened before will happen again, which is no better founded than the horse's belief that you will take the turning you usually take. It is not altogether easy to see what is to replace these pseudo-principles in the practice of science; but perhaps the theory of relativity gives us a glimpse of the kind of thing we may expect. Causation, in the old sense, no longer has a place in theoretical physics. There is, of course, something else which takes its place, but the substitute appears to have a better empirical foundation than the old principle which it has superseded. . . .

Assuming the utmost that can be claimed for physics, it does not tell us what it is that changes, or what are its various states; it only tells us such things as that changes follow each other periodically, or spread with a certain speed. Even now we are probably not at the end of the process of stripping away what is merely imagination, in order to reach the core of true scientific knowledge. The theory of relativity has accomplished a very great deal in this respect, and in doing so has taken us nearer and nearer to bare structure, which is the mathematician's goal—not because it is the only thing in which he is interested as a human being, but because it is the only thing that he can express in mathematical formulae. But far as we have travelled in the direction of abstraction, it may be that we shall have to travel farther still. . . .

To the non-mathematical mind, the abstract character of our physical knowledge may seem unsatisfactory. From an artistic or imaginative point of view, it is perhaps regrettable, but from a practical point of view it is of no consequence. Abstraction, difficult as it is, is the source of practical power. A financier, whose dealings with the world are more abstract than those of any other "practical" man, is also more powerful than any other practical man. He can deal in wheat or cotton without needing ever to have seen either: all he needs to know is whether they will go up or down. This is abstract mathematical knowledge, at least as compared to the knowledge of the agriculturist. Similarly the physicist, who knows nothing of matter except certain laws of its movements, nevertheless knows enough to enable him to manipulate it. After working through whole strings of equations, in which the symbols stand for things whose intrinsic nature can never be known to us, he arrives at last at a result which can be interpreted in terms of our own perceptions, and utilized to bring about desired effects in our own lives. What we know about matter, abstract and schematic as it is, is enough, in principle, to tell us the rules according to which it produces perceptions and feelings in ourselves; and it is upon these rules that the *practical* uses of physics depend.

The final conclusion is that we know very little, and yet it is astonishing that we know so much, and still more astonishing that so little knowledge can give us so much power.

NOTES AND COMMENTS

Russell successfully avoids the twin dangers of popularizing a complicated idea: he doesn't baffle the layman with technical terms and intricate mathematics, while hinting mysteriously that still more significant material lies beyond the reader's grasp, nor does he oversimplify or distort ideas to make them more intelligible. Do you find his metaphors clear—or merely charming? Would you agree that the concepts he discusses are easier to grasp for your generation, which "grew up with them," than for your parents'?

What do you think of Russell's philosophic outlook, as revealed in his closing remarks? Do you think it is widely shared? Is it a point of view only a mathematician would have? Are most scientists more dogmatic? Do you see anything anti-religious in such views?

JULIAN HUXLEY

1887-

Julian Huxley is an English biologist and writer, the older brother of Aldous Huxley (see the biographical note, page 264). Like Bertrand Russell, he has written many books and articles elucidating modern scientific thought for the layman. About this essay, written in 1941, he has said: "It illustrates better than any of my writings my central preoccupation with scientific humanism, which seeks to combine a rigorously scientific approach with a recognition of the many-sidedness of human nature."

The Uniqueness of Man

MAN'S OPINION of his own position in relation to the rest of the animals has swung pendulum-wise between too great or too little a conceit of himself, fixing now too large a gap between him-self and the animals, now too small. The gap, of course, can be diminished or increased at either the animal or the human end. One can, like Descartes, make animals too mechanical, or, like most unsophisticated people, humanize them too much. Or one can work at the human end of the gap, and then either dehu-manize one's own kind into an animal species like any other, or superhumanize it into beings a little lower than the angels.

After Darwin, man could no longer avoid considering himself as an animal; but he is beginning to see himself as a very peculiar and in many ways a unique animal. The analysis of man's biological uniqueness is as yet incomplete. This essay is an attempt to review its present position.

The first and most obviously unique characteristic of man is his capacity for conceptual thought; if you prefer objective terms, you will say his employment of true speech, but that is only another way of saying the same thing.

This basic human property has had many consequences. The most important was the development of a cumulative tradition. The beginnings of tradition, by which experience is transmitted from one generation to the next, are to be seen in many higher animals. But in no case is the tradition cumulative. Offspring learn from parents, but they learn the same kind and quantity of lessons as they, in turn, impart; the transmission of experience never bridges more than one generation. In man, however, tradition is an independent and potentially permanent activity, capable of indefinite improvement in quality and increase in quantity. It constitutes a new accessory process of heredity in evolution, running side by side with the biological process, heredity of experience to supplement the universal heredity of living substance.

The existence of a cumulative tradition has as its chief consequence—or if you prefer, its chief objective manifestation—the progressive improvement of human tools and machinery. Many animals employ tools; but they are always crude tools employed in a crude way. Elaborate tools and skilled technique can develop only with the aid of speech and tradition.

In the perspective of evolution, tradition and tools are the characters which have given man his dominant position among organisms. This biological dominance is, at present, another of man's unique properties. Since the early Pleistocene, widespread extinction has diminished the previously dominant group of placental mammals, and man has not merely multiplied, but has evolved, extended his range, and increased the variety of his modes of life.

Biology thus reinstates man in a position analogous to that conferred on him as Lord of Creation by theology. There are, however, differences, and differences of some importance for our general outlook. In the biological view, the other animals have not been created to serve man's needs, but man has evolved in such a way that he has been able to eliminate some competing types, to enslave others by domestication, and to modify physical and biological conditions over the larger part of the earth's land area. The theological view was not true in detail or in many of its implications; but it had a solid biological basis.

Speech, tradition, and tools have led to many other unique properties of man. These are, for the most part, obvious and well known, and I propose to leave them aside until I have dealt with some less familiar human characteristics. For the human species, considered as a species, is unique in certain purely biological attributes; and these have not received the attention they deserve, either from the zoological or the sociological standpoint.

In the first place, man is by far the most variable wild species known. Domesticated species like dog, horse, or fowl may rival or exceed him in this particular, but their variability has obvious reasons, and is irrelevant to our inquiry.

In correlation with his wide variability, man has a far wider range than any other animal species, with the possible exception of some of his parasites. Man is also unique as a dominant type. All other dominant types have evolved into many hundreds or thousands of separate species, grouped in numerous genera, families, and larger classificatory groups. The human type has maintained its dominance without splitting: man's variety has been achieved within the limits of a single species.

Finally, man is unique among higher animals in the method of his evolution. Whereas, in general, animal evolution is divergent, human evolution is reticulate. By this is meant that in animals, evolution occurs by the isolation of groups which then become progressively more different in their genetic characteristics, so that the course of evolution can be represented as a divergent radiation of separate lines, some of which become extinct, others continue unbranched, and still others divergently branch again. Whereas in man, after incipient divergence, the branches have come together again, and have generated new diversity from their Mendelian recombinations, this process being repeated until the course of human descent is like a network.

Let us remind ourselves that superposed upon this purely biological or genetic variability is the even greater amount of variability due to differences of upbringing, profession, and personal tastes. The final result is a degree of variation that would be staggering if it were not so familiar. It would be fair to say that, in respect to mind and outlook, individual human beings are separated by differences as profound as those which distinguish the major groups of the animal kingdom. This enormous range of individual variation in human minds often leads to misunderstanding and even mutual incomprehensibility; but it also provides the necessary basis for fruitful division of labour in human society.

Another biological peculiarity of man is the uniqueness of his evolutionary history. Writers have indulged their speculative fancy by imagining other organisms endowed with speech and conceptual thought—talking rats, rational ants, philosophic dogs, and the like. But closer analysis shows that these fantasies are impossible. A brain capable of conceptual thought could not have been developed elsewhere than in a human body.

Evolution consists of an enormous number of blind alleys, with a very occasional path of progress. It is like a maze in which almost all turnings are wrong turnings. The goal of the evolutionary maze, however, is not a central chamber, but a road which will lead indefinitely onwards.

If now we look back upon the past history of life, we shall see that the avenues of progress have been steadily reduced in number, until by the Pleistocene period, or even earlier, only one was left. Let us remember that we can and must judge early progress in the light of its latest steps. The most recent step has been the acquisition of conceptual thought, which has enabled man to dethrone the non-human mammals from their previous position of dominance. It is a biological fact that conceptual thought could never have arisen save in a mammal.

Most mammalian lines, however, cut themselves off from indefinite progress by one-sided evolution, turning their limbs and jaws into specialized and therefore limited instruments. And, for the most part, they relied mainly on the crude sense of smell, which cannot present as differentiated a pattern of detailed knowledge as can sight. Finally, the majority continued to produce their young several at a time, in litters. As J. B. S. Haldane has pointed out, this gives rise to an acute struggle for existence in the prenatal period, a considerable percentage of embryos being aborted or resorbed. Such intra-uterine selection will put a premium upon rapidity of growth and differentiation, since the devil takes the hindmost; and this rapidity of development will tend automatically to be carried on into postnatal growth.

As everyone knows, man is characterized by a rate of development which is abnormally slow as compared with that of any other mammal. The period from birth to the first onset of sexual maturity comprises nearly a quarter of the normal span of his life, instead of an eighth, a tenth or twelfth, as in some animals. This again is in one sense a unique characteristic of man, although from the evolutionary point of view it represents merely the exaggeration of a tendency which is operative in other Primates. In any case, it is a necessary condition for the evolution and proper utilization of rational thought. If men and women were, like mice, confronted with the problems of adult life and parenthood after a few weeks, or even, like whales, after a couple of years, they could never acquire the skills of body and mind that they now absorb from and contribute to the social heritage of the species.

This slowing (or "foetalization," as Bolk has called it, since it prolongs the foetal characteristics of earlier ancestral forms into postnatal development and even into adult life) has had other important by-products for man. Here I will mention but one—his nakedness. The distribution of hair on man is extremely similar to that on a late foetus of a chimpanzee, and there can be little doubt that it represents an extension of this temporary anthropoid phase into permanence. Hairlessness of body is not a unique biological characteristic of man; but it is unique among terrestrial mammals, save for a few desert creatures, and some others which have compensated for loss of hair by developing a pachydermatous skin. In any case, it has important biological consequences, since it must have encouraged the comparatively defenceless human creatures in their efforts to protect themselves against animal enemies and the elements, and so has been a spur to the improvement of intelligence.

Now, foetalization could never have occurred in a mammal producing many young at a time, since intra-uterine competition would have encouraged the opposing tendency. Thus we may conclude that conceptual thought could develop only in a mammalian stock which normally brings forth but one young at a birth. Such a stock is provided in the Primates—lemurs, monkeys, and apes.

The Primates also have another characteristic which was necessary for the ancestor of a rational animal—they are arboreal. It may seem curious that living in trees is a prerequisite of conceptual thought. But Elliot Smith's analysis has abundantly shown that only in an arboreal mammal could the forelimb become a true hand, and sight become dominant over smell. Hands obtain an elaborate tactile pattern of what they handle, eyes an elaborate visual pattern of what they see. The combination of the two kinds of pattern, with the aid of binocular vision, in the higher centres of the brain allowed the Primate to acquire a wholly new richness of knowledge about objects, a wholly new possibility of manipulating them. Tree life laid the foundation both for the fuller definition of objects by conceptual thought and for the fuller control of them by tools and machines.

Higher Primates have yet another prerequisite of human intelligence—they are all gregarious. Speech, it is obvious, could never have been evolved in a solitary type. And speech is as much the physical basis of conceptual thought as is protoplasm the physical basis of life.

For the passage, however, of the critical point between subhuman and human, between the biological subordination and the biological primacy of intelligence, between a limited and a potentially unlimited tradition—for this it was necessary for the arboreal animal to descend to the ground again. Only in a terrestrial creature could fully erect posture be acquired; and this was essential for the final conversion of the arms from locomotor limbs into manipulative hands. Furthermore, just as land life, ages previously, had demanded and developed a greater variety of response than had been required in the water, so now it did the same in relation to what had been required in the trees. An arboreal animal could never have evolved the skill of the hunting savage, nor ever have proceeded to the domestication of other animals or to agriculture.

We are now in a position to define the uniqueness of human evolution. The essential character of man as a dominant organism is conceptual thought. And conceptual thought could have arisen only in a multicellular animal, an animal with bilateral symmetry, head and blood system, a vertebrate as against a mollusc or an arthropod, a land vertebrate among vertebrates, a mammal among land vertebrates. Finally, it could have arisen only in a mammalian line which was gregarious, which produced one young at a birth instead of several, and which had recently become terrestrial after a long period of arboreal life.

There is only one group of animals which fulfills these conditions—a terrestrial offshoot of the higher Primates. Thus not merely has conceptual thought been evolved only in man: it could not have been evolved except in man. There is but one path of unlimited progress through the evolutionary maze. The course of human evolution is as unique as its result. It is unique not in the trivial sense of being a different course from that of any other organism, but in the profounder sense of being the only path that could have achieved the essential characters of man. Conceptual thought on this planet is inevitably associated with a particular type of Primate body and Primate brain.

A further property of man in which he is unique among higher animals concerns his sexual life. Man is prepared to mate at any time: animals are not.

Another of the purely biological characters in which man is unique is his reproductive variability. In a given species of animals, the maximum litter-size may, on occasions, reach perhaps double the minimum, according to circumstances of food and temperature, or even perhaps threefold. But during a period of years, these variations will be largely equalized within a range of perhaps fifty per cent, either way from the average, and the percentage of wholly infertile adults is very low. In man, on the other hand, the range of positive fertility is enormous—from one to over a dozen, and in exceptional cases to over twenty; and the number of wholly infertile adults is considerable. This fact, in addition to providing a great diversity of patterns of family life, has important bearings on evolution. It means that in the human species differential fertility is more important as a basis for selection than is differential mortality; and it provides the possibility of much more rapid selective change than that found in wild animal species. Such rapidity of evolution would, of course, be effectively realized only if the stocks with large families possessed a markedly different hereditary constitution from those with few children; but the high differential fertility of unskilled workers as against the professional classes in England, or of the French Canadians against the rest of the inhabitants of Canada, demonstrates how rapidly populations may change by this means.

Still another point in which man is biologically unique is the length and relative importance of his period of what we may call "post-maturity." If we consider the female sex, in which the transition from reproductive maturity to non-reproductive post-maturity is more sharply defined than in the male, we find, in the first place, that in animals a comparatively small percentage of the population survives beyond the period of reproduction; in the second place, that such individuals rarely survive long, and so far as known never for a period equal to or greater than the period during which reproduction was possible; and thirdly, that such individuals are rarely of importance in the life of the species. The same is true of the male sex, provided we do not take the incapacity to produce fertile gametes as the criterion of post-maturity, but rather the appearance of signs of age, such as the beginnings of loss of vigour and weight, decreased sexual activity, or greying hair.

But in civilized man the average expectation of life now includes over ten post-mature years, and about a sixth of the population enjoys a longer post-maturity than maturity. What is more, in all advanced human societies, a large proportion of the leaders of the community are always post-mature. All the members of the British War Cabinet were in their post-maturity.

This is truly a remarkable phenomenon. Through the new social mechanisms made possible by speech and tradition, man has been able to utilize for the benefit of the species a period of life which in almost all other creatures is a mere superfluity. We know that the dominance of the old can be overemphasized; but it is equally obvious that society cannot do without the post-mature. To act on the slogan "Too old at forty"—or even at forty-five— would be to rob man of one of his unique characteristics, whereby he utilizes tradition to best advantage.

We have now dealt in a broad way with the unique properties of man both from the comparative and the evolutionary point of view. Now we can return to the present and the particular and discuss these properties and their consequence a little more in detail. First, let us remind ourselves that the gap between human and animal thought is much greater than is usually supposed. The tendency to project familiar human qualities into animals is very strong, and colours the ideas of nearly all people who have not special familiarity both with animal behaviour and scientific method.

Man is more intelligent than the animals because his brain mechanism is more plastic. This fact also gives him, of course, the opportunity of being more nonsensical and perverse: but its primary effects have been more analytical knowledge and more varied control.

This increase of flexibility has also had other psychological consequences which rational philosophers are apt to forget: and in some of these, too, man is unique. It has led, for instance, to the fact that man is the only organism normally and inevitably subject to psychological conflict. You can give a dog neurosis, as Pavlov did, by a complicated laboratory experiment: you can find cases of brief emotional conflict in the lives of wild birds and animals. But, for the most part, psychological conflict is shirked by the simple expedient of arranging that now one and now another instinct should dominate the animal's behaviour.

When we reach the human level, there are new complications; for, as we have seen, one of the peculiarities of man is the abandonment of any rigidity of instinct, and the provision of association-mechanisms by which any activity of the mind, whether in the spheres of knowing, feeling, or willing, can be brought into relation with any other. It is through this that man has acquired the possibility of a unified mental life. But, by the same token, the door is opened to the forces of disruption, which may destroy any such unity and even prevent him from enjoying the efficiency of behaviour attained by animals.

I need not pursue the subject further. Here I am only concerned to show that the great biological advantages conferred on man by the unification of mind have inevitably brought with them certain counterbalancing defects. The freedom of association between all aspects and processes of the mind has provided the basis for conceptual thought and tradition; but it has also provided potential antagonists, which in lower organisms were carefully kept apart, with the opportunity of meeting face to face, and has thus made some degree of conflict unavoidable.

In rather similar fashion, man's upright posture has brought with it certain consequential disadvantages in regard to the functioning of his internal organs and his proneness to rupture. Thus man's unique characteristics are by no means wholly beneficial.

In close correlation with our subjection to conflict is our proneness to laughter. So characteristic of our species is laughter that man has been defined as the laughing animal. It is true that, like so much else of man's uniqueness, it has its roots among the animals, where it reveals itself as an expression of a certain kind of general pleasure—and thus in truth perhaps more of a smile than a laugh. And in a few animals—ravens, for example—there are traces of a malicious sense of humour. Laughter in man, however, is much more than this. There are many theories of laughter, most of them containing partial truth. But biologically the important feature of human laughter seems to lie in its providing a release for conflict, a resolution of trouble-some situations.

Those of man's unique characteristics which may better be called psychological and social than narrowly biological spring from one or another of three characteristics. The first is his capacity for abstract and general thought: the second is the relative unification of his mental processes, as against the much more rigid compartmentalization of animal mind and behaviour: the third is the existence of social units, such as tribe, nation, party, and church, with a continuity of their own, based on organized tradition and culture.

There are various by-products of the change from pre-human to the human type of mind which are, of course, also unique biologically. Let us enumerate a few: pure mathematics; musical gifts; artistic appreciation and creation; religion; romantic love.

Mathematical ability appears, almost inevitably, as something mysterious. Yet the attainment of speech, abstraction, and logical thought, bring it into potential being. It may remain in a very rudimentary state of development; but even the simplest arith-metical calculations are a manifestation of its existence. Like any other human activity, it requires proper tools and machinery. Arabic numerals, algebraic conventions, logarithms, the differential calculus, are such tools: each one unlocks new possibilities of mathematical achievement. But just as there is no essential dif-ference between man's conscious use of a chipped flint as an implement and his design of the most elaborate machine, so there is none between such simple operations as numeration or addition and the comprehensive flights of higher mathematics.

Again, some people are by nature more gifted than others in this field; yet no normal human being is unable to perform some mathematical operations. Thus the capacity for mathematics is, as I have said, a by-product of the human type of mind.

We have seen, however, that the human type of mind is distinguished by two somewhat opposed attributes. One is the capacity for abstraction, the other for synthesis. Mathematics is one of the extreme by-products of our capacity for abstraction. Arithmetic abstracts objects of all qualities save their enumerability; the symbol π abstracts in a single Greek letter a complicated relation between the parts of all circles. Art, on the other hand, is an extreme by-product of our capacity for synthesis. In one unique production, the painter can bring together form, colour, arrangement, associations of memory, emotion, and idea. Dim adumbrations of art are to be found in a few creatures such as bower-birds; but nothing is found to which the word can rightly be applied until man's mind gave the possibility of freely mingling observations, emotions, memories, and ideas, and subjecting the mixture to deliberate control.

But it is not enough here to enumerate a few special activities. In point of fact, the great majority of man's activities and characteristics are by-products of his primary distinctive characteristics, and therefore, like them, biologically unique.

On the one hand, conversation, organized games, education, sport, paid work, gardening, the theatre; on the other, conscience, duty, sin, humiliation, vice, penitence—these are all such unique by-products. The trouble, indeed, is to find any human activities which are not unique. Even the fundamental biological attributes such as eating, sleeping, and mating have been tricked out by man with all kinds of unique frills and peculiarities.

There may be other by-products of man's basic uniqueness which have not yet been exploited. For let us remember that such by-products may remain almost wholly latent until demand stimulates invention and invention facilitates development. It is asserted that there exist human tribes who cannot count above two; certainly some savages stop at ten. Here the mathematical faculty is restricted to numeration, and stops short at a very rudimentary stage of this rudimentary process. Similarly, there are human societies in which art has never been developed beyond the stage of personal decoration. It is probable that during the first half of the Pleistocene period, none of the human race had developed either their mathematical or their artistic potentialities beyond such a rudimentary stage.

It is perfectly possible that today man's so-called super-normal or extra-sensory faculties are in the same case as were his mathematical faculties during the first or second glaciations of the Ice Age—barely more than a potentiality, with no technique for eliciting and developing them, no tradition behind them to give them continuity and intellectual respectability. Even such simple performances as multiplying two three-figure numbers would have appeared entirely magical to early Stone Age men.

It is only exceptionally that men have dared to uphold their uniqueness and to be proud of their human superiority to the impersonality of the rest of the universe. It is time now, in the light of our knowledge, to be brave and face the fact and the consequences of our uniqueness. That is the view of Dr. Everett of the University of California, as it was also that of T. H. Huxley in his famous Romanes lecture. I agree with them; but I would suggest that the antinomy between man and the universe is not quite so sharp as they have made out. Man represents the culmination of that process of organic evolution which has been proceeding on this planet for over a thousand million years. That process, however wasteful and cruel it may be, and into however many blind alleys it may have been diverted, is also in one aspect progressive. Man has now become the sole representative of life in that progressive aspect and its sole trustee for any progress in the future.

Meanwhile it is true that the appearance of the human type of mind, the latest step in evolutionary progress, has introduced both new methods and new standards. By means of his conscious reason and its chief offspring, science, man has the power of substituting less dilatory, less wasteful, and less cruel methods of effective progressive change than those of natural selection, which alone are available to lower organisms. And by means of his conscious purpose and his set of values, he has the power of substituting new and higher standards for change than those of mere survival and adaptation to immediate circumstances, which alone are inherent in pre-human evolution. To put the matter in another way, progress has hitherto been a rare and fitful by-product of evolution. Man has the possibility of making it the main feature of his own future evolution, and of guiding its course in relation to a deliberate aim.

But he must not be afraid of his uniqueness. There may be other beings in this vast universe endowed with reason, purpose, and aspiration: but we know nothing of them. So far as our knowledge goes, human mind and personality are unique and constitute the highest product yet achieved by the cosmos. Let us not put off our responsibilities on to the shoulders of mythical gods or philosophical absolutes, but shoulder them in the hopefulness of tempered pride. In the perspective of biology, our business in the world is seen to be the imposition of the best and most enduring of our human standards upon ourselves and our planet. The enjoyment of beauty and interest, the achievement of goodness and efficiency, the enhancement of life and its variety —these are the harvest which our human uniqueness should be called upon to yield.

NOTES AND COMMENTS

Ever since evolution was first advanced as a scientific theory, opposition to it has centered around the feeling that a purely biological view of man debases him. Huxley, staying within scientific bounds, seeks to elevate man, emphasizing that his true superiority over the animals is not diminished by their common origin. Do you find fanciful Huxley's suggestion that "super-normal or extra-sensory faculties" may be latent in man and subject to future development? Do you feel that his conclusion is overly optimistic?

Contrast the impersonality of Julian Huxley on the biological process and the very personal feeling that Stevenson has about death. Whose style do you think is more effective? Whose point of view do you find more attractive?

MARTIN CYRIL D'ARCY

1888-

Martin Cyril D'Arcy, S.J., priest and philosopher, has lectured on philosophy at Oxford, served as provincial (head) of the Society of Jesus in England and has taught in America at Fordham, Notre Dame, and the Institute for Advanced Study at Princeton. One of his principal preoccupations as a philosopher has been human love: its capacity and limitations. In *The Mind and Heart of Love* he attempts to synthesize the conflicting claims of Eros, the masculine principle in human life and love with its insistence upon self-fulfillment, and Agape, the feminine desire to lose oneself in self-abnegation and ecstasy.

"The Varieties of Human Love" considers an even broader synthesis: a welding of scientific discovery and Judeo-Christian doctrine into a new explanation of man and the cosmos, an explanation as all-encompassing as that achieved by the scholastic philosophers of the Middle Ages. The philosophy of St. Thomas Aquinas, for instance, grew from the Bible, the wisdom of earlier Christian thinkers, the humanistic legacy of ancient Greece and Rome, and the scientific knowledge of his own day. Father D'Arcy discusses the efforts of religious thinkers to accomplish the same feat for the twentieth century, especially those of Pierre Teilhard de Chardin, the French priest and paleontologist (1881-1955), who, in *The Phenomenon of Man*, sought to yoke together the scientific vision of evolution and the tenets of Christianity.

The Varieties of Human Love

CARVED ON THE GATES of Harvard University are the words:
". . . Dreading to leave an illiterate Ministry to the Churches
when our present Ministers shall lie in the Dust." These words
show the intention of the founders to educate students in "knowledge and godliness." Until recent times, culture and religion went
hand in hand. In early societies, kings were usually high priests
and the wise men were seers and prophets. Western culture had
its beginning in the schools of the Benedictines and the bishops;
in the middle ages the scholars were tonsured clerics. "The Lord
is my Light" is Oxford University's motto, and to this day we can
see the influence on the democratic institutions in the west of the
Christian philosophy and outlook. The contrast is striking today
when we behold in one large part of the world a violently atheist
system, and in the other a secular culture which may be neutral
or friendly or hostile to religion.

Religion, then, has obviously lost its former place in culture.
Owing to their having held prescriptive rights in so many fields
of learning, Christian theologians were slow in relinquishing some
of the positions they held, and clashed with scientists on dis-
putable points. Hence religion and science have been taken to be
chronic adversaries. Science, however, is by now secure in its
rights, and the more pertinent question at the moment is whether
a new alliance is not due. The democracies need a unifying and
invigorating philosophy of life, and human beings without belief
are subject to bad dreams. If only the Christian religion could
bring out from its stores what is new as well as what is old, and
adapt its treasures to our modern predicaments, there would be
hope of a new and vigorous culture.

Growth in religious and philosophic ideas follows a different
rule from that of science. Scientists do not as yet agree as to the
methods which they pursue in their studies of a physical nature.
There is still dispute both as to the relation of their discoveries to
nature and as to the function of the hypotheses upon which these

discoveries are based. But what is clear is that the scientist holds to hypotheses so long as they serve to unify the data and predict the future. As soon as new data appear which do not conform with these hypotheses, new ones must be sought.

Now in religion and philosophy, hypothesis does not play the same part. Here, knowledge grows by a form of speculation which consists in poring over an often well-known truth, discovering further horizons to it as well as hitherto unsuspected connections with other truths. It is as if the obvious were continually taking one by surprise, and at times an analytical thinker, like George Edward Moore, of Cambridge, will show us how carelessly we have been thinking about such a simple idea as "goodness"; or a metaphysician, like the late Alfred North Whitehead, will bring together in one synthesis ideas and objects which we had assumed to be quite unconnected. Philosophy deals principally with what is immemorially true, and religion has for its field such subjects as God and man, conscience, doctrine and experience, providence and the afterlife.

The human mind, like human sensibility, has its fashions, and grows bored with one aspect of an idea. It is a mark of genius not to throw away the idea and put in its place something new or artificial, but to show a new aspect of the *same* idea and to associate with it what no one so far had suspected. Platitude, then, which the positivists rejected, is the cornerstone of his philosophy! Truth, like beauty, therefore, should be "ever ancient and ever fresh," and it is quite possible for a lover to use, for example, only the one word "love" and never to repeat himself.

Any genuine philosophical or religious idea would serve to exemplify this; we have but to think of this word "love" or of "human personality" to see how in the course of centuries, their meaning, though ever the same, has grown clearer and fuller. The Christian religion claims to teach revealed truth, and therefore Christian doctrine, in a manner all its own, is said to develop without revealed or external contradiction.

Today this claim is better understood by the educated public, with the result that the quarrel between science and the Christian religion has abated. Much of the former bickering was based on a misunderstanding, on the belief that the subject matter of science and religion was necessarily the same. Both sides erred here. The scientist was not sufficiently aware of the limitation imposed upon his subject matter by the yardstick he used, and the Christian did not notice that the formal object or specific aspect of his faith depended upon a special kind of insight. What this means can be seen easily if we think with what different eyes a farmer, a scientist and a painter look at an acre of farmland, or how the sound issuing from a violin can be described as the rubbing of the hair of a dead horse over the intestines of a dead cat or as a concerto by Beethoven. The crowds round the foot of the Cross, as Saint Augustine said, saw a condemned man dying; the Christian sees in the same scene a God redeeming. What are common in the two interpretations are the facts, and for a justifiable interpretation the facts must reinforce each other and point in one direction, just as stray evidence can turn into clues in a law court or in a detective story.

For an understanding of the relations between science and religion, it is essential to understand this diversity in method and outlook. The scientist relies upon observation and experiment, and for his purpose measurement by highly developed techniques is all-important. Though employing such measurements he did not, until recent times, discard some of the old common-sense philosophical notions of nature as uniform in its causes. Now, however, the scientist has purified his science of all that does not belong to it. Instead of the language of cause he deals with mathematical equations, and his predictions are of the nature of mathematical probability. The successes of this method have been beyond belief, but they have been bought at a price; for if asked what they are talking about, many distinguished scientists would answer that they do not know. Most would admit to an "animal faith" in the presence of things and their awareness of them, but once "things" have been broken down and then reconstituted as measurable quantities, very different worlds begin to appear.

Nor should we expect a mathematical world to be a complete representation of the infinitely variegated world of quality we live in, any more than we should expect the information given by a weighing machine to cover all our manhood. Every science uses a yardstick, and the results tell us nothing beyond the yardstick's capacity. What has beguiled and helped philosophers from early times has been the far-reaching applicability of the mathematical or measurable, the power it provides for dealing with almost everything that is human. Whether living matter be radically different from the inorganic or not, we can treat them both by the scientific methods. The quality of music has its own value and its own criterion, but it can be translated into quantitative mathematical terms. Similarly in economics and sociology, and to some extent in experimental psychology, it has become the habit to use statistical methods. Attempt has even been made by philosophers of science and some schools of positivists to reduce mind to some form of behaviorism.

Throughout this procedure what is distinct in its own right is transformed into a mathematical or measurable substitute. Time is described in terms of distance. We speak of light as waves.

"Light itself," writes Bertrand Russell, "the thing which seeing people experience and blind people do not, is not supposed by science to form any part of the world that is independent of us and our senses." Scientists treat organic growth in terms of physical aggregates, and learn much, but they have to ignore the fact that physical aggregates do not grow. The atomic particles that make up the aggregate remain what they are all the time, whereas in the growth of living matter what was there at the beginning is still there at the end, but in a completer form of itself; the ugly duckling *becomes* the handsome swan. If then the quantitative and the qualitative, the inorganic and the organic can be treated for some purposes as one, and nevertheless also be different, it would appear that there are different ways of approaching the real world, and one explanation need not contradict the other, as a triangle includes an angle, and a square with a diagonal includes both.

This possibility brings us back to the varying standpoints and insights of the scientist and the religious philosopher. Now not only do they approach the same objects with different yardsticks and different interests; their very attitude to certainty and truth may differ. The modern scientist, as already pointed out, has given up the dogmatism of his predecessors; he does not pretend to reveal to us the nature of reality. His subject matter is at least one remove from the real, and all he claims is to be consistent with his initial postulates. Modern science is pragmatic, hoisting hypotheses on high, and later replacing them by other flags. On the other hand, it has been a characteristic of philosophy and theology to keep their gaze fixed on basic or ultimate truths and to concern themselves with the origin and destiny of man, the nature of goodness and freedom, and the relation of man to nature and to God. Christian theologians are particularly interested in providing a coherent and adequate setting for the doctrines contained in the Creeds. Here, they would say, is to be found an air in which man can breathe and grow, a true and a more abundant life.

The Christian philosopher, therefore, supports humanism against any attempt to rob man of his rights, his freedom and his personal responsibilities. This being so, in the long drawn-out crisis of the twentieth century, when many of the old forms of civilization are in danger, and its high codes threatened; when, too, a large proportion of the human race is being conditioned to accept a subhuman status, the religious thinker is anxious not so much to defend his position as to make a positive contribution to truth, which will serve his fellow men.

Christianity, if it be a live religion, must ever grow, and do so by keeping its identity, and at the same time enlivening itself with all that is best in the modern world. As we still live upon the ground of a Christian culture, there is no antecedent reason why the church should not bring an intellectual concord into society, as it did in the dark ages, but now with a much more complicated and rich material to work upon.

Another function of philosophy is to discover an order in reality, one based on the principles which govern the whole of reality in so far as it is known to us. This interest of the mind can be called synthetic. It unifies, and is comparable with what the artist or writer or musician tries to do in any composition. In the past we notice how the metaphysicians differ from one another, Aristotle from Plato, Marx from Hegel. Aristotle believed that in his distinction of matter and form, of potency and act, he had discovered characteristics of the real order which permitted him to make a scale running from prime matter to pure thought. Hegel found the vital clue in a form of dialectic, in the clash of apparent opposites which brought as a result a richer unity in the synthesis of these opposites. The scientific philosopher, on the other hand, is inclined to rely upon a general form of evolution to provide a framework of order.

To judge from the religious ideas now current, and the boldness of some of them, a new synthesis, or an old synthesis with a new look, is being premeditated. What else can explain the fearless effort of the late Père Teilhard de Chardin to rope together evolution and the Christian religion? Other writers have offered ingenious solutions of the fall of man, and of nature too, in terms of evolution, but Père Teilhard goes much further and argues that man is still developing, and, under the direction of Christianity, is evolving into a higher species.

As a scientist of high repute, one of those responsible for the verdict on the Peking man, and at the same time a distinguished priest of the Catholic Church, Père Teilhard was in the happy position of being able to speak with some authority as a scientist and as a Christian. He was convinced that the secret of the universe lay in evolution, which he regarded as "regular, continuous and total." There is, he reasoned, a continuous, upward process from matter to the organic, and from the organic to Homo sapiens and still higher. Man is the end product, so far, of nature, and able, therefore, to reflect and discover the truth about nature and himself. Mankind is one, but is not invariant. Owing to the power of reflection, man is in the process of evolving into a new superorganism or species, which will individually and collectively mirror reality in its mind. It will be coconscious and one in truth and affection. To use Père Teilhard's own words, "There will be only one science, one ethic and one passion, that is to say, one mystique." The present time may seem to be a melting pot; but, "man is in process of re-emerging . . . as the head of nature. The reason is that by being in this way cast into the general current of a convergent Cosmogenesis, he acquires the power and the quality of forming, in the very heart of Time and Space, a central and singular gathering-point of the whole stuff of the universe." This cosmos of affection and thought must in turn be centered around One, who is the Word by and in whom all things were made and have their meaning.

That scientists of many countries should have willingly supported the publication of Père Teilhard's ideas shows the general respect for these ideas. Few probably would entirely concur with them. The Catholic theologians, on their side, are also critical; not so much, I think, because of any distaste for the theme as for the defects in the argument. I believe that more work has still to be done by both philosophers and scientists before evolution can pass from a working hypothesis to a general philosophical theory.

The obscurities of the evolutionary hypothesis are apparent in

Père Teilhard's gallant work. He goes beyond the territory of the biologists and extends the hypothesis to mind and inorganic matter as well as to living organisms. As a result he finds himself forced to attribute some form of mind to the simplest material elements. It is a desperate measure. It cannot be verified; it is based on no empirical evidence, and it runs counter to common sense, making meaningless the distinctions on which human intercourse depends. If the rocket to be fired to the moon, or the table at which I write or the dust collecting on the window has some form of consciousness, meaning is taken out of what we call consciousness, and we are as illogical as the Oriental who drinks water filled with micro-organisms though he refuses to destroy any form of living thing.

Yet to make the general theory of evolution coherent, there is need to introduce consciousness at the earliest possible stage; otherwise there is no continuity, no one thing which evolves. When John Tyndall, an advocate of Darwin's views, said that he discerned "Plato, Shakespeare, Newton and Raphael potential in the fires of the sun," he was emphasizing this necessary continuity between mind and matter. If evolution be extended to everything, there must be something implicit in undeveloped matter or organisms, which will later be revealed. On the other hand, any talk about mind, as about vitalism, is abhorred by the strict biologist as a *deus ex machina*. He prefers to keep the physical and chemical laws, and assumes that there is a continuing physical thing, or aggregate of physical things, throughout the uninterrupted generation of germ cells. But there is no material unit which persists as the subject of the process, whether we take the growth of an individual from a fertilized egg cell, or an individual from a remote ancestor of different form. An electron may continue unchanged in all kinds of combinations; if so, it has no development. So far as the history of the germ plasm is concerned, nothing physical continues throughout all the generations. At this crucial point the biologist falls back on metaphor and writes, for example, of "molecules carrying genetic information from one generation to the next." One might as well call a rain cloud a continual development, because the aggregate which composes it is forever changing, and then, to add to the fun, ask with Bertrand Russell whether it is raining between the drops.

Nevertheless, Père Teilhard surely strikes a rich vein in in-

sisting on the new world of communication and unity opened up
by the advent of mind. In far-off times, tribe was separated from
tribe; the stranger was an enemy. Then slowly came the development of communication by speech and writing, and also the
facility to travel. Now there is no distance which cannot be
covered easily, and instead of human beings living in little
worlds apart, we have one in which all men can share knowledge.
Père Teilhard did not greatly exaggerate when he said that mankind has developed what is almost a new form of life and may be
moving into a new phase of coconsciousness.

He saw, too, that the most vital problem of the future is
that of society or the state and the freedom and development of
the individual. Here, in presenting a picture of man reaching full
consciousness and forming a spiritual hive, utterly unlike the
classless society envisaged by Marx, he followed the trend of
Christian theology today. That trend is toward personal freedom
and love.

If we are to believe certain anthropologists, the individual
members of primitive tribes behaved and thought coconsciously
and collectively. Like sheep moving through a gate, the tribe,
almost somnambulistically, carried out the routine of its daily
life. The coming of a full, independent will and consciousness
must be gradual, and, even when freedom of will is realized, the
mind works with the general and the universal in order to arrive
at truths. Even in Greek philosophical literature there was no
proper conception of the individual nor any satisfactory account
of the will as freely choosing. The Greek was interested in the
universal and the necessary, and only with the advent of Christianity did the value of the individual come to full recognition.

The Christian belongs to a community, a holy people. Nevertheless, so sacred is each member that he has to be regarded as an
individual, free and with the highest obligations, and commanded
to love his neighbor as himself. A primitive coconsciousness, therefore, has been succeeded by the splendor and dangers of individual
and independent life. Furthermore, to complete the story of man,
a new and higher form of coconsciousness is promised, and is
said to be already inaugurated in the sacred community. This new
form is to combine the unity of the human race with the complete freedom of the individual, and the image of this unity is a
body with human members and with Christ as its head.

Such union, however, though it be initiated in this life, belongs for the full experience to life after death. On this point, what the theologians say fits in very well with the ideal of a new species, because they teach that as Christ was God and man, so through our incorporation into his life we shall be able to share finitely in the supreme life of divinity.

Consider how we evolve from conception to death. There is a rhythm of self-renewal. At first the embryo, grafted in the womb upon another life, exercises the movements necessary to its birth. Birth breaks the primitive symbiosis and provides the first stage of liberty and selfhood. There remains, however, a total dependence for food, for language and race on what is not itself. New freedoms are acquired at puberty and manhood, new struggles of spirit and body at marriage and companionship, and slowly, where there is a good will, the body and soul form a harmony and the body assists the movements of the spirit to be unimpeded, preparing it for the new birth, the *dies natalis* of death, when, in a last great option, the self will pass from a chrysalis stage to a new selfhood and be coconscious with a new humanity in Christ.

This new form of existence is in process of development here and now. We know what it is to think with another person and, better still, to experience another person thinking with us and being at one with us. Where there is the marriage of true minds, one and one do not make two, but infinity. Such infinity does not, however, take us out of ourselves into a nonhuman state; it increases our humanity. It is along these lines that Christian philosophers are now thinking. They are only too aware that the growth of large states and corporations, of vast and complicated machinery, has made personal and full life more difficult. As science develops, those who think in its terms tend to regard human beings as numbers, commodities and things. This habit lies behind the sharp distinction which the theologians, Martin Buber and Gabriel Marcel, made between what they call the I-It and the I-Thou relation. The scientist, the doctor, the employer and the economist must treat many people as if they had no individuality. This is the I-It relation. But when I "face" another person as I-Thou, I meet the other person, and in the meeting I become an "I" for the first time. Marcel also dwells on the extraordinary force of love as between persons, where I do not seek to possess the other, but wish to be present with him and with an open heart.

What with the dialectical materialism of Marx and the evidence produced by Freud that even spiritual love belonged to the libido, it seemed as if there would be no breathing space for the old true love. But that is not so. The French philosopher Jean Guitton tells us that for a while he found something scandalous in the close association of the ideals of love and the mechanism of reproduction. Even to the biologist this is disconcerting, as it does not fit in with the neat, laborsaving development demanded by evolution. Parthenogenesis would have been so much simpler, mating restricted to certain phases and seasons.

Nevertheless, the closer one looks at the various manifestations of human love the more one is conscious of a congruity between spiritual love and sex. Guitton argues that these various manifestations are not haphazard; they disclose a sequence as unified and progressive as a symphony of music by a great master. It is as if some presiding genius of the species were watching over the expressions of love and regulating the human lottery. Sex proves to be the surest means of arousing and sustaining love. The permanence of the species is assured, and at the same time the greatest variety of the individual encouraged. The vital energies allow themselves to be transformed into something spiritual. What was begun in carnality ends in heaven; what seemed to be mere animal breeding partakes of spirituality, and what appears at first to be just a bodily function acquires a value of its own above even that of knowledge. So it comes about that the vital energies can be enlisted in the service of the soul, and the highest spiritual experiences await those who are faithful to the institutes of nature. The art of loving is not in the least what the libertine tradition would have us believe. It is rather the science of making the fleeting loves of youth endure and multiply in fresh waves of experience throughout the course of a long human life. Love is no episode, it imposes itself like a divinity, regulating, inspiring, and offering the promise of an undreamed-of perfection.

Lastly, there is the philosophy of the two loves, encompassing all life, eternity and time, heaven and hell. Saint Augustine wrote of the two loves, which make two cities, the city of God and the city of unregenerate man. In this philosophy the relation between libido and the highest personal love can be traced. At the same time, it prepares the way for a reconciliation between the religious love and the noblest ambitions of man capable of realization in the life of family or society. According to this view, two loves rule every individual in different measures. In theological language, the first is called Agape, the second, Eros. Psychologically they represent the masculine and feminine elements which are present in every human being. Eros is possessive and self-assertive, its end that of self-realization, its virtues those of honor, independence and self-respect. Agape is submissive, and, disregarding the measures imposed by reason and propriety, would lose itself in the emotion of a herd or the ecstasy of religious faith, in wooing death and darkness, or in a total self-surrender for love's sake.

These two loves make up the warp and woof of life lived in common. They have their dark descents, and they are in harmony; they are in the gentle relation of love between individuals, where each can give and receive the other's love. But in everything human there is imperfection, a coming to be and a passing away, and a chamber of loneliness which cannot be entered. This very incompleteness points to something beyond it, giving a glimpse of a love without misunderstanding, where each lives by the life of the other. This would be the supreme Agape. But the divine Agape is not an image or shadow. It is the rainbow in the sky and the sunlight in the heart.

NOTES AND COMMENTS

If a synthesis between science and philosophy is possible, the first step, says Father D'Arcy, must be an understanding by scientists and philosophers of the methods and limitations of each discipline. As Bertrand Russell would agree, the scientist can know only quantitatively; he must leave qualitative judgments to others—the philosopher or the artist. A physicist, for example, could describe a Mozart symphony solely in terms of physics; consider how different this description would be from an analysis of the same symphony by a perceptive music critic. Are the two kinds of knowledge represented by two such descriptions complementary or contradictory? Would D'Arcy accept all the conclusions of the two scientific articles in this section—Russell's and Huxley's—as based on scientific evidence, or would he find that to reach some of them, the authors rely on the method of philosophy?

In Darwin's day evolution was the battleground for science and religion; now it may prove to be the lantern by which philosophers will see an old synthesis in a new light. Father D'Arcy discusses in detail the new perspective developed by Teilhard de Chardin from evolutionary theory and Christian doctrine. Do you think this "new synthesis" is convincing, or do you find D'Arcy's criticism of it valid? Does it provide a view of man and his place in the universe as complete and inclusive as the older, traditional Christian view? Looking at it from the point of view of the scientist, to what extent is Teilhard's theory in agreement with the ideas in Julian Huxley's essay? In this connection, you might find it interesting to read Huxley's introduction to Teilhard's major work, *The Phenomenon of Man.*

Note also D'Arcy's discussion of the problem of individuality in an age that emphasizes the collective. Using Teilhard de Chardin's notion of co-consciousness, he presents an answer based on Christian theology. What would some of the other writers in this book who are concerned with the same question—Macdonald, Ortega y Gasset, Russell in his essay on education, C. S. Lewis—have to say about this answer?

THE PERSONAL
ESSAY

◄§ The essay is at its most engaging when its author writes not about the necessary business of life, but, so to speak, off the record, inviting the reader to share with him a mood, a memory, or an insight. He may himself be appreciating the world around him, as Addison delights (albeit satirically) in the city, Thoreau in the country, or Chesterton in the fact that men have legs. He may be remembering his youth with the nostalgia of Dylan Thomas, with Mark Twain's wit, or with E. B. White's gentleness. He may be laughing, like Sullivan, Thurber and, again, Twain, at the propensity of human beings to become involved in the ridiculous. Or he may ask of his reader not laughter but sympathy, like Charles Lamb, who dreams poignantly of what his life might have been.

The key word in describing this sort of essay is *invite*. Most of the material in the other sections of this book persuades, discusses, criticizes, even exhorts. The authors (with few exceptions) do these things politely, for they are gentlemen and sufficiently men of the world to know that no reader can be bludgeoned into agreement. But their essays seek to convince. They expect assent to the propositions they present because they are demonstrating them to be true. The essays which follow seek instead to beguile. Even the funniest of them can touch upon matters which are serious and profound, but the touch is light, graceful, and undemanding, for no reader will share a mood, a memory, an insight unless he is invited to share it in a way which offers delight.

JOSEPH ADDISON

1672-1719

Though Addison was a poet, dramatist, and critic, his fame rests on the papers he wrote with Sir Richard Steele for *The Tatler* and *The Spectator*. A fuller discussion of these periodicals and their contribution to the development of the essay form can be found in "Of Essays."

"The Cries of London" is one of the Sir Roger de Coverley papers (see below). Though it mentions the club's members only incidentally, it is otherwise quite typical of the series. In it Addison is the Spectator, benevolent but detached from the people and the society he comments about. The mask or *persona* (rhetorical terms for this sort of assumed personality) presents the author as objective, as one whose disinterestedness gives validity as well as good humor to his gentle critique of London life.

The Cries of London

THERE IS NOTHING which more astonishes a foreigner and frights a country squire than the Cries of London. My good friend Sir Roger often declares that he cannot get them out of his head, or go to sleep for them, the first week that he is in town. On the contrary, Will Honeycomb[1] calls them the *Ramage de la Ville*,[2] and prefers them to the sounds of larks and nightingales, with all the music of the fields and woods. I have lately re-

---

[1 The "gallant" of the Sir Roger de Coverley club, who loved the night life of London and whose talk was all of women.—*Ed.*]

[2 *Ramage de la Ville*, bird-songs of the city.— *Ed.*]

ceived a letter from some very odd fellow upon this subject, which
I shall leave with my reader, without saying anything further of it.

"Sir,—

"I am a man of all business, and would willingly turn my
head to anything for an honest livelihood. I have invented several
projects for raising many millions of money without burthening
the subject, but I cannot get the parliament to listen to me, who
look upon me, forsooth, as a crack and a projector; so that despairing to enrich either myself or my country by this public-spirited-
ness, I would make some proposals to you relating to a design
which I have very much at heart, and which may procure me a
handsome subsistence, if you will be pleased to recommend it to
the cities of London and Westminster.

"The post I would aim at is to be Comptroller-general of the
London Cries, which are at present under no manner of rules or
discipline. I think I am pretty well qualified for this place, as being
a man of very strong lungs, of great insight into all the branches
of our British trades and manufactures, and of a competent skill
in music.

"The cries of London may be divided into vocal and instru-
mental. As for the latter, they are at present under a very great
disorder. A freeman of London has the privilege of disturbing a
whole street for an hour together, with the twanking of a brass
kettle or a frying-pan. The watchman's thump at midnight startles
us in our beds, as much as the breaking in of a thief. The sow-
gelder's horn has indeed something musical in it, but this is
seldom heard within the liberties. I would therefore propose that
no instrument of this nature should be made use of which I have
not tuned and licensed, after having carefully examined in what
manner it may affect the ears of her Majesty's liege subjects.

"Vocal cries are of a much larger extent, and, indeed, so full
of incongruities and barbarisms that we appear a distracted city
to foreigners, who do not comprehend the meaning of such
enormous outcries. Milk is generally sold in a note above *ela*,[1]
and in sounds so exceedingly shrill that it often sets our teeth
on edge. The chimney-sweeper is confined to no certain pitch; he
sometimes utters himself in the deepest bass, and sometimes in

_____

[1 The second E above middle C.—*Ed.*]

the sharpest treble; sometimes in the highest, and sometimes in the lowest note of the gamut. The same observation might be made on the retailers of small coal, not to mention broken glasses or brick-dust. In these, therefore, and the like cases, it should be my care to sweeten and mellow the voices of these itinerant tradesmen, before they make their appearance in our streets, as also to accommodate their cries to their respective wares; and to take care in particular that those may not make the most noise who have the least to sell, which is very observable in the venders of card-matches, to whom I cannot but apply that old proverb of 'Much cry, but little wool.'

"Some of these last mentioned musicians are so very loud in the sale of these trifling manufactures, that an honest splenetic gentleman of my acquaintance bargained with one of them never to come into the street where he lived: but what was the effect of this contract? why, the whole tribe of card-matchmakers which frequent that quarter passed by his door the very next day, in hopes of being bought off after the same manner.

"It is another great imperfection in our London cries, that there is no just time nor measure observed in them. Our news should, indeed, be published in a very quick time, because it is a commodity that will not keep cold. It should not, however, be cried with the same precipitation as 'fire': yet this is generally the case. A bloody battle alarms the town from one end to another in an instant. Every motion of the French is published in so great a hurry that one would think the enemy were at our gates. This likewise I would take upon me to regulate in such a manner that there should be some distinction made between the spreading of a victory, a march, or an encampment, a Dutch, a Portugal, or a Spanish mail. Nor must I omit, under this head, those excessive alarms with which several boisterous rustics infest our streets in turnip season; and which are more inexcusable because these are wares which are in no danger of cooling upon their hands.

"There are others who affect a very slow time, and are, in my opinion, much more tunable than the former; the cooper, in particular, swells his last note in an hollow voice, that is not without its harmony: nor can I forbear being inspired with a most agreeable melancholy when I hear that sad and solemn air with which the public are very often asked if they have any chairs to mend? Your own memory may suggest to you many other lamentable ditties of the same nature, in which the music is wonderfully languishing and melodious.

"I am always pleased with that particular time of the year which is proper for the pickling of dill and cucumbers; but, alas, this cry, like the song of the nightingale, is not heard above two months. It would, therefore, be worth while to consider whether the same air might not in some cases be adapted to other words.

"It might likewise deserve our most serious consideration, how far, in a well-regulated city, those humorists are to be tolerated who, not contented with the traditional cries of their forefathers, have invented particular songs and tunes of their own: such as was, not many years since, the pastry-man, commonly known by the name of the colly-molly-puff; and such as is at this day the vender of powder and wash-balls, who, if I am rightly informed, goes under the name of Powder Watt.

"I must not here omit one particular absurdity which runs through this whole vociferous generation, and which renders their cries very often not only incommodious, but altogether useless to the public; I mean that idle accomplishment which they all of them aim at, of crying so as not to be understood. Whether or no they have learned this from several of our affected singers, I will not take upon me to say; but most certain it is, that people know the wares they deal in rather by their tunes than by their words; insomuch, that I have sometimes seen a country boy run out to buy apples of a bellows-mender, and ginger-bread from a grinder of knives and scissors. Nay, so strangely infatuated are some very eminent artists of this particular grace in a cry, that none but their acquaintance are able to guess at their profession; for who else can know that 'Work if I had it' should be the signification of a corn-cutter?

"Forasmuch, therefore, as persons of this rank are seldom men of genius or capacity, I think it would be very proper that some man of good sense and sound judgment should preside over these public cries, who should permit none to lift up their voices in our streets that have not tunable throats, and are not only able to overcome the noise of the crowd, and the rattling of coaches, but also to vend their respective merchandise in apt phrases, and in the most distinct and agreeable sounds. I do therefore humbly recommend myself as a person rightly qualified for this post: and if I meet with fitting encouragement, shall communicate some other projects which I have by me, that may no less conduce to the emolument of the public.

"I am, Sir, &c.

RALPH CROTCHET."

C.

NOTES AND COMMENTS

Addison's London, seen in retrospect, may have the charm of quaintness, but surely twentieth-century cities have noises which suggest even more emphatically the need for a Comptroller-general of Cries. Try writing a modern American version of this essay.

HENRY DAVID THOREAU

1817-1862

For Thoreau, to live close enough to nature to be aware of its richness and of the simplicity of human needs was not a vacation project,
as it would be for many of us, but a necessary condition for a sound
view of the business of life, a conviction he propounds in *Walden*,
from which this selection is taken. He would, therefore, probably
regard as frivolous the vacation attitude with which most readers approach his book. However, for most of us a fourteen-month sojourn
in the woods near a pond, sheltered by a hut built for $28.12½, would
not be the feasible venture it was for Thoreau. If we are to profit at
all from his experiment in living "deliberately," confronting "only the
essential facts of life," we will do so in all likelihood not during
business hours, but in the hours reserved for considering what we
don't *have* to think about. And who's to say those hours shouldn't
yield a profit, too?

FROM *Brute Neighbors*

WHY DO PRECISELY these objects which we behold make a
world? Why has man just species of animals for his neighbors;
as if nothing but a mouse could have filled this crevice? I suspect
that Pilpay & Co. have put animals to their best use, for they are
all beasts of burden, in a sense, made to carry some portion of our
thoughts.

The mice which haunted my house were not the common
ones, which are said to have been introduced into the country, but
a wild native kind not found in the village. I sent one to a distinguished naturalist, and it interested him much. When I was

building, one of these had its nest underneath the house, and before I had laid the second floor, and swept out the shavings, would come out regularly at lunch time and pick up the crumbs at my feet. It probably had never seen a man before; and it soon became quite familiar, and would run over my shoes and up my clothes. It could readily ascend the sides of the room by short impulses, like a squirrel, which it resembled in its motions. At length, as I leaned with my elbow on the bench one day, it ran up my clothes, and along my sleeve, and round and round the paper which held my dinner, while I kept the latter close, and dodged and played at bopeep with it; and when at last I held still a piece of cheese between my thumb and finger, it came and nibbled it, sitting in my hand, and afterward cleaned its face and paws, like a fly, and walked away.

A phœbe soon built in my shed, and a robin for protection in a pine which grew against the house. In June the partridge (*Tetrao umbellus*), which is so shy a bird, led her brood past my windows, from the woods in the rear to the front of my house, clucking and calling to them like a hen, and in all her behavior proving herself the hen of the woods. The young suddenly disperse on your approach, at a signal from the mother, as if a whirlwind had swept them away, and they so exactly resemble the dried leaves and twigs that many a traveller has placed his foot in the midst of a brood, and heard the whir of the old bird as she flew off, and her anxious calls and mewing, or seen her trail her wings to attract his attention, without suspecting their neighborhood. The parent will sometimes roll and spin round before you in such a dishabille, that you cannot, for a few moments, detect what kind of creature it is. The young squat still and flat, often running their heads under a leaf, and mind only their mother's directions given from a distance, nor will your approach make them run again and betray themselves. You may even tread on them, or have your eyes on them for a minute, without discovering them. I have held them in my open hand at such a time, and still their only care, obedient to their mother and their instinct, was to squat there without fear or trembling. So perfect is this instinct, that once, when I had laid them on the leaves again, and one accidentally fell on its side, it was found with the rest in exactly the same position ten minutes afterward. They are not callow like the young of most birds, but more perfectly developed and precocious

even than chickens. The remarkably adult yet innocent expressions
of their open and serene eyes is very memorable. All intelligence
seems reflected in them. They suggest not merely the purity of
infancy, but a wisdom clarified by experience. Such an eye was not
born when the bird was, but is coeval with the sky it reflects. The
woods do not yield another such a gem. The traveller does not
often look into such a limpid well. The ignorant or reckless sportsman often shoots the parent at such a time, and leaves these innocents to fall a prey to some prowling beast or bird, or gradually
mingle with the decaying leaves which they so much resemble. It
is said that when hatched by a hen they will directly disperse on
some alarm, and so are lost, for they never hear the mother's call
which gathers them again. These were my hens and chickens.

It is remarkable how many creatures live wild and free though
secret in the woods, and still sustain themselves in the neighborhood of towns, suspected by hunters only. How retired the otter
manages to live here! He grows to be four feet long, as big as a
small boy, perhaps without any human being getting a glimpse of
him. I formerly saw the raccoon in the woods behind where my
house is built, and probably still heard their whinnering at night.
Commonly I rested an hour or two in the shade at noon, after
planting, and ate my lunch, and read a little by a spring which
was the source of a swamp and of a brook, oozing from under
Brister's Hill, half a mile from my field. The approach to this
was through a succession of descending grassy hollows, full of
young pitch pines, into a larger wood about the swamp. There, in
a very secluded and shaded spot, under a spreading white pine,
there was yet a clean, firm sward to sit on. I had dug out the spring
and made a well of clear gray water, where I could dip up a pailful
without roiling it, and thither I went for this purpose almost every
day in midsummer, when the pond was warmest. Thither, too, the
woodcock led her brood, to probe the mud for worms, flying but
a foot above them down the bank, while they ran in a troop beneath; but at last, spying me, she would leave her young and
circle round and round me, nearer and nearer till within four or
five feet, pretending broken wings and legs, to attract my attention, and get off her young, who would already have taken up
their march, with faint, wiry peep, single file through the swamp,
as she directed. Or I heard the peep of the young when I could not
see the parent bird. There too the turtle doves sat over the spring,

or fluttered from bough to bough of the soft white pines over my head; or the red squirrel, coursing down the nearest bough, was particularly familiar and inquisitive. You only need sit still long enough in some attractive spot in the woods that all its inhabitants may exhibit themselves to you by turns.

I was witness to events of a less peaceful character. One day when I went out to my wood-pile, or rather my pile of stumps, I observed two large ants, the one red, the other much larger, nearly half an inch long, and black, fiercely contending with one another. Having once got hold they never let go, but struggled and wrestled and rolled on the chips incessantly. Looking farther, I was surprised to find that the chips were covered with such combatants, that it was not a *duellum*, but a *bellum*, a war between two races of ants, the red always pitted against the black, and frequently two red ones to one black. The legions of these Myrmidons covered all the hills and vales in my wood-yard, and the ground was already strewn with the dead and dying, both red and black. It was the only battle which I have ever witnessed, the only battle-field I ever trod while the battle was raging; internecine war; the red republicans on the one hand, and the black imperialists on the other. On every side they were engaged in deadly combat, yet without any noise that I could hear, and human soldiers never fought so resolutely. I watched a couple that were fast locked in each other's embraces, in a little sunny valley amid the chips, now at noonday prepared to fight till the sun went down, or life went out. The smaller red champion had fastened himself like a vise to his adversary's front, and through all the tumblings on that field never for an instant ceased to gnaw at one of his feelers near the root, having already caused the other to go by the board; while the stronger black one dashed him from side to side, and, as I saw on looking nearer, had already divested him of several of his members. They fought with more pertinacity than bulldogs. Neither manifested the least disposition to retreat. It was evident that their battle-cry was "Conquer or die." In the meanwhile there came along a single red ant on the hillside of this valley, evidently full of excitement, who either had despatched his foe, or had not yet taken part in the battle; probably the latter, for he had lost none of his limbs; whose mother had charged him to return with his shield or upon it. Or perchance he was some Achilles, who had nourished his wrath apart, and had now come to avenge or rescue his Patroclus. He saw this unequal combat from afar,—for the blacks were nearly twice the size of the red,—he drew near with rapid pace till he stood on his guard within half an inch of the combatants; then, watching his opportunity, he sprang upon the black warrior, and commenced his operations near the root of his right fore leg, leaving the foe to select among his own members; so there were three united for life, as if a new kind of attraction had been invented which put all other locks and cements to shame. I should not have wondered by this time to find that they had their respective musical bands stationed on some eminent chip, and playing their national airs the while, to excite the slow and cheer the dying combatants. I was myself excited somewhat even as if they had been men. The more you think of it, the less the difference. And certainly there is not the fight recorded in Concord history, at least, if in the history of America, that will bear a moment's comparison with this, whether for the numbers engaged in it, or for the patriotism and heroism displayed. For numbers and for carnage it was an Austerlitz or Dresden. Concord fight! Two killed on the patriots' side, and Luther Blanchard wounded! Why here every ant was a Buttrick,—"Fire! for God's sake fire!"—and thousands shared the fate of Davis and Hosmer. There was not one hireling there. I have no doubt that it was a principle they fought for, as much as our ancestors, and not to avoid a three-penny tax on their tea; and the results of this battle will be as important and memorable to those whom it concerns as those of the battle of Bunker Hill, at least.

I took up the chip on which the three I have particularly described were struggling, carried it into my house, and placed it under a tumbler on my window-sill, in order to see the issue. Holding a microscope to the first-mentioned red ant, I saw that, though he was assiduously gnawing at the near fore leg of his enemy, having severed his remaining feeler, his own breast was all torn away, exposing what vitals he had there to the jaws of the black warrior, whose breastplate was apparently too thick for his to pierce; and the dark carbuncles of the sufferer's eyes shone with ferocity such as war only could excite. They struggled half an hour longer under the tumbler, and when I looked again the black soldier had severed the heads of his foes from their bodies, and the still living heads were hanging on either side of him like ghastly trophies at his saddle-bow, still apparently as firmly fastened as ever, and he was endeavoring with feeble struggles, being without feelers and with only the remnant of a leg, and I know not how many other wounds, to divest himself of them; which at length, after half an hour or more, he accomplished. I raised the glass, and he went off over the window-sill in that crippled state. Whether he finally survived that combat, and spent the remainder of his days in some Hôtel des Invalides, I do not know; but I thought that his industry would not be worth much thereafter. I never learned which party was victorious, nor the cause of the war; but I felt for the rest of that day as if I had had my feelings excited and harrowed by witnessing the struggle, the ferocity and carnage, of a human battle before my door.

Kirby and Spence tell us that the battles of ants have long been celebrated and the date of them recorded, though they say that Huber is the only modern author who appears to have witnessed them. "Æneas Sylvius," say they, "after giving a very circumstantial account of one contested with great obstinacy by a great and small species on the trunk of a pear tree," adds that " 'this action was fought in the pontificate of Eugenius the Fourth, in the presence of Nicholas Pistoriensis, an eminent lawyer, who related the whole history of the battle with the greatest fidelity.' A similar engagement between great and small ants is recorded by Olaus Magnus, in which the small ones, being victorious, are said to have buried the bodies of their own soldiers, but left those of their giant enemies a prey to the birds. This event happened previous to the expulsion of the tyrant Christiern the Second from Sweden." The battle which I witnessed took place in the Presidency of Polk, five years before the passage of Webster's Fugitive-Slave Bill.

Many a village Bose, fit only to course a mud-turtle in a victualling cellar, sported his heavy quarters in the woods, without the knowledge of his master, and ineffectually smelled at old fox burrows and woodchucks' holes; led perchance by some slight cur which nimbly threaded the wood, and might still inspire a natural terror in its denizens;—now far behind his guide, barking like a canine bull toward some small squirrel which had treed itself for scrutiny, then, cantering off, bending the bushes with his weight, imagining that he is on the track of some stray member of the jerbilla family. Once I was surprised to see a cat walking along the stony shore of the pond, for they rarely wander so far from

home. The surprise was mutual. Nevertheless the most domestic
cat, which has lain on a rug all her days, appears quite at home in
the woods, and, by her sly and stealthy behavior, proves herself
more native there than the regular inhabitants. Once, when berry-
ing, I met with a cat with young kittens in the woods, quite wild,
and they all, like their mother had their backs up and were fiercely
spitting at me. A few years before I lived in the woods there was
what was called a "winged cat" in one of the farmhouses in
Lincoln nearest the pond, Mr. Gilian Baker's. When I called to
see her in June, 1842, she was gone a-hunting in the woods, as was
her wont (I am not sure whether it was a male or female, and so
use the more common pronoun), but her mistress told me that she
came into the neighborhood a little more than a year before, in
April, and was finally taken into their house; that she was of a dark
brownish-gray color, with a white spot on her throat, and white
feet, and had a large bushy tail like a fox; that in the winter the
fur grew thick and flatted out along her sides, forming strips ten
or twelve inches long by two and a half wide, and under her chin
like a muff, the upper side loose, the under matted like felt, and
in the spring these appendages dropped off. They gave me a pair
of her "wings," which I keep still. There is no appearance of a
membrane about them. Some thought it was part flying squirrel or
some other wild animal, which is not impossible, for, according to
naturalists, prolific hybrids have been produced by the union of
the marten and domestic cat. This would have been the right kind
of cat for me to keep, if I had kept any; for why should not a
poet's cat be winged as well as his horse?

  In the fall the loon (*Colymbus glacialis*) came, as usual, to
moult and bathe in the pond, making the woods ring with his
wild laughter before I had risen. At rumor of his arrival all the
Mill-dam sportsmen are on the alert, in gigs and on foot, two by
two and three by three, with patent rifles and conical balls and
spy-glasses. They come rustling through the woods like autumn
leaves, at least ten men to one loon. Some station themselves on
this side of the pond, some on that, for the poor bird cannot be
omnipresent; if he dive here he must come up there. But now the
kind October wind rises, rustling the leaves and rippling the surface of the water, so that no loon can be heard or seen, though his
foes sweep the pond with spy-glasses, and make the woods resound
with their discharges. The waves generously rise and dash angrily,

taking sides with all waterfowl, and our sportsmen must beat a retreat to town and shop and unfinished jobs. But they were too often successful. When I went to get a pail of water early in the morning I frequently saw this stately bird sailing out of my cove within a few rods. If I endeavored to overtake him in a boat, in order to see how he would manoeuvre, he would dive and be completely lost, so that I did not discover him again, sometimes, till the latter part of the day. But I was more than a match for him on the surface. He commonly went off in a rain.

As I was paddling along the north shore one very calm October afternoon, for such days especially they settle on to the lakes, like the milkweed down, having looked in vain over the pond for a loon, suddenly one, sailing out from the shore toward the middle a few rods in front of me, set up his wild laugh and betrayed himself. I pursued with a paddle and he dived, but when he came up I was nearer than before. He dived again, but I miscalculated the direction he would take, and we were fifty rods apart when he came to the surface this time, for I had helped to widen the interval; and again he laughed long and loud, and with more reason than before. He manoeuvred so cunningly that I could not get within half a dozen rods of him. Each time, when he came to the surface, turning his head this way and that, he coolly surveyed the water and the land, and apparently chose his course so that he might come up where there was the widest expanse of water and at the greatest distance from the boat. It was surprising how quickly he made up his mind and put his resolve into execution. He led me at once to the widest part of the pond, and could not be driven from it. While he was thinking one thing in his brain, I was endeavoring to divine his thought in mine. It was a pretty game, played on the smooth surface of the pond, a man against a loon. Suddenly your adversary's checker disappears beneath the board, and the problem is to place yours nearest to where his will appear again. Sometimes he would come up unexpectedly on the opposite side of me, having apparently passed directly under the boat. So long-winded was he and so unweariable, that when he had swum farthest he would immediately plunge again, nevertheless; and then no wit could divine where in the deep pond, beneath the smooth surface, he might be speeding his way like a fish, for he had time and ability to visit the bottom of the pond in its deepest part. It is said that loons have been caught

in the New York lakes eighty feet beneath the surface, with hooks
set for trout,—though Walden is deeper than that. How surprised
must the fishes be to see this ungainly visitor from another sphere
speeding his way amid their schools! Yet he appeared to know his
course as surely under water as on the surface, and swam much
faster there. Once or twice I saw a ripple where he approached
the surface, just put his head out to reconnoitre, and instantly
dived again. I found that it was as well for me to rest on my oars
and wait his reappearing as to endeavor to calculate where he
would rise; for again and again, when I was straining my eyes over
the surface one way, I would suddenly be startled by his unearthly
laugh behind me. But why, after displaying so much cunning, did
he invariably betray himself the moment he came up by that loud
laugh? Did not his white breast enough betray him? He was indeed a silly loon, I thought. I could commonly hear the splash of
the water when he came up, and so also detected him. But after
an hour he seemed as fresh as ever, dived as willingly, and swam
yet farther than at first. It was surprising to see how serenely he
sailed off with unruffled breast when he came to the surface, doing
all the work with his webbed feet beneath. His usual note was this
demoniac laughter, yet somewhat like that of a water-fowl; but
occasionally, when he had balked me most successfully and come
up a long way off, he uttered a long-drawn unearthly howl, probably more like that of a wolf than any bird; as when a beast puts
his muzzle to the ground and deliberately howls. This was his
looning,—perhaps the wildest sound that is ever heard here, making the woods ring far and wide. I concluded that he laughed in
derision of my efforts, confident of his own resources. Though the
sky was by this time overcast, the pond was so smooth that I could
see where he broke the surface when I did not hear him. His white
breast, the stillness of the air, and the smoothness of the water
were all against him. At length, having come up fifty rods off, he
uttered one of those prolonged howls, as if calling on the god of
loons to aid him, and immediately there came a wind from the
east and rippled the surface, and filled the whole air with misty
rain, and I was impressed as if it were the prayer of the loon answered, and his god was angry with me; and so I left him disappearing far away on the tumultuous surface.

For hours, in fall days, I watched the ducks cunningly tack
and veer and hold the middle of the pond, far from the sportsman;

tricks which they will have less need to practise in Louisiana bayous. When compelled to rise they would sometimes circle round and round and over the pond at a considerable height, from which they could easily see to other ponds and the river, like black motes in the sky; and, when I thought they had gone off thither long since, they would settle down by a slanting flight of a quarter of a mile on to a distant part which was left free; but what beside safety they got by sailing in the middle of Walden I do not know, unless they love its water for the same reason that I do.

NOTES AND COMMENTS

Thoreau seems to do little in this selection other than observe carefully the animals with whom he shared the neighborhood of Walden Pond. Such observation, however, involves more by way of preparation and attitude than first consideration suggests. Thoreau calls the animals "neighbors." Does his attitude toward them bear out the accuracy of the term? How much of the charm of the essay depends upon this attitude?

The battle of the ants might be called an epic in miniature, especially in view of the allusions by which Thoreau endows his warriors with significance. Such apparently simple passages as this and the one about the checker-game with the loon invite imitation.

CHARLES LAMB

1775-1834

Charles Lamb's essays—signed with the pen name "Elia"—are in the personal, subjective tradition of Montaigne. The life of this most loved of the English Romantic essayists was overshadowed by a family tragedy: when he was twenty-one his sister Mary, in a fit of insanity, killed their mother. As a result Lamb gave up the idea of marriage to Ann Simmons, the girl he loved, and devoted himself to caring for his sister. His personal situation lends poignance to a number of his essays, especially to "Dream Children." The "fair Alice" of the essay is Ann Simmons; "Bridget" is Mary Lamb; and "John L——" is Lamb's elder brother John, who had recently died.

Dream Children: A Reverie

CHILDREN LOVE to listen to stories about their elders, when *they* were children; to stretch their imagination to the conception of a traditionary great-uncle, or grandame, whom they never saw. It was in this spirit that my little ones crept about me the other evening to hear about their great-grandmother Field, who lived in a great house in Norfolk (a hundred times bigger than that in which they and papa lived) which had been the scene—so at least it was generally believed in that part of the country—of the tragic incidents which they had lately become familiar with from the ballad of the Children in the Wood. Certain it is that the whole story of the children and their cruel uncle was to be seen fairly carved out in wood upon the chimney-piece of the great hall, the whole story down to the Robin Redbreasts; till a foolish rich person pulled it down to set up a marble one of modern invention in its stead, with no story upon it. Here Alice put out one of her dear mother's looks, too tender to be called upbraiding. Then I went on to say, how religious and how good their great-grand-mother Field was, how beloved and respected by everybody, though she was not indeed the mistress of this great house, but had only the charge of it (and yet in some respects she might be said to be the mistress of it too) committed to her by the owner, who preferred living in a newer and more fashionable mansion which he had purchased somewhere in the adjoining county; but still she lived in it in a manner as if it had been her own, and kept up the dignity of the great house in a sort while she lived, which afterwards came to decay, and was nearly pulled down, and all its old ornaments stripped and carried away to the owner's other house, where they were set up, and looked as awkward as if some one were to carry away the old tombs they had seen lately at the Abbey, and stick them up in Lady C.'s tawdry gilt drawing-room. Here John smiled, as much as to say, "that would be foolish indeed." And then I told how, when she came to die, her funeral was attended by a concourse of all the poor, and some of the gentry too, of the neighbourhood for many miles round, to show their respect for her memory, because she had been such a good and religious woman; so good indeed that she knew all the Psaltery by heart, ay, and a great part of the Testament besides. Here little Alice spread her hands. Then I told what a tall, upright, graceful person their great-grandmother Field once was; and how in her youth she was esteemed the best dancer—here Alice's little right foot played an involuntary movement, till, upon my looking grave, it desisted—the best dancer, I was saying, in the county, till a cruel disease, called a cancer, came, and bowed her down with pain; but it could never bend her good spirits, or make them stoop, but they were still upright, because she was so good and religious. Then I told how she was used to sleep by herself in a lone chamber of the great lone house; and how she believed that an apparition of two infants was to be seen at midnight gliding up and down the great staircase near where she slept, but she said "those innocents would do her no harm"; and how frightened I used to be, though in those days I had my maid to sleep with me, because I was never half so good or religious as she—and yet I never saw the infants. Here John expanded all his eye-brows and tried to look courageous. Then I told how good she was to all her grandchildren, having us to the great house in the holy-days, where I in particular used to spend many hours by myself, in gazing upon the old busts of the Twelve Cæsars, that had been Emperors of Rome, till the old marble heads would seem to live again, or I to be turned into marble with them; how I never could be tired with roaming about that huge mansion, with its vast empty rooms, with their worn-out hangings, fluttering tapestry, and carved oaken panels, with the gilding almost rubbed out—sometimes in the spacious old-fashioned gardens, which I had almost to myself, unless when now and then a solitary gardening man would cross me —and how the nectarines and peaches hung upon the walls, without my ever offering to pluck them, because they were forbidden fruit, unless now and then,—and because I had more pleasure in strolling about among the old melancholy-looking yew-trees, or the firs, and picking up the red berries, and the fir-apples, which were good for nothing but to look at—or in lying about upon the fresh grass with all the fine garden smells around me—or basking in the orangery, till I could almost fancy myself ripening too along with the oranges and the limes in that grateful warmth—or in watching the dace that darted to and fro in the fish-pond, at the bottom of the garden, with here and there a great sulky pike hanging midway down the water in silent state, as if it mocked at their impertinent friskings,—I had more pleasure in these busy-idle diversions than in all the sweet flavours of peaches, nectarines, oranges, and such-like common baits of children. Here John slyly deposited back upon the plate a bunch of grapes, which, not unobserved by Alice, he had meditated dividing with her, and both seemed willing to relinquish them for the present as irrelevant. Then, in somewhat a more heightened tone, I told how, though their great-grandmother Field loved all her grandchildren, yet in an especial manner she might be said to love their uncle, John L——, because he was so handsome and spirited a youth, and a king to the rest of us; and, instead of moping about in solitary corners, like some of us, he would mount the most mettlesome horse he could get, when but an imp no bigger than themselves, and make it carry him half over the county in a morning, and join the hunters when there were any out—and yet he loved the old great house and gardens too, but had too much spirit to be always pent up within their boundaries—and how their uncle grew up to man's estate as brave as he was handsome, to the admiration of everybody, but of their great-grandmother Field most especially; and how he used to carry me upon his back when I was a lame-footed boy—for he was a good bit older than me—many a mile when I could not walk for pain;—and how in after life he became lame-footed too, and I did not always (I fear) make allowances enough for him when he was impatient and in pain, nor remember sufficiently how considerate he had been to me when I was lame-footed, and how when he died, though he had not been dead an hour, it seemed as if he had died a great while ago, such a distance there is betwixt life and death; and how I bore his death as I thought pretty well at first, but afterwards it haunted and haunted me; and though I did not cry or take it to heart as some do, and as I think he would have done if I had died, yet I missed him all day long, and knew not till then how much I had loved him. I missed his kindness, and I missed his crossness, and wished him to be alive again, to be quarrelling with him (for we quarrelled some-times), rather than not have him again, and was as uneasy with-out him, as he, their poor uncle, must have been when the doctor took off his limb.—Here the children fell a crying, and asked if their little mourning which they had on was not for uncle John, and they looked up, and prayed me not to go on about their uncle, but to tell them some stories about their pretty dead mother. Then I told how for seven long years, in hope sometimes, some-times in despair, yet persisting ever, I courted the fair Alice W—n; and as much as children could understand, I explained to them what coyness, and difficulty, and denial, meant in maidens—when suddenly turning to Alice, the soul of the first Alice looked out at her eyes with such a reality of re-presentment, that I became in doubt which of them stood there before me, or whose that bright hair was; and while I stood gazing, both the children gradually grew fainter to my view, receding, and still receding, till nothing at last but two mournful features were seen in the uttermost dis-tance, which, without speech, strangely impressed upon me the effects of speech: "We are not of Alice, nor of thee, nor are we children at all. The children of Alice call Bartrum father. We are nothing; less than nothing, and dreams. We are only what might have been, and must wait upon the tedious shores of Lethe mil-lions of ages before we have existence, and a name"—and immedi-ately awaking, I found myself quietly seated in my bachelor arm-chair, where I had fallen asleep, with the faithful Bridget un-

changed by my side—but John L. (or James Elia) was gone for
ever.

NOTES AND COMMENTS

Perhaps one of the most moving ways for a writer to be auto-
biographical is to describe what might have been. In his "reverie"
does Lamb avoid sentimentality and self-pity, the usual dangers inherent in this type of writing? If so, how?

Is this essay powerful in the sense that De Quincey used the
term? Consider the difference between Lamb's use of personal materials and that of Dylan Thomas or Mark Twain. In what ways is
Lamb subtler and more delicate?

G. K. CHESTERTON

1874-1936

Gilbert Keith Chesterton enjoyed a diversified and highly successful career as a novelist, poet, essayist and literary critic. Like his close friend Hilaire Belloc, he was at his happiest defending with wit and gusto positions many of his contemporaries felt had already been abandoned. This selection, from *Tremendous Trifles*, is informed with his whimsy, his delight in paradox, and his unabashed joy in being alive, especially when he was confronted not with life at its most equable but as it is more frequently—disjointed, asymmetrical, and for him at least, more interesting.

The Advantages of Having One Leg

A FRIEND OF MINE who was visiting a poor woman in bereavement and casting about for some phrase of consolation that should not be either insolent or weak, said at last, "I think one can live through these great sorrows and even be the better. What wears one is the little worries." "That's quite right, mum," answered the old woman with emphasis, "and I ought to know, seeing I've had ten of 'em." It is, perhaps, in this sense that it is most true that little worries are most wearing. In its vaguer significance the phrase, though it contains a truth, contains also some possibilities of self-deception and error. People who have both small troubles and big ones have the right to say that they find the small ones the most bitter; and it is undoubtedly true that the back which is bowed under loads incredible can feel a faint addition to those loads; a giant holding up the earth and all its animal creation might still find the grasshopper a burden. But I am afraid that the maxim that the smallest worries are the worst is sometimes used or abused by people, because they have nothing but the very smallest worries. The lady may excuse herself for reviling the crumpled rose-leaf by reflecting with what extraordinary dignity she would wear the crown of thorns—if she had to. The gentleman may permit himself to curse the dinner and tell himself that he would behave much better if it were a mere matter of starvation. We need not deny that the grasshopper on man's shoulder is a burden; but we need not pay much respect to a gentleman who is always calling out that he would rather have an elephant when he knows there are no elephants in the country. We may concede that a straw may break the camel's back, but we like to know that it really is the last straw and not the first.

I grant that those who have serious wrongs have a real right to grumble, so long as they grumble about something else. It is a singular fact that if they are sane they almost always do grumble about something else. To talk quite reasonably about your own quite real wrongs is the quickest way to go off your head. But people with great troubles talk about little ones, and the man who complains of the crumpled rose leaf very often has his flesh full of the thorns. But if a man has commonly a very clear and happy daily life then I think we are justified in asking that he shall not make mountains out of molehills. I do not deny that molehills can sometimes be important. Small annoyances have this evil about them, that they can be more abrupt because they are more invisible; they cast no shadow before, they have no atmosphere. No one ever had a mystical premonition that he was going to tumble over a hassock. William III. died by falling over a molehill; I do not suppose that with all his varied abilities he could have managed to fall over a mountain. But when all this is allowed for, I repeat that we may ask a happy man (not William III.) to put up with pure inconveniences, and even make them part of his happiness. Of positive pain or positive poverty I do not here speak. I speak of those innumerable accidental limitations that are always falling across our path—bad weather, confinement to this or that house or room, failure of appointments or arrangements, waiting at railway stations, missing posts, finding unpunctuality when we want punctuality, or, what is worse, finding punctuality when we don't. It is of the poetic pleasures to be drawn from all these that I sing—I sing with confidence because I have recently been experimenting in the poetic pleasures which arise from having to sit in one chair with a sprained foot, with the only alternative course of standing on one leg like a stork—a stork is a poetic simile; therefore I eagerly adopted it.

To appreciate anything we must always isolate it, even if the thing itself symbolise something other than isolation. If we wish to see what a house is it must be a house in some uninhabited landscape. If we wish to depict what a man really is we must depict a man alone in a desert or on a dark sea sand. So long as he is a single figure he means all that humanity means; so long as he is solitary he means human society; so long as he is solitary he means sociability and comradeship. Add another figure and the picture is less human—not more so. One is company, two is none. If you wish to symbolise human building draw one dark tower on the horizon; if you wish to symbolise light let there be no star in the sky. Indeed, all through that strangely lit season which we call our day there is but one star in the sky—a large, fierce star which we call the sun. One sun is splendid; six suns would be only vulgar. One Tower of Giotto is sublime; a row of Towers of Giotto would be only like a row of white posts. The poetry of art is in beholding the single tower; the poetry of nature in seeing the single tree; the poetry of love in following the single woman; the poetry of religion in worshipping the single star. And so, in the same pensive lucidity, I find the poetry of all human anatomy in standing on a single leg. To express complete and perfect leggishness the leg must stand in sublime isolation, like the tower in the wilderness. As Ibsen so finely says, the strongest leg is that which stands most alone. This lonely leg on which I rest has all the simplicity of some Doric column. The students of architecture tell us that the only legitimate use of a column is to support weight. This column of mine fulfils its legitimate function. It supports weight. Being of an animal and organic consistency, it may even improve by the process, and during these few days that I am thus unequally balanced, the helplessness or dislocation of the one leg may find compensation in the astonishing strength and classic beauty of the other leg. Mrs. Mountstuart Jenkinson in Mr. George Meredith's novel might pass by at any moment, and seeing me in the stork-like attitude would exclaim, with equal admiration and a more literal exactitude, "He has a leg." Notice how this famous literary phrase supports my content touching this isolation of any admirable thing. Mrs. Mountstuart Jenkinson, wishing to make a clear and perfect picture of human grace, said that Sir Willoughby Patterne had a leg. She delicately glossed over and concealed the clumsy and offensive fact that he had really two legs. Two legs were superfluous and irrelevant, a reflection, and a confusion. Two legs would have confused Mrs. Mountstuart Jenkinson like two Monuments in London. That having had one good leg he should have another—this would be to use vain repetitions as the Gentiles do. She would have been as much bewildered by him as if he had been a centipede.

All pessimism has a secret optimism for its object. All surrender of life, all denial of pleasure, all darkness, all austerity, all desolation has for its real aim this separation of something so that it may be poignantly and perfectly enjoyed. I feel grateful for the slight sprain which has introduced this mysterious and fascinating division between one of my feet and the other. The way to love anything is to realise that it might be lost. In one of my feet I can feel how strong and splendid a foot is; in the other I can realise how very much otherwise it might have been. The moral of the thing is wholly exhilarating. This world and all our powers in it are far more awful and beautiful than even we know until some accident reminds us. If you wish to perceive that limitless felicity, limit yourself if only for a moment. If you wish to realise how fearfully and wonderfully God's image is made, stand on one leg. If you want to realise the splendid vision of all visible things —wink the other eye.

NOTES AND COMMENTS

Chesterton is on the surface not a writer remarkable for his terseness. But this short essay in its discursiveness touches with no sense of haste several topics which could be essays in themselves: "The Right to Complain," "On Bearing with the Small," "The Pleasures of Inconvenience," "The Poetry of One," "The Optimism of Pessimists," "The Exhilaration of Limit."

Chesterton's accomplishment lies not just in the variety he presents but in his synthesis of subjects so diverse. Note how his use of paradox and puns enables him to achieve unity.

MARK TWAIN

1835-1910

Mark Twain (Samuel Langhorne Clemens) was not merely the frontier humorist, popular lecturer, and author of "boys' books": he was also, particularly toward the end of his life, a penetrating social critic with a bitterly satiric and pessimistic turn of mind. In the two essays which follow the serious writer speaks through the humorist. Both the frank recollection of an episode from Twain's youth ("The Mesmerizer," from his *Autobiography*) and the deliberately satiric address prepared for a club meeting ("On the Decay of the Art of Lying") are charming, informal, and laugh-provoking. But underlying both are profound questions answered harshly.

The Mesmerizer

AN EXCITING EVENT in our village was the arrival of the mesmerizer. I think the year was 1850. As to that I am not sure but I know the month—it was May; that detail has survived the wear of fifty years. A pair of connected little incidents of that month have served to keep the memory of it green for me all this time; incidents of no consequence and not worth embalming, yet my memory has preserved them carefully and flung away things of real value to give them space and make them comfortable. The truth is, a person's memory has no more sense than his conscience and no appreciation whatever of values and proportions. How-

ever, never mind those trifling incidents; my subject is the mesmerizer now.

He advertised his show and promised marvels. Admission as
usual: 25 cents, children and negroes half price. The village had
heard of mesmerism in a general way but had not encountered it
yet. Not many people attended the first night but next day they
had so many wonders to tell that everybody's curiosity was fired
and after that for a fortnight the magician had prosperous times.
I was fourteen or fifteen years old, the age at which a boy is willing to endure all things, suffer all things short of death by fire,
if thereby he may be conspicuous and show off before the public;
and so, when I saw the "subjects" perform their foolish antics on
the platform and make the people laugh and shout and admire
I had a burning desire to be a subject myself.

Every night for three nights I sat in the row of candidates on
the platform and held the magic disk in the palm of my hand and
gazed at it and tried to get sleepy, but it was a failure; I remained
wide awake and had to retire defeated, like the majority. Also, I
had to sit there and be gnawed with envy of Hicks, our journey-
man; I had to sit there and see him scamper and jump when
Simmons the enchanter exclaimed, "See the snake! See the
snake!" and hear him say, "My, how beautiful!" in response to the
suggestion that he was observing a splendid sunset; and so on—
the whole insane business. I couldn't laugh, I couldn't applaud; it
filled me with bitterness to have others do it and to have people
make a hero of Hicks and crowd around him when the show was
over and ask him for more and more particulars of the wonders
he had seen in his visions and manifest in many ways that they
were proud to be acquainted with him. Hicks—the idea! I
couldn't stand it; I was getting boiled to death in my own bile.

On the fourth night temptation came and I was not strong
enough to resist. When I had gazed at the disk a while I pretended to be sleepy and began to nod. Straightway came the professor and made passes over my head and down my body and
legs and arms, finishing each pass with a snap of his fingers in
the air to discharge the surplus electricity; then he began to
"draw" me with the disk, holding it in his fingers and telling me
I could not take my eyes off it, try as I might; so I rose slowly,
bent and gazing, and followed that disk all over the place, just as
I had seen the others do. Then I was put through the other paces.

Upon suggestion I fled from snakes, passed buckets at a fire, became excited over hot steamboat-races, made love to imaginary girls and kissed them, fished from the platform and landed mud cats that outweighed me—and so on, all the customary marvels. But not in the customary way. I was cautious at first and watchful, being afraid the professor would discover that I was an imposter and drive me from the platform in disgrace; but as soon as I realized that I was not in danger, I set myself the task of terminating Hicks's usefulness as a subject and of usurping his place.

It was a sufficiently easy task. Hicks was born honest, I without that incumbrance—so some people said. Hicks saw what he saw and reported accordingly, I saw more than was visible and added to it such details as could help. Hicks had no imagination; I had a double supply. He was born calm, I was born excited. No vision could start a rapture in him and he was constipated as to language, anyway; but if I saw a vision I emptied the dictionary onto it and lost the remnant of my mind into the bargain.

At the end of my first half-hour Hicks was a thing of the past, a fallen hero, a broken idol, and I knew it and was glad and said in my heart, "Success to crime!" Hicks could never have been mesmerized to the point where he could kiss an imaginary girl in public or a real one either, but I was competent. Whatever Hicks had failed in, I made it a point to succeed in, let the cost be what it might, physically or morally. He had shown several bad defects and I had made a note of them. For instance, if the magician asked, "What do you see?" and left him to invent a vision for himself, Hicks was dumb and blind, he couldn't see a thing nor say a word, whereas the magician soon found out that when it came to seeing visions of a stunning and marketable sort I could get along better without his help than with it.

Then there was another thing: Hicks wasn't worth a tallow dip on mute mental suggestion. Whenever Simmons stood behind him and gazed at the back of his skull and tried to drive a mental suggestion into it, Hicks sat with vacant face and never suspected. If he had been noticing he could have seen by the rapt faces of the audience that something was going on behind his back that required a response. Inasmuch as I was an imposter I dreaded to have this test put upon me, for I knew the professor would be "willing" me to do something, and as I couldn't know what it was, I should be exposed and denounced. However, when my time came, I took my chance. I perceived by the tense and expectant faces of the people that Simmons was behind me willing me with all his might. I tried my best to imagine what he wanted but nothing suggested itself. I felt ashamed and miserable then. I believed that the hour of my disgrace was come and that in another moment I should go out of that place disgraced. I ought to be ashamed to confess it but my next thought was not how I could win the compassion of kindly hearts by going out humbly and in sorrow for my misdoings, but how I could go out most sensationally and spectacularly.

There was a rusty and empty old revolver lying on the table among the "properties" employed in the performances. On May Day two or three weeks before there had been a celebration by the schools and I had had a quarrel with a big boy who was the school bully and I had not come out of it with credit. That boy was now seated in the middle of the house, halfway down the main aisle. I crept stealthily and impressively toward the table, with a dark and murderous scowl on my face, copied from a popular romance, seized the revolver suddenly, flourished it, shouted the bully's name, jumped off the platform and made a rush for him and chased him out of the house before the paralyzed people could interfere to save him. There was a storm of applause, and the magician, addressing the house, said, most impressively—

"That you may know how really remarkable this is and how wonderfully developed a subject we have in this boy, I assure you that without a single spoken word to guide him he has carried out what I mentally commanded him to do, to the minutest detail. I could have stoped him at a moment in his vengeful career by a mere exertion of my will, therefore the poor fellow who has escaped was at no time in danger."

So I was not in disgrace. I returned to the platform a hero and happier than I have ever been in this world since. As regards mental suggestion, my fears of it were gone. I judged that in case I failed to guess what the professor might be willing me to do, I could count on putting up something that would answer just as well. I was right, and exhibitions of unspoken suggestion became a favorite with the public. Whenever I perceived that I was being willed to do something I got up and did something—anything that occurred to me—and the magician, not being a fool, always ratified it. When people asked me, "How *can* you tell what he is willing you to do?" I said, "It's just as easy," and they always said admiringly, "Well, it beats *me* how you can do it."

Hicks was weak in another detail. When the professor made passes over him and said "his whole body is without sensation now—come forward and test him, ladies and gentlemen," the ladies and gentlemen always complied eagerly and stuck pins into Hicks, and if they went deep Hicks was sure to wince, then that poor professor would have to explain that Hicks "wasn't sufficiently under the influence." But I didn't wince; I only suffered and shed tears on the inside. The miseries that a conceited boy will endure to keep up his "reputation"! And so will a conceited man; I know it in my own person and have seen it in a hundred thousand others. That professor ought to have protected me and I often hoped he would, when the tests were unusually severe, but he didn't. It may be that he was deceived as well as the others, though I did not believe it nor think it possible. Those were dear good people but they must have carried simplicity and credulity to the limit. They would stick a pin in my arm and bear on it until they drove it a third of its length in, and then be lost in wonder that by a mere exercise of will power the professor could turn my arm to iron and make it insensible to pain. Whereas it was not insensible at all; I was suffering agonies of pain.

After that fourth night, that proud night, that triumphant night, I was the only subject. Simmons invited no more candidates to the platform. I performed alone every night the rest of the fortnight. Up to that time a dozen wise old heads, the intellectual aristocracy of the town, had held out as implacable unbelievers. I was as hurt by this as if I were engaged in some honest occupation. There is nothing surprising about this. Human beings feel dishonor the most, sometimes, when they most deserve it. That handful of overwise old gentlemen kept on shaking their heads all the first week and saying they had seen no marvels there that could not have been produced by collusion; and they were pretty vain of their unbelief too and liked to show it and air it and be superior to the ignorant and the gullible. Particularly old Dr. Peake, who was the ringleader of the irreconcilables and very formidable; for he was an F.F.V., he was learned, white-haired and venerable, nobly and richly clad in the fashions of an earlier and courtlier day, he was large and stately, and he not only seemed wise but was what he seemed in that regard. He had great influence and his opinion upon any matter was worth much more than that of any other person in the community. When I conquered him at last, I knew I was undisputed master of the field; and now after more than fifty years I acknowledge with a few dry old tears that I rejoiced without shame.

In 1847 we were living in a large white house on the corner of Hill and Main Streets—a house that still stands but isn't large now although it hasn't lost a plank; I saw it a year ago and noticed that shrinkage.[1] My father died in it in March of the year mentioned but our family did not move out of it until some months afterward. Ours was not the only family in the house; there was another, Dr. Grant's. One day Dr. Grant and Dr. Reyburn argued a matter on the street with sword canes and Grant was brought home multifariously punctured. Old Dr. Peake calked the leaks and came every day for a while to look after him.

The Grants were Virginians, like Peake, and one day when Grant was getting well enough to be on his feet and sit around in the parlor and talk, the conversation fell upon Virginia and old times. I was present but the group were probably unconscious of me, I being only a lad and a negligible quantity. Two of the group—Dr. Peake and Mrs. Crawford, Mrs. Grant's mother—had been of the audience when the Richmond theater burned down thirty-six years before, and they talked over the frightful details of that memorable tragedy. These were eyewitnesses, and with their eyes I saw it all with an intolerable vividness: I saw the black smoke rolling and tumbling toward the sky, I saw the flames burst through it and turn red, I heard the shrieks of the despairing, I glimpsed their faces at the windows, caught fitfully through the veiling smoke, I saw them jump to their death or to mutilation worse than death. The picture is before me yet and can never fade.

In due course they talked of the colonial mansion of the Peakes, with its stately columns and its spacious grounds, and by odds and ends I picked up a clearly defined idea of the place. I was strongly interested, for I had not before heard of such palatial things from the lips of people who had seen them with their own eyes. One detail, casually dropped, hit my imagination hard. In the

[1 Written in 1903.—*Ed.*]

wall by the great front door there was a round hole as big as a saucer—a British cannon ball had made it in the war of the Revolution. It was breathtaking; it made history real; history had never been real to me before.

Very well, three or four years later, as already mentioned, I was king bee and sole "subject" in the mesmeric show; it was the beginning of the second week; the performance was half over; just then the majestic Dr. Peake with his ruffled bosom and wristbands and his gold-headed cane entered, and a deferential citizen vacated his seat beside the Grants and made the great chief take it. This happened while I was trying to invent something fresh in the way of vision, in response to the professor's remark—

"Concentrate your powers. Look—look attentively. There— don't you see something? Concentrate—concentrate! Now then —describe it."

Without suspecting it, Dr. Peake, by entering the place, had reminded me of the talk of three years before. He had also furnished me capital and was become my confederate, an accomplice in my frauds. I began on a vision, a vague and dim one (that was part of the game at the beginning of a vision; it isn't best to see it too clearly at first, it might look as if you had come loaded with it). The vision developed by degrees and gathered swing, momentum, energy. It was the Richmond fire. Dr. Peake was cold at first and his fine face had a trace of polite scorn in it; but when he began to recognize that fire, that expression changed and his eyes began to light up. As soon as I saw that, I threw the valves wide open and turned on all the steam and gave those people a supper of fire and horrors that was calculated to last them one while! They couldn't gasp when I got through—they were petrified. Dr. Peake had risen and was standing—and breathing hard. He said, in a great voice:

"My doubts are ended. No collusion could produce that miracle. It was totally impossible for him to know those details, yet he has described them with the clarity of an eyewitness—and with what unassailable truthfulnes God knows I know!"

I saved the colonial mansion for the last night and solidified and perpetuated Dr. Peake's conversion with the cannon-ball hole. He explained to the house that I could never have heard of that small detail, which differentiated this mansion from all other

Virginian mansions and perfectly identified it, therefore the fact stood proven that I had *seen* it in my vision. Lawks!

It is curious. When the magician's engagement closed there was but one person in the village who did not believe in mesmerism and I was the one. All the others were converted but I was to remain an implacable and unpersuadable disbeliever in mesmerism and hypnotism for close upon fifty years. This was because I never would examine them, in after life. I couldn't. The subject revolted me. Perhaps it brought back to me a passage in my life which for pride's sake I wished to forget; though I thought, or persuaded myself I thought, I should never come across a "proof" which wasn't thin and cheap and probably had a fraud like me behind it.

The truth is I did not have to wait long to get tired of my triumphs. Not thirty days, I think. The glory which is built upon a lie soon becomes a most unpleasant incumbrance. No doubt for a while I enjoyed having my exploits told and retold and told again in my presence and wondered over and exclaimed about, but I quite distinctly remember that there presently came a time when the subject was wearisome and odious to me and I could not endure the disgusting discomfort of it. I am well aware that the world-glorified doer of a deed of great and real splendor has just my experience; I know that he deliciously enjoys hearing about it for three or four weeks and that pretty soon after that he begins to dread the mention of it and by and by wishes he had been with the damned before he ever thought of doing that deed. I remember how General Sherman used to rage and swear over "While we were marching through Georgia," which was played at him and sung at him everywhere he went; still, I think I suffered a shade more than the legitimate hero does, he being privileged to soften his misery with the reflection that his glory was at any rate golden and reproachless in its origin, whereas I had no such privilege, there being no possible way to make mine respectable.

How easy it is to make people believe a lie and how hard it is to undo that work again! Thirty-five years after those evil exploits of mine I visited my old mother, whom I had not seen for ten years; and being moved by what seemed to me a rather noble and perhaps heroic impulse, I thought I would humble myself and confess my ancient fault. It cost me a great effort to make up my mind; I dreaded the sorrow that would rise in her

face and the shame that would look out of her eyes; but after long
and troubled reflection, the sacrifice semed due and right and I
gathered my resolution together and made the confession.

To my astonishment there were no sentimentalities, no dra-
matics, no George Washington effects; she was not moved in the
least degree; she simply did not believe me and said so! I was not
merely disappointed, I was nettled to have my costly truthfulness
flung out of the market in this placid and confident way when I
was expecting to get a profit out of it. I asserted and reasserted,
with rising heat, my statement that every single thing I had done
on those long-vanished nights was a lie and a swindle; and when
she shook her head tranquilly and said she knew better, I put up
my hand and *swore* to it—adding a triumphant, "*Now* what do
you say?"

It did not affect her at all; it did not budge her the fraction
of an inch from her position. If this was hard for me to endure,
it did not begin with the blister she put upon the raw when she
began to put my sworn oath out of court with *arguments* to prove
that I was under a delusion and did not know what I was talking
about. Arguments! Arguments to show that a person on a man's
outside can know better what is on his inside than he does himself. I had cherished some contempt for arguments before, I have
not enlarged my respect for them since. She refused to believe
that I had invented my visions myself; she said it was folly: that
I was only a child at the time and could not have done it. She
cited the Richmond fire and the colonial mansion and said they
were quite beyond my capacities. Then I saw my chance! I said
she was right—I didn't invent those, I got them from Dr. Peake.
Even this great shot did not damage. She said Dr. Peake's evidence
was better than mine, and he had said in plain words that it was
impossible for me to have heard about those things. Dear, dear,
what a grotesque and unthinkable situation: a confessed swindler
convicted of honesty and condemned to acquittal by circumstantial
evidence furnished by the swindled!

I realized with shame and with impotent vexation that I was
defeated all along the line. I had but one card left but it was a
formidable one. I played it and stood from under. It seemed
ignoble to demolish her fortress after she had defended it so
valiantly but the defeated know not mercy. I played that master
card. It was the pinsticking. I said solemnly—

"I give you my honor, a pin was never stuck into me without causing me cruel pain."

She only said—

"It is thirty-five years. I believe you do think that now but I was there and I know better. You never winced."

She was so calm! and I was so far from it, so nearly frantic.

"Oh, my goodness!" I said, "let me *show* you that I am speaking the truth. Here is my arm; drive a pin into it—drive it to the head—I shall not wince."

She only shook her gray head and said with simplicity and conviction—

"You are a man now and could dissemble the hurt; but you were only a child then and could not have done it."

And so the lie which I played upon her in my youth remained with her as an unchallengeable truth to the day of her death. Carlyle said "a lie cannot live." It shows that he did not know how to tell them. If I had taken out a life policy on this one the premiums would have bankrupted me ages ago.

On the Decay of the Art of Lying

Essay, for Discussion, Read at a meeting of the Historical and Antiquarian Club of Hartford, and Offered for the Thirty-Dollar Prize. Now First Published.[1]

OBSERVE, I do not mean to suggest that the *custom* of lying has suffered any decay or interruption—no, for the Lie, as a Virtue, a Principle, is eternal; the Lie, as a recreation, a solace, a refuge in time of need, the fourth Grace, the tenth Muse, man's best and surest friend, is immortal, and cannot perish from the earth while this Club remains. My complaint simply concerns the decay of the *art* of lying. No high-minded man, no man of right feeling, can contemplate the lumbering and slovenly lying of the present day without grieving to see a noble art so prostituted. In

---

[1] Did not take the prize.

this veteran presence I naturally enter upon this scheme with diffidence; it is like an old maid trying to teach nursery matters to the mothers in Israel. It would not become me to criticize you, gentlemen, who are nearly all my elders—and my superiors, in this thing—and so, if I should here and there *seem* to do it, I trust it will in most cases be more in a spirit of admiration than of fault-finding; indeed, if this finest of the fine arts had everywhere received the attention, encouragement, and conscientious practice and development which this Club has devoted to it, I should not need to utter this lament or shed a single tear. I do not say this to flatter: I say it in a spirit of just and appreciative recognition.

[It had been my intention, at this point, to mention names and give illustrative specimens, but indications observable about me admonished me to beware of particulars and confine myself to generalities.]

No fact is more firmly established than that lying is a necessity of our circumstances—the deduction that it is then a Virtue goes without saying. No virtue can reach its highest usefulness without careful and diligent cultivation—therefore, it goes without saying that this one ought to be taught in the public schools —at the fireside—even in the newspapers. What chance has the ignorant, uncultivated liar against the educated expert? What chance have I against Mr. Per—against a lawyer? *Judicious* lying is what the world needs. I sometimes think it were even better and safer not to lie at all than to lie injudiciously. An awkward, unscientific lie is often as ineffectual as the truth.

Now let us see what the philosophers say. Note that venerable proverb: Children and fools *always* speak the truth. The deduction is plain—adults and wise persons never speak it. Parkman, the historian, says, "The principle of truth may itself be carried into an absurdity." In another place in the same chapter he says, "The saying is old that truth should not be spoken at all times; and those whom a sick conscience worries into habitual violation of the maxim are imbeciles and nuisances." It is strong language, but true. None of us could *live* with an habitual truth-teller; but, thank goodness, none of us has to. An habitual truth-teller is simply an impossible creature; he does not exist; he never has existed. Of course there are people who *think* they never lie, but it is not so—and this ignorance is one of the very things that

shame our so-called civilization. Everybody lies—every day; every
hour; awake; asleep; in his dreams; in his joy; in his mourning; if
he keeps his tongue still, his hands, his feet, his eyes, his attitude,
will convey deception—and purposely. Even in sermons—but that
is a platitude.

In a far country where I once lived the ladies used to go
around paying calls, under the humane and kindly pretense of
wanting to see each other; and when they returned home, they
would cry out with a glad voice, saying, "We made sixteen calls
and found fourteen of them out"—not meaning that they found
out anything against the fourteen—no, that was only a colloquial
phrase to signify that they were not at home—and their manner
of saying it expressed their lively satisfaction in that fact. Now
their pretense of wanting to see the fourteen—and the other
two whom they had been less lucky with—was that commonest
and mildest form of lying which is sufficiently described as a
deflation from the truth. Is it justifiable? Most certainly. It is
beautiful, it is noble; for its object is, *not* to reap profit, but to
convey a pleasure to the sixteen. The iron-souled truth-monger
would plainly manifest, or even utter the fact, that he didn't want
to see those people—and he would be an ass, and inflict a totally
unnecessary pain. And next, those ladies in that far country—but
never mind, they had a thousand pleasant ways of lying, that
grew out of gentle impulses, and were a credit to their intelligence
and an honor to their hearts. Let the particulars go.

The men in that far country were liars, every one. Their
mere howdy-do was a lie, because *they* didn't care how you did,
except they were undertakers. To the ordinary inquirer you lied
in return; for you made no conscientious diagnosis of your case,
but answered at random, and usually missed it considerably. You
lied to the undertaker, and said your health was failing—a wholly
commendable lie, since it cost you nothing and pleased the other
man. If a stranger called and interrupted you, you said with your
hearty tongue, "I'm glad to see you," and said with your heartier
soul, "I wish you were with the cannibals and it was dinner-time."
When he went, you said regretfully, "*Must* you go?" and followed
it with a "Call again"; but you did no harm, for you did not
deceive anybody nor inflict any hurt, whereas the truth would
have made you both unhappy.

I think that all this courteous lying is a sweet and loving art, and should be cultivated. The highest perfection of politeness is only a beautiful edifice, built, from the base to the dome, of graceful and gilded forms of charitable and unselfish lying.

What I bemoan is the growing prevalence of the brutal truth. Let us do what we can to eradicate it. An injurious truth has no merit over an injurious lie. Neither should ever be uttered. The man who speaks an injurious truth, lest his soul be not saved if he do otherwise, should reflect that that sort of a soul is not strictly worth saving. The man who tells a lie to help a poor devil out of trouble is one of whom the angels doubtless say, "Lo, here is an heroic soul who casts his own welfare into jeopardy to succor his neighbor's; let us exalt this magnaminous liar."

An injurious lie is an uncommendable thing; and so, also, and in the same degree, is an injurious truth—a fact which is recognized by the law of libel.

Among other common lies, we have the *silent* lie—the deception which one conveys by simply keeping still and concealing the truth. Many obstinate truth-mongers indulge in this dissipation, imagining that if they *speak* no lie, they lie not at all. In that far country where I once lived, there was a lovely spirit, a lady whose impulses were always high and pure, and whose character answered to them. One day I was there at dinner, and remarked, in a general way, that we are all liars. She was amazed, and said, "Not *all?*" It was before "Pinafore's" time, so I did not make the response which would naturally follow in our day, but frankly said, "Yes, *all*—we are all liars; there are no exceptions." She looked almost offended, and said, "Why, do you include *me?*" "Certainly," I said, "I think you even rank as an expert." She said, "'Sh!—'sh! the children!" So the subject was changed in deference to the children's presence, and we went on talking about other things. But as soon as the young people were out of the way, the lady came warmly back to the matter and said, "I have made it the rule of my life to never tell a lie; and I have never departed from it in a single instance." I said, "I don't mean the least harm or disrespect, but really you have been lying like smoke ever since I've been sitting here. It has caused me a good deal of pain, because I am not used to it." She required of me an instance—just a single instance. So I said:

"Well, here is the unfilled duplicate of the blank which the Oakland hospital people sent to you by the hand of the sick-nurse when she came here to nurse your little nephew through his dangerous illness. This blank asks all manner of questions as to the conduct of that sick-nurse: 'Did she ever sleep on her watch? Did she ever forget to give the medicine?' and so forth and so on. You are warned to be very careful and explicit in your answers, for the welfare of the service requires that the nurses be promptly fined or otherwise punished for derelictions. You told me you were perfectly delighted with that nurse—that she had a thousand perfections and only one fault: you found you never could depend on her wrapping Johnny up half sufficiently while he waited in a chilly chair for her to rearrange the warm bed. You filled up the duplicate of this paper, and sent it back to the hospital by the hand of the nurse. How did you answer this question—'Was the nurse at any time guilty of a negligence which was likely to result in the patient's taking cold?' Come—everything is decided by a bet here in California: ten dollars to ten cents you lied when you answered that question." She said, "I didn't; *I left it blank!*" "Just so—you have told a *silent* lie; you have left it to be inferred that you had no fault to find in that matter." She said, "Oh, was that a lie? And how *could* I mention her one single fault, and she so good?—it would have been cruel." I said, "One ought always to lie when one can do good by it; your impulse was right, but your judgment was crude; this comes of unintelligent practice. Now observe the result of this inexpert deflection of yours. You know Mr. Jones's Willie is lying very low with scarlet fever; well, your recommendation was so enthusiastic that that girl is there nursing him, and the worn-out family have all been trustingly sound asleep for the last fourteen hours, leaving their darling with full confidence in those fatal hands, because you, like young George Washington, have a reputa— However, if you are not going to have anything to do, I will come around to-morrow and we'll attend the funeral together, for, of course, you'll naturally feel a peculiar interest in Willie's case—as personal a one, in fact, as the undertaker."

But that was all lost. Before I was half-way through she was in a carriage and making thirty miles an hour toward the Jones mansion to save what was left of Willie and tell all she knew about the deadly nurse. All of which was unnecessary, as Willie wasn't sick; I had been lying myself. But that same day, all the same, she sent a line to the hospital which filled up the neglected blank, and stated the *facts*, too, in the squarest possible manner.

Now, you see, this lady's fault was *not* in lying, but only in lying injudiciously. She should have told the truth, *there*, and made it up to the nurse with a fraudulent compliment further along in the paper. She could have said, "In one respect the sick-nurse is perfection—when she is on watch, she never snores." Almost any little pleasant lie would have taken the sting out of that troublesome but necessary expression of the truth.

Lying is universal—we *all* do it; we all *must* do it. Therefore, the wise thing is for us diligently to train ourselves to lie thoughtfully, judiciously; to lie with a good object, and not an evil one; to lie for others' advantage, and not our own; to lie healingly, charitably, humanely, not cruelly, hurtfully, maliciously; to lie gracefully and graciously, not awkwardly and clumsily; to lie firmly, frankly, squarely, with head erect, not haltingly, tortuously, with pusillanimous mien, as being ashamed of our high calling. Then shall we be rid of the rank and pestilent truth that is rotting the land; then shall we be great and good and beautiful, and worthy dwellers in a world where even benign Nature habitually lies, except when she promises execrable weather. Then— But I am but a new and feeble student in this gracious art; I cannot instruct *this* Club.

Joking aside, I think there is much need of wise examination into what sorts of lies are best and wholesomest to be indulged, seeing we *must* all lie and *do* all lie, and what sorts it may be best to avoid—and this is a thing which I feel I can confidently put into the hands of this experienced Club—a ripe body, who may be termed, in this regard, and without undue flattery, Old Masters.

NOTES AND COMMENTS

These pieces present lying from two different aspects. "The Mesmerizer" considers the effect of lying on the liar; "On the Decay of the Art of Lying" considers the role lying plays in society. The first essay is personal, colloquially humorous, yet sad in tone; the second is removed, satiric, unemotional. Which do you think better conveys Twain's philosophic pessimism? If these essays are considered as a unit in which one describes a youthful experience and the other an adult attitude, what do they reveal about why Twain became a pessimist?

It would be interesting to compare Twain's role as a social critic with the position of modern humorists like Thurber and E. B. White. Are they less serious in their way than Twain is in his, or do we read modern humorists for different reasons?

DYLAN THOMAS

1914-1953

Dylan Thomas was one of the few real poets whose lives conformed to the Romantic idea of a poet most people have unconsciously accepted since the days of Byron. A Welshman, he lived recklessly, cherishing experience and transmuting it into poetry marked with an exuberant delight in the richness and variety of nature. Unfortunately, though burning the candle at both ends may, as Millay phrased it, "make a lovely light," it is very hard on the candle. Thomas died in New York at the age of thirty-nine, and with him died one of the few authentic lyric gifts of the twentieth century.

Thomas's prose is the prose of a poet, rich in image, alliteration, internal rhyme, and singing rhythms. This selection from *Quite Early One Morning* was written originally to be read over the British Broadcasting Company's famous Third Programme.

Holiday Memory

AUGUST BANK HOLIDAY[1]—a tune on an ice-cream cornet. A slap of sea and a tickle of sand. A fanfare of sunshades opening. A wince and whinny of bathers dancing into deceptive water. A tuck of dresses. A rolling of trousers. A compromise of paddlers. A sunburn of girls and a lark of boys. A silent hullabaloo of balloons.

Reprinted from *Quite Early One Morning* by Dylan Thomas. Copyright 1954 by New Directions. By permission of the publisher, New Directions, and J. M. Dent & Sons Ltd., London.
[1 One of six legal holidays in Great Britain on which the banks are closed.—*Ed.*]

I remember the sea telling lies in a shell held to my ear for a whole harmonious, hollow minute by a small, wet girl in an enormous bathing suit marked Corporation Property.

I remember sharing the last of my moist buns with a boy and a lion. Tawny and savage, with cruel nails and capacious mouth, the little boy tore and devoured. Wild as seedcake, ferocious as a hearthrug, the depressed and verminous lion nibbled like a mouse at his half a bun and hiccupped in the sad dusk of his cage.

I remember a man like an alderman or a bailiff, bowlered and collarless, with a bag of monkeynuts in his hand, crying "Ride 'em, cowboy!" time and again as he whirled in his chairaplane giddily above the upturned laughing faces of the town girls bold as brass and the boys with padded shoulders and shoes sharp as knives; and the monkeynuts flew through the air like salty hail.

Children all day capered or squealed by the glazed or bashing sea, and the steam-organ wheezed its waltzes in the threadbare playground and the waste lot, where the dodgems dodged, behind the pickle factory.

And mothers loudly warned their proud pink daughters or sons to put that jellyfish down; the fathers spread newspapers over their faces; and sandfleas hopped on the picnic lettuce; and someone had forgotten the salt.

In those always radiant, rainless, lazily rowdy and skyblue summers departed, I remember August Monday from the rising of the sun over the stained and royal town to the husky hushing of the roundabout music and the dowsing of the naphtha jets in the seaside fair: from bubble-and-squeak to the last of the sandy sandwiches.

There was no need, that holiday morning, for the sluggardly boys to be shouted down to breakfast; out of their jumbled beds they tumbled, and scrambled into their rumpled clothes; quickly at the bathroom basin they catlicked their hands and faces, but never forgot to run the water loud and long as though they washed like colliers; in front of the cracked looking-glass, bordered with cigarette cards, in their treasure-trove bedrooms, they whisked a gap-tooth comb through their surly hair; and with shining cheeks and noses and tidemarked necks, they took the stairs three at a time.

But for all their scramble and scamper, clamour on the landing, catlick and toothbrush flick, hairwhisk and stair-jump, their

sisters were always there before them. Up with the lady lark, they had prinked and frizzed and hot-ironed; and smug in their blossoming dresses, ribboned for the sun, in gymshoes white as the blanco'd snow, neat and silly with doilies and tomatoes they helped in the higgledy kitchen. They were calm; they were virtuous; they had washed their necks; they did not romp, or fidget; and only the smallest sister put out her tongue at the noisy boys.

And the woman who lived next door came into the kitchen and said that her mother, an ancient uncertain body who wore a hat with cherries, was having one of her days and had insisted, that very holiday morning, in carrying, all the way to the tram-stop, a photograph album and the cutglass fruitbowl from the front room.

This was the morning when father, mending one hole in the thermos-flask, made three; when the sun declared war on the butter, and the butter ran; when dogs, with all the sweet-binned backyards to wag and sniff and bicker in, chased their tails in the jostling kitchen, worried sandshoes, snapped at flies, writhed between legs, scratched among towels, sat smiling on hampers.

And if you could have listened at some of the open doors of some of the houses in the street you might have heard:—

"Uncle Owen says he can't find the bottle-opener—"

"Has he looked under the hallstand?"

"Willy's cut his finger—"

"Got your spade?"

"If somebody doesn't kill that dog—"

"Uncle Owen says why should the bottle-opener
      be under the hallstand?"

"Never again, never again—"

"I know I put the pepper somewhere—"

"Willy's bleeding—"

"Look, there's a bootlace in my bucket—"

"Oh come *on*, come *on*—"

"Let's have a look at the bootlace in your bucket—"

"If I lay my hands on that dog—"

"Uncle Owen's found the bottle-opener—"

"Willy's bleeding over the cheese—"

And the trams that hissed like ganders took us all to the beautiful beach.

There was cricket on the sand, and sand in the spongecake,

sandflies in the watercress, and foolish, mulish, religious donkeys on the unwilling trot. Girls undressed in slipping tents of propriety; under invisible umbrellas, stout ladies dressed for the male and immoral sea. Little naked navvies dug canals; children with spades and no ambition built fleeting castles; wispy young men, outside the bathing-huts, whistled at substantial young women and dogs who desired thrown stones more than the bones of elephants. Recalcitrant uncles huddled, over luke ale, in the tiger-striped marquees. Mothers in black, like wobbling mountains, gasped under the discarded dresses of daughters who shrilly braved the gobbling waves. And fathers, in the once-a-year sun, took fifty winks. Oh, think of all the fifty winks along the paper-bagged sand.

Liquorice allsorts, and Welsh hearts, were melting. And the sticks of rock, that we all sucked, were like barbers' poles made of rhubarb.

In the distance, surrounded by disappointed theoreticians and an ironmonger with a drum, a cross man on an orange-box shouted that holidays were wrong. And the waves rolled in, with rubber ducks and clerks upon them.

I remember the patient, laborious, and enamouring hobby, or profession, of burying relatives in sand.

I remember the princely pastime of pouring sand, from cupped hands or bucket, down collars of tops of dresses; the shriek, the shake, the slap.

I can remember the boy by himself, the beachcombing lone-wolf, hungrily waiting at the edge of family cricket; the friendless fielder, the boy uninvited to bat or to tea.

I remember the smell of sea and seaweed, wet flesh, wet hair, wet bathing-dresses, the warm smell as of a rabbity field after rain, the smell of pop and splashed sunshades and toffee, the stable-and-straw smell of hot, tossed, tumbled, dug and trodden sand, the swill-and-gaslamp smell of Saturday night, though the sun shone strong, from the bellying beer-tents, the smell of the vinegar on shelled cockles, winkle-smell, shrimp-smell, the dripping-oily back-street winter-smell of chips in newspapers, the smell of ships from the sundazed docks round the corner of the sandhills, the smell of the known and paddled-in sea moving, full of the drowned and herrings, out and away and beyond and further still towards the

antipodes that hung their koala-bears and Maoris, kangaroos and boomerangs, upside down over the backs of the stars.

And the noise of pummelling Punch and Judy falling, and a clock tolling or telling no time in the tenantless town; now and again a bell from a lost tower or a train on the lines behind us clearing its throat, and always the hopeless, ravenous swearing and pleading of the gulls, donkey-bray and hawker-cry, harmonicas and toy trumpets, shouting and laughing and singing, hooting of tugs and tramps, the clip of the chair-attendant's puncher, the motorboat coughing in the bay, and the same hymn and washing of the sea that was heard in the Bible.

"If it could only just, if it could only just," your lips said again and again as you scooped, in the hob-hot sand, dungeons, garages, torture-chambers, train tunnels, arsenals, hangars for zeppelins, witches' kitchens, vampires' parlours, smugglers' cellars, trolls' grog-shops, sewers, under the ponderous and cracking castle, "If it could only just be like this for ever and ever amen." August Monday all over the earth, from Mumbles where the aunties grew like ladies on a seaside tree to brown, bear-hugging Henty-land and the turtled Ballantyne Islands.

"Could donkeys go on the ice?"

"Only if they got snowshoes."

We snowshoed a meek, complaining donkey and galloped him off in the wake of the ten-foot-tall and Atlas-muscled Mounties, rifled and pemmicanned, who always, in the white Gold Rush wastes, got their black-oathed-and-bearded Man.

"Are there donkeys on desert islands?"

"Only sort-of-donkeys."

"What d'you mean, sort-of-donkeys?"

"Native donkeys. They hunt things on them!"

"Sort-of walruses and seals and things?"

"Donkeys can't swim!"

"These donkeys can. They swim like whales, they swim like anything, they swim like—"

"Liar."

"Liar yourself."

And two small boys fought fiercely and silently in the sand, rolling together in a ball of legs and bottoms. Then they went and saw the pierrots, or bought vanilla ices.

Lolling or larriking that unsoiled, boiling beauty of a common day, great gods with their braces over their vests sang, spat pips, puffed smoke at wasps, gulped and ogled, forgot the rent, embraced, posed for the dicky-bird, were coarse, had rainbow-coloured armpits, winked, belched, blamed the radishes, looked at Ilfracombe, played hymns on paper and comb, peeled bananas, scratched, found seaweed in their panamas, blew up paper-bags and banged them, wished for nothing. But over all the beautiful beach I remember most the children playing, boys and girls tumbling, moving jewels, who might never be happy again. And "happy as a sandboy" is true as the heat of the sun.

Dusk came down; or grew up out of the sands and the sea; or curled around us from the calling docks and the bloodily smoking sun. The day was done, the sands brushed and ruffled suddenly with a sea-broom of cold wind. And we gathered together all the spades and buckets and towels, empty hampers and bottles, umbrellas and fishfrails, bats and balls and knitting, and went—oh, listen, Dad!—to the Fair in the dusk on the bald seaside field.

Fairs were no good in the day; then they were shoddy and tired; the voices of hoopla girls were crimped as elocutionists; no cannonball could shake the roosting coconuts; the gondolas mechanically repeated their sober lurch; the Wall of Death was safe as a governess-cart; the wooden animals were waiting for the night.

But in the night, the hoopla girls, like operatic crows, croaked at the coming moon; whizz, whirl, and ten for a tanner, the coconuts rained from their sawdust like grouse from the Highland sky; tipsy the griffon-prowed gondolas weaved on dizzy rails, and the Wall of Death was a spinning rim of ruin, and the neighing wooden horses took, to a haunting hunting tune, a thousand Beecher's Brooks as easily and breezily as hooved swallows.

Approaching, at dusk, the Fair-field from the beach, we scorched and gritty boys heard above the belabouring of the batherless sea the siren voices of the raucous, horsy barkers.

"Roll up, roll up!"

In her tent and her rolls of flesh the Fattest Woman in the World sat sewing her winter frock, another tent, and fixed her little eyes, blackcurrants in blanc-mange, on the skeletons who filed and sniggered by.

"Roll up, roll up, roll up to see the Largest Rat on the Earth, the Rover or Bonzo of vermin."

Here scampered the smallest pony, like a Shetland shrew. And here the Most Intelligent Fleas, trained, reined, bridled, and bitted, minutely cavorted in their glass corral.

Round galleries and shies and stalls, pennies were burning holes in a hundred pockets. Pale young men with larded hair and Valentino-black sidewhiskers, fags stuck to their lower lips, squinted along their swivel-sighted rifles and aimed at ping-pong balls dancing on fountains. In knife-creased, silver-grey, skirt-like Oxford bags, and a sleeveless, scarlet, zip-fastened shirt with yellow horizontal stripes, a collier at the strength-machine spat on his hands, raised the hammer, and brought it Thor-ing down. The bell rang for Blaina.

Outside his booth stood a bitten-eared and barndoor-chested pug with a nose like a twisted swede and hair that startled from his eyebrows and three teeth yellow as a camel's, inviting any sportsman to a sudden and sickening basting in the sandy ring or a quid if he lasted a round; and wiry, cocky, bowlegged, coal-scarred, boozed sportsmen by the dozen strutted in and reeled out; and still those three teeth remained, chipped and camel-yellow in the bored, teak face.

Draggled and stout-wanting mothers, with haphazard hats, hostile hatpins, buns awry, bursting bags, and children at their skirts like pop-filled and jam-smeared limpets, screamed, before distorting mirrors, at their suddenly tapering or tubular bodies and huge ballooning heads, and the children gaily bellowed at their own reflected bogies withering and bulging in the glass.

Old men, smelling of Milford Haven in the rain, shuffled, badgering and cadging, round the edges of the swaggering crowd, their only wares a handful of damp confetti. A daring dash of schoolboys, safely, shoulder to shoulder, with their fathers' trilbies cocked at a desperate angle over one eye, winked at and whistled after the procession past the swings of two girls arm-in-arm: always one pert and pretty, and always one with glasses. Girls in skulled and crossboned tunnels shrieked, and were comforted. Young men, heroic after pints, stood up on the flying chairaplanes, tousled, crimson, and against the rules. Jaunty girls gave sailors sauce.

All the Fun of the Fair in the hot, bubbling night. The Man in the sand-yellow Moon over the hurdy of gurdies. The swing-boats swimming to and fro like slices of the moon. Dragons and Hippogriffs at the prows of the gondolas breathing fire and Sousa. Midnight roundabout riders tantivying under the fairy-lights, huntsmen on billygoats and zebras hallooing under a circle of glow-worms.

And as we climbed home, up the gas-lit hill, to the still house over the mumbling bay, we heard the music die and the voices drift like sand. And we saw the lights of the Fair fade. And, at the far end of seaside field, they lit their lamps, one by one, in the caravans.

NOTES AND COMMENTS

Thomas makes the summer day real to the reader through appeal to all five senses. The sights and sounds and smells in turn evoke his childhood emotions. And the child's wistful plea, "If it could only just be like this for ever and ever amen," is linked with the author's adult nostalgia for a day when he and the rest of the world were on holiday.

It would stretch anyone's capacity for vivid and imaginative description to reminisce in imitation of the first seven paragraphs, or any other unified section, of Thomas's essay, particularly if he really tried to join in the author's delight in word play.

E. B. WHITE

1899-

E. B. White came to New York and eventually to the staff of *The New Yorker* after a stint as a reporter for the Seattle *Times*. According to a sketch James Thurber wrote about him, he left that paper because when he quite accurately reported that a man on finding his wife dead cried, "By God, it's her!" his editor changed it to "By God, it's she!" Editors since, and readers too, have appreciated his care for the truth of words, especially in the *New Yorker* column, "The Talk of the Town," and later in a department for *Harper's*, "One Man's Meat," in which the following essay originally appeared.

October, 1939

First World War

I KEEP FORGETTING that soldiers are so young. I keep thinking of them as my age, or Hitler's age. (Hitler and I are about the same age.) Actually, soldiers are often quite young. They haven't finished school, many of them, and their heads are full of the fragile theme of love, and underneath their bluster and swagger everything in life is coated with that strange beautiful importance that you almost forget about because it dates back so far. The other day some French soldiers on the western front sent a request to a German broadcasting studio asking the orchestra to play "*Parlez moi d'amour.*" The station was glad to oblige, and all along the Maginot Line and the Siegfried Line the young men were listening to the propaganda of their own desire instead of attending to the fight. So few people speak to the young men of love any more, except the song writers and scenarists. The leaders speak always of raw materials and *Lebensraum*. But the young men in uniforms do not care much for raw materials (except tobacco) and they are thinking of *Liebestraum*, and are resolving their dream as best they can. I am trying hard to remember what it is like to be as young as a soldier.

When war was getting under way in 1914, I was in high school. I was translating Cæsar, studying ancient history, working with algebraic equations, and drawing pictures of the bean, which is a dicotyledonous seed, and of the frog, an amphibian. In those days I kept a journal. My life and activities and thoughts were dear to me, and I took the trouble to set them down. I still have this journal, and the outbreak of the present war has started me going through its pages to refresh my memory. The entries are disappointingly lacking in solid facts. Much of the stuff is sickening to read, but I have a strong stomach and a deep regard for the young man that was I. Everyone, I believe, has this tolerance and respect if he is worth anything, and much of life is unconsciously an attempt to preserve and perpetuate this youth, this strange laudable young man. Though my journal is a mass of horrid little essays, moral in tone and definitely on the pretty side, I cannot bring myself to throw it away. Just now I like to consult it to rediscover what the impact of a world war means to one young fellow in the 1914-1918 period—how important each step seemed, what preposterous notions I held, how uncertain and groping and unscathed I was.

At first, before the United States entered the fray, the War seemed to mean mighty little. In those years, war was remote, implausible—a distant noise or threat, something that was ahead perhaps, like college or marriage or earning one's living, but not near enough to be of any immediate concern. In the early pages of my journal I was thinking and writing about keeping pigeons, about going skating, about the comings and goings of people on the same block with us. After a couple of years of it the War begins to take shape and I begin swelling with large thoughts. On March 16, 1917, carefully described as a "rainy Saturday," I pasted into my journal an editorial from the *Globe* on the emancipation of Russia, which spoke of the sunlight of freedom shining over the Russian steppes. "Father thinks it will be an important factor in the ultimate results of the war," I wrote. "I have always wondered what the purpose—in the bigger sense—of the war was. Perhaps this is it."

Russian freedom probably occupied my mind upward of ten minutes. The next entry in the journal was concerned with plans for a canoe trip down the Housatonic (which I never took) and with the rehearsals of a Pinero farce in which I acted the part of an English servant.

On Palm Sunday, 1917, with a bad cold in the head, I reported the advent of springtime, and the flags flying from houses all along the block. "War and springtime are being heralded with one breath and the thoughts of the people are in confusion." My own thoughts, however, were not in any particular confusion. They came to an orderly, if not monumental, focus in the composition, on the same page, of a love poem of twenty-four lines, celebrating an attachment to a girl I had met on an ice pond.

On April 3rd, with America still three days away from war, I speculated on the possibility of another canoe trip, for August —a journey on which I proposed to carry "a modified form of miner's tent." Apparently I was spending more time reading sporting goods catalogues and dreaming of the woods than studying news accounts of hostilities in Europe. I was also considering the chances of getting a summer job. Next fall I was to enter college.

Springtime and wartime! Of the two, springtime clearly took precedence. I was in love. Not so much actively as retrospectively. The memory of winter twilights when the air grew still and the pond cracked and creaked under our skates, was enough to sustain me; and the way the trails of ice led off into the woods, and the little fires burning along the shore. It was enough, that spring, to remember what a girl's hand felt like, suddenly ungloved in winter. I never tried to pursue the acquaintanceship off the pond. Without ice and skates, there seemed no reason for her existence. Lying on my back on the settee in the hall, I listened to Liszt on the pianola.

I wrote half a dozen nature poems, got a haircut, read *Raymond* by Sir Oliver Lodge, and heard one of Billy Sunday's workers in church on the text: "Follow me and I will make you fishers of men." One of my friends enlisted in the Naval Reserve. Another became wireless operator on a mosquito boat. Dimly, dimly I became aware that something was going on.

April 26, 1917. I suppose this little Journal ought to be filled with war talk, because that is what people are all thinking about now. It is believed that there will be a shortage of food soon, and so the State is supervising a "Farm Cadet" movement.

I joined the cadets that July, and served in Hempstead, L. I. It never seemed to me that the farmers were particularly pleased with the arrangement.

May 14, 1917. Yesterday I heard Billy Sunday deliver his booze sermon.

May 27, 1917. I don't know what to do this summer. The country is at war and I think I ought to serve. Strange that the greatest war in the history of the world is now going on, and it is hard to get men to enlist.

June 3, 1917. I'm feeling extraordinarily patriotic to-night, after having read the papers. I think tomorrow I shall buy a Liberty Bond and get a job on a farm. The struggle in Europe isn't over by any means, and so much history is being made every minute that it's up to every last one of us to see that it's the right kind of history. It is my firm conviction that only the unstinted giving of time, money, and resources of the American people can save this world from its most terrible doom.

June 7, 1917. I guess there is no place in the world for me. I've been trying to get a job since Monday, and have failed. Yesterday afternoon I applied at G———'s School of Popular Music for a job playing piano at a summer hotel in the Catskills. This was in answer to an ad that I had seen in the paper. When I got there, I couldn't play the kind of music he gave me, so I started for the door, but not before he had handed me a circular showing how, by his method, ragtime piano playing might be taught in 20 lessons. However, when I arrived home, I discovered that the little town in the Catskills was not on the map. I don't weigh enough to join the Army, and a job on a farm would probably be hard on my hay fever. I want to join the American Ambulance Corps, but I'm not eighteen and I've never had any experience driving a car, and Mother doesn't think I ought to go to France. So here I am, quite hopeless, and undeniably jobless. I think either I must be very stupid or else I lack faith in myself and in everything else.

My morale at this point had sunk so low that I pasted into the journal a clipping called "Foolishness of Worry," a reprint from *The White Road to Verdun*, by Kathleen Burke.

June 10, 1917. To-morrow I am going to the city to find out facts concerning the American Ambulance Corps. Somewhere in Europe there must be a place for me, and I would rather save men than destroy them. Father and L——— have just come back from the city where they went in a fruitless attempt to hear Billy Sunday.

July 5, 1917. I can think of nothing else to do but to run away. My utter dependence galls me, and I am living the life of a slacker, gorging my belly with food which others need. I wish I were old enough to be drafted.

July 11, 1917. My birthday! Eighteen, and still no future! I'd be more contented in prison, for there at least I would know precisely what I had to look forward to.

September 4, 1917. To-night I have been reading about aviation tests—I think I would like to fly, but as with everything else I have thought of, I lack the necessary qualifications.

Leaving the war behind, I packed my suitcase and went off to college, itself no small adventure. I took along the strip of bicycle tape which she and I used to hang onto in our interminable circuit of the pond the winter before. I was homesick. After the football games on Saturday afternoons I would walk down the long streets into the town shuffling through the dry leaves in the gutters, past children making bonfires of the piles of leaves, and the spirals of sweet, strong smoke. It was a golden fall that year, and I pursued October to the uttermost hill.

October 13, 1917. My English prof said the other day that bashfulness was a form of vanity, the only difference being that vanity is the tendency to overestimate your worth, and bashfulness to underestimate it: both arising from the over-indulgence of self-consciousness. The days are getting colder.

November 10, 1917. The war still continues in this its third autumn. [I couldn't even count—it was the *fourth* autumn.] Our troops are in the trenches on a relatively quiet sector of the west front. Just the other day I read that the first American Sammy had been killed. More are being trained by experienced officers in back of the line, and still more are in this country training in the several cantonments for the National Draft Army. It is a wonderful thing. The Russians have again overthrown their new-born republic and are showing themselves incapable of meeting the crises that are being put in their way. The Italian Army has been outguessed by the combined Austro-German forces and has retreated to the Piave River. The French and English lines show little change. Now, after more than three years of intensive warfare, Germany stands, solidly defying three-fourths of the countries of the world. They all look to us as the only hope of salvation, and I firmly believe that, slow as we are to foresee danger and loath as we seem to be to give up our pleasures and amusements, once in the struggle for fair we will live up to the examples set by our sturdy fore-fathers and will shed the last drop of blood for the great cause for which the whole world is now shedding blood.

November 21, 1917. I've been feeling sick for the past week and I think I must have consumption. If I have, I will leave college and travel for my health.

December 25, 1917. I have just finished *Over the Top* by Arthur Guy Empey. On the last page of his narrative he confirms what I have always sensed as truth, that strength comes surely at the critical hour, that anticipation far exceeds the realization of the utmost trial; and that man, despite his recent gentle breeding and flabby ways, when called, is not found wanting, nor untrue when facing death.

December 31, 1917. I find myself thinking the same thoughts and wishing the same wishes that I thought and wished this night a year ago. I'm wondering if I'm any nearer my ultimate goal—certainly still a long way off inasmuch as the goal itself is an unknown quantity.

February 18, 1918. The talk is of Universal Peace after the war—everlasting peace through the medium of an international council. Nations will be ruled by brotherly love and divine principle, arms will be laid down forever and man will return to the ploughshare. Bosh!

March 26, 1918. Sunday was the beginning of the immense German offensive along a 50-mile front which is threatening the civilized world and which is paralyzing the stoutest of hearts in the enormity of its plan and the apparent success of its execution. The grimness of impending danger is settling slowly over the American people. I had begun to think that perhaps I would not be called to war, but now I am not so sure. In fact, it seems almost inevitable that I will go. Things are happening on a tremendous scale.

April 13, 1918. I heard ex-President Taft speak in Bailey Hall this morning. He spoke on the war—nothing else is spoken of in these days. Now the question is, shall I set out, at the close of this academic year, to fit myself for some branch of the service so that at the age of 21 I will be trained in military or war work, or shall I wait still longer in the hope that peace will come?

On April 25th I inscribed a short nature poem, celebrating spring. On May 11th, while other freshmen were burning their caps, I recorded the belief that the greatest period of my life was past and gone. The school year was drawing to a close and again I was left stranded for the summer. "I don't even know that I'll return in the fall. I ought to want to, but I'm not sure that I do. I am never sure of anything."

I settled this feeling of uncertainty by buying a second-hand Oldsmobile and taking a job in my father's store, in the credit department. But I could feel the War in my bowels now.

July 14, 1918. I have been thinking of a sentence I read somewhere: "Destiny makes no mistakes."

Armed with a copy of *Marcus Aurelius*, I accompanied my family to Bellport, Long Island, for the month of August. There was a noticeable dearth of young men at the summer resort. The sea washed over me, the sun struck down, the wind blew at me, in an attempt to dispel the fearful mists of indecision. On the first of September we returned to the cicada-laden streets of our suburb; the month in Bellport had become a memory of sea and sky and doubt. On August 31st I wrote a poem strongly advising myself to get killed in action. On September 12th, with thirteen million other Americans, I registered for the draft.

September 21, 1918. My serial number is 3751 and I don't understand what it means, except that I can remember the days when I didn't used to have a number. The harvest moon is full to-night . . . and looking through the window 3751 enjoys the splendor.

The War, and my own travail, were both drawing to a close. I returned to Ithaca and enlisted in the Army. The enemy turned out to be an epidemic of flu—which I met stoically with a bag of licorice drops. I can't remember who told me that licorice fended off flu germs, but he was right.

November 12, 1918. Yesterday was one of the greatest days in the history of the world. The war came to an end at 2:15 o'clock in the morning. At half-past five a hand pushed against me in the darkness and a voice whispered "The whole town of Ithaca must be on fire— listen to the bells!" I sat up in bed. Just at that moment the chimes in the library tower rang out "The Star Spangled Banner" and someone down below yelled "The war is over!" . . . The terms are little less than unconditional surrender. Germany is brought to her knees, and is no longer in a position to menace the safety of other European nations. Peace with victory has been established, to the everlasting glory of all the allied countries who stood side by side in the greatest conflict of history.

For another month we had to go on drilling as though nothing had happened. As a parting blessing, the War Department vaccinated all of us for smallpox, shot us with a triple dose of typhus serum, and confined us to barracks. It was dark when I walked out of the Army and the lights were beginning to twinkle in the valley. I strode away from the mess hall in a mantle of serenity.

December 25, 1918. Christmas Day. I argued with father for about an hour and a half after breakfast, and just as is always the case we came to no agreement. He believes that the plans now being formulated for a League of Nations will be the means of preventing war in the future for all time. I cannot believe that that is so. He believes that a new era has dawned, that our President and his associate representatives of other nations have a great vision, that all the countries of the world will be united by a bond so strong that there can be no war. Father did most of the talking.

December 28, 1918.
> The pines hang dark by a little pond
> Where the ice has formed in the night
> And the light in the west fades slowly out
> Like a bird in silent flight.
> The memory of the sun that's gone
> Is just the glow in the sky,
> And in the dusk beyond the trees
> A figure is skating by.

I was still in love. The great world war had come and gone. *Parlez moi d'amour.*

NOTES AND COMMENTS

White's mixed emotions about the young man he once was give this piece its character. If he finds his youthful prose embarrassing, his youthful idealism and uncertainty are touching and his young pomposity amusing. But is the piece simply reminiscence, or does the fact that it was written in October 1939 give it a significance it might not otherwise have?

White's early journal has documentary value, for its writer is now one of America's finest stylists. The differences between his youthful and his mature prose appear in tone, syntax, vocabulary, and even punctuation. But can you discern in the journal the seeds of the craftsman White was to become?

JAMES THURBER

1894-1961

Anyone as devoted as James Thurber was to the strange byways of human behavior almost had to investigate in detail the oddities of English grammar.

FROM *Ladies' and Gentlemen's Guide to Modern English Usage*

Inspired by Mr. H. W. Fowler's excellent *Dictionary of Modern English Usage*.

THE SPLIT INFINITIVE. Word has somehow got around that a split infinitive is always wrong. This is of a piece with the sentimental and outworn notion that it is always wrong to strike a lady. Everybody will recall at least one woman of his acquaintance whom, at one time, or another, he has had to punch or slap. I have in mind a charming lady who is overcome by the unaccountable desire, at formal dinners with red and white wines, to climb up on the table and lie down. Her dinner companions used at first to pinch her, under cover of the conversation, but she pinched right back or, what is even less defensible, tickled. They finally learned that they could make her hold her seat only by fetching her a smart downward blow on the head. She would then sit quietly through the rest of the dinner, smiling dreamily and nodding at people, and looking altogether charming.

A man who does not know his own strength could, of course, all too easily overshoot the mark and, instead of producing the delightful languor to which I have alluded, knock his companion completely under the table, an awkward situation which should be avoided at all costs because it would leave two men seated next each other. I know of one man who, to avert this *faux pas*, used to punch his dinner companion in the side (she would begin to cry during the red-wine courses), a blow which can be executed, as a rule, with less fuss, but which has the disadvantage of almost always causing the person who is struck to shout. The hostess, in order to put her guest at her ease, must shout too, which is almost certain to arouse one of those nervous, high-strung men, so common at formal dinners, to such a pitch that he will begin throwing things. There is nothing more deplorable than the spectacle of a formal dinner party ending in a brawl. And yet it is surprising how even the most cultured and charming people can go utterly to pieces when something is unexpectedly thrown at table. They instantly have an overwhelming desire to "join in." Everybody has, at one time or another, experienced the urge to throw a plate of jelly or a half grapefruit, an urge comparable to the inclination that suddenly assails one to leap from high places. Usually this tendency passes as quickly as it comes, but it is astounding how rapidly it can be converted into action once the spell of dignity and well-bred reserve is broken by the sight of, say, a green-glass salad plate flying through the air. It is all but impossible to sit quietly by while someone is throwing salad plates. One is stirred to participation not only by the swift progress of the objects and their crash as they hit something, but also by the cries of "Whammy!" and "Whoop!", with which most men accompany the act of hurling plates. In the end someone is bound to be caught over the eye by a badly aimed plate and rendered unconscious.

My contemporary, Mr. Fowler, in a painstaking analysis of the split infinitive, divides the English-speaking world into five classes as regards this construction: those who don't know and don't care, those who don't know and do care, those who know and approve, those who know and condemn, and those who know and discriminate. (The fact that there was no transition at all between the preceding paragraph and this one does not mean that I did not try, in several different ways, to get back to the split infinitive logically. As in a bridge hand, the absence of a reëntry is not always the fault of the man who is playing the hand, but of the way the cards lie in the dummy. To say more would only make it more difficult than it now is, if possible, to get back to Mr. Fowler.) Mr. Fowler's point is, of course, that there are good split infinitives and bad ones. For instance, he contends that it is better to say "Our object is to further cement trade relations," thus splitting "to cement," than to say "Our object is further to cement trade relations," because the use of "further" before "to cement" might lead the reader to think it had the weight of "moreover" rather than of "increasingly." My own way out of all this confusion would be simply to say "Our object is to let trade relations ride," that is, give them up, let them go. Some people would regard the abandonment of trade relations, merely for the purpose of avoiding grammatical confusion, as a weak-kneed and unpatriotic action. That, it seems to me, is a matter for each person to decide for himself. A man who, like myself, has no knowledge at all of trade relations, cannot be expected to take the same interest in cementing them as, say, the statesman or the politician. This is no reflection on trade relations.

ONLY AND ONE. Where to use "only" in a sentence is a moot question, one of the mootest questions in all rhetoric. The purist will say that the expression: "He only died last week," is incorrect, and that it should be: "He died only last week." The purist's contention is that the first sentence, if carried out to a natural conclusion, would give us something like this: "He only died last week, he didn't do anything else, that's all he did." It isn't a natural conclusion, however, because nobody would say that and if anybody did it would be likely to lead to stomping of feet and clapping of hands, because it is one of those singy-songy expressions which set a certain type of person to acting rowdy and becoming unmanageable. It is better just to let the expression go, either one way or the other, because, after all, this particular sentence is of no importance except in cases where one is breaking the news to a mother. In such cases one should begin with: "Mrs. Gormley, your son has had an accident," or: "Mrs. Gormley, your son is not so good," and then lead up gently to: "He died only last week."

The best way is often to omit "only" and use some other expression. Thus, instead of saying: "He only died last week," one could say: "It was no longer ago than last Thursday that George L. Wodolgoffing became an angel." Moreover, this is more explicit and eliminates the possibility of a misunderstanding as to who died. The greatest care in this regard, by the way, should be taken with the verbs "to die," "to love," "to embezzle," and the like. In this connection, it is well never to use "only" at the beginning of a sentence—"Only one person loves me," for example. This of course makes it necessary to capitalize "Only" and there is the risk of a hurried reader taking it for a proper noun and confusing it with the late Richard Olney, who was Secretary of State under Cleveland.

The indefinite "one" is another source of trouble and is frequently the cause of disagreeable scenes. Such a sentence as "One loves one's friends" is considered by some persons to be stilted and over-formalized, and such persons insist that "One loves his friends" is permissible. It is not permissible, however, because "one" is indefinite and "his" is definite and the combination is rhetorically impossible. This is known as hendiadys and was a common thing in Latin. Rare examples of it still exist and are extremely valuable as antiques, although it is usually unsafe to sit or lie down on one.

The chief objection to a consistent, or "cross-country" use of "one" is that it tends to make a sentence sound like a trombone solo—such as: "One knows one's friends will help one if one is in trouble, or at least one trusts one's friends will help one." Even though this is correct, to the point of being impeccable, there is no excuse for it. The "one" enthusiast should actually take up the trombone and let it go at that.

"One" is, as a matter of fact, too often used for the personal pronoun. What, for example, could be sillier than to write a lady like this: "One loves you and one wonders if you love one." Such a person is going to get nowhere. "I love you. Do you love me?" is a much simpler and better way to say it, except, of course, that there is always the danger here of drifting into a popular ballad of the "Ramona" type.

Some persons use neither the indefinite "one" nor the definite pronoun, but substitute a pet name and get some such result as "Mopsy loves Flopsy and wonders if Flopsy loves Mopsy." This usage frequently gets into the newspapers and becomes famous, particularly if Flopsy is an ambitious blonde and Mopsy a wealthy mop-handle manufacturer. The fault here, however, is not so much with the nouns or pronouns as with the verb, "to love." Nothing can be done about the verb "to love."

THE SUBJUNCTIVE MOOD. The importance of correct grammar in the home can not be over-estimated. Two young people should make sure that each is rhetorically sound before they get married, because grammatical precision, particularly in mood, is just as important as anything else. Rhetoric and sex, in fact, are so closely related that when one becomes confused they both become confused. Take the subjunctive. Fowler, in his book on modern English usage, says the subjunctive is dying, but adds that there are still a few truly living uses, which he groups under "Alives, Revivals, Survivals, and Arrivals." Curiously enough, he leaves out Departures, which it seems to me are just as important as Arrivals. Let us examine the all too common domestic situation where the husband arrives just after another gentleman has departed—or just after he thinks another gentleman has departed (Suppositional Departures lead to just as much bitterness, and even more subjunctives, than Actual Departures).

The wife, in either case, is almost sure to go into the subjunctive—very likely before any accusation is made. Among the most common subjunctives which she will be inclined to use are those of indignation and hauteur, such as "Be that as it may," "Far be it from me," etc. For the moment, she is safe enough in the subjunctive, because her husband has probably gone into it, too, using "Would God I were," "If there be justice," and so on. Wives select the subjunctive usually because it is the best mood in which to spar for time, husbands because it lends itself most easily to ranting and posturing. As long as they both stay in it they are safe. Misunderstandings are almost certain to arise, however, when the husband goes into the indicative, as he is pretty sure to do. He usually does this preparatory to dismissing his suspicions, a step toward which every husband is impelled by his natural egotism. First he will begin with a plain past-tense indicative if-clause— just to show that he knows who the man is—prior to dismissing him.

"If George Spangrell was here," the husband will begin, lighting a cigarette, "I . . ."

"Well, what would you do if he *were?*" demands the wife.

The confusion, which begins at this point, is pretty intricate. The husband has gone into the indicative, but his wife has stayed in the subjunctive and, furthermore, she thinks that he is still there, too. Thus she thinks he intended to say: "If George Spangrell was here [that is, now] I would tell him what I think of him, the low scoundrel." There is no excuse for a wife prematurely imputing such a suspicion or such a rhetorical monstrosity to her husband. What he probably intended to say was merely something like this: "If George Spangrell was here, I wouldn't like it, but of course I know he wasn't, dear." However, misunderstandings now begin to pile up. The husband is instantly made suspicious by her "What would you do if he *were?*" He considers her "were" tantamount to "is." (This quick-tempered construction, of course, makes the "would" in his wife's sentence ridiculous, for, had she meant "is" instead of "were," she would have substituted "will" for "would.") The situation is much too involved now, however, for the husband to make an effort to parse anything. He instantly abandons all grammatical analysis, and begins to look about, peering into the wardrobe, swishing under beds with a cane or umbrella.

His wife now has the advantage of him, not only in mood, but in posture. A woman must naturally view with disdain and contempt any man who is down on all fours unless he has taken that position for the purpose of playing horse with some children —an extenuation which we need not discuss here. To meet her on even terms, the husband should walk, not crawl, from wardrobe to chaise-longue, using the mandatory subjunctive in a firm voice, as follows: "If anyone be in (or under) there, let him come out!" ["Come out" is better here than "emerge" because stronger, but a husband should not fall into the colloquial "Come on out of that!" He may, however, if he so wishes, address the gentleman, whether he be present or not, as "Spangrell" but never "Mr. Spangrell" (Hypocritical Dignification) and certainly never as "George"—the use of the given name being in extreme bad taste where no endearment is intended.]

The wife of course will resent all these goings-on, and the quarrel that results will probably last late into the night.

There are several ways to prevent a situation like this. In the first place, when a husband says "was" a wife should instantly respond with "wasn't." Most husbands will take a "wasn't" at its face value, because it preserves their egotism and self-respect. On the other hand, "if . . . were" is always dangerous. Husbands have come to know that a wife's "if . . . were" usually means that what she is presenting as purely hypothetical is, in reality, a matter of fact. Thus, if a wife begins, one evening after an excellent dinner, "Dear, what would you do, if I were the sort of woman who had, etc.," her husband knows full well that it is going to turn out that she is the sort of woman who has. Husbands are suspicious of all subjunctives. Wives should avoid them. Once a woman has "if . . . were'd" a Mr. Spangrell, her husband is, nine times out of ten, going to swish under the chaise-longue. Even if he finds no one, the situation becomes extremely awkward, and there is of course always the plaguey hundredth chance that he may discover a strange cane or pair of gloves.

The best of all ways out is for the husband to go instantly into the future indicative and say, with great dignity, "I shall go down to the drugstore." Ordinarily, his wife would reply, "Oh, no you won't," but with all the doubt and suspicion in the air, she will be inclined to humor him and let him have his way. She is certain to, if Spangrell is in the clothes hamper.

NOTES AND COMMENTS

Almost anything one says about Thurber on grammar, be it never so subjunctive, will probably serve to only confuse the issue further. However, you (that takes care of the "one," anyway) might try to analyze these exercises in a-logic or excursions into irrelevance in terms of their tone of serious, muddle-headed helpfulness or their amazingly consistent slips into *non sequitur*.

And you might try Fowler or *A Dictionary of American Usage*, by Bergen and Cornelia Evans, should you feel in need of guidance more certain than Thurber's.

FRANK SULLIVAN

1892-

Frank Sullivan writes regularly for *The New Yorker*, especially about situations in which a man is tyrannized by things he ought to be able to control. He has suffered at the hands of an imaginary secretary named Martha Hepplethwaite, whose *Life and Times* he chronicled, and he has observed with scientific care America's capitulation to the cliché. He is considering here the kind of learning that can be a dangerous thing.

A Garland of Ibids

I HAVE JUST FINISHED reading a book[1] which struck me as being one of the finest books I have read since I read "The Flowering of New England," by the same author.[2] But there is a fly in the ointment. I have been rendered cockeyed by the footnotes. There seem to be too many of them, even for a book largely about Boston.[3] I do not know why the author had to have so many foot-

---

[1] "New England: Indian Summer."

[2] Van Wyck Brooks, author of "New England: Indian Summer," "The Flowering of New England," "The Life of Emerson," "The Ordeal of Mark Twain," and other books.

[3] Sometimes referred to as The Hub. Capital and chief city of Massachusetts. Scene of the Boston Tea Party and the arrest of Henry L. Mencken. Bostonians are traditionally noted for their civic pride, or, as an envious New York critic once termed it, their parochial outlook. It is related that on an occasion when Saltonstall Boylston learned that his friend L. Cabot Lowell was leaving for a trip around the world, he inquired of Lowell, "Which route

notes. Maybe he had a reason for each one, but I suspect the footnote habit has crept up on him, for I got out his book on Emerson,[4] published in 1932, and he used practically no footnotes in it.

You read along in "New England: Indian Summer," interested to the hilt in what Van Wyck Brooks is telling you about Longfellow,[5] Thoreau,[6] Phillips,[7] James,[8] Alcott,[9] Lowell,[10]

---

shall you take, L.C.?" "Oh, I shall go by way of Dedham, of course," replied Mr. Lowell. On another occasion, the old Back Bay aristocrat Ralph Waldo Mulcahy said to Oliver Wendell Rooney, "By the way, Rooney, did your ancestors come over on the Mayflower?" "Oh, no," replied Mr. Rooney. "They arrived on the next boat. They sent the servants over on the Mayflower."

[4] Ralph Waldo Emerson, Sage of Concord and famous transcendentalist philosopher, not to be confused with Ralph McAllister Ingersoll, editor of *PM*.

[5] Henry Wadsworth Longfellow, Good Gray Poet. Longfellow was no footnote addict. He preferred foot*prints*. Cf. his "Psalm of Life":

> And, departing, leave behind us
> Footprints on the sands of time.

[6] Henry David Thoreau, philosopher who lived at Walden Pond for two years on carrots, twigs, nuts, minnows, creek water, and, as Margaret Fuller suspected (booming it out at Brook Farm in that full, rich voice of hers, to the dismay of William Ellery Channing, Henry Wadsworth Longfellow, Edward Everett Hale, John Lothrop Motley, Charles Eliot Norton, and William Lloyd Garrison), sirloin steaks and creamery butter smuggled to him by Emerson. Suffering as he did from a vitamin deficiency, the result of too much moss in his diet, Thoreau became somewhat of a misanthrope and would often creep up behind members of the Saturday Club and shout "Boo!," or, as some authorities maintain, "Pooh!" The matter is not clarified very much, one must admit, by a letter Mrs. Harriet Beecher Stowe wrote to her son, Harriet Beecher Stowe, Jr. (not to be confused with Herbert Bayard Swope), on June 7, 1854, in which she states: "Not much to write home about, as the saying goes. Dave Thoreau here for supper last nite [sic]. He got into an argument with John Greenleaf Whittier, the Good Gray Poet, as to whether snow is really ermine too dear for an earl, and Greenleaf called him a Communist. Dave then crept up behind Greenleaf and shouted either 'Boo!' [sic] or 'Pooh!' [sic], I couldn't make out wich [sic]. All well here except F. Marion Crawford, Sarah Orne Jewett, Charles Dudley Warner, Thomas Wentworth Higginson, and William Dean Howells, who complain of feeling sic [sic]. Your aff. mother, H. B. Stowe, Sr."

[7] Wendell Phillips. He was about the only Bostonian of his time who wore no middle name and he was therefore considered half naked. Even Mark Twain, when he went to visit Howells in Boston, registered as Samuel Langhorne Clemens.

[8] Probably not Jesse James. Probably is either William James, deviser of Pragmatic Sanctions, or his brother Henry, the novelist. It was about this time that Henry James was going through his transition period, and could

Adams,[11] and other great figures of the Periclean Age of The Hub,[12] when suddenly there is a footnote.

The text is in fine, clear type. The footnotes are in small type. So it is quite a chore to keep focussing up and down the page, especially if you have old eyes or a touch of astigmatism.[13] By and by you say to yourself, "I be damn if I look down at any more footnotes!," but you do, because the book is so interesting you don't want to miss even the footnotes.[14]

When you get to the footnote at the bottom of the page, like as not all you find is *ibid. Ibid* is a great favorite of footnote-mad authors.[15] It was a great favorite with Gibbon.[16] How come writers

---

not make up his mind whether he was in England living in America or in America living in England.

[9] Amos Bronson Alcott, educator and bad provider. The Mr. Micawber of his day. Not to be confused with Novelist Bus Bronson of Yale or Mrs Chauncey Olcott.

[10] James Russell Lowell, poet, essayist, and kinfolk of late rotund, cigar-smoking Back Bay Poetess Amy Lowell, no rhymester she.

[11] Henry Adams, author of "The Education of Henry Adams," by Henry Adams. Not to be confused with Henry Adams, Samuel Adams, John Adams, John Quincy Adams, Abigail Adams, Charles Edward Adams (not to be confused with Charles Francis Adams, Charles Henry Adams, or Henry Adams), Maude Adams, Franklin Pierce Adams, Samuel Hopkins Adams, Bristow Adams, George Matthew Adams, James Truslow Adams, Adams Express, Adams & Flanagan, Horace Flanagan, or Louis Adamic.

[12] Sometimes referred to as Boston. One is reminded of the famous quatrain:
Here's to the City of Boston,
The home of Filene and the Card.,
Where the Rileys speak only to Cabots
And the Cabots speak only to God!

[13] In this connection, it is interesting to note that Louisa May Alcott had a touch of astigmatism, if we are to accept the word of Charles Eliot Norton. Edward Everett Hale states in his Letters, Vol. XV, Ch. 8, pp. 297 *et seq.*, that William Cullen Bryant told Oliver Wendell Holmes that on one occasion when the fun was running high at Thomas Wentworth Higginson's home and all barriers were down, Thomas Bailey Aldrich had put the question bluntly to Charles Eliot Norton, saying, "Now listen, has Louisa May Alcott got astigmatism or hasn't she?" Charles Eliot Norton answered, perhaps un-wisely, "Yes." Cf. the famous dictum of General William Tecumseh Sherman, sometimes erroneously ascribed to General Ulysses Simpson Grant: "Never bring up a lady's name in the mess."

[14] Ah there, Van Wyck!

[15] So is cf.

[16] Edward Gibbon, English historian, not to be confused with Cedric Gibbons, Hollywood art director. Edward Gibbon was a great hand for foot-notes, especially if they gave him a chance to show off his Latin. He would come sniffing up to a nice, spicy morsel of scandal about the Romans and

of fiction do not need footnotes? Take Edna Ferber.[17] She doesn't use footnotes. Suppose Edna Herford [18] took to writing her novels in this manner:

"Cicely Ticklepaw* sat at her dressing table in a brown study. She had 'a very strange feeling she'd ne'er felt before, a kind of a grind of depression.' † Could it be love? ‡ If so, why had she sent him§ away? She sighed, and a soft cry of 'Aye me!' ‖ escaped her. Seizing a nail file desperately, she commenced hacking away at her fingernails, when a voice behind her said, 'O! that I were a glove upon that hand, that I might touch that cheek!' $ Cicely reddened, turned. It was Cleon Bel Murphy! Softly, she told him, 'What man art thou, that, thus bescreen'd in night, so stumblest on my counsel?' " &

What would Van Wyck Brooks say if Edna Ferber wrote like that? [19] Yes. Exactly. Now, where were we? [20] No, I was not. I know what I was saying. You keep out of this. You're a footnote.[21]

---

then, just as the reader expected him to dish the dirt, he'd go into his Latin routine, somewhat as follows: "In those days vice reached depths not plumbed since the reign of Caligula and it was an open secret that the notorious Empress Theodora in *tres partes divisa erat* and that she was also addicted to the *argumentum ad hominem!*" Gibbon, prissy little fat man that he was, did that just to tease readers who had flunked Caesar.

[17] Edna Cabot Ferber, contemporary New England novelist. It is related of Edna Ferber that she once met Oliver Herford in Gramercy Park and recoiled at the sight of an extremely loud necktie he was wearing. "Heavens above, Oliver Herford!" exclaimed Miss Ferber, never one not to speak her mind. "That is a terrible cravat. Why do you wear it?" "Because it is my wife's whim that I wear it," explained Oliver Herford. "Well, land sakes alive, before I'd wear a tie like that just on account of a wife's whim!" jeered Miss Ferber. "You don't know my wife," said Oliver Herford. "She's got a whim of iron." Miss Ferber later made this incident the basis of the dramatic battle between the husband and wife in her novel "The Cravat."

[18] No, no, no, not Edna Herford! Edna *Ferber!* Edna Herford is the fellow who had the wife with the iron whim.

* Blonde, lovely, and twenty-one.

† See "I'm Falling in Love with Someone"—Victor Herbert.

‡ Sure.

§ Cleon Bel Murphy, the man she loves.

‖ "Romeo and Juliet," Act II, Scene 2.

$ *Ibid.*

& *Ibid.*

[19] And what would Edna Ferber say if Edna Ferber wrote like that?

[20] You were saying Louisa May Alcott had astigmatism.

[21] Yeah? And how far would you have got in this article without footnotes?

Yeah? Well, just for that, no more footnotes. Out you go! [22] I am, that's who.[23] See what I mean, Van Wyck? Give a footnote an inch and it'll take a foot.[24] I give up. They got me. And they'll get you too in the end, Van Wyck. You may think you're strong enough to keep 'em under control; you may think you can take a footnote or leave it. All I say is, remember Dr. Jekyll! Lay off 'em, Van. I'm telling you for your own good.

—UNEASY BROOKS FAN[25]

---

[22] Who's gonna put me out?
[23] Yeah? You and who else?
[24] Yoo-hoo! Footnote!
[25] Frank Saltonstall Sullivan.

NOTES AND COMMENTS

Though he expresses it differently, Sullivan shares with Newman[1] the conviction that the province of learning is open to the pedant as well as to the scholar.[2] Is there a way to distinguish the two? [3] To discourage the former? [4]

---

[1] Q.v., pp. 281.
[2] *Ibid.*
[3] Of course.
[4] Yes, but it isn't easy.

A NOTE ON THE TYPE

This book is set in Electra, a Linotype face designed by W. A. Dwiggins. This face cannot be classified as either modern or old-style. It is not based on any historical model, nor does it echo any particular period or style. It avoids the extreme contrasts between thick and thin elements that mark most modern faces, and attempts to give a feeling of fluidity, power, and speed.